Palgrave Studies in Comparative Global History

This series proposes a new geography of Global History research using Asian and Western sources, welcoming quality research and engaging outstanding scholarship from China, Europe and the Americas. Promoting academic excellence and critical intellectual analysis, it offers a rich source of global history research in sub-continental areas of Europe, Asia (notably China, Japan and the Philippines) and the Americas and aims to help understand the divergences and convergences between East and West.

More information about this series at
http://www.palgrave.com/gp/series/15711

Rafael Dobado-González ·
Alfredo García-Hiernaux
Editors

The Fruits of the Early Globalization

An Iberian Perspective

palgrave
macmillan

Editors
Rafael Dobado-González
Department of Economía Aplicada
Universidad Complutense de Madrid
Madrid, Spain

Alfredo García-Hiernaux
Department of Economía Cuantitativa
Universidad Complutense de Madrid
Madrid, Spain

ISSN 2662-7965 ISSN 2662-7973 (electronic)
Palgrave Studies in Comparative Global History
ISBN 978-3-030-69665-8 ISBN 978-3-030-69666-5 (eBook)
https://doi.org/10.1007/978-3-030-69666-5

Cover credit: World History Archive/Alamy Stock Photo

This Palgrave Macmillan imprint is published by the registered company Springer Nature Switzerland AG
The registered company address is: Gewerbestrasse 11, 6330 Cham, Switzerland

"Most parts of this book were finished under the difficult days of COVID-19 lockdown, 2020. We feel somehow obliged to dedicate it to all victims of the pandemic."

Acknowledgments

We are vastly grateful to Andrés Calderón, Violeta Barrientos, and Gerardo Esquivel, who have restless revised and edited the last versions of the book. The editors are grateful to Manuel Pérez García and Lucio De Sousa—editors of the Palgrave Studies in Comparative Global History—to the authors that have contributed to this volume and to the Palgrave staff.

Contents

Notes on Contributors

Leticia Arroyo Abad is an Associate Professor of Economics at City University of New York. She has held positions at the London School of Economics, Carlos III University, and the Argentine Department of Industry. Her research interests are the long-term economic development of the Americas. She has published articles on inequality, living standards, economic growth, and immigration in outlets such as the *Journal of Economic History*, *Explorations in Economic History*, the *Economic History Review*, and *Cliometrica*. Originally from Buenos Aires, Argentina, she resides in New York City now.

Pim de Zwart is Assistant Professor at Wageningen University in The Netherlands. He wrote *Globalization and the Colonial Origins of the Great Divergence* (2016) and *The Origins of Globalization* (2018, with Jan Luiten van Zanden). In 2016, he was awarded the Thirsk-Feinstein Prize by the Economic History Society. He has written various articles on the role of trade in the economic history of Asia and he is currently working on a research project in which he analyzes the relationship between globalization and within-country economic inequality in Southeast Asia in the nineteenth and twentieth centuries.

Rafael Dobado-González is Professor of Economic History, Complutense University of Madrid, Spain. He was Tinker Visiting Professor at the Institute for Latin American Studies, Columbia University, New York, USA, in the second semester of 2010, and Visiting Scholar at the David Rockefeller Center for Latin American Studies, Harvard University, USA, on several occasions. He has numerous publications in economic history journals and books.

Nadia Fernandez de Pinedo is a Senior Lecturer at the Universidad Autónoma of Madrid (Spain). She is also a Research Associate of the Historical Archive of the Spanish Patent Office (EOPM) and member of the IBC Network (http://www.ibcnetwork.org). She participates in various cross-disciplinary projects (GECEM) where she has embarked on several researches for examining technology transfer processes, institutions, and consumption patterns. Among publications "Technology Transfer Networks in the First Industrial Age: The Case of Derosne & Cail and the Sugar Industry (1818–1871)", *Business History* (2019); "Visualising Defence and War in Economic History Journals (1989–2018)", *Scandinavian Economic History Review* (2019); "The Royal House of Isabel I of Castile;(1492–1504): Use of Silk, Wool and Linen According to the Accounts of Gonzalo deBaeza", *Conservar Património.* Special Issue: Studies in Historical Textile 31 (2019); "Global Commodities in Early Modern Spain", in Pérez-García, Manuel; de Sousa, Lucio (eds.), *Global History and New Polycentric Approaches. Europe, Asia and the Americas in a World Network System*, Palgrave Macmillan, (2018), "A Contribution to the Analysis of Historical Economic Fluctuations (1870–2010): Filtering, Spurious Cycles, and Unobserved Component Modeling", Cliometrica. *Journal of Historical Economics and Econometric History* (2017).

Maria João Ferreira holds a Ph.D. in History of Portuguese Art at the Faculty of Letters of the University of Porto. Currently, she is Curator at Museu de São Roque in Lisbon and member of the Centre International d'Étude des Textiles Anciens (CIETA) and of the Textile Society of America. She is also member of CHAM—Centro de Humanidades, FCSH Universidade NOVA de Lisboa, and the author of several studies in the fields of production and consumption of Asian textiles in Portugal during the early modern period, especially the Indian and Chinese for the export market. Recently, she co-authored with Ana Claro, "Chinese Textiles for the Portuguese Market: Rethinking Their History Through Dye Analysis", *The Textile MuseumJournal*, Washington, 47 (2020).

Dennis O. Flynn Emeritus Economics Professor at University of Pacific (1979–2014) and current Director, Pacific World History Institute

(2000 to present), wrote *The Spanish Price Revolution and the Monetary Approach to the Balance of Payments (1977)*, a Ph.D. dissertation that linked international monetary theory with silver history. In response to decades of inconsistencies between historical evidence and standard theory, Flynn co-created a new economic model that gradually evolved into dynamic Laws of Supplies and Demands (Flynn 2019) and a Price Theory of Monies (Flynn 2018). In the spirit of Classical economics, monies and non-monies are theoretically reunited via mechanisms that illustrate historical roots of accumulated wealth components, wealth accumulation in general, and wealth inequality. His unconventional model also encourages reinterpretation of relationships among economic forces and environmental studies.

Alfredo García-Hiernaux is Associate Professor at Universidad Complutense de Madrid, Spain, and Researcher at Complutense Institute of Economic Analysis (ICAE). His research interests include econometrics and economic history. He has published theoretical papers in journals such as the *International Journal of Forecasting, Journal of Time Series Analysis, Computational Statistics, Journal of Statistical Computation and Simulation* or *Mathematics and Computers in Simulation*, and applied some of these methods to a variety of fields whose publications include *Cliometrica, Journal of Economic History, Journal of Sports Economics, Economics and Human Biology* or *Economic Modelling*. He is also co-author of the book *State-Space Methods for Time Series Analysis: Theory, Applications and Software* (2016).

Arturo Giráldez is Professor of Modern Languages and Literature Department, University of the Pacific (Stockton-CA). He is the author of *The Age of Trade: The Manila Galleons and the Dawn of the Global Economy* and with D. O. Flynn China and the Birth of Globalization in the sixteenth century.

Herbert S. Klein is Gouverneur Morris Professor Emeritus of History at Columbia University and Hoover Research Fellow and Latin American Curator at the Hoover Archives and was Professor of History and Director of the Center for Latin American Studies at Stanford University. He has published some 185 articles and authored several books on *Bolivia: Parties and Political Change in Bolivia, 1880–1952* (1969, 2009); *Revolution and the Rebirth of Inequality* (co-author) (1981); *Haciendas and Ayllus* (1993); and *A Concise History of Bolivia* (2nd edition 2011).

His recent work is on *Slavery includes African Slavery in Latin American and the Caribbean* (2nd edition co-authored 2007); *The Middle Passage: Comparative Studies in the Atlantic Slave Trade* (1969); *The Atlantic Slave Trade* (2nd edition 2009); *Escravismo em São Paulo e Minas Gerais* (co-authored 2009); and *Slavery in Brazil* (co-authored, 2009). On Brazil his most recent books include co-authored *Economic and Social History of Brazil Since 1889* (2014), *Brazil 1964–1985, The Military Regimes of Latin America in the Cold War* (2017), *Feeding the World, The Rise of Modern Brazilian Agriculture* (2019), and *Modern Brazil: A Social History* (2020). He has also written on Latin American colonial fiscal history and is the author of *A Population History of the United States* (2nd edition, 2012).

Nuno Palma is a Senior Lecturer (Associate Professor) in the Department of Economics at the University of Manchester, a Research Fellow at ICS, University of Lisbon, and a Research Affiliate at CEPR, London. He was previously Assistant Professor in the Department of Economics, Econometrics, and Finance, University of Groningen, and a Max Weber Fellow at the European University Institute. He holds an undergraduate degree from the University of Lisbon and M.Sc. and Ph.D. degrees from the London School of Economics. His research interests include economic history, development and growth, macroeconomics and monetary economics, and political economy. He has published in journals such as *Journal of Economic History*, *Economic History Review*, *Financial History Review*, and *European Review of Economic History*. He has been the recipient of several international awards, including the inaugural Stiglitz Award given by the International Economic Association.

Renate Pieper is Full Professor of Social and Economic History at the Institute of History at Graz University. Her main fields of research are the Spanish Empire and its European connections, especially cultural networks, manuscript communication, minging, prices, and State finances. She is a member of the Academia Europea. Among her most recent publications are R. Pieper, C. de Lozanne Jefferies, M. Denzel (ed.), *Mining, Money and Markets in the Early Modern Atlantic. Digital Approaches and New Perspectives*. Cham (Palgrave) 2019.

João Teles e Cunha is currently an auxiliary investigator in the School of Arts and Humanities of the University of Lisbon, hired to be the post-Ph.D. researcher of the project "*Res Sinicae*. A Database of Latin and

Portuguese Sources on China (sixteenth to eighteenth century). Survey, Edition, Translation and Studies" (PTDC/LLT-OUT /31941/2017), based in the Centre for Classical Studies. He is also member of CHAM Centro de Humanidades FCSH Universidade NOVA de Lisboa and of the Academia de Marinha (Lisbon). He has several studies in the area of the History of the Portuguese Empire in Asia, particularly with India, the Persian Gulf, Safavid Iran, and the Indian Ocean. Recently, he co-authored with Maria João Ferreira, "Spreading Desire, Linking the World: Pintados and the Portuguese, 1500–1800", in Sarah Fee, ed., *Cloth that Changed the World. The Art and Fashion of Indian Chintz*. New Haven: Yale University Press—Royal Ontario Museum, 2019.

Corinne Thépaut-Cabasset is an art historian specialized in the decorative arts; she is a Research Associate at the Palace of Versailles. In 2010, she was recruited by the V&A museum in London to work on the European research project funded by HERA (2010–2013) *Fashioning the Early Modern: Creativity and Innovation in Europe 1500–1800*. In 2015, her research project "Dressing the New World: The Trade and the Culture of Clothing in the New Spanish Colonies 1600–1800" was awarded the European grant Marie Sklodowska Curie (Horizon 2020), hosted at the University of Copenhagen SAXO Institute (2015–2017). In 2017, she received a research residency at the Bard Graduate Center, New York. Since 2019, Corinne Thépaut-Cabasset was elected Chair of the international committee ICOM Costume (for the museums and collections of Costume).

List of Figures

The Fruits of the Early Globalization: An Iberian Perspective

The Significance of Early Globalization: Arguments and Evidence

International Migrations to Latin America and the Caribbean Until 1820

The Fruits of *El Dorado*: The Global Impact of American Precious Metals

Prices and Money in the Globalization of the Early Modern Era

Weaving a Global Trade Pattern: The Portuguese Role in the Globalisation on Asian Textiles, 1500–1800

Memoirs of the Fruits of Globalization: The Markets for Chinese Textiles in New Spain by Jean de Monségur

List of Tables

Memoirs of the Fruits of Globalization: The Markets for Chinese Textiles in New Spain by Jean de Monségur

Introduction

The Fruits of the Early Globalization: An Iberian Perspective

Rafael Dobado-González and Alfredo García-Hiernaux

Introduction[1]

This volume reflects the increasing interest on the *Early Globalization* among historians and economic historians. By the term Early Globalization we refer to the centuries-long process that multiplied interactions of many types—e.g., biological, demographic, cultural, technological, economic, religious and political—between all the most populated parts of the world at an unprecedented scale.[2] It started with the arrivals

[1] Editors' opinions expressed in this Introduction are not necessarily shared by the rest of authors.

[2] To the best of our knowledge, among economic historians, the expression "Early Globalization" appeared for the first time in Flynn and Giráldez (2008, pp. 359–387). It was also used independently in Dobado et al. (2013).

R. Dobado-González (✉)
Department of Economía Aplicada, Estructura e Historia, Universidad Complutense de Madrid, Madrid, Spain
e-mail: rdobadog@ucm.es

A. García-Hiernaux
Department of Economía Cuantitativa, Universidad Complutense de Madrid, Madrid, Spain
e-mail: agarciah@ccee.ucm.es

R. Dobado-González and A. García-Hiernaux (eds.), *The Fruits of the Early Globalization*, Palgrave Studies in Comparative Global History,
https://doi.org/10.1007/978-3-030-69666-5_1

of both Spaniards and Portuguese to, respectively, America—1492—and Asia—1498—and lasted until the disruption of the international economy caused by the French Revolutionary and Napoleonic wars (1793–1815). This process had an important economic component indeed. Economic interactions within and across continents reached novel levels in trade, circulation of Hispanic American silver, technological transfers, free and forced migration, entrepreneurial creativity, and international mobilization of capital. They deeply changed human history for the centuries to come. Thus, for good reasons, this book is mainly an essay on economic history.

However, we do not overlook other dimensions of the Early Modern Globalization. Some of them are captured by the concept of Columbian Exchange (Crosby 1972). It alludes to the "exchange of diseases, ideas, food crops, and populations between the New World and the Old World" that resulted from the Columbus's travels across the Atlantic (Nunn and Qian 2019, p. 163). In turn, the transfer of American species—corn, sweet potatoes, peanuts and tobacco—throughout the Pacific has been termed Magellan Exchange.

The notion of "Iberian Globalization" proposed by the French historian Serge Gruzinski privileges the worldwide cultural miscegenation that, especially during the Iberian Union (1580–1640), accompanied the expansion of the Spanish and Portuguese empires (Gruzinski 2010). For instance, as early as ca. 1520, Chinese porcelain from Jingdezhen was already being produced for the Portuguese market—see Illustration 1. A few years before, several tons of Chinese silk and other fabrics were shipped from Kochi—Kerala—to Portugal (Pacheco 2013). In the second half of the sixteenth century, the renting of Macau by the Portuguese increased the flow of Chinese textiles with European motifs to the Iberian Peninsula—see Illustration 2. Since 1598, Chinese folding screens could be found in the interiors of Mexico City houses (Curiel 2012). By the early seventeenth century, screens were already being produced in Mexico City and competed with those imported from Asia (Baena 2012). Some of the domestic-made screens were inspired in the Japanese ***nanban*** (Southern Barbarians) artistic style, which may be considered the first global art, since it received influences through the Portuguese and Spanish transoceanic routes (see Illustration 3; Rivero 2005). Even one of the most famous pictures ever painted, *Las Meninas* (1656) by Diego Velázquez, depicts the offering to the Infanta Doña Margarita of a *búcaro*, or *barro de Indias*—burnished earthenware from

Illustration 1 Jug with Portuguese arms. *ca.* 1520–1540, Hard-paste porcelain with cobalt blue under transparent glaze (Jingdezhen ware), Helena Woolworth McCann Collection, Purchase, Winfield Foundation Gift, 1961 (*Source* The Metropolitan Museum of Art. Accession number 61.196. https://www.metmuseum.org/art/collection/search/202581)

New Spain. Other European painters, such as Van der Hamen—see Illustration 4, Antonio de Pereda, Andrea Belvedere, and Giuseppe Reco, also showed Hispanic American ceramics in their pictures (Curiel 1994, p. 196). Porcelain, textiles, paintings and screens were not only material

Illustration 2 Textile with crowned double-headed eagles, second half of the sixteenth century. Lampas, silk, Rogers Fund, 1912 (*Source* The Metropolitan Museum of Art. Accession number 12.55.4. https://www.metmuseum.org/exhibitions/objects?exhibitionId=%7B063a1aa2-5a4e-439a-a332-046e00e8bd73%7D#!?offset=0&perPage=20)

goods for trade but also cultural artifacts that circulated across continents and frequently adopted mestizo cultural forms. An epitome of this global mestizaje is the folding screen made in New Spain by late seventeenth century—see Illustration 5. It depicts an amazing amalgamation of indigenous—the flying pole and the Moctezuma dance—and Spanish ceremonies—the Catholic wedding—and costumes. The background of the painting, European in style, shows the persistence of the pre-Hispanic transportation in boats, well-adapted to the lacustrine ecosystem surrounding Tenochtitlan/Mexico City. Western quadrupeds are also visible. Idealized syncretism or complex mestizo reality? Likely, a changing combination of both. As Alberto Baena states:

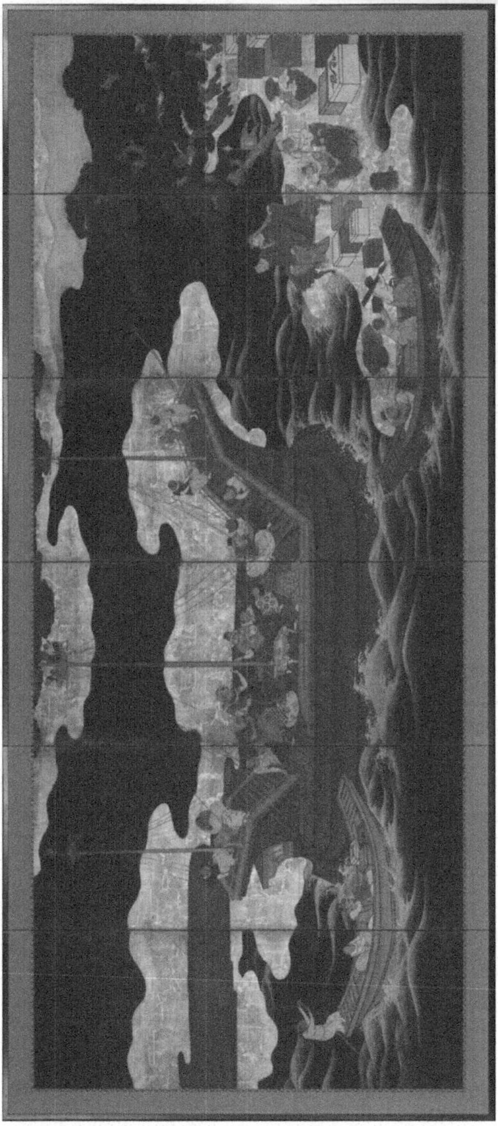

Illustration 3 "The arrival of Europeans to Japan", first quarter of the seventeenth century, Nanban folding screen, Mary Griggs Burke Collection, Gift of the Mary and Jackson Burke Foundation, 2015 (*Source* The Metropolitan Museum of Art. Accession number 2015.300.109.1, .2. https://www.metmuseum.org/art/collection/search/65417)

Illustration 4 "Still Life with Sweets and Pottery" Juan van der Hamen y León (1596–1631), oil on canvas (*Source* National Gallery of Art. Samuel H Kress Collection. N° 1961.9.75. https://www.nga.gov/collection/art-object-page.46174.html)

> The birth in the seventeenth century of a production of folding screens in New Spain and its export to the rest of Hispanic-America and Europe explain the vitality of the processes triggered by economic exchanges. Similarly, the subsequent development of other local manufactures in Hispanic-America, such as those in Peru, Guatemala or Colombia, reflects the artistic maturity that by the eighteenth century had been reached in the continent. (Baena 2012, p. 58)[3]

The historical significance of the Early Globalization and the pioneering role played by the Iberian empires from its earliest stages were already recognized by Adam Smith in *The Wealth of Nations*.[4] Possible exaggeration apart, "the voyages Smith referred to marked one of the

[3] Translated from Spanish by the authors.

[4] "The Discovery of America, and that of a passage to the East Indies by the Cape of Good Hope, are the two greatest and most important events recorded in the history of mankind" (Smith 2008, p. 590).

Illustration 5 Folding Screen with Indian Wedding and Flying Pole. N/A. *ca.* 1690. Oil on canvas (*Source* Los Ángeles County Museum of Art. https://collections.lacma.org/node/209529?parent=589011)

major turning points in world history", as it has been pointed out by Findlay and O'Rourke (2007, p. 143).

As recently as in 2019, the fifth centenary of the Magellan-Elcano expedition from 1519 to 1522 which, unintendedly, turned out to be the first circumnavigation of the world, was commemorated. Magellan, an experienced and knowledgeable Portuguese mariner, was appointed by King Charles I of Spain as commander of the five-vessel fleet dispatched from Seville to find the Western route to the East Indies. After his death at the hands of the aboriginals of Mactan Island (Philippines), Elcano, a Spanish soldier and merchant, led two vessels and a small group of members of the expedition from the Moluccas to Seville, across the Indic and the Atlantic Oceans. This part of the voyage was complicated by the need of sailing away from the various Portuguese enclaves along the route. In fact, one of the vessels, the *Trinidad*, was captured and the crew kept in captivity until an agreement on the Moluccas was reached between Portugal and Spain—Treaty of Zaragoza in 1529. The conflict between the two Iberian Empires turned around the possession of the *Islas de la Especiería*—the Moluccas, which remained in Portuguese hands. Not the same happened with the by then less valuable Philippines, that went to Spanish hands.

From their bases in the Indian Peninsula and Southeast Asia, the Portuguese proceeded with their eastward expansion throughout this commercially flourishing part of the world. They conquered Malacca in 1511, arrived to Tanegashima in 1542 and, after several decades of complicated relations with China, were allowed to settle in Macau in 1557. As a result, Lisbon became an unprecedented destination for a variety of Asian goods. A significant part of them was re-exported from Lisbon to other European ports. This successful trade had a powerful demonstration effect on the Netherlands and England.

In contrast, the access to Asia by the Spaniards had to be different. They launched from America successive expeditions across the unknown and immense Pacific Ocean. They finally succeeded in establishing a permanent settlement in the Philippines. The capital was founded in Manila in 1571. It is then that "*globalization began*" according to Flynn and Giráldez (2004, p. 82). A nautical feat, the "*tornaviaje*" between the Philippines and New Spain—some 20,000 km of uninterrupted sailing across the Pacific—was achieved for the first time in 1566. This voyage permitted the opening of a lasting (1565–1815) trade route between Hispanic America and East Asia, commonly known as the "Manila

Galleon" or the "Nao de China". According to Arturo Giráldez, this route "originated the first planetary economy, the intercontinental market from which emerges the globalized world in which we live" (Giráldez 2015, p. 191). It also constituted the main vehicle for the Magellan Exchange. Huge quantities of Hispanic American silver crossed the Pacific in exchange for the porcelain, silk, cotton, screens and other furniture, species, and ivory transported by the galleons. By the early seventeenth century, thousands of Chinese were already established in the *Parián*, the part of Manila inhabited by migrants coming mainly from Fujian (ibid., pp. 160–168).

Asian goods did not only remain in New Spain. From Acapulco, they were sent to Spain—via Mexico City and Veracruz—and other territories of the Hispanic Monarchy in America (Bonialian 2012, 2014). Earlier and more intensely than usually recognized by most of specialists, Asian goods circulated across the Iberian empires. They deeply influenced tastes and consumption patterns of both the rich and the poor. Although it has never been considered in the mainstream literature, the idea that the revolution in consumption of the Early Modern era started in Hispanic America, most likely in New Spain, deserves careful attention.[5] This is yet an insufficiently explored field of Iberian American economic history despite the increasing body of evidence pointing in that direction. In this respect, once again art history proves helpful:

> Colonial Latin America was more directly and profoundly affected by Asia culture than Europe ever was (…) More than a century before chinoiserie took hold in Europe, colonial societies in Spanish and Portuguese America were captivated by the arts of Japan, China, and India, of which they had extensive firsthand knowledge (…) much of the furniture, ceramics, and textiles that adorned colonial homes and churches –whether in Potosi, Bolivia, or Pernambuco, Brazil– either came from Asia or was inspired by Asian art. (Bailey 2006, p. 57)

Thus, we accept the above-mentioned proposition by Flynn and Giráldez (2004) regarding the "birth of globalization" and its historically inclusive meaning. Accepting it entails that the definition of globalization

[5] This hypothesis is explored in the ongoing research conducted by Calderón et al. in a preliminary paper entitled "Asian goods in New Spain: An Early Consumer Revolution?", which is available upon request to the authors.

defended by O'Rourke and Williamson turns out to be very restrictive: "the only irrefutable evidence that globalisation is taking place is a decline in the international dispersion of commodity prices or what might be called commodity price convergence" (O'Rourke and Williamson 2002, p. 26). Their definition of globalization, termed "hard" by De Vries (2010), is empirically demanding: "Where there is evidence of price convergence of spices between Malacca and Amsterdam, or of fine cotton goods between Calcutta and London, or of silver taels between China and Mexico, or of opium chests between Calcutta and Shanghai, then world market integration is at work" (O'Rourke and Williamson 2004, p. 109). In their view, globalization was a sudden phenomenon that started at some point after 1815. This exclusively economic interpretation of globalization has been, and still is, very popular among economic historians and economists. Notwithstanding, the stimulating intellectual threat posed by the notion of "hard globalization" has been responded in their own terms in two ways.

On the one hand, Flynn and Giráldez have found worldwide convergence of silver prices "not once but twice prior to the nineteenth century, by 1640, then again around 1750" (Flynn and Giráldez 2004, p. 87). Silver plays a protagonist role in their version of globalization, labelled "soft" by De Vries (2010) to distinguish it from the "hard" definition of globalization (see Flynn and Giráldez 1995). In fact, the globalization of the Early Modern era disposed of its own currency: the "*reales de a ocho*" or "Spanish dollars". They were coined by billions in Spanish America and circulated all over the world. Brazil's gold production, particularly during the eighteenth century, made a significant contribution to the global money supply too. Chopped "*reales de a ocho*" coined mainly in Mexico City and Lima, in particular during the reigns of Charles III and Charles IV—the "*Carolus pesos*"—may be found all across the world, in Africa, America, Asia, and Oceania.[6]

[6] "*Reales de a ocho*" were re-stamped by the Bank of England with the head of King George III in 1797 with a wide acceptance by the public as a remedy for the shortage of money caused by the Bank Restriction Act and the consequent suspension of the gold standard. At a smaller scale, "*reales de a ocho*" were also re-stamped by private firms in the county of Refrenswhire and, in particular, in the commercial town of Greenock by the late eighteenth and the early nineteenth centuries. Even more economically significant, the "*real de a ocho*" was declared legal tender in the United States in 1793 and it remained so, along with its successor, the Mexican peso, until 1857.

On the other hand, world integration of markets other than the market for silver before the nineteenth century has also been found by some authors. Klas Rönnbäck claims that:

> If convergence is measured by the coefficient of variation, several of the most important commodities –such as tea, textiles, tobacco, sugar and slaves– do experience trends of price convergence prior to the nineteenth century. If convergence is measured in the form of the deflated standard deviation, most of the commodities studied in this article experience trends of convergence. (Rönnbäck 2009, p. 13)

Similarly, Dobado, García-Hiernaux and Guerrero conclude that

> the beginning of globalization is perceptible several decades before the start of the canonical period. It began as commodity price synchronization between distant markets in the eighteenth century. After periods of disintegration (1792–1815) and transition (1815–1846), commodity price convergence is also found. This view may be considered a partial revision of the standard version of globalization since it emphasizes an earlier origin, a nonexplosive initial development, a longer duration, and a non-monotonic evolution over almost two centuries from the first half of the eighteenth century to 1913. (Dobado et al. 2012, p. 697)

Pim De Zwart also finds evidence of price convergence—i.e., "hard globalization"—in the Early Modern era:

> I show that for a majority of commodities in the Dutch-Asiatic trade, prices in Europe and Asia converged. There were limits to this process; some prices diverged and mark-ups remained high. Total trade volumes were much larger and price convergence was faster and more universal in the nineteenth century, nonetheless, if one considers a steady growth of trade and price convergence in a significant share of that trade to be a sufficient condition for globalization, then these results suggest early modern origins for globalization. (De Zwart 2016, p. 544)

Therefore, it is our contention that the concept of early globalization is supported by substantial research even if the rather narrow limits imposed by the identification of globalization with international market integration are not surpassed. Additionally, the notion of early globalization is consistent with the "soft" version of globalization.[7] This version, defended by Flynn and Giráldez (2008), emphasizes the relevance of the sustained interactions across continents that emerged circa 1500 as the cornerstone of globalization. Therefore, our formulation of the early globalization is more inclusive of the variety of new factors that influenced human existence during the three centuries that precede the beginning of the canonical period of "hard" globalization. Some of those factors are taking into consideration in this volume—migrations across the Atlantic, silver production in Hispanic America and international prices, or Asian goods consumption in the Iberian Empires. The very notion of early globalization implies a multidisciplinary approach, which is the one adopted in this book.

In our view, estimating the net effect of the Early Globalization on global well-being is not easy, if only because of methodological difficulties. Thus, we disagree with the emphatic claim by De Zwart and Van Zanden that "there is not much doubt that the net effect of globalization on global well-being –particularly when we include the effects of warfare and conquest– was strongly negative" (De Zwart and Van Zanden 2018, p. 278). To start with, it is doubtful that warfare in the Early Modern era was caused only, or even mainly, by the Early Globalization—e.g., the Thirty Years War. Others factors—i.e., dynastic politics and religious intolerance—seem more likely explanations of this lasting and costly intra-European armed conflict. Moreover, was the conquest of Ming China by the Manchu in mid seventeenth century connected to the early globalization? We are rather inclined to answer negatively. More instances of conflict might be adduced as well—e.g., Ottoman and Mughal expansions or interstate warfare in Africa.

On the contrary, we partially agree with their statements that:

> The realignment and distribution that occurred during these three centuries of globalization had large consequences for the well-being of the peoples involved. As always, there were winners and losers. In general, it can be said that the winners were mainly located in Western Europe […] Compared with these modest gains in well-being achieved by the

[7] "Evocations of a compressed and intensified world may be called 'soft globalization'" (De Vries 2010, p. 711).

> "winners" of globalization, there were also real losers in the process who suffered immeasurably. (De Zwart and Van Zanden 2018, p. 278)

Certainly, there were winners and losers. However, how to measure their respective gains and losses in terms of welfare is far from being an easy task. No satisfactory unit of measurement may be used for estimating the net global effect of globalization on human well-being. Likely, this methodological problem will never find an acceptable solution. Generally, the literature on the Early Modern era focuses on the losses—slavery, demographic disasters, violence, etc. However, some positive consequences for non-Europeans might have been overlooked. We will briefly consider the cases of China and West Africa and pay some more attention to Hispanic America.

As to China, producing tea, silk textiles and porcelain for the Western markets in exchange for the Hispanic American silver permitted the existence of a flourishing economy, at least until the nineteenth century. Therefore, participating in the Early Globalization does not seem to have been a bad business for China, which constituted the biggest economy and population in the world. The early adoption of American plants—corn, sweet potatoes and peanuts—significantly contributed to its rapid population growth during the Early Modern era, since they can be cultivated in non-irrigated land. A renowned specialist in Chinese economic history offers a clearly positive view on the "economic boom of the eighteenth century", a period that was also one of "remarkable domestic tranquility" (Von Glahn 2016, p. 322). In any case, placing China among the losers of the Early Globalization is questionable. Something stronger may be said with respect to Japan and Korea, since the two countries decided to close their economies to a significant degree in the seventeenth century. On the contrary, there are irrefutable reasons to include large parts of South Eastern Asia in the losers' side—i.e. the Banda Islands genocide by the Dutch East India Company, highlighted by De Zwart and Van Zanden (2018).

Certainly, Africa paid a high price in the form of slavery since more than ten million Africans were transported to the Americas across the Atlantic. Slavery might have had pervasive effects on economic development of large parts of the continent (Nunn 2017). Diamond (1997) offers a geo-ecological ultimate explanation of the "outcome of Africa's collision with Europe" based on: (a) the lower availability of domesticable animals and plants; and (b) the retardation in the diffusion of food production and innovation caused by the morphological dominance of the north–south axis, as compared with the much more favorable east-west axis in Eurasia.

However, the Early Globalization did not have only negative effects on Africa. In Herbert Klein's own words

> the introduction of American food crops to the African continent would revolutionize food production here as much as did the American potato in Europe and Asia. Early in the period of slave trade, manioc and maize were introduced into Africa. Manioc, which originated in Brazil, had a revolutionary impact on the forest agriculture, providing a crucial new food crop ideal for forest cultivation and one that could dependably feed and maintain more dense populations. In turn, maize became an important food crop on the savanna. Tobacco, cacao, peanuts, and a host of other American plants were also introduced, many of which become important African commercial export crops in later centuries. (Klein 2010, p. 64)

Obviously, we agree with De Zwart and Van Zanden's (2018) affirmation that plantation economies offered the African slaves that were forced to cross the Atlantic, as well as their descendants, "a dramatic decline in their well-being". Slavery was certainly important in the Caribbean and Brazil, but not so in Hispanic America.

As to this part of the world, any attempt to discuss the net effect of a constitutive element of the Early Globalization as the Spanish conquest requires nuanced and comprehensive thinking. Here we can only present our arguments in reduced form.

In the first place, the notion of *Pax Hispanica* turns out to be useful to understand the costs and benefits of belonging to the Spanish Empire. After the conquest and the intense associated violence, a period of nearly three centuries of peace—not without some exceptions that seem minor if compared with Europe at the time—contrasts with the pre-Hispanic and post-independence periods.

Enrique Semo reckons that for the Mexicas, appropriation of plunder and extraction of tribute from the submitted peoples "were an essential part of the national wealth" and that military activity played "a fundamental role in the education and occupation of males" (Semo

2006, p. 237).[8] According to Peter Bakewell, when referring to the Aztecs/Mexicas:

> the violence accompanying conquest, and the marching of armies across the land en route to the expanding frontier, had a usefully intimidating effect on previously subjugated polities. So did the constant cutting and plucking of captive's hearts and the cascading of their blood down the temple stairways in Tenochtitlan. [...] War, religion, politics and economics thus intertwined to reinforce one another, and also what became after 1428, Aztec triumphal expansionism. (Bakewell 2004, p. 30)

For this author, the Incas drew on violence less frequently than the Mexicas. However, in their nearly continuous expansion since the mid-fifteenth century, they managed to extend the limits of their rule from the Maule River to contemporary Ecuador, and this expansion needed "a military power that no one could oppose" that "swept all before it" (Klein 2006, pp. 19–20). Along with territorial gains, the expansion of the Inca Empire had an economic goal: "Tribute collection was a major purpose of the imperial enterprise. Tribute was not set directly in goods, but in labor obligations that produced goods" (Bakewell 2004, p. 35).

Thus, the expansion of the Mexica and the Inca empires was inseparable of long decades of almost permanent warfare of high or low intensity. It brought about the oppression of aboriginal peoples that supported the system imposed by the conquerors. In fact, some of those peoples actively cooperated with the Spaniards against their former lords.

After independence, with the exception of Brazil and Chile, the new republics were plagued during most of the nineteenth century with numerous international and civil conflicts.[9] Thus, in our opinion, the centuries-long *Pax Hispanica* should play a role in the explanation of the finding by Arroyo and Van Zanden that "[...] there was much more economic growth between 1550 and 1780 than previously assumed. Major indices of economic development such as urbanization rates, real wages of unskilled labors, literacy, and numeracy confirm this picture" (Arroyo and Van Zanden 2016, p. 1183).

[8] Translated from Spanish by the authors.

[9] Hispanic America "experienced almost continuous war and civil strife between the 1820s and the 1870s" (Coatsworth and Williamson 2002, p. 11).

Mining, through what has been termed "*mining-led growth*" by Dobado and Marrero (2011), was the main engine of a particular kind of Smithian growth. It was especially intense and widespread in eighteenth-century Mexico. No convincing empirical evidence supports the claim that growth did not improve economic and biological living conditions of the lower segments of the society. Rather the contrary seems to be true according to Arroyo et al. (2012), Dobado and García-Montero (2014), Dobado (2015), Challú and Gómez-Galvarriato (2015), Dobado and García-Hiernaux (2017), and Llorca-Jaña et al. (2018). If measured through numeracy, levels of human capital formation in central New Spain by late-eighteenth century were comparable with those of the less advanced European countries (Calderón-Fernández et al. 2020).

Confirming previous studies, Arroyo and Van Zanden offer an "optimistic" view on real wages. They often were higher in the "colonies" than in the metropolis:

> From the numerous historical studies, we know that certain cities in Latin America had relatively high wages by mid-seventeenth century. Starting at or below subsistence level in early colonial times (ca. 1550s) real wages in Mexico City and Potosi climbed to higher levels than in Madrid. The Peruvian living standards had a more moderate trend even though they exceeded Madrid's levels by 1750s. (Arroyo and Van Zanden 2016, p. 1199)

In some case, the *Pax Hispanica* permitted the resettlement of population from locations justified in times of war—e.g. rugged terrain—to better ones in terms of conducting economic activities (García 2006).

The generally accepted—if empirically untested—view of Hispanic America as the quintessence of inequality has been also questioned by Coatsworth (2008), Dobado and García-Montero (2010) and Williamson (2015). A logical inference from these studies is that the extractive character of the institutions in Hispanic America has probably been overestimated. The meaning of John Coatsworth's words are unequivocal:

> the Spanish and Portuguese colonial societies were less unequal, social hierarchies far more contested, and settler elites therefore far less powerful than is suggested in the new work, and much of the old historiography. In the Amerindian colonies of Mesoamerica and the Andes, for example, the creole settler elite did not control the indigenous peasantry's access to land. Colonial officials and magistrates were explicitly and repeatedly

> instructed to issue land titles to indigenous villages and to defend village lands against usurpation and encroachment. In contrast to Britain and the European continent, most of the arable land in the predominantly indigenous colonies of Spanish America belonged to indigenous peasants and their communities until long after independence. In the Andes, moreover, most of the highland pastures with their immense llama herds also remained under indigenous ownership and control throughout the colonial era. (Coatsworth 2008, p. 556)

In the same vein, Herbert Klein shares the idea that in Charcas, free Indian communities "remained the dominant form of social organization and landownership" (Klein 2006, p. 49).

Moreover, along with large-scale slavery—a new form of coerced labor that came to be added to others previously existing, markets for production factors appeared for the first time in the Americas as a result of the partial transfer of European institutions made by the Iberians. This institutional progress is increasingly perceptible over the three centuries preceding the independence, probably more in New Spain than elsewhere in Iberian America. Not much attention has been paid so far to the increase in economic efficiency resulting from the creation *ex nihilo* of markets for land, labor, and capital. On the contrary, institutions based on pre-existing practices, such as the *mita*, the *encomienda* or the *repartimiento* have frequently been presented as epitomes of labor extraction that basically persisted from conquest to independence and beyond, i.e. Acemoglu et al. (2002) and Engerman and Sokoloff (2005). When those institutions are historicized, instead of taking them as a constant, another picture arises. Of decreasing importance over time—some of them were legally suspended, they were progressively displaced by an enlarging market for free labor.

A case in point is mining. In Potosí, supposedly the most infamous mining center of the Early Modern era, *mitayos* were very well paid by international standards. Besides, after staying at Potosí the time established by the *mita* norms, they often decided to stay in town and become free miners earning still higher wages (Bakewell 1989; Klein 2006; Dobado and García-Montero 2012). Moreover, other Andean mining centers were *mita*-less (Bakewell 2004). In New Spain, especially in the northern mining centers, since its very discovery by mid-sixteenth century and during the "golden age" of the eighteenth century, coerced work, if anything, was marginal (Klein 2006). Besides, New Spain miners also constituted a very well paid and movable labor force.

Additionally, a significant—but also difficult to measure—part of the efficiency gains for Hispanic America after the conquest is related to the adoption of new technologies. The technological backwardness of Pre-Hispanic Mexico is recognized by Semo (2006). Other American civilizations did not fare any better in terms of their technical progress before the Early Modern era. The arrival of some plants—wheat, rice, etc.—and animals—horses, mules, cows, sheep, hens—along with new technologies—iron tools, wheels, cranes, mills, printing press, etc.—improved the poor living standards, both economic and biological, of most of the pre-Hispanic population, particularly in the Mexica Empire and surrounding areas. Erecting impressive pyramids and other magnificent buildings or transporting goods in the absence of metals, cranes, and animal power must have been extremely demanding in terms of human effort. The anthropometric history of the pre-Hispanic period shows a pessimistic view on health and nutrition (Steckel 2005). It points to a highly unequal distribution of work effort and access to food between the elite and the commoners in Central America. Besides, from mid-fifteenth century, the nutritional situation of the Valley of Mexico seems to have seriously worsened (Knight 2002; Calderón-Fernández 2016).

Thus, technology transfer, human capital accumulation and institutional development brought by the settlers to Iberian America help to explain a "reversal of fortune" which is exactly the opposite to the one proposed by Acemoglu et al. (2002). According to Comín et al.

> Latin American countries were behind the median country in the overall technology adoption level in 1500, but today they are middle income countries. This very likely has something to do with the long period of European settlement in Latin America, even though the European settlers were generally a minority of the population (Comín et al. 2010, p. 82)

In other words, Hispanic America has today a level of GDP per capita which is higher than the one that could be expected according to its development in 1500. The reason for this positive difference is the rather poor adoption in Pre-Columbian times of main technologies in such significant fields for economic growth as "writing and records", "technological specialization"—chiefly metalworks, "land transport", and "agriculture".

That poor state was improved substantially by the rapid diffusion of relatively advanced technologies brought by the conquerors.

Thus, Hispanic America economic gains from the Early Globalization might well be more than modest. Certainly, a demographic catastrophe occurred in the Americas. This is the "original sin" of the conquest and, along with massive slavery, represents the dark side of the early globalization in this part of the world. The dramatic decline in population in Hispanic America is a fact beyond any doubt. However, its magnitude and causes (violence, epidemics, and exploitation) are debatable and they varied from place to place. The magnitude of the disaster is, and will be, difficult to estimate. First of all, there is not consensus about the size of pre-1492 population. Figures differ enormously: from more than a hundred million to less than ten for the whole continent (Livi 2006). Therefore the estimates of the demographic losses are also subject to high uncertainty. Livi recognizes the extreme difficulty of inferring from the known (the first fiscal registers elaborated not late after the conquest) to the unknown (the population of the Mexica Empire). Nonetheless, he claims that, in New Spain, there were "little more than one million inhabitants, less than a century after the Conquest, compared to the initial 5, 10 or more" (ibid., pp. 165–166).[10]

A differential feature of the Andean case with respect to the rest of the Americas is that the demographic decline started before the arrival of the Spaniards. According to Livi (2006), evaluating the change in population in the Andean region is additionally complicated by the fact that "terrible wars of succession" between two sons of the Inca Huayna Capac "had devastated the country and destroyed the geographic integration." All in all, estimating the population of the Inca Empire before the conquest is an "almost impossible enterprise". In spite of it, he proposes a figure of ten million as most likely. By the 1560s it would have fallen to 2 ~ 2.5 million. The Andean population continued to decline and it did not reach 1.5 million circa 1600; it is to say "a fraction of the initial population […] a disaster" (Livi 2006, p. 227).

Even accepting the most pessimistic estimates, important questions remains: what were the causes of the disaster? Did they result from the Early Globalization? Our answer to the first question is conventional: a

[10] For this source, the authors have provided their translation from the Spanish version.

combination of violence, epidemics, and mistreatment—or exploitation—of the aboriginal population. As to the second question, some ambiguity is inevitable since no assertive reply can capture its intricacy. Both questions are interrelated.

In turn, the inquiry into the causes of the disaster leads to one more question: which of the three above-mentioned causes was the most important? In our attempt to respond we will suggest some general considerations based on comparative history and economic thinking.

The role of violence was probably, and relatively, not very important. On the one hand, it was a constitutive element of the imperial expansion of the Incas and, especially, the Mexicas. On the other hand, significant decreases in population have taken place historically in the absence of violence due to worldwide epidemics –the Black Death, the "Spanish" flu and AIDS—or repeated huge famines in Asia. In this respect, Hawaii in the nineteenth century is an instance that is worth being considered. Not a conquest comparable to that of the Spaniards in America was necessary for the demographic catastrophe experienced by the Hawaiian population in the century following the arrival in 1778 of James Cook. As it might be expected, estimates of the pre-contact population vary from 200,000 to 1 million (Swanson 2016). For this author, "the sudden appearance of a highly infectious and deadly disease" might be the cause of a reduction of roughly 6 per cent in Native Hawaiians in two years after 1778 (ibid., p. 10). The short-term losses would be dramatically increased by those that appeared over the long term. The nearly 700,000 inhabitants in 1778 had declined to less than 30,000 in 1900. This decline widely surpasses the most pessimistic estimates for Hispanic America.[11] As opposed to the latter, the long-term growth of Part-Hawaiians (from zero in 1779 to roughly 8,000 in 1900) did not compensate for the demographic losses.[12] In summary, intense violence was neither new in American lands and nor needed to originate its dramatic demographic crisis.

As to the other two explanatory causes, the mistreatment or exploitation of the aboriginals will be discussed in a brief manner on two grounds. On the one hand, even accepting that extreme mistreatment might have occurred, especially in the Caribbean—Hispaniola Island might be a case

[11] Other estimates reduce the departure number to a range between 100,000 and 150,000. See Dye (1994).

[12] In the long run, the relative and absolute increase of the *mestizo* population in Hispanic America significantly contributed to cushion the effect of the demographic crisis.

in point, the quantitative support offered by original sources is not solid enough as to safely infer that it was a chief factor of mortality in the rest of Hispanic America. In fact, to the best of our knowledge, a well-founded comparison between the rates of exploitation of the tributaries by pre-Hispanic and Hispanic elites is still missing. On the other hand, economic rationality should be taken into account. This approach is based on the one adopted to study slavery in the United States by Fogel and Engerman (1974). Beside the limits legally established by the *Leyes Nuevas* in 1542, it was in the best interest of the recipients—Spanish conquerors or Indian caciques—of any form of tribute—labor or otherwise—no to destroy their allotments. Likely, the fall in population strengthened the need for this restriction to overexploitation of the—paid or unpaid—coerced labor force. Livi claims that:

> the conquerors [...] did not plan a genocide. They prospered through the natives work and violence was functional for imposing their domination over them. Gratuitous cruelty was certainly inflicted [...], but not as generally as to be considered an important cause of mortality. (Livi 2006, pp. 139–140)

Once violence and exploitation are discarded as main factors of the drastic depopulation of the continent, epidemics remain as the most convincing explanation. In fact, consensus among specialists exists on this matter (Pérez Moreda 2012). Some of the deadliest were imported (e.g. smallpox) while others were endemic. The latter have been overlooked in the literature. However, according to Barbi and McCaa (2003), they were important factors of depopulation. On top of violence and exploitation, whatever their importance was, epidemics were amplified by poor health and nutritional stress.

Bearing this in mind, we can now answer the second question posed above: should the Early Globalization be blamed for the demographic disaster in the Americas? In our view, it should not. As in other "immunological islands", such as late-medieval and eighteenth-century Iceland and the nineteenth-century Pacific Ocean, the dramatic decrease in the American population was not caused by the Early Globalization itself. It was the long-lasting isolation of the Americas from the rest of the world which made the catastrophe quite inevitable. Sooner or later, any other historically plausible contact between aboriginal Americans and Asians or Europeans—be them Iberians or not—would have had not very different results, since epidemics were until not so far back in time almost unstoppable.

Thus, in our interpretation, abundant evidence supports our certainly limited optimism on the world-wide economic effects of the early globalization. In any case, a close look to the Iberian Empires turns out to be fully justified.

Book's Structure and Short Summary of the Chapters

Beside this introductory chapter (Part I), the volume consists of two parts. The first one is titled "The Early Globalization: Description and Some Consequences" and comprises six chapters. The second part includes three chapters and bears "Trade and Consumption of Textiles in the Early Globalization" as title.

Part II. The Early Globalization: Description and Some Consequences

In "The Significance of Early Globalization: Arguments and Evidence", Dennis Flynn and Pim de Zwart review the two notions of globalization. They show evidence in favor of price convergence across international markets prior to the nineteenth century. Notwithstanding, these authors defend a wider definition of globalization that encompasses not only purely economic aspects whose significance still reverberates—e.g. epidemics and its consequences across the Atlantic as well as changes in agriculture and population resulting from the diffusion of species throughout the world. Their main conclusions are first, that globalization started as early as in the sixteenth century, and second, that some dimensions of the twenty-first century globalization were originated by the interactions between the Eastern and Western hemispheres from the beginning of the Early Globalization almost five centuries ago.

The Early Globalization brought about unprecedented displacements of population from Europe and Africa to the Americas. Herbert Klein's chapter, "International Migrations to Latin America and the Caribbean Until 1820", quantitatively examines some important dimensions of the free and coerced migration waves that crossed the Atlantic from the sixteenth to the beginning of the nineteenth centuries. Thus, major changes over time and space in the migration of Iberians and Africans are found. Economic and social factors determined the characteristics of

Iberian migrants—most of them adult, urban males—and their regions of destination. In continental Spanish America the persistence of a large Indian population and the increasing number of *mestizos* explains the difference in slavery with respect to the Hispanic Caribbean and Brazil: many less African slaves, and mainly urban. With the decrease in the Iberian and African migration, native-born *mestizos* and *castas* became the majority of a population with pre-modern demographic characteristics.

The chapter by Leticia Arroyo and Nuno Palma, "The Fruits of *El Dorado*: The Global Impact of the American Precious Metals", analyses the effect of the unprecedentedly large production of gold and silver in Iberian America during the Early Modern era on the international economy. To do that, they examine short-, medium- and long-term economic effects on several countries and parts of the world. Quantitative methods as used to estimate those effects, as well as a counterfactual (a metal-less empire). They conclude that, among European countries, England and the Netherlands benefited most. On the contrary, neither Portugal nor Spain, the colonizers *par excellence*, were able to make a profitable use of their overseas expansion. Less assertive is their conclusion regarding Iberian America. Certainly, its economic outcomes and institutions would have been different in the absence of such a large mining sector. As to the impact on Africa and Asia, the authors claim it was negligible.

In "Prices and Money in the Globalization of the Early Modern Era", Rafael Dobado and Alfredo García-Hiernaux posit that one of the main manifestations of the Early Globalization was the worldwide circulation of the "*real de a ocho*". Circa 1800 New Spain reached a historical record of coining: nearly 60% of the world total. After the beginning in 1810 of the conflict that led to independence, Mexican silver production dramatically decreased. However, the country remained an important producer. As most silver was exported, production in New Spain/Mexico directly influenced prices in the "open economies". Long term similar upward and downward movements of grain prices (with an inflection point in the mid-1810s) across the Atlantic economy and China are found, albeit not in the comparatively "closed" Japan and Korea. Thus, in most cases, statistical analysis confirms that price series are cointegrated.

Renate Pieper starts his chapter, "The Impact of Early Iberian Globalisation on Austrian Mining Ventures", with the famous Habsburg's motto: "*Bella gerant alii, tu felix Austria, nube*". It condenses into a few words the marriage policy of the famous royal family. It continues: "*Nam quse*

Mars aliis, dat tibi regna Venus." And yes, it describes the marriage policy of the Austrian Habsburgs towards the Iberian kingdoms from the beginning of the Early Globalization. This policy pursued not only political goals but also economic ones which are less well-known. From commercial ventures in Asia to exports of mercury to be used in silver production in Hispanic America, the economic connections between the Austrian Habsburg and the Iberian empires in the Early Modern era are thoroughly examined.

Part III. Trade and Consumption of Textiles in the Early Globalization

Arturo Giráldez, in "The Last Link of an Emergent Global Economy: The Manila Galleon", deals with one of the most important vehicles of the Early Globalization: the commercial route that during nearly 250 years connected Asia with Hispanic America, more precisely Acapulco with Manila. Tellingly, it was known, in Spanish, as the *Galeón de Manila* or the *Nao* (vessel) *de China*. Its operation from the second half of the sixteenth century added an unprecedented Pacific dimension to the network of intercontinental exchanges that already included the rest of the world. With Manila as entrepôt, this intra-Spanish Empire would have been impossible without China. The hunger for silver of the largest economy of the Early Modern era fueled long-lasting transactions, consisting basically in manufactured goods, especially textiles, in exchange for Hispanic American silver. Those Pacific-crossing galleons may be linked to the contemporary globalization.

"Weaving a Global Trade Pattern: The Portuguese Role in the Globalisation on Asian Textiles, 1500–1800", by João Teles e Cunha and Maria João Ferreira, presents an overview of the early leadership of Portugal in the circulation of Asian textiles outside the Indian Ocean. Textiles were not monopolized by the Crown. After 1560, New Christians of Jewish origin took an important part in establishing, for the first time, permanent trade connections between the Indian and the Atlantic Oceans. Thus, cheap Indian cottons were introduced in the slave trade. From 1600, other Europeans also participated in this new, and long-lasting, business. Brazil became an important market for Asian textiles: fine Chinese and Indian silk and cotton fabrics for the upper segments of the population, as well as inexpensive clothing for slaves and the less well-off commoners.

"Mass consumption" of Asian textiles appeared in Portugal in the second half of the eighteenth century.

One of the clearest signs of the Early Globalization was the increase in international trade. A significant part of the growing commercial exchanges corresponded to textiles, particularly from Asia. Nadia Fernández de Pinedo and Corinne Thépaut-Cabasset's "Memoirs of the Fruits of Globalization: The Markets for Chinese Textiles in New Spain by Jean de Monségur" studies the particular case of the New Spain at the beginning of the eighteenth century. The source used is a detailed report of the time: the *Nouveaux memoires touchant le Mexique ou la Nouvelle-Espagne*, of the French captain Jean de Monségur. The manuscript was presented to the king of Spain in 1709, following his visit to New Spain in 1707–1708. Monségur worked for the French intelligence services and had been commissioned to New Spain by the Comte of Pontchartrain, Louis XIV's minister of the Navy. In his work, Monségur describes the trade of textiles between New Spain and Asia. The authors put the travellers' data and reflections in the wider context of textile trade in and with Europe and Western clothing fashion.

Bibliography

Acemoglu, Daren, James Robinson, and Simon Johnson. 2002. "Reversal of Fortune: Geography and Institutions in the Making of the Modern World Income Distribution." *Quarterly Journal of Economics* 117 (4): 1231–1294.

Arroyo, Leticia, and Jan Luiten Van Zanden. 2016. "Growth Under Extractive Institutions? Latin American Per Capita GDP in Colonial Times." *The Journal of Economic History* 76 (4): 1182–1215.

Arroyo, Leticia, Elwyn Davies, and Jan Luiten van Zanden. 2012. "Between Conquest and Independence: Real Wages and Demographic Change in Spanish America, 1530–1820." *Explorations in Economic History* 49: 149–166.

Baena, Alberto. 2012. "Un ejemplo de mundialización: El movimiento de biombos desde el Pacífico hasta el Atlántico (s. XVII–XVIII)." *Anuario de Estudios Americanos* 62 (1): 32–61.

Bailey, Gauvin Alexander. 2006. "Asia in the Arts of Latin America." In *The Arts in Latin America, 1492–1820*, organized by Joseph J. Rishel with Suzanne Stratton-Pruitt. Philadelphia: Philadelphia Museum of Arts.

Bakewell, Peter. 1989. *Mineros de la Montaña Roja. El trabajo de los indios en Potosí, 1545–1650*. Madrid: Alianza América.

Bakewell, Peter. 2004. *A History of Latin America*. Oxford: Blackwell.

Barbi, Elisabetta, and Robert McCaa. 2003. "1491: Paradise, Purgatory and Hell: Health and Nutrition in the Americas Before and After Colombu." Presentation available at: https://users.pop.umn.edu/~rmccaa/. Visited on April 15, 2020.

Bonialian, Mariano. 2012. *El Pacífico hispanoamericano. Política y comercio asiático en el imperio español, 1670–1784*. Mexico City: El Colegio de México.

Bonialian, Mariano. 2014. *China en la América colonial. Bienes, mercados, comercio y cultura del consumo. Desde México hasta Buenos Aires*. Mexico City: Instituto Mora.

Calderón-Fernández, Andrés. 2016. "La crisis demográfica de la Nueva España en el siglo XVI: nuevas perspectivas de un viejo debate". In *Mirando a Nueva España en otros espejos. Cuatro ensayos sobre demografía y niveles de vida*, Ph.D. thesis, Universidad Complutense de Madrid, 55–126.

Calderón-Fernández, Andrés, Rafael Dobado-González, and Alfredo García-Hiernaux. 2020. "Numeracy in Central New Spain During the Enlightment." *Revista de Historia Económica/Journal of Iberian and Latin American Economic History* 38: 369–403.

Challú, Amílcar, and Aurora Gómez-Galvarriato. 2015. "Mexico's Real Wages in the Age of the Great Divergence, 1730–1930." *Revista De Historia Económica/Journal of Iberian and Latin American Economic History* 33 (1): 83–122.

Coatsworth, John. 2008. "Inequality, Institutions and Economic Growth in Latin America." *Journal of Latin American Studies* 40 (3): 545–569.

Coatsworth, John, and Jeffrey Williamson. 2002. "The Roots of Latin American Protectionism: Looking Before the Great Depression." NBER Working Paper No. 8999.

Comín, Diego, William Easterly, and Erick Gong. 2010. "Was the Wealth of Nations Determined in 1000 BC?" *American Economic Journal: Macroeconomics* 2 (3): 65–97.

Crosby, Alfred. 1972. *The Columbian Exchange: Biological and Cultural Consequences of 1492*. Westport: Greenwood Press.

Curiel, Gonzalo. 1994. "El ajuar doméstico del tornaviaje." In *México en el mundo de las colecciones de arte. Volumen 3*, directed by María Luisa Sabau. Mexico City: Editorial Azabache.

Curiel, Gonzalo. 2012. "Lenguajes artísticos transcontinentales en objetos suntuarios de uso cotidiano. El caso de la Nueva España." In *Pintura de los Reinos. Identidades compartidas en el mundo hispánico, miradas varias, siglos XVI–XIX*, coordinated by Andrés Calderón and Rafael Dobado. Mexico City: Fomento Cultural Banamex.

De Vries, Jan. 2010. "The Limits of Globalization in the Early Modern World." *Economic History Review* 63 (3): 710–733.

De Zwart, Pim. 2016. "Globalization in the Early Modern Era: New Evidence from the Dutch-Asiatic Trade, c. 1600–1800." *The Journal of Economic History* 76 (2): 520–558.

De Zwart, Pim, and Jan Van Zanden. 2018. *The Origins of Globalization. World Trade in the Making of the Global Economy, 1500–1800*. Cambridge: Cambridge University Press.

Diamond, Jared. 1997. *Guns, Germs, and Steel. The Fates of Human Societies*. New York: W. W. Norton.

Dobado, Rafael. 2015. "Pre-independence Spanish Americans: Poor, Short and Unequal... or the Opposite?" *Revista de Historia Económica/Journal of Iberian and Latin American Economic History* 33 (1): 15–59.

Dobado, Rafael, and Gustavo Marrero. 2011. "The role of the Spanish imperial state in the mining-led growth of Bourbon Mexico's economy." *The Economic History Review* 64 (3): 855–884.

Dobado, Rafael, and Héctor García-Montero. 2012. "Neither So Low No So Short: Wages and Heights in Bourbon Spanish America from an International Comparative Perspective." *Journal of Latin American Studies* 46: 291–321.

Dobado, Rafael, and Alfredo García-Hiernaux. 2017. "Two Worlds Apart: Determinants of Height in Late 18th Century Central Mexico." *Economics & Human Biology* 24: 153–163.

Dobado, Rafael, and Héctor García-Montero. 2010. "Colonial Origins of Inequality in Hispanic America? Some Reflections Based on New Empirical Evidence." *Revista de Historia Económica/Journal of Iberian and Latin American Economic History* 28 (2): 258–277.

Dobado, Rafael, and Héctor García-Montero. 2014. "Neither So Low nor So Short: Wages and Heights in Bourbon Spanish America from an International Comparative Perspective." *Journal of Latin American Studies* 46 (2): 291–321.

Dobado, Rafael, Alfredo García-Hiernaux, and David Guerrero. 2012. "The Integration of Grain Markets in the Eighteenth Century: Early Rise of Globalization in the West." *The Journal of Economic History* 72 (3): 671–707.

Dobado, Rafael, Alfredo García-Hiernaux, and David Guerrero. 2013. "West Versus East: Early Globalization and the Great Divergence." DT CCEE 1308. https://eprints.ucm.es/22528/1/13-08.pdf.

Dye, Tom. 1994. "Population Trends in Hawai'i Before 1778." *The Hawaiian Journal of History* 28: 1–20.

Engerman, Stanley, and Kenneth Sokoloff. 2005. "Colonialism, Inequality, and Long-Run Paths of Development." NBER Working Paper No. 11057.

Findlay, Ronald, and Kevin O'Rourke. 2007. *Power and Plenty. Trade, War, and the World Economy in the Second Millenium*. Princeton: Princeton University Press.

Flynn, Dennis, and Arturo Giráldez. 1995. "*Born with a 'Silver Spoon'*: The Origin of World Trade in 1571." *Journal of World History* 6 (2): 201–221.

Flynn, Dennis, and Arturo Giráldez. 2004. "Path Dependence, Time Lags, and the Birth of Globalisation: A Critique of O'Rourke and Williamson." *European Review of Economic History* 8 (1): 82.

Flynn, Dennis, and Arturo Giráldez. 2008. "Born Again: Globalization's Sixteenth Century Origins (Asian/Global Versus European Dynamics)." *Pacific Economic Review* 13 (3): 359–387.

Fogel, Robert, and Stanley Engerman. 1974. *Time on the Cross: The Economics of American Negro Slavery*. Boston: Little, Brown.

García Martínez, Bernardo. 2006. "La creación de la Nueva España." In *Historia General de México*. Mexico City: Centro de Estudios Históricos, El Colegio de México.

Giráldez, Arturo. 2015. *The Age of Trade. The Manila Galleons and the Dawn of the Global Economy*. Lanham: Rowman & Littlefield.

Gruzinski, Serge. 2010. *Las cuatro partes del mundo. Historia de una mundialización*. Mexico City: Fondo de Cultura Económica.

Klein, Herbert. 2006. *A Concise History of Bolivia*. Cambridge: Cambridge University Press.

Klein, Herbert. 2010. *The Atlantic Slave Trade*. Cambridge: Cambridge University Press.

Knight, Alan. 2002. *Mexico. From the Beginning to the Spanish Conquest*. Cambridge: Cambridge University Press.

Livi, Massimo. 2006. *Los estragos de la conquista*. Barcelona: Crítica.

Llorca-Jaña, Manuel, Juan Navarrete-Montalvo, Federico Droller, and Roberto Araya-Valenzuela. 2018. "Height in Eighteenth-Century Chilean Men: Evidence from Military Records, 1730–1800s." *Economics & Human Biology* 29: 168–178.

Nunn, Nathan. 2017. "Understanding the Long-Run Effects of Africa's Slave Trades." VOX, CEPR Policy Portal. https://voxeu.org/article/understanding-long-run-effects-africa-s-slave-trades. Visited on May 6, 2020.

Nunn, Nathan, and Nancy Qian. 2019. "The Columbian Exchange: A History of Disease, Food, and Ideas." *Journal of Economic Perspectives* 24 (2): 163–188.

O'Rourke, Kevin, and Jeffrey Williamson. 2002. "When Did Globalization Begin?" *European Review of Economic History* 6 (1): 23–50.

O'Rourke, Kevin, and Jeffrey Williamson. 2004. "Once More: When Did Globalization Begin?" *European Review of Economic History* 8 (1): 109–117.

Pacheco, Maria. 2013. "Chinese Textiles for Portuguese Tastes." In *Interwoven Globe*, edited by Amelia Peck. New York: The Metropolitan Museum of Art.

Pérez Moreda, Vicente. 2012. "La población de España y las Indias en los siglos XVI y XVII." In *Pintura de los Reinos: Identidades compartidas en el mundo hispánico, miradas varias, siglos XVI–XIX*, coordinated by Andrés Calderón and Rafael Dobado. Mexico City: Fomento Cultural Banamex.

Rivero, Rodrigo. 2005. *El arte namban en el México virreinal*. Madrid: Turner.

Rönbäck, Klas. 2009. "Integration of Global Commodity Markets in the Early Modern Era." *European Review of Economic History* 13 (1): 95–120.

Semo, Enrique. 2006. "Los orígenes." In *Historia Económica de México*, coordinated by Enrique Semo. Mexico: UNAM.

Smith, Adam. 2008. *The Discovery of America, and That of a Passage to the East Indies by the Cape of Good Hope, Are the Two Greatest and Most Important Events Recorded in the History of Mankind*. New Delhi: Atlantic.

Steckel, Richard. 2005. "Health and Nutrition in Pre-Columbian America: The Skeletal Evidence." *Journal of Interdisciplinary History* 36 (1): 1–32.

Swanson, David. 2016. "The Number of Native Hawaiians and Part Hawaiians in Hawaii, 1778–1900: Demographic Estimates by Age, with Discussion (Conference Paper)."

Von Glahn, Richard. 2016. *The Economic History of China*. Cambridge: Cambridge University Press.

Williamson, Jeffrey. 2015. "Latin American Inequality: Colonial Origins, Commodity Booms, or a Missed 20th Century Leveling?" NBER Working Paper No. 20915.

The Early Globalization: Description and Some Consequences

The Significance of Early Globalization: Arguments and Evidence

Pim de Zwart and Dennis O. Flynn

Introduction

To what extent can the early modern period be viewed as a first age of globalization? This question has been at the centre of an academic debate among economic historians over the past two decades. The answer to the question is, of course, crucially influenced by the definition of globalization. Two definitions have dominated the literature to date. The first, put forth by Dennis O. Flynn and Arturo Giráldez (2004, 2008), defines globalization as sustained interaction among all of the world's heavily populated land masses on a scale that generated deep and lasting impacts. Their geographical definition emphasizes a multidimensional process that includes economic, environmental, epidemiological, demographic and cultural aspects. A second definition offered by Kevin O'Rourke and Jeff Williamson (2002, 2004) describes the process in much narrower terms. They suggest that globalization means integration of markets, and that

P. de Zwart (✉)
Wageningen University, Wageningen, The Netherlands
e-mail: pim.dezwart@wur.nl

D. O. Flynn
Pacific World History Institute, San Francisco, CA, USA
e-mail: doflynn@pacific.edu

R. Dobado-González and A. García-Hiernaux (eds.), *The Fruits of the Early Globalization*, Palgrave Studies in Comparative Global History,
https://doi.org/10.1007/978-3-030-69666-5_2

evidence for market integration can be found in analysis of convergence of prices across the globe. Jan de Vries (2010) dubbed the former definition "soft" globalization, and the latter "hard" globalization in his review of this debate.

In this chapter, we first demonstrate that the early modern period can be confidently viewed as the first era of globalization according to either definition. In measurable, quantitative "hard" terms, substantial globalization took place prior to 1800: trade volumes increased, prices converged globally, purchase patterns changed, migration increased, and environmental integration ensued. Second, we show that irrespective of "hard" globalization, effects of sustained global interactions were highly significant. In fact, we argue that impacts of "soft" globalization were often much "harder" than impacts of "hard" globalization. We suggest that globalization was a driving force that influenced patterns of global economic divergence prior to the Industrial Revolution, patterns that largely persist into the twenty-first century.

Integration of Global Commodity Markets

Did commodity markets across the globe become increasingly integrated during the early modern period (ca. 1500–1800)?[1] Until recently, the answer to this question has usually been negative: lack of technological progress in shipping, information asymmetries and monopolies (O'Rourke and Williamson 2002, 2004), as well as low trading volumes compared with total population (De Vries 2010), meant that domestic prices remained unaffected by global trade and events. Since prices did not budge, according to this view, effects of globalization were inconsequential. Technological progress involving steamships and railroads, as well as the demise of monopolies by chartered companies, caused commodity prices to converge globally only after the Napoleonic Wars (O'Rourke and Williamson 2002). This view has been highly influential among economists, and some economic historians even refer to the nineteenth century as "the first age of globalization" without bothering to explain it (see e.g. Alexander and Keay 2019; Chilosi and Federico 2019; Pascali 2017).

[1] See also: De Zwart and Van Zanden (2018).

Recent research, however, has put this view in doubt. While it is true that trade grew faster, and prices converged quicker, during the nineteenth century, there is nevertheless evidence of integration of markets along all major trade routes (between America and Europe, Africa and America, America and Asia, and between Europe and Asia). Flynn and Giráldez (1995, 2002, 2004) had long observed convergence of silver prices (expressed in gold) during both the seventeenth and eighteenth centuries, which—since silver was the main medium of exchange globally—clearly indicates integration of global markets. Klas Rönnback (2009) questioned whether patterns of price evidence observed by O'Rourke and Williamson (2002) would hold for all routes if data analyses were expanded. Rönnback's (2009) analysis showed price convergence for sugar between Brazil and Europe, coffee between Asia and Europe, tea between China and Europe, among others. In addition, he finds convergence in prices of slaves between Brazil and Luanda (Angola). This latter finding has been confirmed with figures on slave prices in Africa and Jamaica (De Zwart and Van Zanden 2018). Additional evidence of integrating Atlantic markets came from analysis by Rafael Dobado-González et al. (2012) of a large database of prices in grain markets in the Americas and Europe. They suggest that, at least regarding grain markets, integration across the Atlantic started during the eighteenth century.

Extensive work on trade between Europe and Asia by Pim De Zwart (2016a, b) is based upon new primary materials extracted from Dutch East India Company (VOC) archives. De Zwart analyzed trends in price convergence between Asia and Amsterdam for 16 products that constituted over 90% of total VOC trade. Ten product series showed statistically significant price convergence trends in the period between 1600 and 1800, while five series showed divergence, and only one product showed no significant trend in price gaps. Some goods were of greater importance than others, of course, and constituted a larger share of total trade in terms of volumes or values. VOC price gaps generally showed convergence when weighted by total volumes, invoice values, or in terms of gross margins (the overall difference between the invoice value of all goods purchased in Asia and total income from sale of these goods in the Dutch Republic). Evidence of VOC prices thus show a substantial scope for convergence of prices between Europe and Asia during the seventeenth and eighteenth centuries. At the same time, it becomes clear that there was no uniform development in these price gaps over time (De Zwart 2016a, b).

The extensive database with consistent data from a single company active in various regions of Asia also permits a deeper probe into the question of what determined price convergence, or lack thereof? An important part of this story is, of course, monopsony and/or monopoly powers held by European chartered trading companies (like the VOC, the British East India Company and the Compagnie des Indes), which influenced market conditions and prices. European chartered companies in principle held monopoly rights for sale of Asian goods in their domestic markets. In practice, pricing power of these companies was often limited due to competition from third markets as well as smuggling (De Zwart 2016a). Furthermore, the extent of control by these companies differed in overseas purchase markets, as shown for the VOC. Whereas in many cases VOC traders represented just one party of traders among many others, and therefore had to pay going market rates, in other cases they obtained special trading privileges in return for military support to a local ruler, while again in other cases the VOC became territorial colonial ruler and held complete control over local production.

Combining information on conditions in purchase and sales markets, De Zwart (2016a, b) identified four different types of commodities: free market goods, contract goods, colonial goods and monopoly goods. Prices converged strongly for those commodities bought in competitive markets throughout China and India (some as fast as 1% per year—reducing the mark-up to almost 1 for textiles and tea by the end of the eighteenth century).[2] Figure 1 shows fast price convergence for tea. Price convergence was less impressive, but still present, for most goods acquired by the VOC in areas where it received special trading privileges (like Japan, Sumatra, and Siam), but the VOC was unable to control production in its entirety. Pepper in Fig. 1 provides an example of a "contract good". A third set of commodities were those produced under colonial systems, like coffee in Fig. 1 and also sugar, which meant that the VOC was in complete control of purchase prices and quantities produced. Since these goods still competed on European markets with the same commodities brought in from elsewhere, however, prices could still converge due to large declines in European sales prices (e.g. the case of sugar). The final group of commodities consists of the famous four monopoly spices. These monopolies could seriously hinder the process of price convergence, and

[2] Since the mark-up is a ratio, a mark-up of 1 implies no difference in prices.

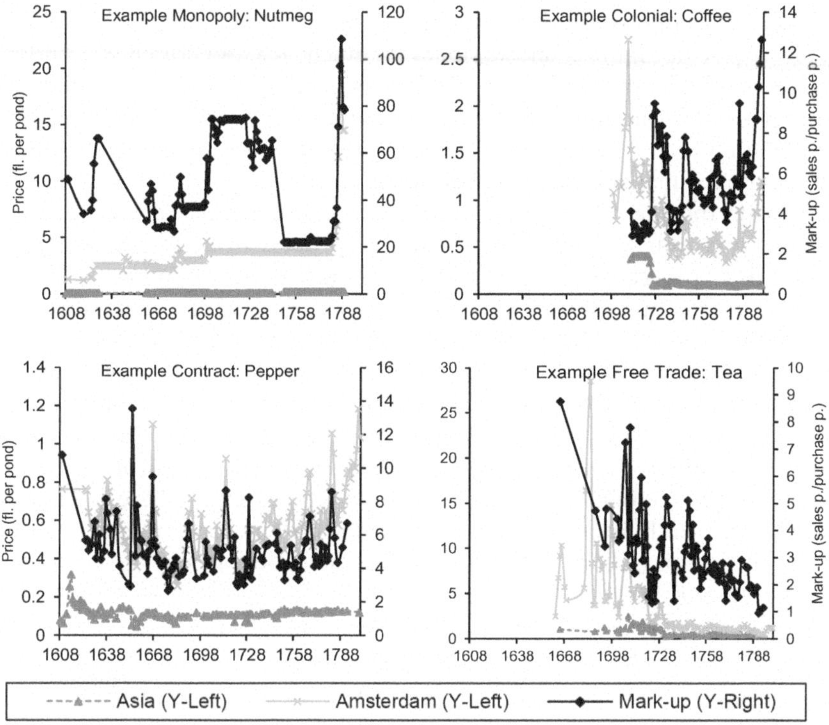

Fig. 1 Purchase and sales prices and the mark-up for example monopoly, colonial, contract and free trade goods (*Source* De Zwart 2016a, b)

mark-ups remained excessively high, as can be seen from the example of nutmeg in Fig. 1.

That no convergence of prices took place (in terms of reductions of the mark-up) for monopolies, however, does not mean that this trade had no impact. In those areas where the VOC hindered increases of prices in production areas, such as the Banda Islands (nutmeg) and Java (coffee) in Indonesia, VOC colonial intrusion in fact had dramatic and long-lasting impacts on local societies. In Banda, for example, almost the entire native population had been killed by the VOC because of its attempt to monopolize production. Furthermore, even in cases where prices may not have converged globally, due to obstacles to the functioning of commodity markets in the Global South, prices in Europe for these "colonial" goods could still decline substantially compared with developments in domestic product prices. Figure 2 shows prices for sugar, tea and coffee in London and Amsterdam deflated by a local consumer price index. It becomes clear from this picture that prices of these global goods declined significantly compared with prices of domestic goods, making global products attainable for many European costumers.

During the age of mercantilism, the rise of colonialism across portions of Asia was thus a major obstacle to the process of price convergence, rather than a force spurring further integration as has often been claimed for the nineteenth century (De Vries 2010). Over the seventeenth and eighteenth centuries the VOC came to be colonial ruler over large parts of Ceylon (present-day Sri Lanka), Java (Indonesia), and the Moluccas (in the eastern part of the Indonesian archipelago). While in some regions, such as Java, the VOC may have been a 'reluctant imperialist' (e.g. Gaastra 2008), in others it deliberately expanded territorial control in order to safeguard its monopoly. Yet for goods produced in areas where European companies held little to no power (as was the case in, for example, most of India and China), there was clearly sufficient scope for prices to converge across the globe.

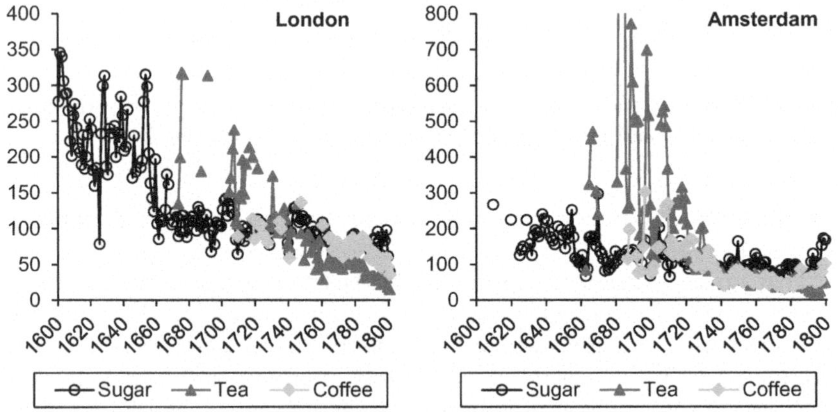

Fig. 2 Prices of sugar, tea and coffee in Amsterdam and London relative to consumer price index, 1600–1800 (*Source* De Zwart and Van Zanden 2018)

The Rise of Global Trade and Migration

Between 1500 and 1800 a boom in global trade and shipping took place (also observed by O'Rourke and Williamson 2009). Trade between Europe and Asia expanded at a rate of about 1% per year (De Vries 2010). Trade between Europe and the Americas, about which data are patchy, possibly increased at twice that rate (ibid.). This growth of trade was quite dramatic when compared with growth of GDP in Western Europe (0.4 per cent per annum) during this same period (Kelly and O' Grada 2019). Total world population between 1500 and 1800 increased a mere 0.25 per cent per annum. Global trade thus became a substantially more important part of European economies, as well as in per capita terms. Most important among commodities traded globally in this period was silver from Spanish American mines. Over these centuries there was a notable increase in both the production and export of American silver across the globe. Because Europeans produced little that was of interest to Asian customers, American silver relieved an important bottleneck of early trade.[3] Silver paid for an ever-increasing volume of pepper, spices, coffee, sugar, silks, and textiles transported from Asia to Europe.[4] Large amounts of coffee and sugar, and later also cotton, were, of course, also produced in the slave economies in the Southern US, Caribbean and Brazil.

Growth of trade was aided by consistent improvements in shipping: ship sizes, labour productivity on ships and ship speeds. First, ocean going ships substantially increased in size over the early modern period. In early decades of the sixteenth century, the average Portuguese ship sailing to India could carry some 280 tons. Later that century, ships with 1,000 tons capacity became the norm. Similarly, VOC ships increased in size from an average of 400 tons in the early seventeenth century to 800 tons by the end of the eighteenth century. Labour productivity also increased, as growth of tonnage was not matched by a similar growth of personnel: as a result, ton-man ratios increased from about 5 to some 9 tons per

[3] On the other hand, Flynn (2019) argues that collapse of the Ming paper money system around 1430 led to expansion of inventory demand for silver, thereby doubling the price of silver within China vis-à-vis European markets. Thus, the great mid-fifteenth century silver mining surge within Europe had already been stimulated by developments within China long before the European voyages of discovery.

[4] See also Palma and Silva (2016) who estimate that without European access to American silver, trade between Europe and Asia would have been significantly lower.

person over the seventeenth and eighteenth centuries—a rather substantial increase in labour productivity. Rönnback (2012) demonstrated that slave ships increased speed from an average of 2 knots in the later seventeenth century to about 4 in the early nineteenth century. In a series of contributions, Peter Solar and co-authors showed the importance of copper sheathing for increased speeds of English ships from the later eighteenth century (Solar 2013; Solar and Hens 2016; Solar and Rönnback 2015; Solar and De Zwart 2017). Morgan Kelly and Cormac O'Grada (2019) confirmed that ship speeds increased from the 1770s on, not only due to coppering, but also as a result of small changes to sails and rigging and improvement of hulls. More speed meant reduction in both capital and labour costs of trade. All this demonstrates that shipping productivity did not stagnate before the Industrial Revolution, even if changes were not as revolutionary as those that followed it.

Finally, no trade can exist without people to organized it, nor can global commodities be produced without labour; thus, the early modern period exhibited an enormous rise in (often forced) migratory flows. The largest flow of people across the Atlantic in the sixteenth century were colonists from Iberia who came to settle in various parts of overseas Spanish and Portuguese empires. Between 1500 and 1600, some 650,000 Iberians crossed the Atlantic. This number was more or less similar in the seventeenth century, and then increased to almost a million in the eighteenth (Lucassen 2016, p. 27). The number of northern Europeans migrating to the (mainly northern) Americas was smaller before the nineteenth century: some 400,000 in the seventeenth century and double that number in the eighteenth (from France, Britain, the Dutch Republic, and Germany combined) (ibid.). A much smaller number of colonists settled in European Asian Empires; according to Giráldez (2013, p. 266), 'in any one year between 1600 and 1740 there were not more than fifty thousand Europeans to be found in the whole of Asia'. Already in the seventeenth century, however, African slaves replaced European colonists as the biggest migratory flow. Whereas in the sixteenth century about 280,000 slaves disembarked in the Americas, this figure increased to almost 2 million in the seventeenth century and 6.5 million in the eighteenth. Taking these migrations together, as well as adding smaller migratory flows between, for example, Asia and Africa,[5] there was a

[5] Based on excellent recent overviews of Richardson (2011) and Lucassen (2016).

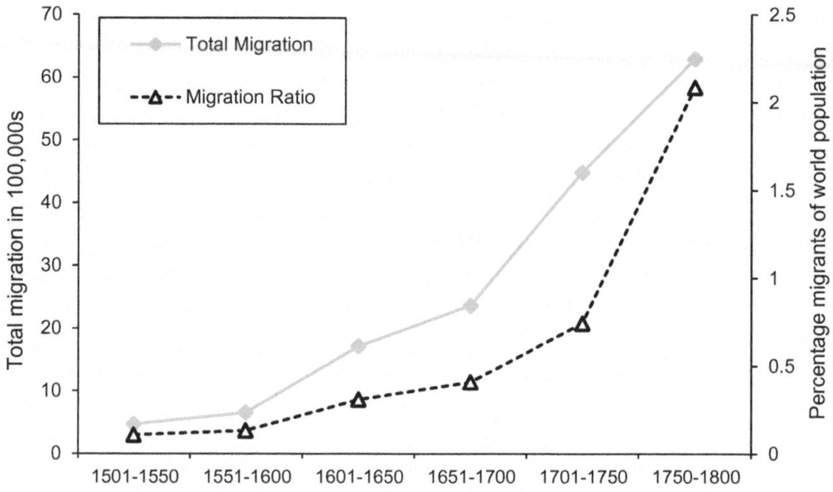

Fig. 3 Total number of intercontinental migrants and migration ratio, 1600–1800 (*Source* De Zwart and Van Zanden 2018)

substantial increase in both total migration and the total migration ratio—that is, migrants as a share of total population—over time (see Fig. 3). This increase in the migration ratio—which can only be an underestimate—provides another clear indication of growing interconnectedness of the early modern world. As a result of this migration, some early modern cities, like Amsterdam and Batavia, transformed into true melting pots where people from all corners of the globe lived together (De Zwart and Van Zanden 2018).

Consequences for Global Development

Debate

Thus far, we have shown how tremendous rise in global trade oftentimes spurred price convergence and thus caused integration of commodity markets, which contradicts the claim of O'Rourke and Williamson (2004, p. 113) that "no evidence" exists in support of price convergence prior to 1820. In this section we review the extent to which early modern globalization affected development across the globe. We argue that the evidence of price convergence is, in fact, not a very good guide for assessing the impacts of global connections on regional, geographic, economic, demographic, political and social developments.[6]

Some decades ago, influential thinkers of world-systems and dependency theories, like Immanuel Wallerstein (1974, 1989) and Andre Gunder Frank (1969, 1970), suggested that as a result of the growing global trading system, patterns of economic development across the globe diverged as clear winners and losers of the (capitalist) global trading system emerged. Frank (1969, 1970) specifically argued that Latin American underdevelopment resulted from inclusion in the capitalist world economy, stating that the closer ties with Europe, the more underdeveloped a country became. Wallerstein emphasized restructuring of the division of labour throughout the European world-system: whereas peripheral countries in the capitalist world-system focused on low-skilled-labour-intensive production of goods that yielded low profits, core countries (i.e. Western Europe) focused on high-skilled production of high-profit goods.[7]

These interpretations were questioned by Patrick O'Brien (1982, p. 18) who argued that intercontinental trade accounted for at most 1% of British GDP, and therefore concluded that "for economic growth at the centre, the periphery was peripheral". In his view, long-distant trade simply amounted to too little quantitatively for it to have a significant impact on patterns of development. Further doubts were raised by studies in the so-called "Great Divergence" debate concerning comparative living standards in Europe and Asia. For example, studies by R. Bin Wong (1997) and Kenneth Pomeranz (2000) on China and Europe, and Prasanan Parthasarathi (1998, 2011) on India and Europe, suggested that differences in living standards between the Europe and China had not yet emerged before 1800, thereby implying absence of divergence in need of explanation via globalization.

More recently, however, the world-systems and dependency theories have regained some ground as a result of research that showed not only

[6] Ning Ma (2017, p. 52), for instance, documents sweeping societal impacts worldwide reflected in the emergence of the novel "East and West" (specifically in China, Japan, and Spain) beginning in the late sixteenth century.

[7] Arguing against application of "Capitalism" terminology in describing global trade connections, Flynn (2020) includes specific criticisms of the European world-system framework promoted by Wallerstein. Readers should also keep in mind that Frank (1998) repudiated his own early views (and those of Wallerstein) late in his career.

direct, but also indirect effects of trade on patterns of economic development in both Europe and other parts of the world. Daron Acemoglu et al. (2001, 2002), for example, emphasized persistent effects of different types of colonial institutions implemented across the Americas, Africa and Asia. They suggest that Europeans implemented 'extractive' institutions, for example systems of forced labour, in areas like Latin America and Africa, that hindered long-run development. While new historical research with more detailed analyses of institutional developments (and their changes over time) in colonial empires has added nuance to this picture, and in some cases contradicted findings of economists, it is clear that impacts of global connections from the sixteenth century on were large.

Africa and the Americas

Dramatic changes resulting from globalization took place in the Americas. The indigenous population of the New World was decimated (up to 90% of the population had perished by the middle of the seventeenth century) due to diseases spread during worldwide biological integration (discussed more extensively below) (Newson 2006, p. 143). The Americas were subsequently repopulated by Europeans and Africans. In the most northern of American colonies, biographic conditions allowed for economies populated by large numbers of Europeans based around fishing and grain production and greater diversification. More difficult climatic and disease conditions for Europeans in the Carolinas, Georgia, the Caribbean and Brazil, however, led those societies to rely extensively on African slave labour for production of commodities that required concentrated labour inputs. In Spanish America, societies largely untouched by market forces (the Incas, for example, seem to have known almost no market exchange) transitioned into market economies. These economies at first retained many indigenous structures of coercion and monopolization, but later "free" labour and commodity markets began to emerge.

While various economists have emphasized negative long-run effects of European "extractive" colonialism in Latin America (e.g. Engerman and Sokoloff 2000; Acemoglu et al. 2001, 2002; Dell 2010), some recent investigations have questioned this. A wide range of evidence on wages and heights suggest living standards in Spanish America were similar or on a par with Europe in the early modern era (Arroyo

Abad et al. 2012; Dobado-González and García-Montero 2014; Challú and Gómez-Galvarriato 2015; Dobado-González and García-Hiernaux 2017). A recent study suggests high levels of human capital formation, as suggested by numeracy rates estimated using age heaping (Calderón-Fernández et al. 2020). Furthermore, it has recently been argued the Spanish colonial state in eighteenth- and nineteenth-century Mexico should be more positively assessed. The imperial government played an active role in stimulating expansion of the mining sector and mining contributed to economic growth, as proxied by growing tax receipts, in this era (Dobado-González and Marrero 2011). New estimates on GDP per capita suggest that there was substantial economic growth in Mexico and Peru between 1550 and 1800 (Arroyo Abad and Van Zanden 2016). Another investigation showed that funds "extracted" from the Spanish colonies and remitted to Spain were actually rather low, as most colonial state revenues were locally spent (Grafe and Irigoin 2012). A recent survey by Klein and Serrano Hernández (2018) bolsters claims of robust economic and demographic growth across Spanish America during most of the seventeenth century. Likewise, Suarez Espinosa (2018, p. 259) documents Peruvian wine sales at Lima or Panama at over one million pesos in 1677 and 1679 (over 3 million pesos at prices in Potosí) alongside massive flows of contraband silver from Peru across the Pacific Ocean.

Scholarly emphasis upon institutional arrangements makes sense, yet institutions are clearly influenced by physical geographies. Flynn and Giráldez (2008, p. 360) invoke "1/3, 1/3, 1/3 logic" to expand discussion of the birth of globalization from economic considerations alone; economic, environmental/ecological, epidemiological, demographic and cultural components emerged in context of transformative geographical realities. The Pacific Ocean spans one-third of Earth's surface. The Americas (including the Atlantic Ocean) comprise another one-third. The Afro-Eurasian "Old World" therefore cannot comprise more than the remaining one-third. Humans already resided on all of today's heavily populated land masses more than 12,000 years ago (Christian 2004, p. 193). When global warming melted ice caps, sea levels rose 300–400 feet, thereby mutually isolating "New World" from "Old World" for over 10,000 years. The significance of more than 100 centuries of isolation is difficult to overstate because flora, fauna, and diseases had evolved along divergent paths in each hemisphere.

From a geographical point of view, modern globalization occurred once permanent linkages were established among all three "1/3 regions" of the globe. Permanent linkages across the Atlantic began with the voyage of Columbus in 1492, while permanent linkages across the Pacific began with establishment of Manila Bay as a Spanish entrepot during 1565–1571.[8] These transoceanic connections unleashed profound forces summarized by prominent historian Alfred Crosby:

> Tradition has limited historians in their search for the true significance of the renewed contact between the Old and New Worlds. Even the economic historian may occasionally miss what any ecologist or geographer would find glaringly obvious after a cursory reading of the basic original sources of the sixteenth century; the most important changes brought on by the Columbian voyages were biological in nature. (Crosby 1972, p. xiv)

Introduction of Old World plants, animals, and diseases transformed physical landscapes across the Western Hemisphere. It is nearly impossible to imagine histories of North America, Central America, or South America without horses, cattle, donkeys, mules, sheep, goats, pigs, large dogs, bees, coffee, wheat, sugar, rice, grapes, oranges, and other fundamental building blocks of American societies. Crosby refers to associated ecological and social transformations as "a revolution more extreme than any seen on this planet since the extinction at the end of the Pleistocene" (Crosby 1986, p. 271). Utilizing stratigraphic records, Lewis and Maslin (2015) argue that decimation of indigenous American populations led inadvertently to reforestation and carbon sequestration, leading to the Little Ice Age of the seventeenth century; these authors claim that this initiated the Anthropocene era—human domination of the global environment—early in the seventeenth century.[9] Irrespective of whether these events ushered in the Anthropocene, historian Geoffrey Parker (2013, p. XXX) claims that the Little Ice Age crisis "increased an imbalance between

[8] Flannery and Ruiz-Stovel (2020) reveal widespread multi-ethnic connections throughout intra-Asian trade during the eighteenth century via micro-historical analysis of an exceptionally wealthy Manila-based merchant and ship owner from Southeastern India, Thomé Gaspar de León.

[9] See Hamilton's (2015) argument against this proposition by Lewis and Maslin; the argument of this chapter does not depend upon which side is correct regarding proper dating of the Anthropocene era.

supply and demand for resources… that would eventually reduce global population by perhaps one-third" during the seventeenth century.

Previously unknown throughout the Afro-Eurasian Old World, American plants and seeds—including corn/maize, potato, sweet potato, peanut, tomato, most beans, peppers, tobacco, and numerous others—physically transformed Afro-Eurasia. One-third to one-half of calories consumed today worldwide by humans and domesticated animals are attributable to New World plants previously unknown in the Old World. Eighteenth-century population explosions worldwide resulted largely from dissemination of American plants and seeds. Thanks in large part to American plants, the landmass of China doubled and Chinese population more than doubled during the eighteenth century, which in turn unleashed both supply-side and demand-side shockwaves globally (Flynn and Giráldez 2008). While circumstances no doubt continued to change fundamentally during the nineteenth century, as numerous scholars point out, it is nonetheless difficult to imagine the Industrial Revolution in the absence of rubber—unknown in the Old World prior to the sixteenth century— essential for manufacture of gaskets, tires, and other industrial applications (Mann 2011, Chapter 7).

Nowhere were impacts of introduction of American foodstuffs more pronounced than in Africa. As Crosby notes:

> The importance of American foods in Africa is more obvious than in any other continent of the Old World… Very few of man's cultivated plants originated in Africa – only 50 out of 640 […] – and so Africa had to import its chief food plants from Asia and America. This has been especially true in the rain forest areas, for practically none of the jungle food crops is native to Africa. (Crosby 1972, p. 185)

Moreover, "new American foods imported by Europeans…slowly replaced or supplemented traditional African foodstuffs, often permitting denser and healthier populations" (Klein 1999, p. 106). In an ironic twist, millions nourished by American foods within Africa were subsequently sent in chains to be nourished further by the same foods in the New World.

> Blacks were with Balboa when he claimed the Pacific,… with Cortes when he marched to Tenochtitlan…and Gonzalo Pizzaro…had up to 400 blacks in his forces…The principal role of Black Africans in the Spanish Empire

> was as mainstay of the economy...In no small measure, the black man created the empire that Spain directed in the New World. (Kamen 2003, pp. 139, 141)

Large exports of labour from Africa, a labour-scarce continent already before the sixteenth century (Austin 2008), significantly impacted local developments there. Impacts of the slave trade different substantially between and within regions. Coastal cities may actually have benefitted from growing commercialization, whereas hinterlands—where the slave raiding took place—were negatively impacted. Some areas exported many more slaves than others. For example, Angola and the Bight of Biafra (Cameroon) were disproportionally affected. In regions most heavily engaged with the Atlantic slave trade, it retarded population growth, commercial development and gave rise to violent conflict.

American silver was the main export product exchanged for imported slaves initially, and since a significant portion of New World silver exports ultimately came to rest in Chinese end-markets, China was therefore involved in the Transatlantic slave trade in an indirect sense. Similarly, African slaves crossed Indian and Pacific Oceans in exchange for silver: "The Portuguese need for silver explains why trading ships carried captives from as far away as Mozambique to sell in Manila, where they exchanged them for American silver" (Seijas 2014, p. 12). During the early modern period, massive flows of cowrie shells (an important global money produced mainly in the Indian Ocean's Maldive islands) flooded into West Africa as a major exchange item with which exported slaves were purchased.[10] *Larin* coins manufactured in Persia (from Spanish American silver), on the other hand, dominated the monetary system of the Maldives. As was true of countless products, coins routinely failed to recognize political boundaries. An important advantage of globalization history is revelation of direct and indirect long-distance interconnections that are routinely overlooked in histories restricted to nation-state analyses.

[10] For the most comprehensive history of cowries throughout the world to date, see Yang (2019).

Asia

Southeast Asia was heavily impacted by globalization. The Philippines and parts of present-day Indonesia (Java and the Moluccas) were especially affected by combined forces of colonialism and globalization. Whereas the region as a whole experienced increases in cash crop production and intensified commercialization, growing production for global markets was associated with increased labour coercion in parts of the region. The Dutch aggressively expanded territorial control in the Moluccas in order to control the world supply of cloves, nutmeg and mace (designed to hinder development of "hard" globalization—and no price convergence can be observed for e.g. nutmeg and mace). Virtually the entire indigenous population of the Banda islands was murdered or expelled and a plantation system was implemented. Large shares of population in Java were brought under Dutch control. Whereas for some this meant increased commercial opportunities, for example work as wage labourers in port towns like Batavia or Semarang, for others it may have meant an increase in forced labour (De Zwart and Van Zanden 2015).

Even seemingly isolated places like New Guinea were, in fact, connected to global processes via ecological forces. Consider these comments by Jared Diamond:

> …in former times New Guinea's available root crops were limiting for calories as well as for protein, because they do not grow well at high elevations where many New Guineans live today. Many centuries ago, however, a new root crop of ultimately South American origin, the sweet potato, reached New Guinea, probably by way of the Philippines, where it had been introduced by the Spaniards. Compared with taro and other presumably older New Guinea root crops, the sweet potato can be grown up to higher elevations, grow more quickly, and gives higher yields per acre cultivated and per hour of labor. The result of the sweet potato's arrival was a highland population explosion. (Diamond 1997, p. 149)

This sweet-potato-instigated population explosion, combined with introduction of European guns, fundamentally transformed expanding New Guinean societies. Although imports probably represented an infinitesimal fraction of GDP, globalization impacts upon the economic foundation of New Guinea were profound.

No region in the world played a more prominent role in the birth of globalization than China, notwithstanding periodic efforts by the Ming

Dynasty to disrupt powerful "silverization" forces stimulated by extraordinarily high silver prices in Chinese markets (Von Glahn 1996; Flynn 1996). Vast quantities of silks, ceramics, tea (later on) and other Chinese products were exported in exchange for enormous imports of silver from Japan and Spanish America. The timing and shape of Early Globalization would have certainly unfolded far differently, in ways that are difficult to imagine, had Chinese end-markets not become the most notorious "silver sinks" on earth (as a result of prior collapse of the Ming paper-money system). At least 10 million mostly freehold farmers or freehold tenants, more than the total population of England, migrated internally to underdeveloped parts of China during the late seventeenth and early eighteenth centuries (Pomeranz 2000, p. 84). Traditional depictions of China as backward/stagnant are contradicted by historical evidence. China's landmass doubled, while population more than doubled during the eighteenth century. China's "population growth in the eighteenth century was speeded up by massive ecological change: the introduction of new crops into China from the New World" (sweet potato, peanut, and maize) (Spence 1990, p. 95).[11]

Given such explosive expansion in eighteenth-century Chinese landmass and population, already "silverized," demand-side forces could not help but stimulate an unprecedented surge in silver mining in New Spain/Mexico (and to a lesser extent in Upper Peru). As is the case for any good, end-market concentrations of silver in particular locations were determined by demand to hold silver, one component of wealth in a region.

There is no consensus concerning long-term impacts of silver imports upon China's economy. Andre Gunder Frank (1998) argued that vast imports of silver, from Japan and Spanish America mostly, stimulated economic growth within China for centuries. In direct contradiction, Flynn and Giráldez (2000) reject cause-effect logic employed by Frank, maintaining instead that *demand to hold* silver within China *caused* import flows required to feed and maintain silver holdings. In short, Frank argued that *supply-side inflows* of silver *caused* Chinese economic growth, whereas Flynn and Giráldez maintain that *demand to hold silver (a wealth component)* within China *caused* its importation of silver. Cause and effect are reversed. Frank's position that silver imports *caused* domestic economic

[11] Impacts of New World crops on Chinese agriculture had long been acknowledged by Ho (1959, p. 268) and Naquin and Rawski (1987, p. 23).

expansion is essentially a restated version of "bullionistic/mercantilistic" views repudiated by Adam Smith and countless others since publication of the *Wealth of Nations* (1776). Flynn and Giráldez agree with the logic of Smith on this issue, since staggering volumes of silver were imported for centuries in exchange for voluminous quantities of Chinese silks, porcelains, tea (later on), and other export objects. Chinese exports represent *costs* associated with, as opposed to *benefits* from, obtaining and maintaining Chinese silver stocks. Cause versus effect, as well as costs versus benefits, are reversed.

Dynamics throughout early modern Chinese history were extraordinary, yet domestic trade among regions was interlinked with Chinese foreign trade in complex ways that are difficult to conceptually disentangle. Consider long-distance trade in grains within China:

> In… China.. the share of the harvest that was marketed over long distances seems to have been considerably higher than in Europe. Wu Chengming has conservatively estimated that 30,000,000 *shi* of grain entered long-distance trade in the 18th century, or enough to feed about 14,000,000 people. This would be more than five times a generous estimate of Europe's long-distance grain trade in a normal year during its heyday…. Eighteenth-century China (and perhaps Japan as well) actually came closer to resembling the neoclassical ideal of a market economy than did western Europe. (Pomeranz 2000, pp. 34, 70)

No one knows rates of profit or wealth accumulations attributable to trade directly or indirectly linked to global connections over these centuries, but we know of no evidence to suggest that Chinese merchants profited less than European merchant counterparts. What is known is that American plants rendered intensive exploitation of resources in former Chinese hinterlands possible. Resource sustainability was practiced in some regions of China, but environmental tragedy evolved in other regions:

> Ming… population increase spurred consolidation of a broader marketing system…. But especially important for the movement of large numbers of Han people from the lowlands into the highlands was the availability of new kinds of foods from the Americas that were especially adapted for those environments. (Marks 2017, p. 229)

High prices in lowland markets induced expansion into frontier regions. Upon exhaustion of soil, Han immigrants moved to nearby lands along with Americans plants (Von Glahn 2016, p. 329), leading to erosion and widespread environmental collapse during the nineteenth century (Marks 2017, Chapter 5, especially pp. 228–247).

Considerable long-term benefits seem to have accrued to Japanese society as a result of Japanese silver mines, which produced about half as much silver as all of Spanish America during the sixteenth and seventeenth centuries. Japanese silver was unsurprisingly exported mainly to Chinese end-markets, and the Shogunate gained control of all Japanese silver mines. Silver mine profits were instrumental in paying for subjugation of more than 250 heavily armed *daimyos* (lords), leading to unification of Japan by the end of the sixteenth century. The Shogun intentionally weakened samurai powers (holding family members hostage in Edo/Tokyo) while collaborating with business interests while turning attention to domestic developments. After a disastrous 160,000 man invasion of Korea in the 1590s CE (in an ill-advised attempt to conquer Ming China), the Tokugawa Shogunate turned attention to heavy investments in domestic land reclamation and other infrastructure projects.

When silver super-profits vanished worldwide during the 1630s, the Shogun replaced troublesome Portuguese intermediaries with compliant Dutch merchants, who were restricted to a small man-made island in Nagasaki Bay, Deshima, a World Heritage Site today. The so-called "closure" of Japan from the late 1630s involved regulation of trade and curtailment of international migration, but portrayal of Tokugawa policy as anti-trade is misleading. Japan subsequently became a major exporter of gold later in the seventeenth century, and also became the world's leading exporter of copper (mainly to China, but to Europe as well).[12] At the same time, it is clear that the Tokugawa government in the eighteenth century effectively curtailed sugar and silk imports in efforts to spurt its domestic industries (Shimba and Hasegawa 2004).

A wayward Portuguese ship had inadvertently introduced European firearms to the Japanese in 1543. Adoption and improvements of guns in Japan was remarkable: "The number of guns produced in Japan in the latter part of the sixteenth century, according to one source, was 300,000. This exceeded the total number of guns in Europe at that time" (Sakae 2001, p. 48). Unthreatened by foreigners, the Shogun subsequently forbade domestic access to military technology; in other

[12] See Shimada (2006, p. 47) for comparison of Japanese and Swedish copper production. Silver mines also shifted to copper production.

words, Japanese took the unprecedented step of giving up the gun.[13] Pax Tokugawa generated relative prosperity through redirection of expanding resources from military to civilian projects:

> Whereas Europe knew only four years of peace during the seventeenth century, and China knew none, Tokugawa Japan knew only four years of war (and none at all after 1638). By avoiding war, the sink that drained the revenues of most other early modern states, the shogun managed to keep tax rates relatively low and yet still accumulate resources. (Parker 2013, p. 497)

Parker (2013, p. XXX) claims that global population decreased by perhaps one-third during the seventeenth-century Little Ice Age, yet Japan's population more than doubled and its urban population quintupled during the seventeenth century (Parker 2013, p. 484). The Japanese managed to expand agricultural production and kept living standards remarkably stable in the face of this fast population growth as a result of low taxes, heavy infrastructure investment, and the most literate population in the world (Parker 2013; Waswo 1986; Yasuba 1986). Equivalent to levels in Europe prior to the Industrial Revolution, a Japanese "Industrious Revolution" generated rising living standards through development of labour-intensive and resource-saving technology, according to Sugihara (2003, p. 115), in contrast to capital-intensive and resource-intensive technologies characteristic of European and American development. Sugihara (2019) updates this argument.

South Asia was highly integrated in the global economy in the early modern period. A lot of the silver mined in the Americas was sent to India. Lacking domestic silver mines, it is unknown what portion of India's imported silver was retained in medieval times because "statistical series on mint production, prices, wages and volume of trade is non-existent" (Haider 2007, p. 195). Significant quantities of European silver definitely entered the subcontinent, but there is little evidence that silver accumulated within India:

[13] See Perrin (1980) for a classic treatment of this topic. A Dutch envoy claimed that the Tokugawa castle itself, however, contained enough weapons to equip 100,000 soldiers, according to Parker (2013, p. 498).

> Bullion and copper coins dominated north Indian markets from the last quarter of the fourteenth century, and a point was reached...when precious metal coinage disappeared from the [Lodi] kingdom...[While there was] a sizeable flow of copper coins (*fils*) from Egypt... Gold disappeared entirely...except for the South, silver gave way to bullion, and currencies reserved for petty transactions, such as copper and cowries, began to compete for a large share of the market. (Haider 2007, pp. 89, 191–192)

If European silver merely passed through India, then where were the ultimate silver end-markets located? One answer seems clear: China.[14] Despite repeated claims of an India "silver famine" by historians, John F. Richards has insisted that market forces worked properly and that evidence "points to the inescapable conclusion that there was no shortage of precious metals in Delhi or in the territories controlled by the Lodis from 1451 to 1526" (Richards 1998, p. 150). Coexistence of vigorous Indian imports of silver alongside relatively modest holdings of silver within India makes sense, however, so long as Indian silver export volumes matched Indian silver import volumes. Unfortunately, estimation of quantities of silver that passed through India in transit to East and Southeast Asian end-markets cannot be assessed directly: "Most documents on which modern surveys are based are revenue registers of major entrepots, which do not cover currency exports because such transactions were often exempted from customs dues" (Haider 2007, p. 187). It is possible that quantities of silver held could be estimated through research of confiscation archives, probate inventories (or their equivalent), or other archival and archaeological records.[15] Extensive market relations are known to have stretched from the Mediterranean to East Asia, where premium silver prices are known to have existed:

> ...the steady, incremental improvement of the efficiency, security, and capacity of the long-distance maritime trade running from the Mediterranean and East Africa to China and Japan... [rendered] India...the fulcrum of this medieval trade... in a burgeoning world maritime commerce. (Richards 1993, p. 296)

[14] For an insightful contrast between introduction of New World crops into China (where demographic impacts were huge) and India (where demographic impacts were muted), see Mazumdar (1999).

[15] See Cao and Flynn (2019) for an initial attempt to estimate silver holdings within China around 1750 CE.

Despite a paucity of documentary evidence concerning quantities of silver that remained within India (even in the seventeenth century), K.N. Chaudhuri nonetheless expressed certainty that silver flowed through India onward to East Asia:

> Since India's trade with Europe was only a part of her total foreign trade, the missing piece of the puzzle is the size of movements in the trade of other areas... There is ample evidence that American silver flowing into India was re-exported to China and South East Asia to be exchanged for the economic products of those regions. (Chaudhuri 1978, pp. 159–160)

There exists a large (and growing) literature on vast Indian textile exports to end-markets in Europe, Africa, and elsewhere, of course, but Indian *imports* from East and Southeast Asia do not seem to have received proportionate attention. The key role of India during the sixteenth-century birth of globalization deserves sustained attention in this regard.[16]

Interestingly, effects of global trade on economic development and living standards of the majority of people was probably limited. While volumes of intercontinental trade were large and there is much evidence of significant price convergence in goods traded between Europe and India (as discussed above), local living standards, as evidenced by estimates of real wages and GDP, were largely determined by developments in agriculture (De Zwart and Van Zanden 2018). India thus provides a good example for our thesis that effects of soft globalization may be larger than those of hard globalization. The most important impact of trade in this era was arguably political: increased revenues from trade earned by local potentates in coastal cities vis-à-vis tax incomes of the Mughal state at the centre of empire shook the delicate balance of power while the empire disintegrated in the eighteenth century (Roy 2013). The British stepped into the void from the late eighteenth century, expanding colonial rule from the north-eastern region of Bengal while dramatically increasing the impact of global contact.

[16] For a useful survey of Indian Ocean trade (including overland connections) in context of global history, see Parthasarathi and Riello (2014).

Europe

For Europe, the impact of globalization was largely positive. Acemoglu et al. (2005) showed that those European economies trading with the Americas, Africa and Asia grew faster than others. Growing trade strengthened interests of commercials classes in society, which consequently pushed for institutional and policy changes conducive to economic growth. Countries that had already checked royal power at the start of trade across the Atlantic (i.e. England and the Dutch Republic) experienced particularly flourishing economies. In absolutist countries like France and Spain, royal families and their entourages were the main beneficiaries of the rise in trade. This trend ties in neatly with evidence on parliamentary activity across Western Europe: in the Dutch Republic and England, parliaments became ever more active over the early modern period, whereas those in absolutist France and Spain stopped meeting almost entirely (Van Zanden et al. 2012). There is also an association between engaging in global trade and levels of urbanization (Acemoglu et al. 2005; Allen 2003; De Pleijt and Van Zanden 2016). Urbanization rates were higher in those areas most heavily engaged in global trade, such as England and the Low Countries. Cities like Amsterdam and London grew rapidly and growth of overseas trade in these cities meant more job opportunities; it increased demand for dockworkers and sailors, ship-owners, merchants and brokers, and many more. City growth also explains higher wages observed for England and the Low Countries, as division of labour was more sophisticated in larger towns (Allen 2001, 2003, 2009).[17] Recent research using a dynamic panel model confirmed that in Spain, Portugal, England and the Dutch Republic, intercontinental trade contributed to urbanization and real wage rates (Palma 2016). Large amounts of capital (partially from earnings in global trade) together with higher wages consequently provided crucial incentives for the Industrial Revolution in Britain in which relatively expensive labour was substituted with cheaper capital (as argued by Allen 2009).

One element that has been underestimated (or, rather, not taken into account) by those who dismiss early modern globalization, is the fact

[17] Although a topic we do not engage here, conversions of actual prices and wages into silver-content counterparts, common now while assessing relative living standards around the world, can be misleading and unnecessary, according to an insightful recent essay by Mayhew (2018).

that purchasing patterns across most parts of Europe changed substantially as a result of the newly emerging global economy. As a result of declining European prices for many goods previously considered luxuries, like coffee, sugar, and tea, purchase of these goods became attainable for large parts of the population. An eighteenth-century French observer noted that "Consumption [of coffee] has tripled in France; there is no bourgeois household where you are not offered coffee, no shopkeeper, no cook, no chambermaid who does not breakfast on coffee with milk in the morning. In public markets and in certain streets and alleys in the capital, women have set themselves up selling what they call *café au lait* to the populace" (cited in Hersh and Voth 2011, p. 13). For Britain, data on sheer quantities of coffee, tea, and, especially, sugar that entered the island in the seventeenth and eighteenth centuries, suggest widespread consumption of these goods: tea consumption grew from almost nothing to about 1.2 kilos per capita annually over the course of the eighteenth century, while sugar consumption increased from about 2 to about 15 kilos per capita in that same period (Hersh and Voth 2011). After-death inventories from a number of cities and towns across the early modern Low Counties showed that over 60% of the lower-middle-class population owned accumulated instruments specifically designed for coffee and/or tea consumption (McCants 2008). The possibility to purchase objects that were previously considered luxuries, at lower and lower prices, not only increased well-being in Europe (Hersh and Voth 2011), but also stimulated many European households to reallocate time from leisure to productive market employment in order to obtain such goods, thus giving rise to an "industrious revolution" in the early modern era (de Vries 2008; Allen and Weisdorf 2011). While connecting demand-side changes to import substitution on the production side, McCants concludes that:

> Although a paucity of source materials will continue to make it difficult for historians to quantify with precision the size and scope of the early modern demand for colonial groceries and Asian manufactures, we risk misunderstanding a critical moment in the globalizing process if we fail to recognize the power of that demand to radically transform European patterns of consumption as well as its processes of production. (McCants 2007, p. 462)

Products imported and sold in Europe also involved global connections that neither contemporary merchant sellers nor end-market purchasers recognized at the time, as was true for the market for French hats in Habsburg Vienna (1650–1750). Research of last wills, probate inventories, letter patents and tax accounts, led Hyden-Hanscho (2016) to label this market "Invisible Globalization" because neither buyers nor sellers were aware that hat components originated in Canada (beaver, processed in Russia prior to re-export through France) or in South America (vicuñas via Lima or Buenos Aires), gum Arabic (from Arabia, Sudan, West and sub-Sahara Africa), and ostrich feathers (from the Levant). Hat quality also varied widely, while low-price segments included second-hand hats (often mended), demonstrating that import goods penetrated much deeper than is normally recognized.

Conclusion

We argue that evidence demonstrating deep impacts of early modern globalization cannot be neglected, including (but not limited to) widespread convergence of prices. While some world regions were less dramatically impacted than others, it is important to recognize that seemingly remote areas such as New Guinea underwent fundamental transformations that stemmed from ecological, epidemiological and demographic forces that should not be ignored. The overall picture is that early modern globalization led to radical ecological and demographic changes in Africa, the Americas, large swaths of Asia, Europe, as well as oceanic islands worldwide. Empires toppled across the Global South, while European industrialization emerged within context of complex global mechanisms that require further exploration. Many Europeans certainly enjoyed fruits of Early Globalization, but non-European merchant intermediaries reaped rewards as well, as did producers within and beyond European borders. From a strictly economic point of view, emphasis upon end-market demand-side forces throughout the globe deserve as much scrutiny as supply-side considerations; to cite just one example, end-market inventory demand to hold silver within China requires explanation on its own terms, as opposed to mere assumption that "precious metals" flowed to abstract "Asia" as a result of *European* trade deficits due, in turn, to dynamic *European* demand-side forces. In sum, effects of "soft" globalization were in many respects "harder" than those of "hard" globalization. Proper interpretation of nineteenth-century globalization patterns—indeed, into the twenty-first century—require acknowledgement of global forces that continue to evolve from sixteenth-century origins.

References

Acemoglu, Daron, Simon Johnson, and James A. Robinson. 2001. "The Colonial Origins of Comparative Development: An Empirical Investigation." *American Economic Review* 102: 3077–3110.

Acemoglu, Daron, Simon Johnson, and James A. Robinson. 2002. "Reversal of Fortune: Geography and Institutions in the Making of the Modern World Income Distribution." *Quarterly Journal of Economics* 117: 1231–1294.

Acemoglu, Daron, Simon Johnson, and James A. Robinson. 2005. "The Rise of Europe: Atlantic Trade, Institutional Change, and Economic Growth." *American Economic Review* 95: 546–579.

Alexander, Patrick D., and Ian Keay. 2019. "Responding to the First Era of Globalization: Canadian Trade Policy, 1870–1913." *Journal of Economic History* 79: 826–861.

Allen, Robert C. 2001. "The Great Divergence in European Wages and Prices from the Middle Ages to the First World War." *Explorations in Economic History* 38: 411–447.

Allen, Robert C. 2003. "Progress and Poverty in Early Modern Europe." *Economic History Review* 56: 403–443.

Allen, Robert C. 2009. *The British Industrial Revolution in Global Perspective*. Cambridge: Cambridge University Press.

Allen, Robert C., and Jacob Weisdorf. 2011. "Was There an 'Industrious Revolution' Before the Industrial Revolution? An Empirical Exercise for England, c. 1300–1830." *Economic History Review* 64: 715–729.

Arroyo Abad, Leticia, and Jan Luiten van Zanden. 2016. "Growth Under Extractive Institutions? Latin American Per Capita GDP in Colonial Times." *Journal of Economic History* 76: 1182–1215.

Arroyo Abad, Leticia, Elwyn Davies, and Jan Luiten van Zanden. 2012. "Between Conquest and Independence: Real Wages and Demographic Change in Spanish America, 1530–1820." *Explorations in Economic History* 49: 149–166.

Austin, Gareth. 2008. "Resources, Techniques, and Strategies South of the Sahara: Revising the Factor Endowments Perspective on African Economic Development, 1500–2000." *Economic History Review* 61 (3): 587–624.

Calderón Fernández, Andés, Rafael Dobado González, and Alfredo García-Hiernaux. 2020. "Numeracy in Central New Spain During the Enlightenment." *Revista de Historia Economica/Journal of Iberian and Latin American Economic History* 38: 369–403.

Cao, Jin, and Dennis O. Flynn. 2019. "Global Quantification and Inventory Demand for Silver in China." *Revista de Historia Economica*: 1–27. https://doi.org/10.1017/S0212610919000181.

Challú, Amilcar E., and Aurora Gómez Galvarriato. 2015. "Mexico's Real Wages in the Age of the Great Divergence." *Revista de Historia Economica/Journal of Iberian and Latin American Economic History* 33: 83–122.

Chaudhuri, Kirti N. 1978. *The Trading World of Asia and the English East India Company, 1660–1760.* Cambridge: Cambridge University Press.

Chilosi, David, and Giovanni Federico. 2019. "The Effects of Market Integration During the First Globalization: A Multi-market Approach." CEPR, discussion paper #13818.

Christian, David. 2004. *Maps of Time: An Introduction to Big History*. Berkeley, Los Angeles and London: University of California Press.

Crosby, Alfred W. 1972. *The Columbian Exchange: Biological and Cultural Consequences of 1492.* Greenwood Press.

Crosby, Alfred W. 1986. *Ecological Imperialism: The Biological Expansion of Europe, 900–1900.* Cambridge: Cambridge University Press.

Dell, Melissa. 2010. "The Persistent Effects of Peru's Mining Mita." *Econometrica* 78: 1863–1903.

De Pleijt, Alexandra M., and Jan Luiten Van Zanden. 2016. "Accounting for the Little Divergence: What Drove Economic Growth in Pre-industrial Europe, 1300–1800?" *European Review of Economic History* 20: 387-409.

De Vries, Jan. 2008. *The Industrious Revolution. Consumer Behavior and the Household Economy, 1650 to the present*. Cambridge: Cambridge University Press.

De Vries, Jan. 2010. "The Limits of Globalization in the Early Modern World." *Economic History Review* 63: 710–733.

De Zwart, Pim. 2016a. "Globalization in the Early Modern Era: New Evidence from the Dutch-Asiatic Trade, 1600–1800." *Journal of Economic History* 76: 520–558.

De Zwart, Pim. 2016b. *Globalization and the Colonial Origins of the Great Divergence. Intercontinental Trade and Living Standards in the Dutch East India Company's Commercial Empire, 1600–1800.* Leiden: Brill.

De Zwart, Pim, and Jan Luiten van Zanden. 2015. "Labor, Wages and Living Standards in Java, 1680–1914." *European Review of Economic History* 19: 215–234.

De Zwart, Pim, and Jan Luiten van Zanden. 2018. *The Origins of Globalization: World Trade in the Making of the Global Economy, 1500–1800.* Cambridge: Cambridge University Press

Diamond, Jared. 1997. *Guns, Germs and Steel: A Short History of Everybody for the Last 13,000 Years*. New York: W. W. Norton.

Dobado-González, Rafael, and Alfredo García-Hiernaux. 2017. "Two Worlds Apart: Determinants of Height in Late 18th Century Central Mexico." *Economics & Human Biology* 24: 153–163.

Dobado-González, Rafael, and H. García Montero. 2014. "Neither So Low nor So Short: Wages and Heights in Bourbon Spanish America from an International Comparative Perspective." *Journal of Latin American Studies* 46: 1–31.

Dobado-González, Rafael, and Gaustavo A. Marrero. 2011. "The Role of the Spanish Imperial State in the Mining-Led Growth of Bourbon Mexico's Economy." *Economic History Review* 64: 855–884.

Dobado-González, Rafael, Alfredo García-Hiernaux, and David E. Guerrero. 2012. "The Integration of Grain Markets in the Eighteenth Century: Early Rise of Globalization in the West." *Journal of Economic History* 72: 671–707.

Engerman, Stanley L., and Kenneth L. Sokoloff. 2000. "History Lessons. Institutions, Factor Endowments, and Paths of Development in the New World." *Journal of Economic Perspectives* 14: 217–232.

Flannery, Kristie P., and Guillermo Ruiz-Stovel. 2020. "The Loyal Foreign Merchant Captain: Thomé Gaspar de León and the Making of Manila's Intra-Asian Connections." *Vegueta. Anuario de la Facultad de Geographi e Historia* 20: 189–215.

Flynn, Dennis O. 1996. *World Silver and Monetary History in the 16th and 17th Centuries* (Collected Studies Series). Aldershot: Variorum.

Flynn, Dennis O. 2019. "Fifteenth-Century European Silver and Chinese End-Markets." In *ITALIEN ALS VORBILD? Ökonomische und kulturelle Verflechtungen europäischer Metropolen am Vorabend der, ersten Globalisierung' (1300–1600)*, edited by J. Oberste and S. Ehrich, 163–180. Regensburg: Verlag Schnell & Steiner GmbH.

Flynn, Dennis O. 2020. "Silver, Globalization and Capitalism." In *Capitalisms: Towards a Global History*, edited by K. Yazdani and D. M. Menon, 35–70. New Delhi: Oxford University Press.

Flynn, Dennis O., and Arturo Giráldez. 1995. "*Born with a 'Silver Spoon': The Origin of World Trade in 1571.*" *Journal of World History* 6: 201–221.

Flynn, Dennis O., and Arturo Giráldez. 2000. "Money and Growth Without Development: The Case of Ming China." In *Asian Pacific Dynamism 1550–2000*, edited by A. J. H. Latham and H. Kawakatsu. London: Routledge.

Flynn, Dennis O., and Arturo Giráldez. 2002. "Cycles of Silver: Global Economic Unity Through the Mid-Eighteenth Century." *Journal of World History* 13: 391–427.

Flynn, Dennis O., and Arturo Giráldez. 2004. "Path Dependence, Time Lags and the Birth of Globalization: A Critique of O'Rourke and Williamson." *European Review of Economic History* 8 (1): 81–108.

Flynn, Dennis O., and Arturo Giráldez. 2008. "Born Again: Globalization's Sixteenth Century Origins (Asian/Global Versus European Dynamics)." *Pacific Economic Review* 13: 359–387.

Frank, Andre Gunder. 1969. *Capitalism and Underdevelopment in Latin America: Historical Studies of Chile and Brazil*. New York: Monthly Review Press.

Frank, Andre Gunder. 1970. *Latin America: Underdevelopment or Essays on the Development of Underdevelopment and the Immediate Enemy*. New York: Monthly Review Press.

Frank, Andre Gunder. 1998. *ReORIENT: Global Economy in the Asian Age*. Berkeley, CA: University of California Press.

Gaastra, Femme. 2008. *De Geschiedenis van de VOC*. Zutphen: Walburg Pers.

Giráldez, Arturo. 2013. "A Two-Year Merchant Strike (1636–1637) and the Chinese in Manila: The Seventeenth-Century Crisis in the Philippines." In *Mining, Monies and Culture in Early Modern Societies: East Asian and Global Perspectives*, edited by N. Kim and K. Nagase-Reimer, 261–288. Leiden: Brill.

Grafe, Regina, and Alejandra Irigoin. 2012. "A Stakeholder Empire: The Political Economy of Spanish Imperial Rule in America." *Economic History Review* 65: 609–651.

Haider, Najaf. 2007. "The Network of Monetary Exchange in the Indian Ocean Trade, 1200–1700." In *Cross Currents and Community Networks: The History of the Indian Ocean World*, edited by H. Prabha Ray and E. Alpers, 181–205. Oxford: Oxford University Press.

Hamilton, Clive. 2015. "Getting the Anthropocene So Wrong." *The Anthropocene Review* 2 (2): 102–107.

Hersh, Jonathan, and Hans-Joachim Voth. 2011. "Sweet Diversity: Colonial Goods and the Rise of European Living Standards After 1492." *Mimeo*. https://econ-papers.upf.edu/papers/1163.pdf.

Ho, Ping-ti. 1959. *Studies on the Population of China 1368–1953*. Cambridge, MA: Harvard University Press.

Hyden-Hanscho, Veronika. 2016. "Invisible Globalization: French Hats in Habsburg Vienna, 1650–1750." *Journal of European Economic History* 3: 11–54.

Kamen, Henry. 2003. *Empire: How Spain Became a World Power 1492–1763*. New York: Harper Collins.

Kelly, Morgan, and Cormac O'Grada. 2019. "Speed Under Sail During the Early Industrial Revolution (c. 1750–1830)." *Economic History Review* 72: 459–480.

Klein, Herbert. 1999. *The Atlantic Slave Trade*. Cambridge: Cambridge University Pres.

Klein, Herbert S., and S. T. Serrano Hernández. 2018. "Was There a 17th Century Crisis in Spanish America?" *Revista de Historia Económica/Journal of Iberian and Latin American History*: 43–80. https://doi.org/10.1017/S0212610918000101.

Lewis, Simon, and Mark A. Maslin. 2015. "Defining the Anthropocene." *Nature* 519: 171–180.

Lucassen, Leo. 2016. "Connecting the World. Migration and Globalization in the Second Millennium." In *Explorations in History and Globalization*, edited by C. A. Antunes and K. J. Fatah-Black, 19–46. London: Routledge.

Mann, Charles C. 2011. *1493: Uncovering the New World Columbus Created.* New York: Alfred A. Knopf.

Marks, Robert B. 2017. *China: An Environmental History*. Lanham: Rowman and Littlefield.

Mayhew, Nick. 2018. "Money in England from the Middle Ages to the Nineteenth Century." In *Money, Currency and Crisis: In Search of Trust, 2000 BC to AD 2000*, edited by R. J. van der Spek and Bas van Leeuwen, 185–205. Routeldge.

Mazumdar, Sucheta. 1999. "The Impact of New World Food Crops on the Diet and Economy of China and India, 1600–1900." In *Food in Global History*, edited by R. Grew. Boulder, CO: Westview Press.

McCants, Anne. 2007. "Exotic Goods, Popular Consumption, and the Standard of Living: Thinking About Globalization in the Early Modern World." *Journal of World History* 18 (4): 433–462.

McCants, Anne. 2008. "Poor Consumers as Global Consumers: The Diffusion of Tea and Coffee Drinking in the Eighteenth Century." *Economic History Review* 61: 172–200.

Naquin, Susan, and Evelyn S. Rawski. 1987. *Chinese Society in the Eighteenth Century*. New Haven: Yale University Press.

Newson, Linda A. 2006. "The Demographic Impact of Colonization." In *The Cambridge Economic History of Latin America: Volume 1, The Colonial Era*, edited by V. Bulmer-Thomas, John Coatsworth and Roberto Cortes-Conde. Cambridge: Cambridge University Press.

Ning, Ma. 2017. *The Age of Silver: The Rise of the Novel East and West*. New York: Oxford University Press.

O'Brien, Patrick. 1982. "European Economic Development: The Contribution of the Periphery." *Economic History Review* 35 (1): 1–18.

O'Rourke, Kevin H., and Jeffrey G. Williamson. 2002. "When Did Globalisation Begin?" *European Review of Economic History* 6: 23–50.

O'Rourke, Kevin H., and Jeffrey G. Williamson. 2004. "Once More: When Did Globalisation Begin?" *European Review of Economic History* 8: 109–117.

O'Rourke, Kevin H., and Jeffrey G. Williamson. 2009. "Did Vasco da Gama matter for European markets?" *Economic History Review* 62: 655–684.

Palma, Nuno. 2016. "Sailing Away from Malthus: Intercontinental Trade and European Economic Growth, 1500–1800." *Cliometrica* 10: 129–149.

Palma, Nuno, and André C. Silva. 2016. "Spending a Windfall: American Precious Metals and Euro-Asian Trade, 1531–1810." GGDC Research Memorandum 165.

Pascali, Luigi. 2017. "The Wind of Change: Maritime Technology, Trade, and Economic Development." *American Economic Review* 107: 2821–2854.

Parker, Geoffrey. 2013. *Global Crisis. War, Climate Change and Catastrophe in the Seventeenth Century*. New Haven: Yale University Press.

Parthasarathi, Prasannan. 1998. "Rethinking Wages and Competitiveness in the Eighteenth Century: Britain and South India." *Past and Present* 158: 79–109.

Parthasarathi, Prasannan. 2011. *Why Europe Grew Rich and Asia Did Not. Global Economic Divergence, 1600–1850*. Cambridge: Cambridge University Press.

Parthasarathi, Prasannan, and Giorgio Riello. 2014. "The Indian Ocean in the Long Eighteenth Century." *Eighteenth-Century Studies* 48 (1): 1–19

Perrin, Noel. 1980. *Giving Up the Gun: Japan's Reversion to the Sword, 1543–1879*. Boulder: Shambhala Publications Inc.

Pomeranz, Kenneth. 2000. *The Great Divergence. China, Europe and the Making of the Modern World Economy*. Princeton: Princeton University Press.

Richards, John F. 1993. "Mughal State Finance and the Premodern World Economy." In *Power, Administration and Finance in Mughal India* (Collected Studies Series 419), edited by J. F. Richards, 285–308. Aldershot: Ashgate/Variorum.

Richards, John F. 1998. "The Economic History of the Lodi Period: 1451–1526." In *Money and the Market in India 1100–1700*, edited by S. Subrahmanyam, 137–155. Oxford: Oxford India Paperbacks.

Richardson, David. 2011. "Involuntary Migration in the Early Modern World, 1500–1800." In *The Cambridge World History of Slavery*, vol. 3, edited by D. Eltis and Stanley Engerman, 563–593. Cambridge: Cambridge University Press.

Rönnbäck, Klas. 2009. "Integration of Global Commodity Markets in the Early Modern Era." *European Review of Economic History* 13: 95–120.

Rönnback, Klas. 2012. "The Speed of Ships and Shipping Productivity in the Age of Sail." *European Review of Economic History* 16: 469–489.

Roy, Tirthankar. 2013. *An Economic History of Early Modern India*. London and New York: Routledge.

Sakae, Tsunoyama. 2001. "Sakai, East Asia's Largest Trading City: Where Did All the Riches Go." *Journal of Japanese Trade and Industry*: 46–49. [Reprinted as "Chapter 3" in *Japan and the Pacific, 1540–1920* (2006). Edited by M. Caprio and Matsuda Koichiro. Aldershot: Ashgate/Variorum.]

Seijas, Tatiana. 2014. *Asian Slaves in Colonial Mexico: From Chinos to Indians*. New York: Cambridge University Press.

Shimada, Ryuto. 2006. *The Intra-Asian Trade in Japanese Copper by the Dutch East India Company During the Eighteenth Century*. Leiden: Brill.

Shimba, Hiroshi, and Akira Hasegawa. 2004. "The Dynamics of Market Economy and Production." In *The Economic History of Japan: 1600–1800*, edited by Hayama et al., 159–191. Oxford: Oxford University Press.

Smith, Adam. 2003 (1776). *The Wealth of Nations*. New York: Bantam Dell.

Solar, Peter M. 2013. "Opening to the East: Shipping Between Europe and Asia, 1770–1830." *Journal of Economic History* 73: 625–661.

Solar, Peter M., and Pim de Zwart. 2017. "Why Were Dutch East Indiamen so Slow?" *International Journal of Maritime History* 29: 738–751.

Solar, Peter M., and Luc Hens. 2016. "Ship Speeds During the Industrial Revolution: East India Company Ships, 1770–1828." *European Review of Economic History* 20 (1): 66–78.

Solar, Peter M., and Klas Rönnbäck. 2015. "Copper Sheathing and the British Slave Trade." *Economic History Review* 68 (3): 806–829.

Spence, Jonathan D. 1990. *The Search for Modern China*. New York and London: W. W. Norton.

Suarez Espinosa, M. 2018. "The Alternative Circuits of Silver: Lima and the Inter-Colonial Trade of the Pacific During the 17th Century." In *A Global Trading Network: The Spanish Empire in the World Economy (1580–1820)*, edited by J. Ignacio Martínez Ruiz, 239–260. Seville: Editorial Universidad de Sevilla.

Sugihara, Kaoru. 2003. "The East Asian Path of Economic Development: A Long-Term Perspective." In *The Resurgence of East Asia: 500, 150, and 50 Year Perspectives*, edited by G. Arrighi, T. Hamashita, and M. Selden, 78–123. London and New York: Routledge.

Sugihara, Kaoru. 2019. "Multiple Paths to Industrialization: A Global Context of the Rise of Emerging States." In *Paths to the Emerging State in Asia and Africa*, edited by K. Otsuka and K. Sugihara, 1–34. Singapore: Springer.

Van Zanden, Luiten Jan, Maarten Bosker, and Eltjo Buringh. 2012. "The Rise and Decline of European Parliaments, 1188–1789." *Economic History Review* 65: 835–861

Von Glahn, Richard. 1996. *Fountain of Fortune: Money and Monetary Policy in China, 1000–1700*. Berkeley, Los Angeles, and London: University of California Press.

Von Glahn, Richard. 2016. *The Economic History of China: From Antiquity to the Nineteenth Century*. Cambridge: Cambridge University Press.

Wallerstein, Immanuel. 1974–1989. *The Modern-World System*. 3 vols. Berkeley, CA: University of California.

Waswo, Ann. 1986. "Innovation and Growth in Japanese Agriculture, 1600–1868" In *Pre-conditions to Industrialization in Japan*, edited by A. Hayami, 1–9. Bern, Switzerland.

Wong, Roy Bin. 1997. *China Transformed. Historical Change and the Limits of the European Experience*. Ithaca, NY: Cornell University Press.

Yang, Bin. 2019. *Cowrie Shells and Cowrie Money: A Global History*. London and New York: Routledge.

Yasuba, Yasukichi. 1986. "The Tokugawa Legacy: A Survey." In *Pre-conditions to Industrialization in Japan*, edited by A. Hayami, 1–9. Bern, Switzerland.

International Migrations to Latin America and the Caribbean Until 1820

Herbert S. Klein

Preliminary Draft not for citation 31/VII/2019
Revised 7/III/2020

The transatlantic migration of peoples to the Americas after 1492 was influenced by a series of factors determined by conditions in the regions of origins as well as the zones of arrivals. To begin with both Castile and Portugal were at the height of their empires when the New World was opened up to foreign penetration. There thus existed innumerable opportunities for rural peasants to find employment not only in the economies and growing urban centers of the metropolis, but also to serve in the armies and fleets of these expanding intercontinental empires within Europe and Asia. These Iberian armies and fleets dominated Europe, Asia and parts of Africa in the same period that explorers were reaching America. It was estimated for example, that there were 10,000 Portuguese troops serving in this empire in the sixteenth century (Naylor 2006,

H. S. Klein (✉)
Columbia University, New York City, NY, USA
e-mail: hsk1@columbia.edu; hklein@stanford.edu

Stanford University, Stanford, CA, USA

Palo Alto, CA, USA

R. Dobado-González and A. García-Hiernaux (eds.), *The Fruits of the Early Globalization*, Palgrave Studies in Comparative Global History,
https://doi.org/10.1007/978-3-030-69666-5_3

p. 62), and some 60,000 Spanish troops operating in Europe and North Africa garrisons in the same century (Thompson 2008, p. 258). This was out of an estimated population of just under 1 million Portuguese and 4.8 million Spaniards in 1500 (Freire et al. 2016, p. 54). At the same time the wealth generated by these two powerful states led to major expansion of their urban population in this same period. Portugal had 12% of its population living in urban centers of 5,000 persons or more (Freire et al. 2016, p. 57), and Spain in the seventeenth century increased its share of such cities of 5,000 or more persons from 10% in 1530 to 15% of the population in 1591 (Álvarez-Nogal and Prados 2013, p. 14). There was also a positive rate of population growth in every province in Spain from 1531 to 1590 (Álvarez-Nogal and Prados 2007, p. 329). Not only did these metropolitan populations expand along with their empires, but so did their metropolitan economies along with their agriculture and industrial activities. As late as the 1570s, output per capita in Spain was above that in the United Kingdom, the Netherlands, Germany, France and Sweden (Álvarez-Nogal and Prados 2007, p. 23). In terms of industries, for example, Portugal throughout the seventeenth century had approximately the same amount of shipbuilding capacity as England and the Dutch Republic (Freire et al. 2016, p. 92).

With the availability of alternative occupations in their expanding metropolitan economies and empires, there was less interest in America for most potential European migrants because of its distance and high cost of transport. The factors that changed this equation were the sudden availability of gold and silver, which compensated the major expenses needed to migrate and settle in America. Another influence was the availability of complex peasant Amerindian societies in certain zones of America which could be quickly exploited by a few European settlers to produce the goods needed to sustain the colonies. Finally, a late development was well funded governments which were willing to both protect and subsidize economically fragile colonies in the Americas in order to maintain their rights of possession.

In areas of the Americas which lacked precious metals or an easily available peasant Indian labor source, the costs of settlement were extremely high and resulted in a very slow growth of non-American populations until alternative sources of wealth could be found. Although Amerindian groups existed everywhere in the Americas, they could not all be effectively exploited for agricultural labor as the early conquerors quickly discovered. Most of these Amerindian groups were either semi-nomadic or simple agricultural communities unlike the structured multi-class agrarian societies of Mexico and the Central Andes and they were close to open frontiers uncontrolled by Europeans. In these lands there were also few precious metals to be found and therefore to survive these initially marginal colonies needed both new products in demand in Europe and a new labor force to produce them.

Even after the successful development of the advanced zones of Mexico and Peru there was little demand for European immigrants. As the American colonies matured into permanent settlements in the late sixteenth century and early seventeenth century, they experienced the growth of an intermediate mestizo rural and urban population of mixed European, Amerindian and African ancestry. These mestizos and mulattos became the basis of much of the urban lower classes as well as the majority of small-scale farming which spread throughout the Americas. By the seventeenth century this population could sustain itself not only supplying food to the urban centers, but also engaging in international trade, mostly contraband, in hides, tobacco and other products in demand in Europe. The increasing density of this population inhibited large scale international migrations of Europeans to the Americas until the end of the colonial period, except in unusual periods of thriving commercial activity or special promotions of migration by the state, such as populations of the Canary islands (Morales 1951) being sent to various colonies in the Caribbean area and of Azoreans to the Southern Brazilian frontier (Piazza 2011; Torres 2004).

Thus, the majority of the Iberian migrants who came to America after the middle of the sixteenth century came from urban centers of the Peninsular rather than from its rural areas. Once these American colonies were established there was a steady migration of professionals to all of Latin America and the Caribbean. This included churchmen, government officials, lawyers, notaries, doctors, skilled artisans and of course merchants. Many of them came to "Hacer/Fazer America" and once wealthy returned to the metropolis. This was especially the case of officials, judges and churchmen who worked in a type of civil service with the goal of returning home to a higher occupational status. This was also true of merchants, who were often junior members of major metropolitan commercial houses. As international commerce expanded there was the growth of an important foreign-born commercial class in all the urban centers of America, from Santiago de Chile to Mexico City. For most of the colonial period these merchants were tied to merchant houses in

Seville, Cadiz, or Lisbon. By the late colonial period this also included Catalans and other merchant groups from other regions of Spain.

It was even possible for immigrant journeymen and poorer master craftsmen to quickly accumulate income in the Americas, train mesitzos, Indians and Africans to perform their crafts, and then return to the metropolis to better their position. In the new American colonies, the guild system was weakened and so Indians, mestizos, freedmen of color and even free Africans could easily practice a trade. Those wealthy persons who did not return were the elite conquistadores that found that their wealth did not lead to high social status in the metropolis. But these elite leaders were few in numbers.[1] Although many returned to the metropolis, the majority of immigrants probably remained in America because they could obtain a better life than they could in the home country, especially due to their high status as whites in the multi-racial and multi-*casta* societies being created in the Americas.

Thus, there initially emerged two basic models: the mining and Indian based peasant agricultural societies of the Andes and New Spain under control of Spain with their increasing mestizo populations, and the slave plantation model developed in Brazil by the Portuguese which was later adopted by all the Northern Europeans in their American colonies. This second model took almost a century to develop and needed major private and public funding to be sustained. It would also be based on a different migration stream, that of African slaves, who by the middle of the seventeenth century were more numerous than the free persons migrating to the Americas. It was this Brazilian model which would eventually become the norm in the Caribbean after 1700 and which resulted in the creation of an enormous zone of plantation agriculture stretching from the Rio de la Plata to the Caribbean Sea which produced a host of important exports, from Sugar to tobacco, indigo, cotton and other products which found a ready market in Europe.

Given the high costs of attracting free European labor across the Atlantic, and the ultimate abandonment of American Indian slavery even by the Portuguese, it was African slave labor which would sustain the new agricultural export industries being created in America. In the central provinces of the Spanish American empire with their dense settled Indian

[1] For an interesting discussion of the inability of the wealthy conquerors to return to Spain, see Lockhart (1968).

peasant populations—above all Peru and New Spain - the need for European or African laborers was relatively limited. But even here, European diseases decimated Indian populations, especially along the coasts, and the lack of a poor white migration created a need for skilled and unskilled urban workers. With an excellent supply of precious metals, and a positive trade balance with Europe, the Spaniards of America could afford to experiment with the importation of African slaves to fill in the regions abandoned by Amerindian laborers. They found African slaves useful for the very reasons that they were kinless and totally mobile laborers. Indians could be exploited systematically but they could not be moved from their lands on a permanent basis. Being the dominant cultural group, they were also relatively impervious to Spanish and European norms of behavior. The Africans, in contrast, came from multiple linguistic and cultural groups and were therefore forced to adopt themselves to the European norms. African slaves, in lieu of a cheap pool of European laborers added important strength to the small European urban society which dominated the American Indian peasant masses in Peru and Mexico.

That Africans were the best available pool of labor to be exploited at this time was due to the opening up of the West African coast by the Portuguese. Given the steady export of West African gold and ivory, and the development of Portugal's enormous Asiatic trading empire, the commercial relations between western Africa and Europe now became common. Western Africans brought by sea, had already replaced all other ethnic and religious groups in the European slave markets by the sixteenth century. Although Iberians initially enslaved Canary islanders, these were later freed as were the few Indians who were brought from America. The Moslems who had been enslaved for centuries, were no longer significant as they disappeared from the Iberian Peninsula itself and became powerfully united under independent states of North Africa. The dominance of the Turks in the Eastern Mediterranean also closed off traditional Slavic and Balkan sources for slaves. Even the small numbers of Moslem and Asian slaves brought to America in the sixteenth and seventeenth century were eventually freed by the Spanish Crown. Given the growing efficiency of the Atlantic slave traders, the dependability of African slave supply and the stability of prices, then it would be Africans who would come to be defined almost exclusively as the available slave labor of the sixteenth century (Elbl 1997).

Africans thus came in abundant numbers to these new possessions. Of the Africans arriving in the Americas in the sixteenth century, all

Table 1 Estimated volume of African slaves arriving in America by area, 1501–1820

Period	*Mainland North America*	*Non Hispanic Caribbean*	*Spanish Americas*	*Brazil*	*Total*
1501–1600			169,369	29,275	198,644
1601–1700	15,146	491,466	225,504	784,457	1,516,573
1701–1820	373,098	3,430,836	339,243	2,781,244	6,924,421
Totals	388,244	3,922,302	734,116	3,594,976	8,639,638

Source Slavevoyages estimates accessed July 30, 2019 and found at https://www.slavevoyages.org/assessment/estimates

came to Spanish America and Brazil. In the next century as well these two zones absorbed over two thirds of the arriving Africans, but their share fell to 45% in the eighteenth century with the rise of the Non-Hispanic Caribbean and continental colonies. Over the three centuries of the Atlantic slave trade Spanish America and Brazil accounted for half of all arriving slaves (see Table 1).

The origins of these African slaves changed over time. In the sixteenth century the dominant area would be Senegambia. But as Europeans penetrated regions further south, new areas opened to major migration flows from the Bites of Benin and Biafra in the Gulf of Guinea and then the West Central Coast of Congo and Angola to the South. The Eastern African ports shipped very modest amounts of slaves across the Pacific Ocean and some of them eventually reached Mexico via the Galleon route from the Philippines (Seijas 2014, Chapter 2). But it was only in the post 1800 period that the Portuguese succeeded in establishing a viable South Atlantic route between Mozambique and the coast of Brazil (Klein 1969). Other regions varied considerably from century to century depending on local conditions, such was the case of Senegambia which became important again in the eighteenth century due to a series of religious wars, or the Bite of Benin which only became a major source of African slaves in the eighteenth century (see Table 2).

The relative impact of these African arrivals differed among these colonies, with the total migration stream to the Spanish American region attracting far less Africans than in all the other empires. An estimate for the period 1500–1760 shows that Africans made up only 15% of the total migrants coming to Spanish America in this period, where as they were dominant in all the other empires (see Table 3).

Table 2 Origin of Africans arriving to Brazil and Spanish America, 1501–1820

Period	*Senegambia*	*Sierra Leone*	*Windward Coast*	*Gold Coast*	*Bight of Benin*	*Bight of Biafra*	*West Central Africa*	*Southeast Africa*	*Totals*
1501–1599	103,120	989	1,737	0	0	5,954	86,845	0	198,645
1601–1700	50,771	0	904	11,815	66,635	23,105	848,723	8,008	1,009,961
1701–1820	107,950	32,605	13,890	97,985	749,721	140,672	1,865,576	112,089	3,120,488
Totals	261,841	33,594	16,531	109,800	816,356	169,731	2,801,144	120,097	4,329,094

Source Slavevoyages estimates accessed July 30, 2019 and found at https://www.slavevoyages.org/assessment/estimates

Table 3 Estimate of African and European arrivals in America, by Colonial Empire, 1500–1760 (in thousands)

Nation	*Africans*	*Europeans*	*Total*	*Percentage of Africans*
Spain	120	678	798	15
Portugal	1,779	523	2,302	77
France	535	100	635	84
Netherlands	413	20	433	95
Britain	1,717	746	2,463	70
Total	4,564	2,067	6,631	69

Source David Eltis, "Slavery and Freedom in the Early Modern World," in Stanley L. Engerman, ed., *Terms of Labor. Slavery, Serfdom and Free Labor* (199): 28–29, Table 1

The Sixteenth Century

Migration to America was relative slow until the conquest of Mexico in 1519 by Cortes with an army that eventually counted 900 Spaniards (Lynch 2001, p. 28). Thus from 1493 to 1519 only 5,185 Spaniards legally migrated to America, whereas from 1520 to 1537 the migration more than doubled with 12,172 legal migrants arriving in Spanish America (Boyd-Bowman 1976, p. 166). In this early period, it was mostly younger males seeking their fortunes that joined the various armies of conquest. By the second half of the century migrants more reflected the availabilities of occupations in the new and maturing colonies and thus had more skills. There were also more women coming in the second half of the century than before as more families migrated, though overall women migrants probably represented no more than 30% of the migrants during the century. Eventually some 55,000 immigrants legally arrived in the century. If to this is added an illegal migration of the same size, an assumption that seems to be accepted by many authors as a minimum amount, then the total of immigration was at least 110,000 persons arriving in the period from 1493 to 1600, of which at least 80% were males and mostly from 15 to 30 years of age (Boyd-Bowman 1976, p. 580).[2]

In contrast, the migration of Portuguese to America was much smaller. Initially the Portuguese established only semi-permanent trade "factories" to ship dyewood, Tupi slaves and exotic animals to Europe. But French

[2] For a good survey of all the estimates, see Lemus and Márquez (1992).

interlopers finally forced the Crown to move toward formal settlements in the 1530s, three decades after Cabral's "discovery." The Portuguese government created 15 royal chartered Captaincies granted to leading nobles and well-placed Court leaders, who were required to subsidize the emigration of Portuguese settlers. Only 10 of these captaincies were effectively settled and only two were successful. With few willing to migrate, many of the earlier settlers were either persons legally exiled or "undesirables" of one kind or another. But effective settlement came by mid century with enslavement of the Indians and the development of a thriving sugar plantation system (Johnson 1984; Schwartz 1985). But emigration was still slow. In 1549 when the first royal governor arrived to take over the failing colony there were only 3,000 Europeans. By 1570 the figure had grown to 20,000 mostly concentrated in the Northeastern region, and by 1580 the figure reached 30,000 (Marcílio 1984, p. 45). By 1600, it was estimated that only a third of Portuguese who migrated overseas were living in Brazil (Freire et al. 2016, p. 60).

In Spanish America in the sixteenth century it would appear that the African arrivals may have exceeded the estimated arrivals of Europeans. Using Peter Boyd-Bowman's well-known figures of legal Spanish arrivals and doubling them for illegal migrants, and comparing them to the estimates of Africans arriving to Latin America in the seventeenth century,[3] the results show a long term secular decline in Spanish migrants and a long term secular growth in African arrivals (see Graph 1).

The Spanish migrants to America show a consistent pattern in their origin due to the tight controls of emigration exercised by the Spanish Crown. All studies of this Iberian migration show that for both the legal and illegal migrants from Spain, the primarily region of origin was Andalucía, with the next most important group coming from Extremadura and all the parts of Kingdom of Castile. These three zones in the sixteenth century together accounted for almost nine tenths of all migrants (see Table 4). Most of these migrants were urban dwellers, with the city of Seville being the primary urban center sending out migrants to America.

As for the Africans the dominant region of origin initially was Senegambia region between the Senegal and Niger rivers. Until 1580 it

[3] All the slave trade data comes from the Slave voyage Project estimates which I accessed in July 2019 and to be found at https://www.slavevoyages.org/assessment/estimates.

How these data were constructed can be seen in Borucki et al. (2015, pp. 433–461).

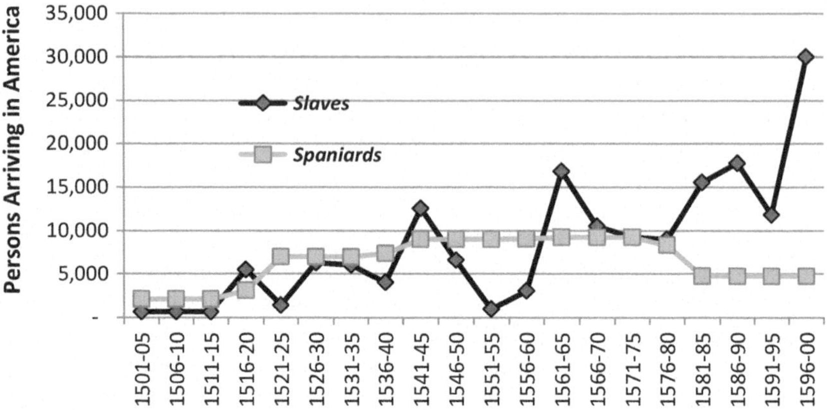

Graph 1 Estimated arrivals of Spanish immigrants and African slaves to Spanish American colonies, 1501–1600 (*Source* see footnote 3)

had relatively little competitions, but after the development of Portuguese Luanda in the 1570s important contingents of slaves from the Congo and Angola began arriving. Also at this point, the Bight of Biafra and the Windward Coast started sending ever more slaves into the market. But the big new source in the following centuries would be West Central African region of Congo and Angola which would prove as dominant as Senegambia was in the seventeenth century, followed by the Benin and Biafra regions in the Gulf of Guinea.

Although the slave trade estimates suggest that there were no Africans brought to the Caribbean islands in the first decades of the sixteenth century, this obviously is not correct. There were already some 1,700 African slaves in Santo Domingo by 1519, even before the opening up of the mainland (Tierra Firme) to Spanish exploitation.[4] The estimates suggest that it was only in the 1530s that a steady stream of slaves arrived to Mexico and the Spanish Caribbean islands. This stream kept increasing throughout the century. In turn Brazil did not see significant slave imports until the last quarter of the century. Thus the seventeenth century migration of Africans was one dominated by the mainland Spanish

[4] Rodríguez Morel, "Apuntes para el estudio de la demografía de la Española. Siglos XVI–XVII," forthcoming.

Table 4 Estimated origins of Europeans arriving in Spanish America by Periods, 1493–1600

Region	*1493–1519*	*1520–1539*	*1540–1559*	*1560–1579*	*1580–1600*	*Totals*
Andalusia	39.6	32.0	36.1	37.2	42.0	36.9
Extremadura	14.0	16.6	15.7	18.7	14.2	16.5
New Castile	8.8	12.0	14.4	19.0	19.2	15.6
Old Castile	18.0	17.6	15.4	11.3	10.2	14.0
León	7.4	7.6	6.2	5.0	4.0	5.9
Basque Provinces	4.7	4.5	4.4	2.9	3.3	3.8
Galicia	2.0	1.5	0.8	1.0	1.2	1.2
Valencia, Catalyunia and Baleric islanda	0.7	1.0	0.7	0.6	0.6	0.7
Aragón	0.6	0.8	0.4	0.6	0.9	0.6
Murcia	0.5	0.9	0.6	0.5	0.5	0.6
Navarra	0.2	0.5	0.9	0.6	0.5	0.6
Asturias	0.7	0.6	0.5	0.5	0.7	0.6
Canarias	0.1	0.2	0.3	0.4	0.3	0.3
Foreigners	2.6	4.2	3.7	1.5	2.4	2.8
Total Percentage	100.0	100.0	100.0	100.0	100.0	100.0
Total *N*	10,962	26,524	18,088	35,172	19,016	109,762

Source Based on Boyd-Bowman (1976): 585, Table 1, with all his figures doubled

colonial empire. It should be stressed that these estimates are based on known ships voyages, and for this reason only approximate the volume of migration. It is also worth mentioning that elite Spaniards brought with them servants and slaves of Moorish origin, the so called Moriscos (Cook 2008), and these small number of Iberian "white slaves" could be found throughout Spanish America in the early seventeenth century (Cáceres 1995) and even as free persons in Inquisition in records later in the century (Cardaillac 1976). Thus, despite their limitations, the slave trade estimates provide a reasonable picture of the importance of the various zones which received African slaves in this period (see Graph 2).

Although the regions of mainland Spanish America had an abundant Amerindian Population which provided the basic agricultural and mining labor, the Spaniards still felt the need for slave laborers and were willing to pay the high cost for their importation. African slaves arrived with the first

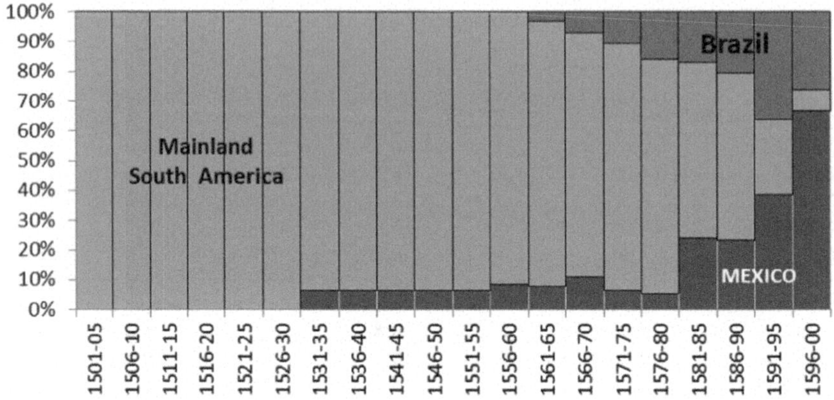

Graph 2 Ratio of slaves arriving to the main regions of Latin America, 1501–1600 (*Source* Slavevoyages estimates accessed July 30, 2019 and found at https://www.slavevoyages.org/assessment/estimates)

Spanish colonists and participated in all the wars of conquest. Cortes and his various armies contained African slaves when they conquered Mexico in the 1520s, while over a thousand African slaves appeared in the armies of Pizarro and Almargo in their conquest of Peru in the 1530s, and in their subsequent civil wars in the 1540s. Although Indians dominated rural life everywhere in Mainland Spanish America, Spaniards found their need for slaves constantly increasing. This was especially true in Peru which was initially both richer, and lost a progressively higher proportion of its coastal Amerindian populations to European diseases than New Spain and thus had abandoned coastal areas which were ideal for such European crops as sugar and grapes. Already by the mid 1550s there were some 3,000 African slaves in the Peruvian viceroyalty, with half of them in the city of Lima and the rest in coastal agriculture. Although African slaves sometimes engaged in agricultural labor, throughout Spanish America these Africans, along with Spaniards, were the most urbanized group in Spanish American society (Bowser 1974, p. 75).

Africans in the viceroyalty of Mexico were also to be found from the first moments in the armies, farms and houses of the Spanish conquerors. As in Peru, the first generation of slaves probably numbered close to the total number of whites. They were also drawn heavily into the local sugar and European commercial crop production in the warmer lowland regions, which were widely scattered in the central zone of the viceroyalty. Also given the discovery of silver in the northern regions of the viceroyalty were there were few settled Indians, Africans were even initially used in silver mining. In a mine census of 1570, 45% of the laboring population consisted of 3,700 Africans slaves, just a few hundred less than the Indian mine workers, and double the number of resident Spaniards (Bakewell 1971, pp. 122–124; Palmer 1976, p. 76). But the increasing availability of free Indian wage labor lessened the need for more expensive African slave labor and they disappeared from the mines by the end of the century. Given the more extensive Indian population in Mexico, Africans were less numerous than in Peru and their relative importance declined over time. Though slaves performed many of the same urban tasks in Mexico City as they did in Lima, the former was essentially an Indian and mestizo town and African slaves never achieved the same importance in the urban labor force.[5]

The relative significance of Mexican slavery was well reflected in the growth of its slave population which peaked at some 35,000 slaves by 1646 when they represented less than 2% of the viceregal population (Aguirre 1972, p. 219). In contrast, the number of slaves within Peru had reached close to 100,000 by mid seventeenth century, where they accounted for between 10 and 15% of the population. By 1650, Peru and New Spain had imported some 250,000 to 300,000 African slaves, a record which they would not repeat in the next century of colonial growth.

The Seventeenth Century and Eighteenth Century

The major demand for African slaves after 1600 came from Portuguese America and the marginal lands which the Spaniards had previously neglected, above all the islands of Cuba and Puerto Rico. With no stable Indian peasant populations to exploit, and few alternative exports in the form of precious metals, successful colonization in these zones required the export of products that Europe could consume, and this would eventually lead to the planting of sugar cane and the massive use of African slave labor. The first to develop the plantation slave model were the Portuguese who took possession of the eastern coastline of South America

[5] For an analysis of African slaves in Mexico, the best surveys are those of Palmer (1976) and Aguirre (1972).

in the early sixteenth century and modeled it along the lines of their Madeira sugar estates. First relaying on Indian slave labor to produce sugar, by the mid 1580s Pernambuco alone reported 2,000 African slaves, comprising one third of the captaincy's sugar labor force (Schwartz 1985, p. 65). With each succeeding decade the percentage of Africans in the slave population increased. By 1630 an estimated 202,000 Africans had arrived in the colony and sugar was now predominantly an African slave labor crop. The decades of the seventeenth century would prove to be the peak years of Brazil's dominance on the European sugar market, and it was this very sugar production monopoly which excited the envy of other European powers and led to the rise of alternative production centers in the Caribbean.

The opening up of the Lesser Antillean islands and the northeastern coast of South America to northern European colonization represented the first systematic challenge to Iberian control of the New World. By 1650, the English had 44,000 whites on their West Indian islands (compared to 53,000 in the settlements of New England),[6] while the French islands of Martinique and Guadeloupe held 15,000 white settlers by the end of the 1650s. At mid century, tobacco and indigo were the primary exports in these islands, and though slaves were present from the beginning, they were still outnumbered by the whites.

The Dutch, who now entered the slave trade in this period, became Portugal's biggest slave trade competitor and were crucial in first supplying slaves to the Non-Hispanic Caribbean islands. The Dutch had been Brazil's major commercial link with Northern Europe, but they turned hostile when Portugal was united with Spain from 1580 to 1640. As early as 1602 they established the East Indies Company to seize control of Portugal's Asian trade, followed in 1621 by the West Indies Company organized to take Portugal's African and American possessions. The Dutch West Indies Company finally captured and held Recife and its interior province of Pernambuco in 1630. They next captured several of Portugal's major African possessions: first the fortress of Elmina on the Gold Coast was taken in 1638 and then Luanda and most of the Angolan region fell to the Dutch in 1641. These conquests profoundly affected the subsequent history of sugar production and African slavery

[6] In fact, the 15,000 Africans on the islands, compared to only 2,000 in British North America at this time, meant that the former were more populated than the latter. McCusker and Menard (1985).

in America. For Brazil, the Dutch occupation resulted in Bahia replacing Pernambuco as the leading slave and sugar province; in the re-emergence of Indian slavery to replace the African slaves lost to the Dutch; with the ensuing Indian slave trade opening up the interior regions of Brazil to exploitation and settlement. For the rest of America, the Dutch would become a major source for the tools, techniques, credit and slaves which would carry the sugar revolution and its slave labor system into the West Indies, especially after the fall of Dutch Pernambuco in 1654.

The transformation which sugar created in the West Indies was truly impressive. The experience of Barbados, the first of the big production islands was typical. On the eve of the introduction of sugar in 1645, there were only 5,680 African slaves. By 1680 there were over 38,000. At this point Barbados was both the most populous and the wealthiest of England's American colonies and averaged some 265 slaves per square mile, compared to less than 2 slaves per square mile in the island of Jamaica which had been captured from the Spanish in 1655 (Meyer 1989, 129).[7] The slave ships were bringing in over 1,300 Africans per annum to Barbados and by the end of the century this tiny island contained over 50,000 slaves.[8] This Barbados experience was quickly emulated by the French. As of 1670 Martinique, Guadeloupe, St. Christopher and the recently settled western half of the island of Santo Domingo, were all producing sugar. By the early 1680s these islands, including Saint Dominque, contained over 18,000 slaves (Schnakenbourg 1977, pp. 44–47; Watts 1987, p. 112).

In Spanish America the seventeenth and especially eighteenth century saw more variation among the Spanish emigrants arriving in the Americas. Andalucía was still the principal origin region in total numbers, along with the traditional Castilian provinces, but Galicia and the Basque region and Navarra were now sending significant numbers of emigrants to America. A survey of emigrants in 1803 found that the Basque Country and Navarra had highest ratio of migrants to resident population which was 7.4 emigrants per 100,000 residents. For larger Andalucía, which had three times the resident population in this year, the ratio was 2.2 migrants per 100,000 residents. The primary destination of these late eighteenth

[7] The density estimates have been converted from those given in square kilometers.

[8] For the demographic history of Barbados, see Dunn (1972). By 1700 there were an estimated 115,000 Black slaves and only 33,000 whites in the British West Indies, see McCusker and Menard (1985).

and early nineteenth century migrants was Mexico and Central America-some 43% of the migrants going there, with the Northern Andean countries being the next most important destination (for 17% of the migrants) and the Hispanic Antilles third with 16% share of the total migrant stream (Lemus and Márquez 1992, pp. 67–68). Interestingly the principal group of legal migrants to Cuba between 1768 and 1817, whose origin was known, were Catalans (46%), followed by Basques (14%). Here too those aged 15–30 years of age represented 56% of the migrants (Tornero 1989, pp. 244–245). Of the 1,263 Catalans who migrated to America in the period 1778–1820, a quarter, the largest contingent, came from the city of Barcelona (Delgado 1982, pp. 136–137). Thus, as in previous centuries, most of the Spanish emigrants came from urban centers, rather than from the rural areas.

The big movements of African slaves to Spanish America throughout most of the seventeenth century was to Mexico, and to a lesser extent mainland South America, with the islands of Cuba and Puerto Rico not becoming major destination for the slave ships until the late eighteenth century. With Brazil dominating the world production of cane sugar for almost a century and them becoming the world's largest gold mining center in the first half of the eighteenth century, African arrivals to this continental Portuguese colony were constantly increasing. By the end of the seventeenth and beginning of the eighteenth century, the French, English and other North European colonies in the Caribbean were finally settled and began producing sugar, tobacco and other crops which were increasingly produced with slave labor. African movements to the Non-Hispanic Caribbean were thus the most important of any region in the eighteenth century and only collapsed with the end of the slave trade in the early nineteenth century (see Graph 3).

For the Spanish American colonies, the seventeenth century slave trade was still dominated by Mexican demand for slaves, with the South American arrivals being second. African slave arrivals to Puerto Rico and Cuba only begin in the second half of the eighteenth century, with Cuba finally becoming the dominant receiver of Africans in the nineteenth century. By the quinquennial of 1815–1820, Cuba accounted for 99% of the 93,000 slaves arriving to Spanish America (see Graph 4).

Within Latin America, Brazil remained the largest single region of African arrivals throughout the seventeenth, eighteenth, and early nineteenth century. Within Brazil the Northeastern ports remained important

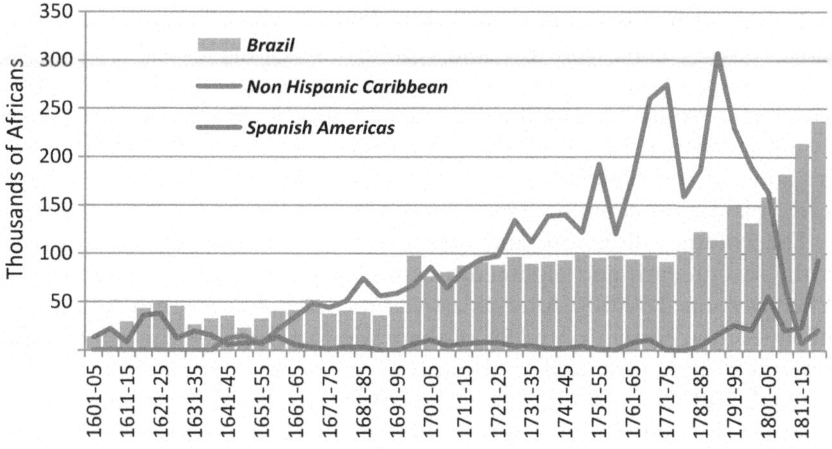

Graph 3 Major regions of African slave arrivals, 1600–1820 (*Source* Slavevoyages estimates accessed July 30, 2019 and found at https://www.slavevoyages.org/assessment/estimates)

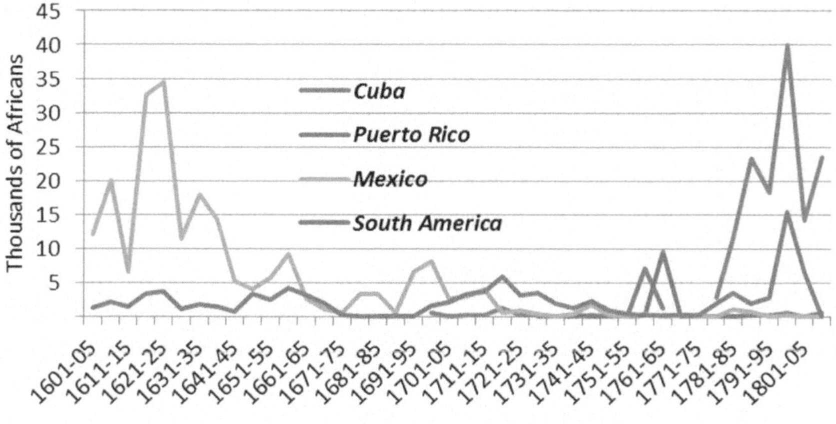

Graph 4 Major regions of Spanish America receiving African slaves, 1601–1815 (*Source* Slavevoyages estimates accessed July 30, 2019 and found at https://www.slavevoyages.org/assessment/estimates)

to 1820, but it was the port of Rio de Janeiro which became the dominant receiving zone from the mid eighteenth century onward. Both the gold mining boom of Minas Gerais and the emergence of a new sugar economy in South Central Brazil in the provinces of Rio de Janeiro, Minas Gerais and São Paulo were absorbing ever more slaves. In turn this was the zone in the nineteenth century which would be the center for the coffee plantation economy (see Graph 5).

The volume, direction, and origin of slaves arriving in the Americas in the seventeenth and eighteenth century showed significant variations. Whereas some 169,000 Africans arrived to Brazil and Spanish America in the sixteenth century, only 15% of them went to Brazil. Although Spanish America steadily increased its absorption of African migrants from an estimated 1,700 slaves in the sixteenth century, to 2,300 per annum in the seventeenth century and 3,400 in the last period, it could not keep pace with Brazilian slave arrivals. Brazil went from 300 or so slaves per annum in the seventeenth century to 8,000 per annum in the next century and 28,000 in the eighteenth century. Thus Brazil took almost four fifths of the Africans disembarked in these two regions in the seventeenth century and its share in the period 1701–1820 rose to 89% of the total African arrivals.

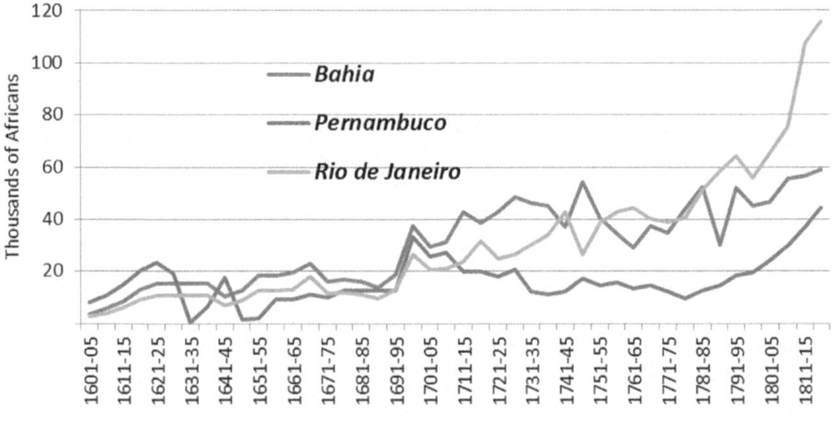

Graph 5 Principal regions of Brazil receiving African slaves, 1600–1820 (*Source* Slavevoyages estimates accessed July 30, 2019 and found at https://www.slavevoyages.org/assessment/estimates)

The origins of Africans also slowly shifted over time. Whereas Senegambia was a major source in the sixteenth century, the two dominant regions of origin in the following periods were the Bight of Biafra and the Congo-Angola area of West Central Africa (see Table 3). Until 1800 the slaves listed as coming from Mozambique came via the Pacific through the Mexican port of Verazcruz. It was only after 1800 that the Portuguese were able to develop a South Atlantic route from this region (Klein 1978, Chapters 3–4).

The migration of Europeans to Spanish America occurred at a much slower pace than the migration of the Africans. Nevertheless, by the standards of the rest of the other European colonizing powers, Spain sent a far higher ratio of European migrants than did the other European nations. The data for the flow of Spanish migrants in the seventeenth century appears to be higher than in the sixteenth century. A recent estimate based on shipping lists places the total number for the first half of the century at 194,816 persons, with the earlier period from 1601–1625 being more intense with an estimated 111,312 arriving. In the second quarter of the century (1626–1650) the numbers dropped to 83,504 (Lemus and Márquez 1992, p. 48). What the volume was for the entire century is difficult to estimate. Some have argued that the total was 100,000, but clearly that is too low (Mörner 1975, p. 12), and given the volume in the first half of the century one can assume that it was at least 200,000 who migrated to the New World. This of course does not include the Portuguese migration to Spanish America during the period when the two kingdoms were united from 1580 to 1640. There are numerous studies of Portuguese merchant communities in all the major Spanish American colonies in this period.[9] All of these numbers of course, also do not count return migration which would have been the norm for officials, clergymen and returning wealthy individuals and their families and servants.

The eighteenth century data are even more sporadic. In this century a study from selected years shows that half of the migrants were illegal. Thus, the best estimate so far gives a figure on the order of 52,000 legal and illegal migrants from Spain going to Spanish America (Lemus and Márquez 1992, p. 49). If this number proves to be correct on further

[9] For a general survey, see Studnicki-Gizbert (2007) and for the important community in Lima, see Sullón (2014).

research, it would mean that there was a major decline of Spanish emigration from earlier centuries. This was also the century when the slave trade declines for Mexico and South America as well.

The Portuguese migration to Brazil in contrast was more intense in the seventeenth and eighteenth centuries. It is estimated that the population of Portuguese residing in Brazil reached 100,000 by 1699 (Marcílio 1984, p. 47). But this was still quite modest compared to the explosive growth in the eighteenth century when gold and Diamonds were discovered in Minas Gerais and Goiás and whole new regions were settled along the entire Atlantic coastline of Brazil from the Amazon to the Rio de la Plata. Some of this migration was subsidized by private companies and others by the state, but the majority were either emigrants paying their own way or African slaves purchased by American settlers. By 1818 when the first full scale enumeration exists for the colony, there were an estimated 2.4 million free persons and 1.1 million slaves. Of these free persons, probably a third were non-whites, which would mean that the Portuguese originated population by then numbered some 1.7 million persons. The majority of this population was native born in Brazil as can be seen by the sex ratio of this free population, which was 98 males per 100 females. Had it been dominated by Portuguese born whites its sex ratio would probably have been as high as the slaves, which was 138 males per 100 females in this same census.[10]

The Structure of Transatlantic Migrations

Except for the occasional migration of elite family, or state sponsored settlements of farmers from the Atlantic islands, all the major migration streams were predominantly young adult males in origin, whether Spanish, Portuguese or African. Moreover, all these migration streams were mostly made up of young adults in their peak working ages. This can be seen in the data of Spanish migrants in several periods. Between 1493 and 1579, for example, there were 37,728 legal male migrants who arrived in America and 7,646 females for a sex ratio of 493 males per 100 females. The dominance of males was also noted by Sánchez Albornoz for the seventeenth century migration citing one estimate for Peru of

[10]This census has been analyzed in Andrade et al. (2008). For a survey of the census materials in this period, see Alden (1963, pp. 173–205).

7 to 8 males for every female among the Spanish residents (Sánchez-Albornoz 1974, 69). In a list of 16,611 migrants who left Spain for America between 1765 and 1820, some 84% were males (for an extraordinary sex ratio of 528 males per 100 females). Of the 9,600 males whose civil status was known, 80% were single. Even among the women migrants some 43% were single. Here as well the prime age group was 16–25, with the next most important being 26–30 years of age (Márquez 1995).

Among the African migrants, young adult males also predominated. One estimate taken from a sample of 1,354 slave ships in the period 1701–1800 found that men and boys made up an estimated 64% of the Africans carried to the New World (Eltis and Engerman 1992, p. 241). This is also reflected in the sex ratio of the African born slaves in the province of São Paulo in 1808. This was a recently expanding state which was beginning to import African slaves on a large scale. Here African born males represented 65% of the immigrant population and the sex ratio was 185 men per 100 women. As their Age Pyramid shows there was a concentration of both males and females in working ages (64% were aged 15–39) among these African born slaves and a significant lack of children, as can be seen in contrast to the Creole, or native-born in Brazil slaves in the same census of 1808 who had a sex ratio of 96 males per 100 females and whose population 15–39 represented only 42% of the total population (see Graphs. 6 and 7).[11]

Conclusion

This survey of the migration of Iberians and Africans to Iberian America shows major variations over time and space. From region of origin to arrival region a series of economic and social factors determined who participated in the migration and to which regions they went. The existence of a large Indian and then mestizo population in the Spanish American colonies meant that Africans were fewer in number and tended to concentrate in the cities and be more totally linked to Spanish white society. Changing legal and socio-economic conditions in the regions of origins also influenced migration flows, though continental Spanish and Portuguese migrants always seemed to come primarily from cities. In the Hispanic Caribbean and Brazil, the migration of Africans was far more

[11] For more detailed analysis of the province's slave population, see Klein and Vidal (2003).

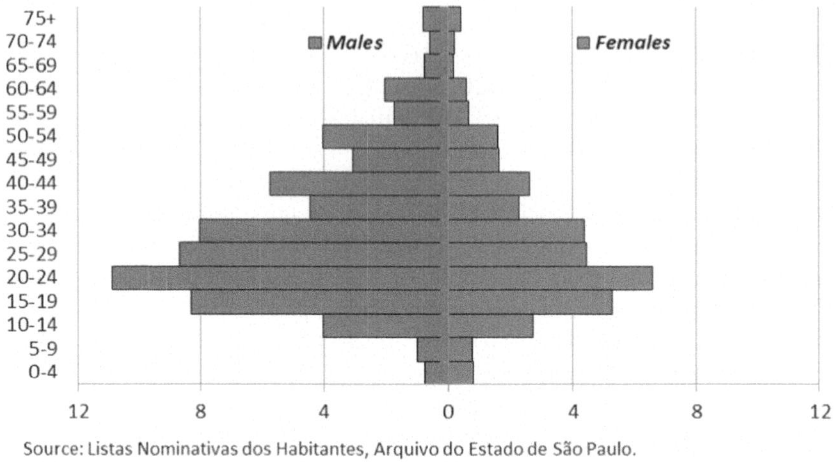

Graph 6 Age pyramid of African born slaves in the province of São Paulo, 1804 (*Source* Listas Nominativas dos Habitantes, Arquivo do Estado de São Paulo)

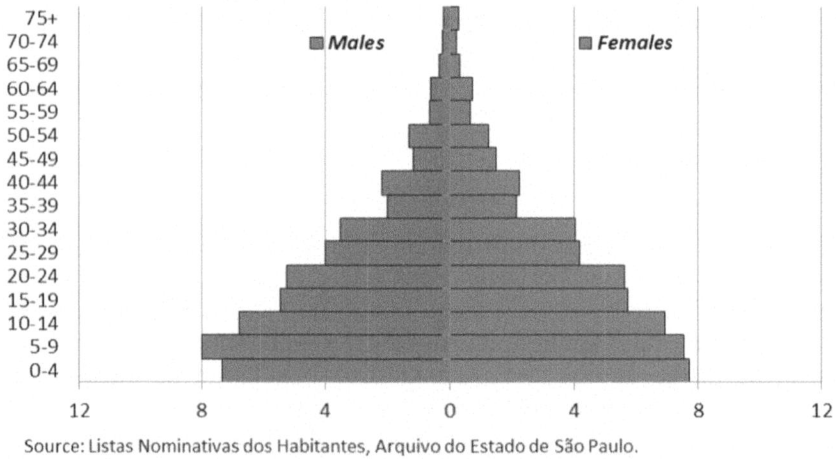

Graph 7 Age pyramid of native born slaves in the province of São Paulo, 1804 (*Source* Listas Nominativas dos Habitantes, Arquivo do Estado de São Paulo)

intense in contrast to mainland South America and brought primarily a rural based population. In these plantation zones Africans, rather than Indians and Mestizos were the primary rural labor force. But whatever the origin of these migrations, the Spaniards, the Portuguese and the Africans arriving in America were always primarily male and adult. It is also worth noting that once the intensity of this migration of Spaniards, Portuguese and Africans slowed, there emerged a dominant creole, or native-born population in these American colonies, and by the end of the colonial period these colonies ended with a balanced population in terms of ages and sexes typical of pre modern societies.

Bibliography

Aguirre, Gonzalo. 1972. *La población negra de Mexico, 1492–1810.* Mexico City: Fondo de Cultura Económica.

Alden, Dauril. 1963. "The Population of Brazil in the Late Eighteenth Century: A Preliminary Study." *The Hispanic American Historical Review* 43 (2): 173–205.

Álvarez-Nogal, Carlos, and Leandro Prados. 2007. "The Decline of Spain (1500–1850): Conjectural Estimates." *European Review of Economic History* 11(3): 319–366.

Álvarez-Nogal, Carlos, and Leandro Prados. 2013. "The Rise and Fall of Spain (1270–1850)." *Economic History Review* 66 (1): 1–37.

Andrade, Clotilde, Tarcísio Botelho, and José Morais. 2008. "Políticas de população no período Joanino." In *A Corte no Brasil: População e Sociedade no Brasil e em Portugal no Início do Século XIX*, 1–16. São Leopoldo: Editora Oikos.

Bakewell, Peter. 1971. *Silver Mining and Society in Colonial Mexico, Zacatecas, 1546–1700.* Cambridge: Cambridge University Press.

Borucki, Alex, David Eltis, and David Wheat. 2015. "Atlantic History and the Slave Trade to Spanish America." *The American Historical Review* 120 (2): 433–461.

Bowser, Frederick. 1974. *The African Slave in Colonial Peru, 1524–1650.* Stanford: Stanford University Press.

Boyd-Bowman, Peter. 1963. "La emigración peninsular aAmérica: 1520 a 1539." *Historia Mexicana* 13 (2): 165–192.

Boyd-Bowman, Peter. 1976. "Patterns of Spanish emigration to the Indies Until 1600." *The Hispanic American Historical Review* 56, 4: 580–604.

Cáceres, Jaime. 1995. "La Mujer Morisca o Esclava Blanca en el Peru del Siglo XVI." *Sharq al-Andalus* 12: 565–574.

Cardaillac, Louis. 1976. "Le Problème Morisque en Amérique." *Mélanges de la Casa de Velázquez* 12: 283–306.

Cook, Karoline. 2008. *Forbidden Crossings: Morisco Emigration to Spanish America, 1492–1650*. PhD thesis, Princeton University.

Delgado, Josep. 1982. "La emigración española a América Latina durante la época del comercio libre (1765–1820): El ejemplo catalán." *Boletín americanista* 32: 115–137.

Dunn, Richard, 1972. *Sugar and Slaves, The Rise of the Planter Class in the English West Indies, 1624–1713*. Chapel Hill: University of North Carolina Press.

Elbl, Ivana, 1997. "The Volume of the Early Atlantic Slave Trade, 1450–1521." *The Journal of African History* 38: 31–75.

Eltis, David, and Stanley Engerman. 1992. "Was the Slave Trade Dominated by Men?" *Journal of Interdisciplinary History* 23 (2): 237–257.

Emory Center for Digital Scholarship. https://www.slavevoyages.org/assessment/estimates. Accessed July 19, 2019.

Freire, Leonor, Pedro Lains, and Susana Münch. 2016. *An Economic History of Portugal, 1143–2010*. Cambridge: Cambridge University Press.

Johnson, Harold. 1984. "The Portuguese Settlement of Brazil, 1500–80." In *Cambridge History of Latin America, Colonial Period*. Cambridge: Cambridge University Press.

Klein, Herbert. 1969. "The Trade in African Slaves to Rio de Janeiro, 1795–1811: Estimates of Mortality and Patterns of Voyages." *Journal of African History* 10 (4): 533–549.

Klein, Herbert. 1978. *Middle Passage: Comparative Studies in the Atlantic Slave Trade*. Princeton: Princeton University Press.

Lemus, Encarnación, Rosario Márquez. 1992. *Los precedentes. Volumen 1: Historia general de la emigración española a Iberoamérica*. Madrid: Ministerio de Trabajo e Inmigración.

Lockhart, James. 1968. *Spanish Peru 1532–1560, A Colonial Society*. Madison: University of Wisconsin Press.

Lynch, John. 2001. *América Latina, entre colonia y nación*. Madrid: Crítica.

Marcílio, Maria. 1984. *The Cambridge History of Latin America. Volume 2: The population of colonial Brazil*, edited by L. Bethell, 37–64. Cambridge: Cambridge University Press.

Márquez, Rosario. 1995. *La emigración española a América, 1765–1824*. Oviedo: Universidad de Oviedo.

McCusker, John, and Russell Menard. 1985. *The Economy of British America, 1607–1789*. Chapel Hill: University of North Carolina Press.

Meyer, Jean. 1989. *Histoire du sucre*. Paris: Editions Desjonquères.

Morales, Francisco. 1951. "Colonos canarios en Indias." *Anuario de Estudios Americanos* 8: 399–441.

Mörner, Magnus. 1975. "La emigración española al Nuevo Mundo antes de 1810. Un informe del estado de la investigación." *Anuario de estudios americanos* 32: 43–131.

Naylor, Michael. 2006. *The Portuguese in India*. Cambridge: Cambridge University Press.

Palmer, Colin A. 1976. *Slaves of the White God. Blacks in Mexico, 1570–1650*. Cambridge: Harvard University Press.

Piazza, Walter F. 2011. "Açorianos e Madeirenses no Sul do Brasil." *Acervo* 10 (2): 119–128.

Rodríguez Morel, Genaro. Forthcoming. "Apuntes para el estudio de la demografía de la Española. Siglos XVI–XVII."

Sánchez-Albornoz, Nicolás. 1974. *The Population of Latin America. A History*. Oakland: University of California Press.

Schnakenbourg, Christian. 1977. "Statistiques pour l'histoire de l'économie de plantation en Guadeloupe et Martinique (1635–1835)." *Bulletin de la Sociétié d'Historie de La Guadeloupe* 21: 3–121.

Schwartz, Stuart. 1985. *Sugar Plantations in the Formation of Brazilian Society: Bahia, 1550–1835*. Cambridge: Cambridge University Press.

Seijas, Tatiana. 2014. *Asian Slaves in Colonial Mexico: From Chinos to Indians*. Cambridge: Cambridge University Press.

Studnicki-Gizbert, Daviken. 2007. *A Nation Upon the Ocean Sea: Portugal's Atlantic Diaspora and the Crisis of the Spanish Empire, 1492–1640*. Oxford: Oxford University Press.

Sullón, Gleydi. 2014. *Vasallos y extranjeros: portugueses en la Lima virreinal, 1570–1680*. PhD thesis, Universidad Complutense de Madrid. https://eprints.ucm.es/27850/1/T35619.pdf.

Thompson, I. A. A. 2008. "Money, Money, and Yet More Money!" Finance, the Fiscal-State, and the Military Revolution: Spain 1500–1650." In *The Military Revolution Debate: Readings on the Military Transformation of Early Modern Europe*, 273–298. Abingdon: Routledge.

Tornero, Pablo. 1989. "Comercio colonial y proyección de la población: la emigración catalana a Cuba en la época del crecimiento azucarero (1790–1817)." *Boletín Americanista* 39: 235–264.

Torres, Luíz. 2004. "A colonização açoriana no Rio Grande do Sul (1752–63)." *Biblos* 16: 177–191.

Klein, Herbert, and Francisco Vidal. 2003. *Slavery and the Economy of São Paulo, 1750–1850*. Stanford: Stanford University Press.

Watts, David. 1987. *The West Indies: Patterns of Development, Culture, and Environmental Change Since 1492*. Cambridge: Cambridge University Press.

The Fruits of *El Dorado*: The Global Impact of American Precious Metals

Leticia Arroyo Abad and Nuno Palma

Introduction

> Behold rich lands! May you know how to govern them well!
> —Hernández Puertocarrero to Cortés in 1519 (Díaz del Castillo 2003, p. 63)

The quest for riches shaped the colonization of the "New World". How did the discovery of large deposits of gold and silver affect the world economy? Many volumes have looked into different aspects and consequences of the phenomenal wave of precious metals that came out of

L. A. Abad
Queens College, City University of New York, New York, NY, USA
e-mail: Leticia.Abad@qc.cuny.edu

N. Palma (✉)
University of Manchester, Manchester, UK
e-mail: nuno.palma@manchester.ac.uk

Instituto de Ciências Sociais, Universidade de Lisboa, Lisbon, Portugal

L. A. Abad · N. Palma
CEPR, London, UK

R. Dobado-González and A. García-Hiernaux (eds.), *The Fruits of the Early Globalization*, Palgrave Studies in Comparative Global History,
https://doi.org/10.1007/978-3-030-69666-5_4

Latin America following the Conquest. The long-run consequences were not the same everywhere. Our task in the present chapter is to present a global view.

In Western Europe, the colonizers *par excellence*—Spain and Portugal—suffered negative consequences in the long run. The Spanish government enjoyed increased revenues, but it squandered those revenues on ultimately unsuccessful European wars. Precious metals enriched a merchant class in both Spain and Portugal, but both economies suffered from the Dutch disease as a result. More seriously, both countries suffered from the political resource curse, as pervasive rent-seeking distorted state institutions. By contrast, England and The Netherlands benefited from the influx of silver coins, which lowered transaction costs and increased fiscal capacity.

In Latin America, silver was the backbone of the colonial enterprise. The colonizers created a complex infrastructure to maximize the proceeds from mineral extraction. Without precious metals, the extent and depth of the Spanish empire would have paled compared to what actually occurred. The wealth from the metal-rich areas supported the imperial fringes and less affluent regions. Local elites, not the Spanish Crown, benefited most from mining and the subsequent growth. In Brazil, the absence of precious metals in the first two centuries gave rise to a plantation economy, which was overshadowed by the discovery of gold in the early 1690s.

American precious metals travelled far, transforming economies and polities in Asia and Africa. American silver lubricated the wheels of trade in Asia. Europeans were able to enjoy silk, tea, and porcelain from China and Japan thanks to silver from Latin America. Mining prosperity in America also fueled the demand for African slaves, contributing to the largest involuntary migration in history (see Klein 2021).[1]

In this chapter, we look into the role and impact of precious metals on economic development. We start with the colonizers *par excellence*, Spain and Portugal. We then turn our attention to other European countries. We then move to detail how the exploitation of precious metals shaped Latin America. Finally, we briefly consider the experience of Asia and Africa.

[1] Later the need for plantation labor would overtake the lower demand driven by American elites, but mining sustained the early trans-Atlantic slave trade.

Impact on European Economies

The trans-Atlantic mining economy consisted largely of silver and gold flowing from the Western Hemisphere. While there was some trade in iron from Europe (and a substantial mercury trade driven entirely by silver production), the overwhelming movement consisted of silver leaving American mines to Europe. Somewhere between 85,000 and 150,000 metric tons of silver were produced between 1500 and 1800 in Spanish America alone, although sources vary as to the exact amount (TePaske 2010; Barrett 1990, p. 236). Whatever the exact amount, the quantities of silver and gold produced in the Americas during the early modern era dwarfed the combined production of the rest of the world (Barrett 1990).

Trade between the colonies and the metropolis consisted of American production in exchange for European goods. In terms of the balance of payments, most of the action were profits remitted in silver and gold by Iberian merchants and, to a lesser extent, tax payments levied by the Portuguese and Spanish imperial governments. In both cases, those remittances mostly took the form of physical shipments of coins across the Atlantic, with all the associated security costs that implied. From early on the Crown needed to protect against unauthorized smuggling and state-sponsored piracy by other European powers (e.g. TePaske 2010, p. 214).

The influx of silver affected Western Europe via three channels. The first was the fiscal impact on the Spanish imperial government. In principle, revenues from the Americas could have subsidized the Crown and thereby given Spain an advantage in its battles to control much of Europe. The second channel was via short and medium-term stimuli to various European economies. Spain (and to a lesser extent Portugal) would be presumed to benefit from the influx of silver, but the increase in demand also produced secondary effects in other European economies. The third would be the longer-term negative effects of the natural resource boom. Those effects would operate through two sub-channels: (1) a loss of competitiveness in other industries via the Dutch disease, and (2) a distortion of political institutions caused by excessive rent-seeking. Let us examine the above channels in turn.

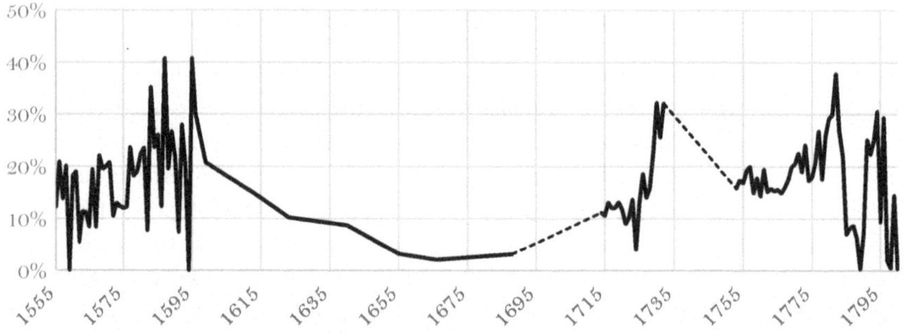

Fig. 1 Tax revenue from precious metals production as a share of Spanish imperial revenue (*Source* 1555–1596 from Drelichman and Voth [2010], Appendix 1; 1599–1688: Ucendo and Lanza García [2020], 1714–1732: Jurado Sánchez [2008], 1753–1788: Gelabert [1999]. Loan proceeds are not included as revenues. Additionally, notice that this only includes direct taxes over metals production, hence excluding other economic activities which appeared as a consequence of that industry)

Fiscal Revenue

The silver resources of the New World were not directly exploited by the Spanish state. Rather, the mines were operated by private entrepreneurs. Anyone who discovered minerals could stake a claim of 160 by 80 *varas* (approximately 440 by 220 feet) along or across the vein and could additionally pursue a continuous vein outside the claim (Lacy 1987, pp. 2–3; see also Elliott 2006, p. 93). Miners had to continuously work their claims and submit production to the treasury for minting and to pay taxes. Taxes consisted of a royalty of at most 20% (the *quinto*), plus additional (but much smaller) assaying, brassage, and seigniorage taxes related to the minting of coins.[2]

These revenues formed a significant portion of the resources available to the Spanish Crown (Fig. 1). Over the course of the colonial era, they averaged approximately a fifth of the empire's fiscal resources.

[2] Mining taxes were initially 1/5 in all Spanish colonies. Mexico negotiated a decrease to 1/10 in 1548, while Peru only obtained that benefit in 1736 (Garner 1988, p. 906). In Brazil, mining taxes remained at 1/5 throughout colonial times, except for a period of about a decade during the mid-eighteenth century, when they were based on the number of slaves used in the mines.

The problem for the Crown was that the revenue stream from the Americas was exceedingly volatile. Production disruptions, enemy naval actions, local labor shortages, access to key raw materials (especially mercury), the vagaries of geology, and changing demands on colonial treasuries (which were also financed by silver) all led to large swings in the silver tax revenue available to the imperial government.

Inasmuch as colonial resources enabled the Spanish Empire to conduct its large-scale military campaigns across Europe, the impact of colonial silver on the Old World was profound indeed. That said, the scale of the Crown's silver income remitted from the New World was not large as a share of the Spanish economy. Silver tax remittances only look large as a share of imperial revenues because the Spanish government was so inefficient at raising revenues from its European territories.[3] Using the lower bound on Spanish GDP from Nogal and Prados de Escosura (2007), Spanish public spending averaged roughly 2.7% of the country's GDP in the sixteenth century and it did not grow appreciably thereafter (Drelichman and Voth 2010, p. 835). As we will discuss below, it is plausible that a Spanish Empire devoid of its access to American silver could have developed alternative revenue sources.

Short and Medium-Term Effects

Most of the revenue from silver and gold production did not accrue to the Spanish state. Rather, it remained in the hands of private miners and merchants. Total production corresponded to a roughly constant 6% of Spain's nominal GDP (see Fig. 2). Not all of this arrived in Spain, because some was retained in the Americas or shipped directly to China (via Manila and the galleon trade; see Giraldez 2021). There is a debate concerning the exact quantities that went to Europe, but whichever figures one adopts, the share of silver remittances flowing back to Spain

[3] In practice, the lion's share of the European revenue collected by the Spanish imperial government came from Castile. Aragón contributed taxes based on light feudal levies dating from the medieval period. The Austrian territories paid little before 1556 and nothing thereafter. Italian revenues were eaten up by local expenses and The Netherlands only paid for imperial expenses if local parliaments agreed. Finally, the nobility throughout the empire was mostly exempt from taxation. After desultory attempts to raise revenues from The Netherlands and Italy, Emperor Charles V made the somewhat astonishing statement in 1540 that "I cannot be sustained except for my realms in Spain." See Reyna (1999, pp. 32–33).

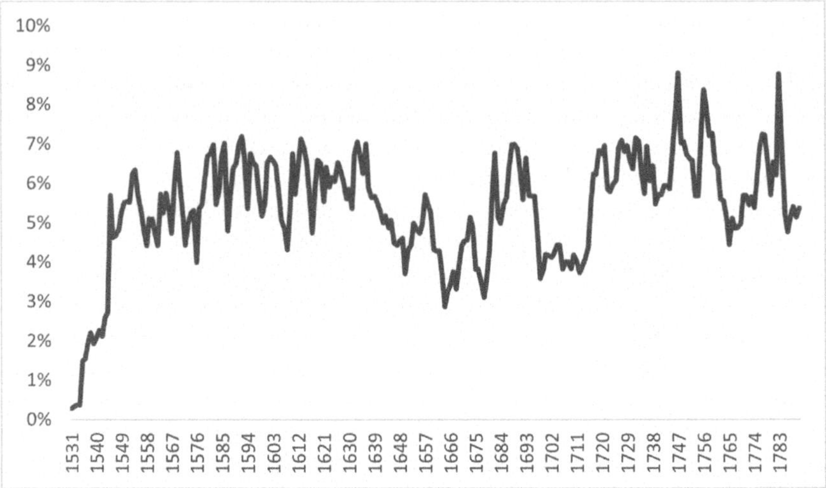

Fig. 2 Precious metal production in the Americas as share of Spanish GDP (*Source* The appendix of Palma [2021])

during the early modern period was never less than half of total American production.[4]

Did the inflows of American silver stimulate the European economy? It is now possible to evaluate the effects of the discovery of silver and gold in the Americas on the Iberian economies thanks to three new interdependent research developments. The first is a series of new datasets on prices and GDP. The second is a set of improved econometric estimation methodologies (Jordà 2005). The third is the usage of historical events that allow for credible identification strategies.

One way to identify the effects on the European economy is to explore exogenous variations in the timing of discovery of new mines and the intensity of production (Palma 2021). Mining discoveries were not driven by European events but by American geology and colonial entrepreneurship. By focusing on a source of variation exogenous to Europe's economy—but which can influence it—this type of strategy is

[4] Hamilton (1934), Morineau (2009), and González (1996) present alternative estimates for arrivals to Seville and Cádiz. For the case of Brazilian gold arriving to Portugal, see Costa et al. (2013).

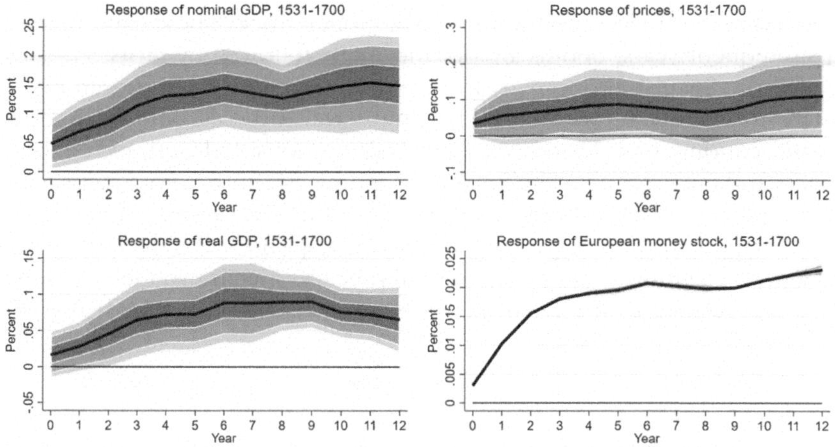

Fig. 3 Response of Nominal GDP, Price level, Real GDP and money stock for a panel of six European countries to a 1% increase in precious metals production relative to stock (1531–1700) (*Note* Country fixed effects are included, and standard errors are clustered by country. One standard deviation, 90% and 95% confidence intervals are shown. The regressions control for four lags of the dependent variable, country-specific quadratic trends, contemporaneous and four lags of temperature, and a dummy variable indicating whether a country is at war with Spain in a given year. *Source* Palma [2021])

immune to the argument that it was population, not American silver, which led to the observable price inflation in Europe (see Munro 2003 for a critical review).

Figure 3 shows the response for a panel of six Western European economies to a (normalized) 1% increase in precious metals production in the Americas relative to the European money stock.[5] The economies included are England, The Netherlands, North and Central Italy, Germany, Spain, and Portugal. Nominal GDP, price levels, and real GDP all respond positively to a silver supply shock. Prices take longer to respond than output. Real output peaks around years 6 to 9, standing at 0.9% higher in response to a 1% increase in production of American

[5] The baseline period does not go beyond 1700 due to the lack of annual gold production data for the eighteenth century. Results are, however, qualitatively similar when including that century.

precious metals relative to the European money stock. These gains remain in subsequent years; booms are not inevitably followed by busts.

Did the Spanish economy react differently from other European ones? There are reasons to believe that it might have. After all, influxes of silver hit its economy first. Moreover, those influxes consisted both of remitted profits and tax revenues. The Spanish economy might therefore be reasonably expected to respond more positively to the silver influxes than other European economies. Figure 4 shows the response of real GDP of six European economies to a 1% increase in precious metals production in the Americas relative to the European money stock. The effect for real GDP

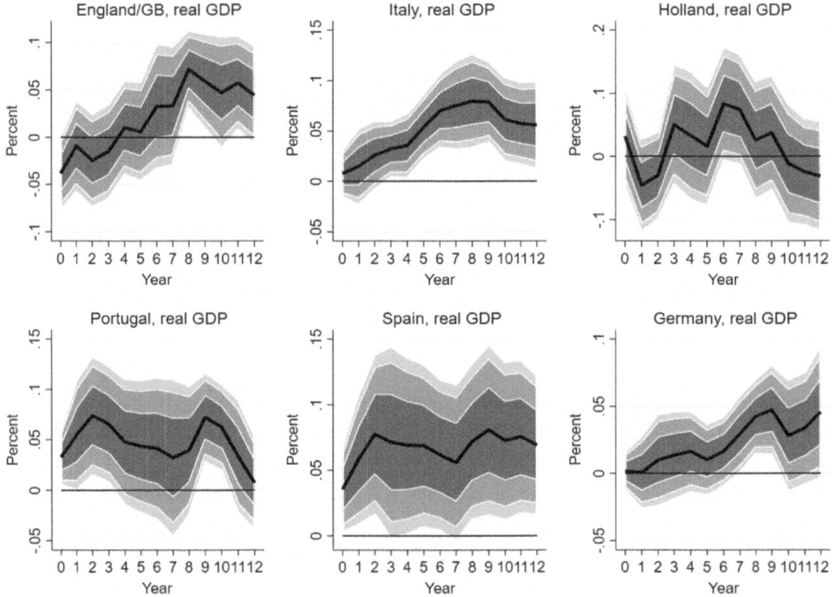

Fig. 4 Response of Real GDP of six European countries to a 1% increase in precious metals production relative to stock (1531–1700) (*Note* Newey-West standard errors are employed. One standard deviation, 90% and 95% confidence intervals are shown. The regressions control for country-specific linear and quadratic trends, contemporaneous and four lags of temperature, four lags of the dependent variable, and a war with Spain dummy. *Source* Based on Palma [2021])

in Spain is initially larger and increases faster than in the second-order receivers such as England and Holland.

It is possible to run the above experiment in reverse when silver fleets were partly shipwrecked or otherwise destroyed. This generates exogenous negative shocks in the growth of the Spanish money supply. Figure 5 shows that a one percentage point reduction in the Spanish money growth rate caused a drop in real output which persisted for several years, with output remaining 1% lower three years later.

What were the mechanisms by which GDP fell when the silver supply was reduced? The first mechanism was a permanent fall in the price level, which occurred with a lag: five years later, prices dropped by 1% in response to the shock (Fig. 6). The failure of prices to adjust immediately

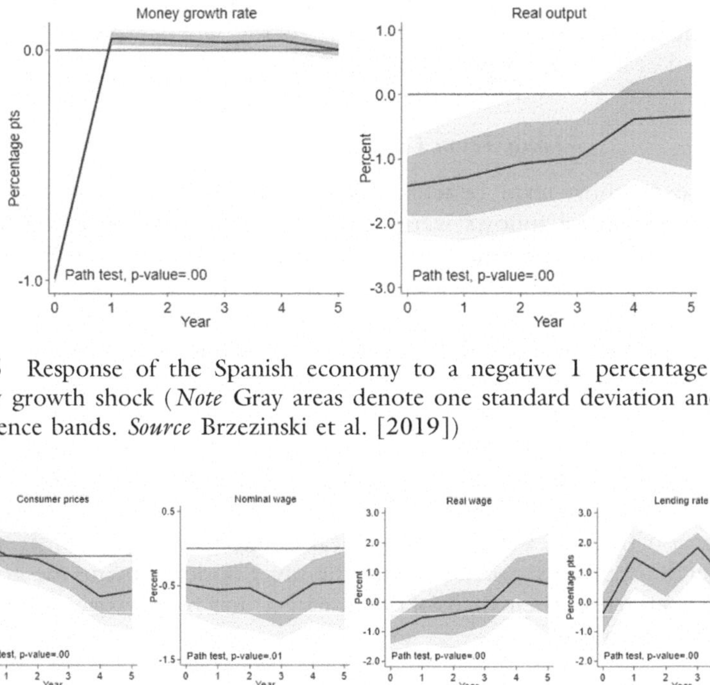

Fig. 5 Response of the Spanish economy to a negative 1 percentage point money growth shock (*Note* Gray areas denote one standard deviation and 90% confidence bands. *Source* Brzezinski et al. [2019])

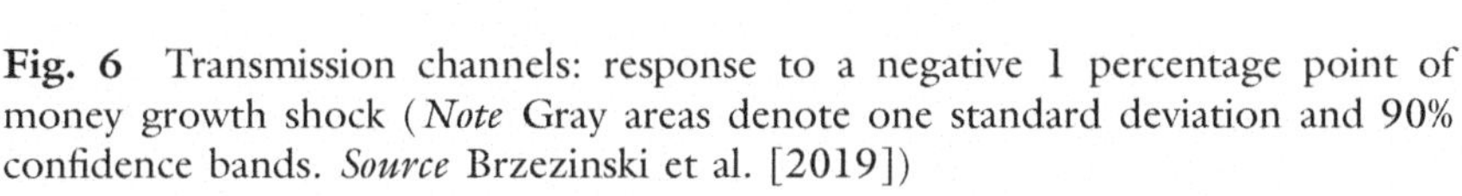

Fig. 6 Transmission channels: response to a negative 1 percentage point of money growth shock (*Note* Gray areas denote one standard deviation and 90% confidence bands. *Source* Brzezinski et al. [2019])

caused part of the fall in GDP. The second mechanism was a temporary tightening of credit markets, with the lending rate more than one percentage points higher one year later. The net effect was the result of a combination of nominal rigidities—prices and wages failing to respond at impact—and credit frictions, with a wave of bankruptcies observed as a consequence of the failure of silver to arrive.

The effect on Spanish price levels warrants additional explanation. Most of the silver coins did not stay in Spain. The initial influx caused Spanish prices to rise faster, but that in turn pushed coins out of Spain via reduced exports, additional imports and increased military payments abroad. When measured in silver units, prices in Spain did rise more than elsewhere (Allen 2001; Karaman et al. 2019; Palma 2019). Much of this rise in Spanish prices (felt first in Andalusia) spilled over to nearby Portugal (e.g. Magalhães 2018, pp. 163–164), which also experienced considerable inflation, particularly when expressed in silver (Karaman et al. 2019; Palma and Reis 2019).

Long-Term Consequences for Iberia

Evidence of short-term benefits does not imply that in the long run the precious metal inflows were good for the Iberian economies. The Spanish economy entered a period of sustained decline and stagnation over the early modern period, and our view is that this can be attributed to a large degree to the negative consequences from large quantities of precious metals from the Americas—the value of which was much larger than other trade (Fig. 7). As a consequence, Spain suffered from Dutch disease and the political form of the resource curse. Dutch disease meant that inflation in silver prices led to a loss of competitiveness of the national industry. In a related process, the influx of precious metals led to widespread rent-seeking, as various groups—with special emphasis on the non-tradable sector such as local religious services, construction, and merchant groups associated with the silver trade lobbying the government—tried to get their share of the bonanza, and progressively weakened Spanish institutions.

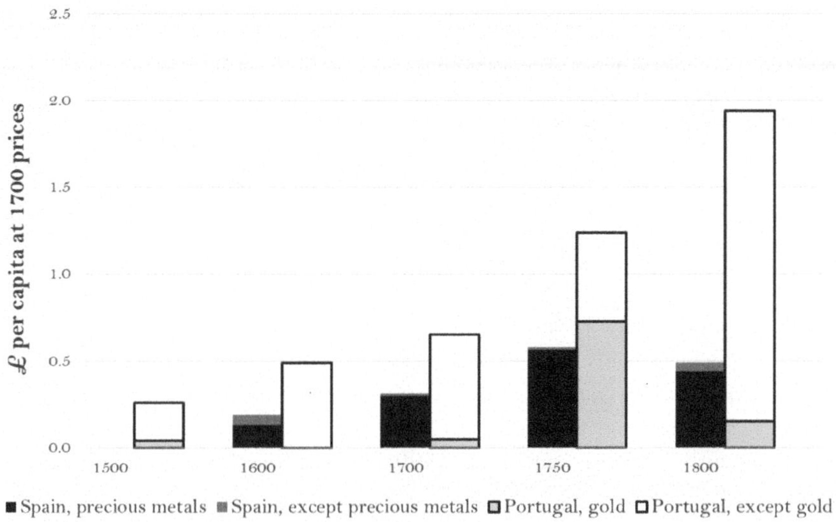

Fig. 7 Per capita inflow of precious metals and trade, in 1700 £ per capita (*Source* Costa et al. [2015])

We start with Dutch disease.[6] Early modern Spanish and European observers did not fail to observe that American treasure was not making Spain as wealthy as it had hoped—and its enemies had feared. On the contrary, after flourishing in the fifteenth and some of the sixteenth century, Spanish industry entered a long period of decline. These impressionistic viewpoints were emphasized in Earl J. Hamilton's work (e.g. Hamilton 1934), and recent scholarship continues to support it (Forsyth and Nicholas 1983; Drelichman 2005a). From 1530 to 1570, when the first large-scale imports of precious metals from the Americas took place, the Spanish economy boomed (Fig. 8). A secular decline and stagnation followed.[7] The Spanish wool industry experienced considerable growth in the fifteenth century (Elliott 2002, p. 42), but then collapsed

[6] It is worth noting that the Iberian economies did not perform much worse than England until 1650 (Henriques and Palma 2019; Álvarez-Nogal and Prados de la Escosura 2013; Broadberry et al. 2015; Palma and Reis 2019).

[7] These patterns confirm the views of Hamilton (1934, pp. 44, 299). Note that 150 years later, Portugal's economy would follow a similar trend with the discovery of gold mines in Brazil in 1690s (Palma and Reis 2019; Palma 2019).

Fig. 8 Spain's GDP per capita (in 1990 "international" GK dollars) (*Source* Prados de la Escosura et al. [2020])

in the sixteenth century. Álvarez-Nogal and Prados de la Escosura (2013, pp. 19–20) describe the effects evocatively:

> American colonization and international trade expansion contributed to the stimulation of economic activity during the 1490s to 1590s [...] The [epoch] ranging from the 1600s to the 1800s, had significantly different features, and the foundations of growth of the previous epoch—wool, trade, and urban activity—would no longer be in place [...] The decline in wool exports after 1570 and the contraction in the purchasing power of American silver from the early seventeenth century forced an inward-looking re-orientation of the Spanish economy. The Dutch disease brought by American silver apparently reinforced low productivity and competitiveness in tradable production [...] Growing taxation from 1575 led towns to increase their indebtedness, which had a negative effect on urban activity, at the time of a decline in wool exports and the disappearance of the Medina del Campo fair. The fiscal system collapsed, as did cities.

The relative price of Spanish nontraded goods began escalating between 1545 and 1550, right when American silver production accelerated. Peninsular Spain became a net importer of commodities that it had formerly exported—including leather and iron goods—and started to import food staples that it had never before imported, such as corn and rice (Drelichman 2005a, p. 8).

The main alternative explanation for Spain's early modern poor economic performance is that initial conditions were not right for growth at the end of the medieval period. Some believe that Spanish (and, in particular, Castilian) culture was particularly biased towards warfare rather than commerce. This viewpoint seems to have been informed by the comparative experience of American conquest and colonization: in particular, how the Spanish American case compared with the English, French and Dutch territories. But in fact, the critical differences were that only Spain settled in highly populated areas and had access to large quantities of precious metals from an early stage. There is no evidence that there was any cultural bias against commerce in either Aragon—heavily involved in medieval Mediterranean trade—or Castile (Elliott 2006, p. 19). Others believe that poor Spanish performance was due to poor initial institutions. Many scholars argue that Iberian political institutions were indeed worse than those of England or The Netherlands by 1500 or earlier (e.g. Ertman 1997; Acemoglu et al. 2005; Acemoglu and Robinson 2012; Hough and Grier 2015; among others).[8] And it is certainly true that the Iberian economies failed to industrialize or enjoy modern economic growth until the twentieth century.

Our view is that Iberian institutions were not absolutist; certainly, they were not worse than those of England or The Netherlands around 1500 (Henriques and Palma 2019). The earlier literature is impressionistic and influenced by Black Legend (*Leyenda Negra*) propaganda, rather than based on systematic quantitative analysis using contemporary sources. By contrast, Henriques and Palma (2019) build a new dataset which allows for a comparison of institutional quality across England, Spain and Portugal over time. They consider the frequency and nature of parliamentary meetings, the frequency and intensity of extraordinary taxation and coin debasement, and real interest rate spreads on public debt. They

[8] By Spanish institutions we mean, to be rigorous, Castilian institutions (Castile corresponds to about three-quarters of Spain), though from the early eighteenth century, institutional differences within Spain become considerably less marked. Additionally, it was Castile that served as an institutional blueprint for the Spanish empire (Elliott 2002, 2006). On a similar note, by "The Netherlands" we mean what the territories of what would become the United Provinces, i.e. the Dutch Republic, which—except for matters related to land reclamation—roughly coincides with the territory of the Kingdom of The Netherlands today. This is more than the province of Holland, as it includes regions such as Friesland, Groningen or Utrecht (only excluding the southern territories which would eventually become Belgium).

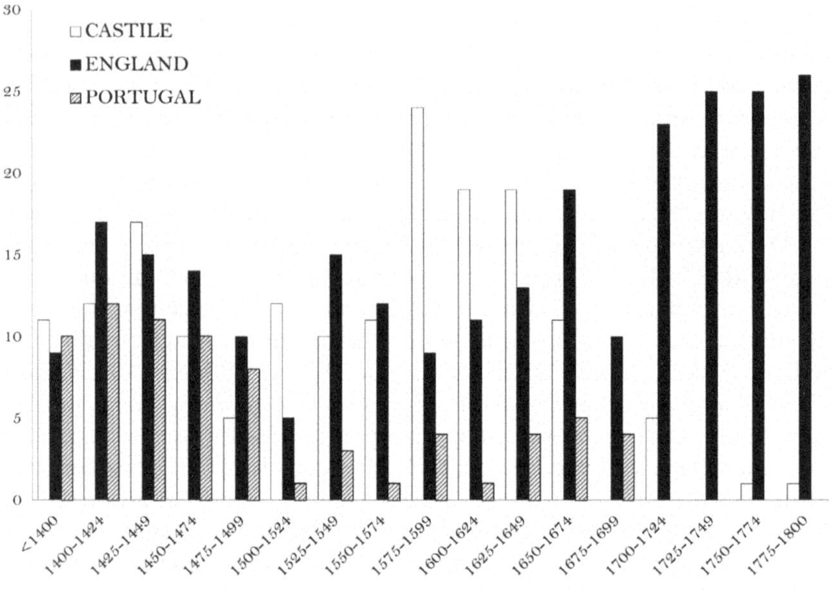

Fig. 9 Years with a parliament meeting (*Source* Henriques and Palma [2019])

find no evidence that the political institutions of Iberia were worse any time before the English Civil War. In Castile, parliaments met about as frequently as in England until the second half of the seventeenth century (see Fig. 9). From the rest of the period, their function was mostly ceremonial with sporadic meetings. In Portugal, parliaments met less frequently but continued to curb executive power. In all cases, the parliaments limited the incidence of extraordinary taxes requested by the rulers until 1700 (Henriques and Palma 2019).

Since there was no difference in the quality of institutions of Iberia vis-à-vis England or The Netherlands in 1500, and given that by 1750 there clearly was, something must have happened during the early modern period itself which changed the nature of the institutions. Spain—in particular Castile—suffered from the political resource curse. This is a situation characterized by state capture from special interests, with consequences for domestic and foreign policy. The special interests were both mercantile (and largely foreign) (Stein and Stein 2000), and internal, associated with the expansion of the non-tradable sector, with an over-ambitious foreign policy, and with the growth of a tax-sheltered nobility (Drelichman 2005b, 2007; Drelichman and Voth 2008). Spanish parliaments declined because the emperor had no need to ask them for revenues before beginning military adventures. Rather, he could use American silver to finance the commitment of Spanish forces and then dare the Cortes to cut them off. As American presidents later discovered, this was a very effective way of undercutting legislative authority. The parliament later attempted to regain some authority over spending but it never succeeded; after 1663 the few parliaments that were called into sessions were purely ceremonial. In addition, the pressures of war—enabled by American silver—prompted the Spanish state to encourage the activities of the Inquisition and ultimately engage in later rounds of expulsions of converted Jews and Muslims (Vidal-Robert 2013).

When the Crown needed to convince the Cortes to raise resources from domestic taxation, it was generally capable of doing so. Those efforts were sporadic and easily abandoned, but they were successful when attempted. The implication is that the Spanish state could have developed a more efficient fiscal system had it not been for its access to American silver.

The case for the negative impact of precious metals is further supported by the experience of Portugal. This country experienced good economic performance until the mid-eighteenth century (Palma and Reis 2019). Large quantities of gold were found in Brazil from the 1690s. This, as had happened in Spain a century and a half earlier, led to a boom lasting about half a century. Income per capita grew until the 1750s, then entering a period of stagnation approximately from the time of the 1755 earthquake, which was in turn followed by a period of secular decline which continued into the nineteenth century, contrasting with the rise of other European economies at the same time (Palma and Reis 2019; Palma 2019; de Macedo 1982; Boxer 1962, pp. 320–321, 323). As with the case of Spain, there is evidence of state capture and institutional deterioration (Madureira 1997).

Long-Term Consequences for Other European Countries

American precious metals traveled to other European economies. England and The Netherlands benefited the most (other European economies appear to have benefitted less, though more research on this matter is

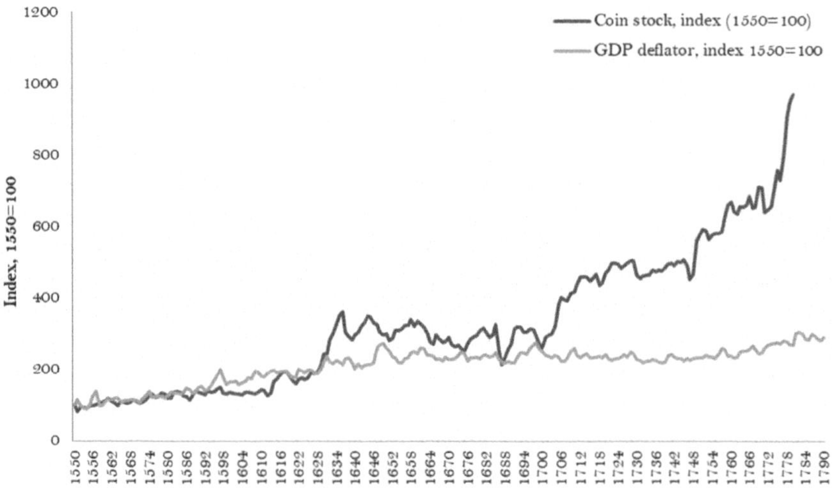

Fig. 10 Coin stock and GDP deflator in England, 1550–1790 (*Note* England here corresponds to England until 1700 and Britain thereafter. *Source* Palma [2018b] and Broadberry et al. [2015])

needed). In The Netherlands and England, the influx of precious metals led to gains in income per capita. Contrary to the Quantity Theory of Money, money supply increases did not fully translate into inflation (see Fig. 10). With no long-run changes in the velocity of money, the influx of money led to sustained economic growth. No other means existed that could have led to the observed growth in the money supply; debasement was constrained and paper money developed only from the late eighteenth century (O'Brien and Palma 2020).

Monetization greased the wheels of economic activity. From the mid-seventeenth century, England's economy enjoyed deep monetization.[9] First, people had access to an adequate money supply for daily payments as evidenced by the sizable share of smaller change present in the English economy (see Fig. 11).[10] Second, by 1630–1670 denominations equal to

[9] Much of the American silver and gold ended up in England, especially after the 1631 Cottington treaty with Spain and the 1703 Methuen treaty with Portugal, both having geopolitical origins which benefited England (Challis 1992; Fisher 1971; Francis 1966; Palma 2018a, b).

[10] See Lucassen (2014) for the case of The Netherlands.

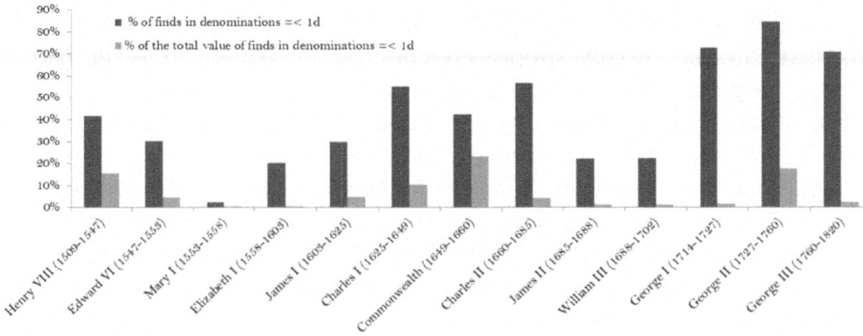

Fig. 11 Distribution of denominations in England (*Source* Palma [2018b])

one hour of waged work existed in large quantities to serve the population (see Fig. 12). The widespread availability of money overall and in small change encouraged market participation and facilitated tax collection (Palma 2018b). At the intensive margin, increased market participation meant that people worked additional days and hours (an industrious revolution). At the extensive level, it took the form of structural change and urbanization (deVries 2008; Palma and Silva 2016). This inflection point

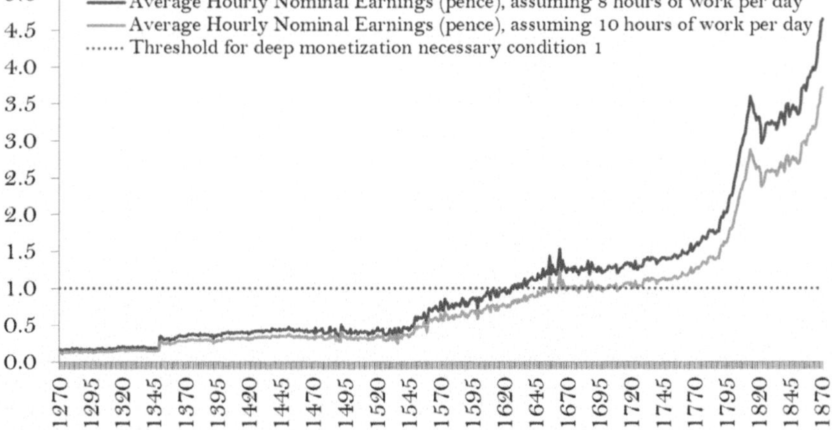

Fig. 12 Deep monetization (*Source* Palma [2018b])

coincides with England's take-off in the mid-seventeenth century.[11] The expansion in the money supply engendered by American silver had a positive long-run effect on economic growth (Palma 2018b).

For other parts of Europe, we do not know much about the long-term impact. Northern Italy and Germany benefited from financing the Spanish Crown. That was, however, a very risky business given its propensity to default. Germany also participated in the trade circuit, especially supplying mercury to Spain (Álvarez-Nogal 1997). France exported textiles and other goods to Spain (much of which was re-exported to the Americas; see Stein and Stein 2000). In more remote parts of Europe, barely any American silver arrived (e.g. Kotilaine 2005).

Impact on Latin America

The search for new trade routes to Asia fueled Spanish westward exploration. But it was the discovery of precious metals in the Americas that shaped its imperial expansion.[12] From gold in the Caribbean to silver in Cerro Rico, the search for *El Dorado* drove both imperial expansion and the need to cement control over vast new territories. In this section, we consider how the production of precious metals shaped labor institutions, the fiscal apparatus, and economic activity. In our view, the weight of the evidence suggests that the Americas would have looked radically different in the absence of gold and silver. Without precious metals the Iberian empires in the Americas would have been substantially smaller in both geographic scope and institutional depth.[13]

The Spanish faced three challenges in exploiting the gold and silver riches of the Americas. First, they needed labor to exploit these resources. Indigenous labor was the answer, but the Spaniards faced a demographic collapse caused by Eurasian diseases, social disruption, and war. The

[11] The timing holds whether we take into account structural change, real wages, or income per head (Wallis et al. 2018; Humphries and Weisdorf 2019; Broadberry et al. 2015).

[12] The division of the Spanish and Portuguese empires was also affected by this process. The search—and eventual discovery—of gold in Brazil from the 1690s was the main responsible factor for the pushing of the border with Spanish America many hundreds of miles westward (Boxer 1962, p. 270). The final borders were much to the west of the 1494 Tordesillas treaty, a fact to which the difficulty of measuring longitude accurately also contributed.

[13] For an alternative view, see Dobado and Marrero (2011).

Caribbean islands were decimated while other locales with abundant indigenous labor—such as Mexico and Peru—experienced death tolls between one-third and nine-tenths of their pre-contact populations.[14] As a result, various sorts of labor coercion became the norm. Second, the Spaniards needed to control labor over a large territory. They therefore founded a vast network of settlements based on their political, economic, and military needs. Finally, financing this enterprise was expensive. As a result, the Spaniards developed a fiscal system to capture rents and distribute revenues across the different corners of the empire.

From Conquest to Colonization

Columbus found an unknown, but highly populated, territory. Soon after his arrival in *La Española*, the newcomers spotted evidence of gold. Those mines were exhausted by the time of Columbus's death. Later, Caribbean expeditions chased the hope of precious metals. Soon after, the new colonies started to fulfill that hope. From 1492 to 1520, the Caribbean produced 162 tons of gold (TePaske 2010; Vilar 1976, ch. 7). But the above number paled in comparison to the riches that came from the main mining centers in what became Mexico and Peru. Cortés and Pizarro quickly found gold and silver. The extraction of precious metals in these new locales resulted in unprecedented yields (Fig. 13). The emergence of the new mining centers reconfigured colonial economic activity, and prompted a vast expansion of the empire.

The mining operations needed labor and the Crown wanted revenue. In a world of declining populations, the solution was to coerce indigenous labor. The need to coerce existing populations over a vast area and ensure that the imperial government received its share of the revenues—particularly those related to precious metals—required a high level of state intervention and control.[15] Indeed, "In the eyes of the colonial authorities, silver production came to take precedence over all other requirements [...] As an early viceroy of Peru put it, 'if there are no mines, there is no Peru'" (Elliott 2006, p. 98). This stands in contrast with the English colonies in North America, where the labor supply came from Europe

[14] The actual magnitude of the demographic collapse in the Americas is contested. For a discussion, see Livi Bacci (2008), Malvido (2006), and Newson (2006).

[15] For an analysis on labor institutions in colonial Peru, see Abad and Maurer (2019).

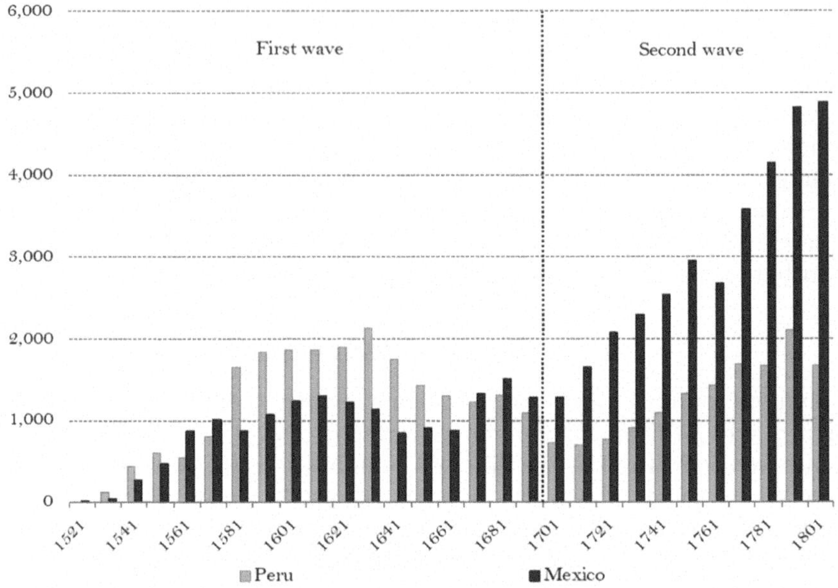

Fig. 13 Silver production in Mexico and Peru, in metric tons (*Source* Based on Abad and van Zanden [2016])

and Africa, the geographic expanses were far smaller, and the direct fiscal benefit for the Crown was almost nonexistent. As a result, the English government's control over institutional development was much laxer.

The Spaniards generally adapted pre-existing labor institutions to secure labor. The extent and prevalence of these institutions varied considerably. The most widespread type of forced labor was the *encomienda*, or "trusteeship," adapted from the Reconquista of the Iberian peninsula.[16] Under this arrangement, Spanish settlers undertook the obligation to "protect" and Christianize indigenous people in return for tribute and labor services. Pizarro and his relatives obtained multiple *encomiendas* with thousands of people under his tutelage (Julien 2000). The *encomienda* was essential to the initial construction of the Spanish empire. Forced labor got roads built, Spanish settlers housed and fed, and initial mining exploitation pursued. The *encomienda* enabled colonial

[16] For a thorough treatment of the encomienda, see Zavala (1935).

expansion at a low fiscal cost, but other factors prompted its abolition by the end of the seventeenth century. First, the cruel treatment of the indigenous people provoked a backlash. Second, the increasing power of the *encomenderos* posed a threat to royal power in the colonies. Nonetheless, the institution informally persisted around some of the fringes of the empire, notably in Paraguay (Service 1951, 1954).

The Spanish also introduced slavery, but it did not prosper in mining. With a few short-lived exceptions—most notably the construction of the Camino de Chagres to carry Peruvian silver across Panama—the Spanish did not impose slavery on the indigenous population.[17] Mine owners in Spanish America found African slavery unprofitable due to high mortality rates (O'Toole 2012, p. 18). As a result, slavery mainly remained confined to plantations and urban centers.[18]

In Peru, the Spanish authorities employed the most infamous compulsory draft—the *mitaminera*—to exploit silver and mercury. As indigenous peoples were not considered slaves, the Crown set a minimum remuneration. The Spanish also tried to coerce labor for mining in Zacatecas in Mexico. The problem was that the *mita* was an adaptation of an Incan practice of drafting labor and soldiers for the Inca Emperor on a regular basis; no such practice existed in Mexico. With no pre-Hispanic institutions to co-opt, the Spanish proved unable to force the indigenous population to comply.

The most radical institutional development was the introduction of free labor (Abad et al. 2012). Mining in Mexico was made possible by using free workers. As time went on, the same became more true for the mines in colonial Peru. While the Potosí *mita* did initially provide much-needed labor, the institution lost its bite throughout the colonial period. Demographic collapse, mass migration, and avoidance became commonplace, resulting in more reliance on free workers.[19] These outside options became far easier as the colonial economy became more sophisticated

[17] For a discussion of the Nicaraguan slave trade in Panama, see Maurer and Yu (2010, pp. 17–21).

[18] This is not to say that the presence of massive precious metal deposits did not increase the prevalence of slavery in Latin America. It did; see later in this chapter for details. An exception was the widespread use of African slaves in Colombian mining (Sharp 1975, p. 469).

[19] Indigenous peoples opted to leave their community and to become an outsider—a "forastero"—in another settlement. Under Spanish law and custom, migrants were subject to neither service, tribute, nor any labor drafts. Migration to avoid the latter became

and outside options for workers expanded, especially in the ever growing urban network.

Building the Backbone of the Empire

Mining was the backbone of the colonial enterprise. Labor, trade, and the administrative system were geared towards the extraction of precious metals. Mining centers attracted people and urban centers proliferated (Map 1). Sparsely populated lands transformed rapidly. Potosí (in today's Bolivia) was the most extreme case. Located in a high desert, the site attracted 120,000 people by 1620s. The population ebbed and flowed with the mining cycle (Fig. 14). Other, more permanent settlements emerged elsewhere, notably in the northwest reaches of Mexico. In Brazil a similar pattern ensued. The discovery of the mines in Ouro Preto in Minas Gerais prompted migration to the Portuguese frontier.

The transportation of precious metals shaped trade routes. Both the Spanish and the Portuguese empires created an institutional framework to centralize trade between the colonies and the metropolis (Álvarez-Nogal 2003). Shipping was left to private hands but cargo ships were heavily guarded by military escorts (e.g. the Spanish Armada) to defend against pirates and hostile nations. In the Spanish empire, only six ports were authorized to trade with Spain: Veracruz and Acapulco in Mexico, Cartagena in Colombia, Portobelo in Panama, El Callao in Peru, and Manila in the Philippines. It was not until the post-1771 Bourbon reforms that more ports were opened for business.

Sustaining mining required mobilizing food and supplies from other locales. Salta in Argentina supplied mules for Potosí, Spain supplied luxury textiles and iron, and a wide array of foodstuffs made their way from Peru and Bolivia. In Mexico, south of Zacatecas, mining prompted the development of lands for grain production and other supplies (including textiles) were drawn from more distant locales. This mercantile circuit shows an important degree of market integration (Bakewell 1971; Assadourian 1982).

commonplace as early as 1590, only two decades after the *mita* began (Abad and Maurer 2019).

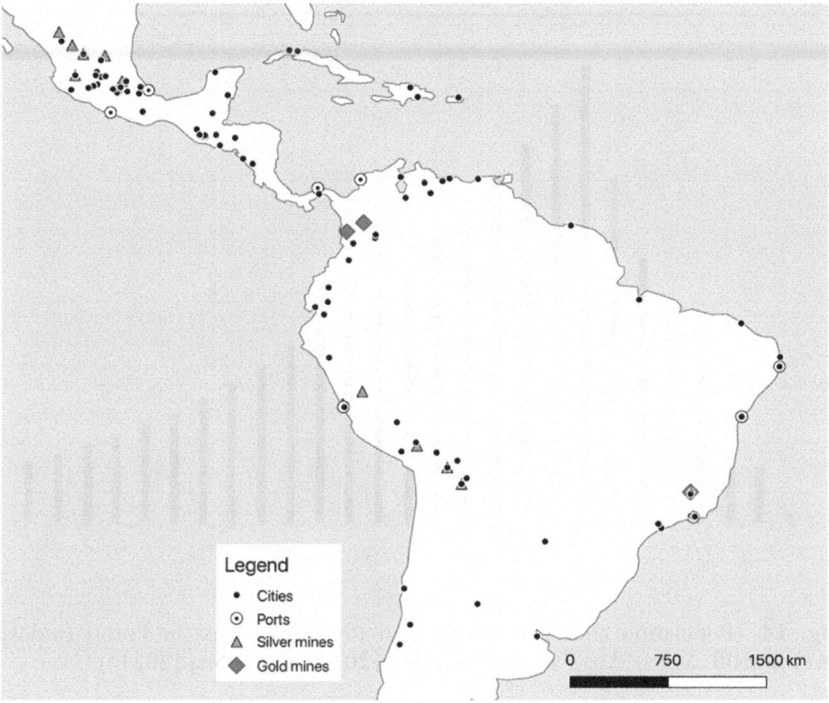

Map 1 Main cities, authorized ports, and mines (*Note* Cities that reached at least 5,000 inhabitants until 1750, and mines that produced at least 100 and 1,500 tons of gold and silver, respectively. *Source* Based on Abad and van Zanden [2016] and Palma [2021])

Imperial Fortunes

The controls on trade had a tangible impact on the cost of living in the colonies. Imported goods from Spain, in particular, were expensive. In Lima, for instance, paper was up to 800% more expensive than in Castile in the early eighteenth century.[20] The regulated trade system spurred regional development for selected sectors, such as textiles. Regional economies hence became increasingly more integrated. An illustrative case

[20]The relative price of paper between Lima and Castile ranged from 2.31 to 9.51 in the 1660–1800 period (Gallo and Newland 2004, p. 581).

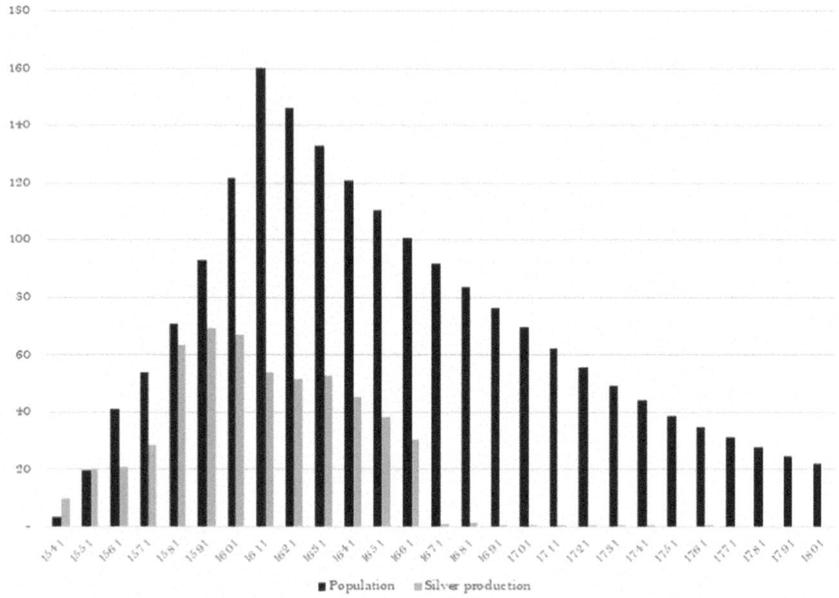

Fig. 14 Population and silver production (in metric tons) in Potosí (index, 1611 = 100. *Source* Abad and van Zanden [2016] and Palma [2021])

is intercolonial trade between Chile and Peru. After the 1687 earthquake in Lima, Peru started importing wheat and Chile imported tobacco and textiles in return (Gallo and Newland 2004). That said, some goods were only available through trade with the motherland, or via contraband.

It would be simplistic to think that the trade monopoly determined prices in Spanish Latin America. Transaction costs raised prices in America, but silver had a sizable independent effect on price and wage levels. Our results in Table 1 suggest that silver production increased price and nominal wage levels. This is in line with existing scholarship. For instance, for Mexico, Garner (1993, p. 19) notes, "An expanding mining industry obviously created an increase in demand for agricultural and manufactured goods [...]. It could also boost inflation because it increased the money supply."

An increase in the production of silver appears to affect nominal wages and prices more in Mexico than in Peru (Table 1). It is conceivable that the rigidity in labor markets in Peru was associated with lower availability

Table 1 Silver production and Prices. Dependent variable: natural logarithm of price level and nominal wages

	Peru			*Mexico*		
Prices						
	(1)	*(2)*	*(3)*	*(4)*	*(5)*	*(6)*
Lag of production	0.105**	0.140**	0.04	0.319***	0.252***	0.024
	(0.037)	(0.047)	(0.074)	(0.053)	(0.056)	(0.253)
R^2	0.244	0.581	0.009	0.44	0.503	0.303
N	187	86	101	243	130	113
Sample	1564–1810	1564–1697	1698–1810	1525–1810	1525–1697	1698–1810
Nominal wages						
	(7)	*(8)*	*(9)*	*(10)*	*(11)*	*(12)*
Lag of production	0.071***	0.289***	0.098***	0.491***	0.409***	-0.024
	(0.009)	(0.042)	(0.019)	(0.057)	(0.043)	(0.018)
R^2	0.680	0.684	0.735	0.708	0.907	0.057
N	175	80	95	277	164	113
Sample	1597–1792	1595–1697	1698–1792	1525–1810	1525–1697	1698–1810

Note Annual (barebone basket) price levels and nominal wages for unskilled labor (in logs) in silver grams for Mexico City and Lima. Annual silver production (in logs, lagged one period) for the viceroyalties of Mexico and Peru. Linear trend included. Robust standard errors. (***), (**) denote levels of significance of 1% and 5% respectively

Source Based on the data of Abad et al. (2012) and Palma (2021)

of free-wage labor. Labor coercion was stronger in Peru than in Mexico, especially in the mining sector. As mining was mostly carried out with free labor in Mexico, the real wage increased accordingly. If we split the sample into two roughly equal periods—the first until the end of the seventeenth century—we can see that these results are driven by the first silver wave in both viceroyalties.[21]

A Counterfactual Metal-Less Empire

So far we have looked at how precious metals shaped the development of the colonial economy. We have documented its remarkable imprint on the patterns of urbanization, the institutional framework, and economic activity. But the main question remains: would the nature of the colonial enterprise have changed in the absence of precious metals?

It is hard to imagine the Spanish empire in the Americas following a similar path in the absence of rich sources of precious metals. Their existence and importance in the cargoes for Spain, "inevitably relegated other commodities, no matter how valuable, to a subordinate status in Spain's transatlantic trade" (Elliott 2006, p. 25). While we cannot speak of a typical Dutch disease situation in this case—since not much industry existed in the Americas to start with—the situation was not conducive to industrial development, regardless of Spain's mercantilist laws.

Mining shaped the economic geography of the continent. In Mexico, the center of economic activity shifted north towards what was then called New Galicia with the discovery of Zacatecas (Bakewell 1971, p. 17). In the Viceroyalty of Peru, Potosí cast a wide net of influence: "[it] stimulated commercial agriculture in the valleys and turned small-scale chacareros into wholesale cereal exporters" (Larson 1998, p. 89). The metal-free corners of the empire were military outposts established in order to contain foreign encroachment or areas of modest agricultural development. The area that became Argentina, for example, was overlooked as "it offered no immediate economic or commercial rewards" (Fisher 1997, p. 25). Buenos Aires only gained some recognition with the creation of the viceroyalty of the Rio de la Plata late in the eighteenth century. Guatemala, similarly, developed an export trade in indigo,

[21] This periodization takes into account the first and second waves in silver production in Latin America.

cacao, and hides for both European and American markets but remained overshadowed by New Spain (Elliott 2006, p. 21).

Would the sun have never set in a metal-less Spanish empire? We know that it was expensive to run an empire and Spain did not profit in the early times. In fact, "the steady export from the peninsula of the basic commodities (primarily flour, oil, wine) which the settlers required for subsistence, together with tools, weapons, animals, seeds, and building materials, tended to be of greater value than the gold and tropical produce which returned" (Fisher 1997, p. 22). Without the silver influx, Spain would have likely been forced to abandon its claims over the fringes of the empire. The wide geographic scope of the Spanish empire was, in part, a product of cross-subsidies from richer to less affluent regions, carried out among regional treasuries. The degree of inter-colonial transfers was remarkable: Grafe and Irigoin (2006, p. 252) find that it was "crucial for the governance of the empire." Without the flow of resources from Mexico and Peru to the periphery, it is hard to imagine Spain maintaining claims on distant territories, leaving them up for grabs by other competing empires.

As it was, the colonists, "having at their disposal silver mines like Guanajuato and Potosí [...] found it to their advantage to specialize in mining and export specie in exchange for importable commodities. The treasure fleets sailed from Spain laden with provisions, wares and all sorts of merchandise. The return cargo comprised small quantities of colonial produce [...] and vast amounts of silver" (Hamilton 1934, p. 33). It is reasonable to conclude that in the absence of precious metals, the Spanish Crown would have attempted to develop commodity cultivation for export where possible. This strategy could have panned out in certain parts of the viceroyalty of Mexico and in the Caribbean, including Venezuela. The fate of the viceroyalty of Peru is less clear. The relatively abundant indigenous population would have been hard to ignore, but given the technology available, exporting agricultural goods would not have been profitable. It is possible that Spain would have retained its claim and let religious orders and eager Spanish colonizers run the place in exchange of tribute. This strategy is consistent with the Crown's attitude towards the Philippines and Paraguay, hence Peru might have become similar to these locations.

Impact on Africa and Asia

The existence of silver and gold in the Americas greatly accelerated European exploration, propelled the settlement of the New World, and stimulated trade. More fundamentally, it fueled the beginning of the largest involuntary migration in history: slave trade. Eltis (2000, pp. 24–25) claims that the influx of precious metals translated into a demand for slaves. This was true, even though African slaves did not become the main source of labor for mining in most Spanish America. At the same time, silver profits did power the importation of slaves to serve as domestic servants in urban centers and in plantations. In Brazil, by contrast, African slaves were essential for the exploitation of the gold mines and alluvial deposits (Klein and Vidal Luna 2009, p. 36) (Map 2).

Much American silver ended up in Asia, and in particular, in China (Palma and Silva 2016). The Manila galleon connected El Callao in Peru, Acapulco in Mexico, and Manila in the Philippines (Giraldez 2021). This route enabled the exchange of silver for silk and porcelain (Fisher 1997, p. 65). While Japan also produced some moderate quantities of silver during part of the early modern period, this was by no means sufficient for the needs of this large part of the world. The impact of the silver coins in the Chinese economy needs further research (see the chapter by De Zwart and Flynn 2020). Paper money no longer circulated by the time the Europeans arrived in the 1500s (Von Glahn 1996). Hence China depended critically of silver for transactions and tax payments. Some scholars claim that the slowdown of silver production in the Americas around the middle of the seventeenth century caused the collapse of the Ming dynasty, while others argue that this was not the case (Flynn and Giráldez 1995; Findlay and O'Rourke 2009). What is certain is that by the early nineteenth century China was awash with Spanish dollars, which were the world's international currency. Once the Spanish Empire broke up following up Napoleon's invasion of Spain, so did the quality of coins produced in the Americas, with negative consequences for the Chinese economy (Irigoin 2013).

During the nineteenth century, Europeans began to systematically colonize much of Africa, and (de-facto) some of China, as well as other regions in Asia. The process had multiple causes, but the experience acquired via the previous history of European interaction with these regions during the early modern era was central. In turn, that previous interaction cannot be separated from the role American precious metals

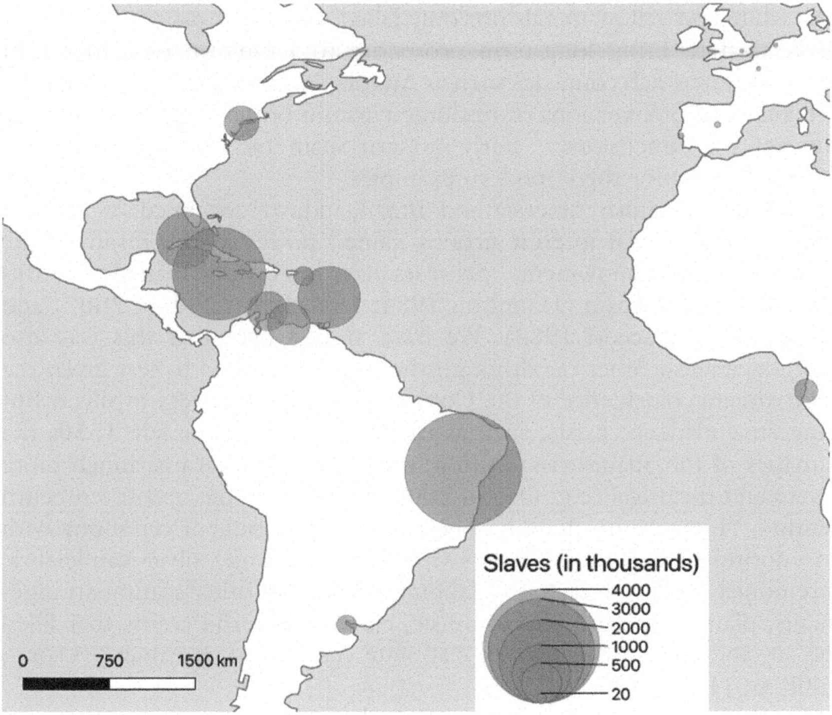

Map 2 Slave trade by main destination of disembarkation (1511–1870) (*Source* Eltis 2018)

played, as we have argued here. The consequences of these interactions still live with us today.

Conclusion

> By the mid-seventeen century, silver was becoming more than a little tarnished. Observers noted how all the silver of America had failed to bring prosperity to Spain.
>
> —Elliott (2006, p. 114)

The white and yellow metals not only failed to bring prosperity to Iberia, they failed to bring long-term prosperity to Latin America. In recent years, resource-rich countries such as Angola, Nigeria, and Venezuela have become textbook versions of resource curse in both in its Dutch disease and political dimensions.[22] Early modern Spain and its empire were the poster children for these modern examples.

In Iberia, Spanish America and Brazil, industry declined or did not flourish, and special interest groups gained power as the result of the silver and gold endowments. Scholars have previously argued that this was the case for Spain (Hamilton 1934; Drelichman 2005b, 2007) and Portugal (de Macedo 1982). We have argued here that this was also true for Spanish America, although the causality is hard to test given the approximate coincidence of the Conquest and the discovery of silver. But suggestive evidence exists, such as the fact that from the late 1550s the activities of the Spanish Inquisition in the Americas became much more severe and theatrical (e.g. Osorio 2008, p. 104). By the mid-seventeenth century, "Lima's auto de fé had become a grandiloquent ceremony with an enormous stage decked out with fine rugs, large silver candelabra, ceremonial candles, crucifixes, elaborate chairs and other seating arrangements, plants, special lighting, music, chants, powerful scents that filled the air, and participants clad in elaborate ceremonial costumes" (Osorio 2008, p. 113).

In the case of Portugal—and Brazil—the later discovery of gold permits a more credible causal attribution. As had happened with Spain (Hamilton 1934, p. 295), the discovery of "treasure" created additional demand for non-tradable sectors, leading to much land being purchased by ecclesiastical institutions. These became special interests which lobbied for policies which were often not in the common interest of society. In the words of Boxer (1962, p. 133): "During the two centuries which elapsed between the time of King João III and that of Pombal, Portugal was probably the most priest-ridden country in Christendom." Boxer (1962, pp. 129, 180) presents similar evidence for Brazil.

The resource curse (whether economic or political) is not inevitable. In the nineteenth century, gold discoveries happened in other parts of the world. A well-known case is that of nineteenth century California.

[22] For some cases such as São Tomé e Príncipe or Brazil, there is direct causal evidence of the mechanism (Vicente 2010; Caselli and Michaels 2013).

But despite the gold rush, precious metals never dominated the well-diversified American economy, which furthermore had, by then, strong institutions (Besley 2006; Elliott 2006; Sargent 2012). The impact of the gold rush distorted neither American nor Californian institutions, and California went on to become one of the most prosperous jurisdictions on Earth.[23]

The search for *El Dorado* shaped European exploration and settlement in the New World. Who reaped the fruits of the discovery of gold and silver? Spain and Portugal, the colonizers *par excellence*, failed to profit from the conquest. It would be a mistake to conclude that the pre-existing Iberian institutions are to blame. The ultimate root cause was state capture by special interests. In contrast, England and The Netherlands benefited the most as a result of increased monetization and fiscal capacity. In the case of Latin America, the exploitation of silver became the backbone of the empire for Spain and pervaded all economic activity. For Brazil, the discovery of gold came later and displaced alternative forms of colonial expansion. Aided by a mercantilist ideology, silver and gold shaped the institutional development and trade patterns in the New World. The influence of precious metals reverberated around the world, lubricating trade from remote corners of the globe.

Acknowledgements We thank Adam Brzezinski, Kivanç Karaman, Alfredo García Hiernaux, and Noel Maurer for their comments and insights.

References

Abad, Leticia, and Noel Maurer. 2019. "The Long Shadow of History? The Impact of Colonial Labor Institutions on Economic Development in Peru." Social Science Research Network, working paper.

Abad, Leticia, and Jan Luiten Van Zanden. 2016. "Growth Under Extractive Institutions? Latin American Per Capita GDP in Colonial Times." *Journal of Economic History* 76 (4): 1182–1215.

Abad, Leticia, Elwyn Davies, Jan Luiten Van Zanden. 2012. "Between Conquest and Independence: Real Wages and Demographic Change in Spanish America, 1530–1820." *Explorations in Economic History* 49 (2): 149–166.

[23] Spanish dollars remained legal tender in the United States until 1857, which reminds us of their prior importance as the world's reserve currency.

Acemoglu, Daron, and James A. Robinson. 2012. *Why Nations Fail: The Origins of Power, Prosperity, and Poverty*. Crown Books.

Acemoglu, Daron, Simon Johnson, and James Robinson. 2005. "The Rise of Europe: Atlantic Trade, Institutional Change and Economic Growth." *American Economic Review* 95: 546–579.

Allen, Robert C. 2001. "The Great Divergence in European Wages and Prices from the Middle Ages to the First World War." *Explorations in Economic History* 3 (4): 411–447.

Álvarez-Nogal, Carlos. 1997. *Los banqueros de Felipe IV y los metales preciosos americanos (1621–1665)*. Banco de España, Servicio de estudios.

Álvarez-Nogal, Carlos. 2003. "Instituciones y desarrollo económico: la Casa de la Contratación y la Carrera de Indias (1503–1790)." Universidad Carlos III Documentos de Trabajo 03–02.

Álvarez-Nogal, Carlos, and Leandro Prados de Escosura. 2007. "The Decline of Spain (1500–1850): Conjectural Estimates." *European Review of Economic History* 11: 319–366.

Álvarez-Nogal, Carlos, and Leandro Prados de la Escosura. 2013. "The Rise and Fall of Spain (1270–1850)." *The Economic History Review* 66 (1): 1–37.

Assadourian, Carlos Sempat. 1982. "El sistema de la economía colonial: mercado interno, regiones y espacio económico." *Estudios Históricos* 10.

Bakewell, Peter J. 1971. *Silver Mining and Society in Colonial Mexico: Zacatecas, 1546–1700*. London: Cambridge University Press.

Barrett, Ward. 1990. "World Bullion Flows, 1450–1800." In *The Rise of Merchant Empires*. Cambridge: Cambridge University Press.

Besley, Tim. 2006. *Principled Agents? The Political Economy of Good Government*. Oxford: Oxford University Press.

Boxer, Charles Ralph. 1962. *The Golden Age of Brazil: Growing Pains of a Colonial Society, 1695–1750*. Berkeley: University of California Press.

Broadberry, Stephen N., Bruce Campbell, Alexander Klein, Mark Overton, and Bas Van Leeuwen. 2015. *British Economic Growth, 1270–1870*. Berkeley: Cambridge University Press.

Brzezinski, Adam, Yao Chen, Nuno Palma, and Felix Ward. 2019. "The Vagaries of the Sea: Evidence on the Real Effects of Money from Maritime Disasters in the Spanish Empire." CEPR, discussion paper 14089.

Caselli, Francesco, and Guy Michaels. 2013. "Do Oil Windfalls Improve Living Standards? Evidence from Brazil." *American Economic Journal: Applied Economics* 5 (1): 208–238.

Challis, Christopher Edgar. 1992. "Lord Hastings to the Great Silver Recoinage, 1464–1699." In *A New History of the Royal Mint*, edited by Christopher Edgar Challis. Cambridge: Cambridge University Press.

Costa, Leonor F., María M. Rocha, and Rita Sousa. 2013. *O Ouro do Brasil*. Lisboa: Imprensa Nacional-Casa da Moeda.

Costa, Leonor F., Nuno Palma, and Jaime Reis. 2015. "The Great Escape? The Contribution of the Empire to Portugal's Economic Growth, 1500–1800." *European Review of Economic History* 19 (1): 1–22.

de Macedo, Jorge Borges. 1982. *Problemas de História da Indústria Portuguesa no Século XVII*. 2nd ed. Lisbon: Querco.

DeVries, Jan. 2008. *The Industrious Revolution: Consumer Behavior and the Household Economy, 1650 to the Present*. Cambridge: Cambridge University Press.

De Zwart, Pin, and Dennis Flynn. 2020. "The Significance of Early Globalization: Arguments and Evidence." In *The Fruits of the Early Globalization*, edited by R. Dobado-González and A. García-Hiernaux. Cham: Palgrave Macmillan.

Díaz del Castillo, Bernal. 2003. *The Conquest of New Spain*. UK: Penguin Classics.

Dobado, Rafael, and Gustavo A. Marrero. 2011. "The Role of the Spanish Imperial State in the Mining–Led Growth of Bourbon Mexico's Economy." *Economic History Review* 64 (3): 855–884.

Drelichman, Mauricio. 2005a. "The Curse of Moctezuma: American Silver and the Dutch Disease." *Explorations in Economic History* 42: 349–380.

Drelichman, Mauricio. 2005b. "All That Glitters: Precious Metals, Rent Seeking and the Decline of Spain." *European Review of Economic History* 9: 313–336.

Drelichman, Mauricio. 2007. "Sons of Something: Taxes, Lawsuits, and Local Political Control in Sixteenth-Century Castile." *Journal of Economic History* 67 (3): 608–642.

Drelichman, Mauricio, and Hans-Joachim Voth. 2008. "Institutions and the Resource Curse in Early Modern Spain." In *Institutions and Economic Performance Elhanan*, edited by Elhanan Helpman. Cambridge: Cambridge University Press.

Drelichman, Mauricio, and Hans-Joachim Voth. 2010. "The Sustainable Debts of Philip II: A Reconstruction of Castile's Fiscal Position, 1566–1596." *Journal of Economic History* 70 (4): 813–842.

Elliott, John Huxtable. 2002. *Imperial Spain 1469–1716*. UK: Penguin.

Elliott, John Huxtable. 2006. *Empires of the Atlantic World: Britain and Spain in America: 1492–1830*. London: Yale University Press.

Eltis, David. 2018. A Brief Overview of the Trans-Atlantic Slave Trade. In *Slave Voyages: The Trans-Atlantic Slave Trade Database*. https://www.slavevoyages.org/voyage/about.

Eltis, David. 2000. *The Rise of African Slavery in the Americas*. Cambridge: Cambridge University Press.

Ertman, Thomas. 1997. *Birth of the Leviathan: Building States and Regimes in Medieval and Early Modern Europe*. Cambridge: Cambridge University Press.

Findlay, Ronald, and Kevin H. O'Rourke. 2009. *Power and Plenty: Trade, War and the World Economy in the Second Millennium*. Princeton: Princeton University Press.

Fisher, Harold Edward S. 1971. *The Portugal Trade: A Study of Anglo-Portuguese Commerce 1700–1770*. London: Methuen & Co Ltd.

Fisher, John. 1997. *The Economic Aspects of Spanish Imperialism in America, 1492–1810*. Cambridge: Cambridge University Press.

Flynn, Dennis O., and Arturo Giráldez. 1995. "Born with a 'Silver Spoon': The Origin of World Trade in 1571." *Journal of World History* 6: 201–221.

Forsyth, Peter J., and Stephen J. Nicholas. 1983. "The Decline of Spanish Industry and the Price Revolution: A Neoclassical Analysis." *Journal of European Economic History* 12: 601–610.

Francis, Alan David. 1966. *The Methuen's and Portugal, 1691–1708*. Cambridge: Cambridge University Press.

Gallo, Andrés, and Carlos Newland. 2004. "Globalización y convergencia de precios en el Imperio Español 1660–1810." *Revista de Historia Económica/Journal of Iberian and Latin American Economic History* 22 (3): 573–596.

Garner, Richard L. 1988. "Long-Term Silver Mining Trends in Spanish America: A Comparative Analysis Of Peru and Mexico." *The American Historical Review* 93 (4): 898–935.

Garner, Richard L. 1993. *Economic Growth and Change in Bourbon Mexico*. Gainesville: University Press of Florida.

Gelabert, Juan. 1999. "Castile, 1504–1808." In *The Rise of the Fiscal State in Europe c. 1200–1815*, edited by R. Bonney. Clarendon Press.

Giraldez, Arturo. 2021. The Last Link of an Emergent Global Economy: The Manila Galleon. In *Globalization and the Early Modern Era: An Iberian Perspective*, edited by R. Doblado and A. Garcia-Hiernaux. Palgrave.

González, Antonio Garcia-Baquero. 1996. "Las remesas de metales preciosos americanos en el siglo XVIII: una aritmética controvertida." *Hispania: Revista española de historia* 56 (192): 203–266.

Grafe, Regina, and Maria Alejandra Irigoin. 2006. "The Spanish Empire and Its Legacy: Fiscal Redistribution and Political Conflict in Colonial and Post-colonial Spanish America." *Journal of Global History* 1 (2): 241–267.

Hamilton, Earl J. 1934. *American Treasure and the Price Revolution in Spain, 1501–1650*. Cambridge, MA: Harvard University Press.

Henriques, Antonio C., and Nuno Palma. 2019. "Comparative European Institutions and the Little Divergence, 1385–1850." CGEH, working paper 84. University of Utrecht.

Hough, Jerry F., and Robin Grier. 2015. *The Long Process of Development*. Cambridge: Cambridge University Press.

Humphries, Jane, and Jacob Weisdorf. 2019. "Unreal Wages? Real Income and Economic Growth in England, 1260–1850." *Economic Journal* 129 (623): 2867–2887.

Irigoin, Maria Alejandra. 2013. "A Trojan Horse in Daoguang China? Explaining the Flows of Silver In and Out of China." Economic History, working papers 173, 13. London, UK: Department of Economic History, London School of Economics and Political Science.

Jordà, Òscar. 2005. "Estimation and Inference of Impulse Responses by Local Projections." *American Economic Review* 95 (1): 161–182.

Julien, Catherine. 2000. "Inca Estates and the Encomienda: Hernando Pizarro's Holdings in Cusco." *Andean Past* 6 (1): 12.

Jurado Sánchez, José. 2008. "Macromagnitudes del sector público en la España del Antiguo Régimen. Las estadísticas del ingreso y el gasto de la Hacienda española en el siglo XVIII." Presented at: IX Congreso de la Asociación Española de Historia Económica, Murcia.

Karaman, Kivanç, Sevket Pamuk, and Seçil Yıldırım-Karaman. 2019. "Money and Monetary Stability in Europe 1300–1914." *Journal of Monetary Economics* 115: 279–300.

Klein, Herbert S., and Francisco Vidal Luna. 2009. *Slavery in Brazil*. Cambridge: Cambridge University Press.

Klein, Herbert S. 2021. International Migrations to Latin America and the Caribbean until 1820. In *Globalization and the Early Modern Era: An Iberian Perspective*, edited by R. Doblado and A. Garcia-Hiernaux. Palgrave.

Kotilaine, Jamo T. 2005. *Russia's Foreign Trade and Economic Expansion in the Seventeenth Century: Windows on the World*. Leiden: Brill.

Lacy, John. 1987. "Early History of Mining in Arizona: Acquisition of Mineral Rights, 1539–1866." In *History of Mining in Arizona*, edited by M. Canty and M. Grealey. Tucson: Mining Club of the Southwest Foundation.

Larson, Brooke. 1998. *Cochabamba, 1550–1900: Colonialism and Agrarian Transformation in Bolivia*. Durham: Duke University Press.

Livi Bacci, Massimo. 2008. *Conquest: The Destruction of the American Indios*. Cambridge: Polity Press.

Lucassen, Jan. 2014. "Deep Monetisation: The Case of The Netherlands 1200–1940." *Tijdschrift voor Sociale en Economische Geschiedenis* 11 (3): 73.

Madureira, Nuno Luis. 1997. *Mercado e Privilégios: A Indústria Portuguesa entre 1750 e 1834*. Lisboa: Editorial Estampa.

Magalhães, Joaquim Romero. 2018. *O Algarve económico durante o século XVI*. Olhão: Sul, Sol e Sal.

Malvido, Elsa. 2006. *La población, siglos XVI al XX*. Mexico: Editorial Oceano.

Maurer, Noel, and Carlos Yu. 2010. *The Big Ditch: How America Took, Built, Ran, and Ultimately Gave Away the Panama Canal*. Princeton, NJ and Woodstock, Oxfordshire: Princeton University Press.

Morineau, Michel. 2009. *Incroyables Gazettes et Fabuleux Métaux: Les Retours des Trésors Américains d'Après les Gazettes Hollandaises (XVI–XVII Siècles).* Cambridge: Cambridge University Press.

Munro, John H. 2003. "The Monetary Origins of the 'Price Revolution': South German Silver Mining, Merchant Banking, and Venetian Commerce, 1470–1540." In *Global Connections and monetary History, 1470–1800*, edited by D. Flynn, A. Giráldez, and R. Von Glahn. Aldershot: Ashgate.

Newson, Linda A. 2006. "The Demographic Impact of Colonization." In *The Cambridge Economic History of Latin America*, edited by V. Bulmer-Thomas, J. Coatsworth, and R. Cortes Conde. Cambridge: Cambridge University Press.

O'Brien, Patrick K., and Nuno Palma. 2020. "Danger to the Old Lady of Threadneedle Street? The Bank Restriction Act and the Regime Shift to Paper Money, 1797–1821." *European Review of Economic History* 24 (2): 390–426.

O'Toole, Rachel Sarah. 2012. *Bound Lives: Africans, Indians, and the Making of Race in Colonial Peru.* Pittsburgh: Pittsburgh University Press.

Osorio, Alejandra B. 2008. *Inventing Lima: Baroque Modernity in Peru's South Sea Metropolis.* New York: Palgrave.

Palma, Nuno. 2018a. "Reconstruction of Money Supply Over the Long Run: The Case of England, 1270–1870." *Economic History Review* 71 (2): 373–392.

Palma, Nuno. 2018b. "Money and Modernization in Early Modern England." *Financial History Review* 25 (3): 231–261.

Palma, Nuno. 2019. "American Precious Metals and Their Consequences for Early Modern Europe." In *Handbook of the History of Money and Currency*, edited by S. Battilossi, Y. Cassis, and K. Yago. Singapore: Springer.

Palma, N. (2021). The real effects of monetary expansions: evidence from a large-scale historical experiment. *Review of Economic Studies*, forthcoming.

Palma, Nuno, and Jaime Reis. 2019. "From Convergence to Divergence: Portuguese Economic Growth, 1527–1850." *Journal of Economic History* 79 (2): 477–506.

Palma, Nuno, and Andre C. Silva. 2016. "Spending a Windfall: American Precious Metals and Euro-Asian Trade 1531–1810." GGDC Research Memorandum 165.

Prados de la Escosura, L., C. Álvarez-Nogal and C. Santiago-Caballero. 2020. Growth Recurring in Preindustrial Spain: Half a Millennium Perspective. CEPR discussion paper.

Reyna, Stephen P. 1999. "The Force of Two Logics: Predatory and Capital Accumulation in the Making of the Great Leviathan 1415–1763." In *Deadly Developments: Capitalism, States and War*, edited by Stephen P. Reyna and R. E. Downs. Amsterdam: Routledge.

Sargent, Thomas J. 2012. "Nobel Lecture: United States Then, Europe Now." *Journal of Political Economy* 120 (1): 1–40.
Service, Elman. 1951. "The Encomienda in Paraguay." *The Hispanic American Historical Review* 31 (2) (May): 230–252.
Service, Elman. 1954. *Spanish-Guarani Relations in Early Colonial Paraguay*. Ann Arbor: University of Michigan Press.
Sharp, William. 1975. The Profitability of Slavery in the Colombian Chocó, 1680–1810. *The Hispanic American Historical Review* 55(3): 468–495.
Stein, Stanley J., and Barbara H. Stein. 2000. *Silver, Trade and War: Spain and America in the Making of Early Modern Europe*. Baltimore: The John Hopkins University Press.
TePaske, John Jay. 2010. *A New World of Gold and Silver*. Leiden: Brill.
Ucendo, José Ignacio, and Ramón Lanza García. 2020. Data on Spanish Crown Finance. The European State Fiscal Database. https://www.esfdb.org/Database.aspx. Accessed on March 20, 2020.
Vicente, Pedro C. 2010. "Does Oil Corrupt? Evidence from a Natural Experiment in West Africa." *Journal of Development Economics* 92 (1): 28–38.
Vidal-Robert, Jordi. 2013. "Historical Institutions and Their Legacy: The Spanish Inquisition's Motivations and Impact on Spanish Economic Development." Ph.D. dissertation, Universitat Pompeu Fabra.
Vilar, Pierre. 1976. *A History of Gold and Money 1450–1920*. London: Verso.
Von Glahn, Richard. 1996. *Fountain of Fortune: Money and Monetary Policy in China, 1000–1700*. Berkeley, CA: University of California Press.
Wallis, Patrick, Justin Colson, and David Chilosi. 2018. "Structural Change and Economic Growth in the British economy Before the Industrial Revolution, 1500–1800." *Journal of Economic History* 78 (3): 862–903.
Zavala, Silvio. 1935. *La encomienda indiana*. Madrid: Imprenta Helenica.

Prices and Money in the Globalization of the Early Modern Era

Alfredo García-Hiernaux and Rafael Dobado-González

Introduction

This chapter intends to test the hypothesis that silver production in New Spain/Mexico (before and after 1821, respectively) had a significant influence on the evolution of prices across the whole world. Silver played a protagonist role in a bimetallic international monetary system and circulated across the global economy of the eighteenth and nineteenth centuries. In particular, the so-called "*reales de a ocho*" (also Spanish pesos or Spanish dollars) massively coined in the mints of the silver-producing territories of Hispanic America, became the international currency from the first half of the sixteenth century until the post-independence decades (Cipolla 1999). Circa 1800, New Spain was, by far, the largest silver world

A. García-Hiernaux
Department of Economía Cuantitativa and ICAE, Universidad Complutense de Madrid, Madrid, Spain
e-mail: agarciah@ccee.ucm.es

R. Dobado-González (✉)
Department of Economía Aplicada, Universidad Complutense de Madrid, Madrid, Spain
e-mail: rdobadog@ucm.es

R. Dobado-González and A. García-Hiernaux (eds.), *The Fruits of the Early Globalization*, Palgrave Studies in Comparative Global History, https://doi.org/10.1007/978-3-030-69666-5_5

producer of silver and reached historical records. After 1811, the production fell dramatically and did not reach the same production levels for the next 40 years in none of the sources analyzed in this study (see Fig. 1). Similarly, it also intensely declined in other independent Hispanic American republics. Previous abundance of silver, then, turned into relative scarcity. Notwithstanding, Mexico continued being the world leader in silver production.

Any version of the quantitative theory of money will predict that world prices in terms of silver should have changed in response to the positive (and negative later) shocks observed in silver supply, of which New Spain production represented an acceptable proxy. Not surprisingly, international prices long-run dynamics moved along the path that might be expected. In fact, prices somehow replicated what had happened in the sixteenth and seventeenth centuries in Europe (price revolution followed by a downward trend). Inflation characterizes the second half of the eighteenth and the beginning of the nineteenth centuries as opposed to the deflation -or stagnation- that started in the mid-1810s.

Given the similarity observed between the two phases of the international economic history mentioned above, our approach to the study of the period 1770–1848 draws on Martín Aceña (1992). We firstly analyze quantitatively the co-movements of prices in silver terms throughout the

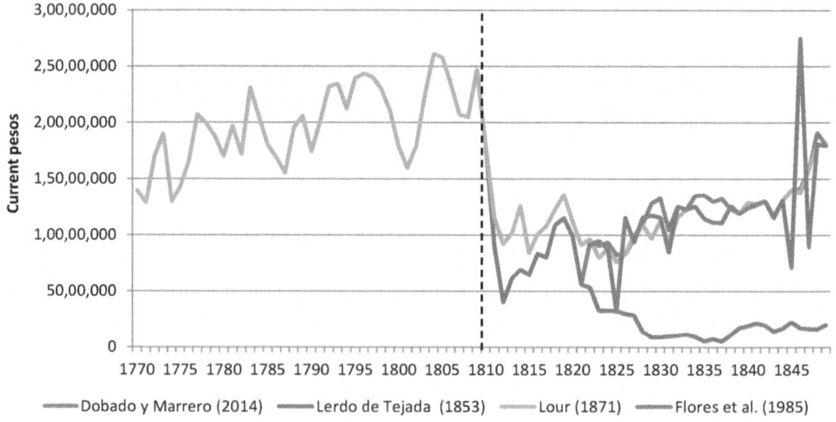

Fig. 1 Different estimates of silver production in New Spain/Mexico, 1770–1848 (*Source* See references)

East (China, Korea and Japan) and the West (the US, New Spain/Mexico, the UK and continental Europe). Next, we make a step forward by proceeding with an attempt to statistically examine the relationship between prices and production of silver in New Spain/Mexico. Although the results are not fully conclusive, there is some evidence in favor of our hypothesis.

The chapter is organized as follows. After this succinct introduction, the next section provides a general overview of the period, and focus on the causes of the fall in silver production in New Spain/Mexico and the rest of Hispanic America from the 1810s to the 1840s. The third part of the chapter deals with the unprecedented silver scarcity, as well as with the coincident international deflation that started in the mid-1810s. After that we show a description of the comovements of prices across a significant number of western and eastern countries—including the "Japanese and Korean exception"—and some insights regarding the century-long importance of the Hispanic American silver—in the form of *reales de a ocho*—as internationally accepted and valued means of payments. We then perform a statistical analysis of those comovements and their correlation with silver production in New Spain/Mexico. Finally, we conclude and outline some potentially promising and complementary avenues for further research.

Golden Age and Collapse of Silver Production

The last decades of the eighteenth century and the first of the nineteenth constitute a period of great importance for the monetary world history. However, it has not attracted so far as much attention from economic historians as it probably deserves. The question is what makes this period so interesting. A satisfactory answer to this question ought to contemplate several factors. In this section we will focus on the geopolitical factors that affected the long-established economic ties across the world.

First, certain main historical events—i.e., French revolution, Napoleonic empire and Hispanic American independence—decisively influenced economic outcomes. In this respect, Dobado et al. (2012) show the long process of grain markets integration across the West, which was initiated in the first half of the eighteenth century but experienced a sharp reversal in 1792–1825. In other words, a process of globalization was on its way before the early 1790s. O'Rourke (2006) points out the significant impact of the French Revolutionary and Napoleonic Wars on the international economy—especially foreign trade—including not only the North Atlantic and Continental Europe, but also Hispanic America and Asia.[1]

A major event taking place in this period was the fragmentation of the American territories of the Hispanic Monarchy. In fact, their independence had unexpected, negative effects at least on the previous monetary and commercial integration within the region. Two reasons of these effects were: (1) the generalized adoption of extremely protectionist policies from independence to World War One by the new republics (Coatsworth and Williamson 2004); (2) the fast breaking of the continental monetary union, based on the silver peso standard that started at the very beginning of the wars between independentists and loyalists (Irigioin 2009a).

One of the most relevant consequences for the global economy related with this event was the collapse of precious metals production in New Spain and Peru. Before the independence, global trade was largely built on the voluminous and continuous exports of Hispanic American silver pesos during the Early Modern Era. In the years preceding the revolts that would end in the independence, Hispanic America reached an all-time record in silver production.[2] In the 1790s, main producers like the viceroyalties of New Spain, Peru and River Plate were, as a whole, producing silver as the world had never seen before. In the 1800s, production slightly decreased but remained close to its historical maximum. In that period New Spain was by far the world leader in silver production. Figures do not lie: 178 millions of fine ounces out of a world total of 286 millions.[3] In other words, more than 60% of total world silver production was obtained in New Spain. Therefore any variation in the viceroyalty's silver production exerted a global influence. In the 1810s silver production in both New Spain and the rest of Hispanic America substantially decreased to 100 and 85 million fine ounces in 1811–1820

[1] Crouzet (1964) explored, as O'Rourke (2006) reckons, the dramatic disruption of international commerce caused by the wars of 1792–1815. In particular, the French economic historian deals with the long-term, far-reaching economic consequences of the British maritime blockade, the "*self-blockade*" of the continent impose by the French and the drastic territorial changes in Germany and Italy.

[2] We draw on data collected by John Garner (https://www.insidemydesk.com/hdd.html, website frequently visited during 2016 and 2017).

[3] White (1930a, b). This is a source that, to the best of our knowledge, has scarcely been mentioned in the specialized literature despite its richness in data.

and 1821–1830, respectively—see Table 1 for the figures and Map 1 for geolocation of major silver mines.

O'Rourke (2006) attributes the fall in New Spain and Hispanic America silver production to "*wartime blockades*" and "*political disorder*". In this respect, some clarification is needed. As to the negative effects of the maritime blockades conducted by the Royal Navy on Spanish shipping across the Atlantic and Caribbean, its importance as a short-termed shock was recognized by Von Humboldt (1814). To him, the causal relationship between blockade and silver production relied on mercury supply to the mining centers. Mercury was the main input in Hispanic American silver production, being Almadén, a village in central Spain, the chief supplier. Thus, shortages of mercury in New Spain caused by "*maritime war*" did happen before 1810 (Dobado and Marrero 2014). However, the fall in silver production—measured by coining in Mexico City mint on a yearly base- in the 1800s was far from important because of the counterbalancing factors such as the previous building of stocks of mercury in years of high imports that were available at the mining centers in years of scarcity or the substitution of smelting for amalgamation in the treatment of certain types of silver ore—see Fig. 1 (ibid.).

Table 1 Production of silver, 1601–1850, in millions of fine ounces

	New Spain/Mexico	*%/World*	*SouthAmerica*	*%/World*	*Hispanic America*	*%/World*	*World total*
1601–1700	306.6	24.1	800.6	62.9	1107.2	87.0	1271.9
1701–1800	1044.5	57.0	598	32.6	1642.5	89.6	1832.8
1801–1810	178	62.1	83.6	29.2	261.6	91.3	286.6
1811–1820	100.3	57.8	48.4	27.9	148.7	85.7	173.4
1821–1830	85.1	55.4	39.7	25.9	124.8	81.3	153.5
1831–1840	106.5	54.0	60.3	30.6	166.8	84.5	197.3
1841–1850	135.4	53.4	72.6	28.6	208	82.1	253.4
1811–1850	427.5	55.0	221.1	28.4	648.6	83.4	777.7

Source White (1930a)

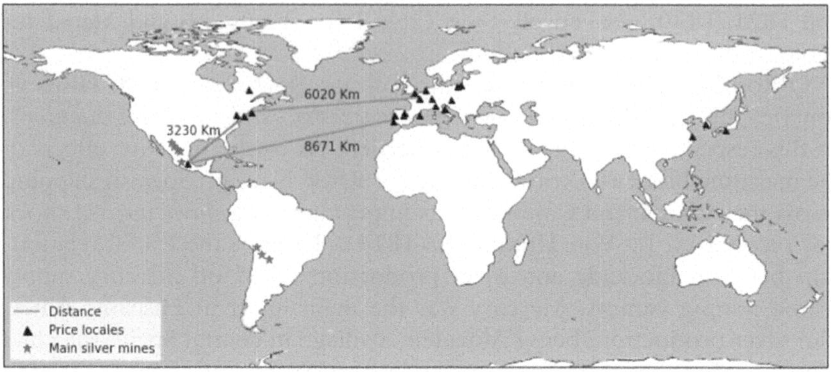

Map 1 Main silver mines and price locales (data) during the eighteenth century

It is true that the registered outflows of silver from New Spain (remittances abroad by private individuals through the ports in the Caribbean including relatively amounts of coined gold) show a high inter-annual variability in response to changes in the relevant circumstances, among them the maritime blockades. Thus, for instance, in 1797, 1801 and 1805 they did not reach one million pesos, far below the average of the years 1796–1815. However, silver exports from New Spain also showed impressive recoveries in "normal" years: e.g., 29.3, 16.9, 19.3 and 21.8 million pesos in, respectively, 1802, 1804, 1807 and 1809. Exports of silver to Asia from Acapulco, via the *Galeón de Manila*, are unknown for most of this period. However, it is safe to assume that, at least, after 1785 they never reached the volume corresponding to the outflows through the Caribbean and that diminished from 1785 until the last voyage of the *Galeón de Manila* in 1815. Smuggling of silver certainly existed, albeit in quantities difficult to estimate. In any case, it is unlikely that they altered with much significance the general picture depicted by the figures of the legal trade. Total registered exports of silver from Mexico, between 1825 and 1849, remained almost constant at a yearly average of nine million pesos. This figure is not only lower than that of 1766–1789 (more than fourteen million pesos) but also even that of the "abnormal" 1800s (nearly twelve million); see Lerdo de Tejada (1967) and Romero (1997).

The spectacular fall in silver production began circa 1810 and was directly related to the civil war—commonly known as *Insurgencia*—that started in that year. Its effects on silver production were simply devastating, see Fig. 1. Moreover, they were accompanied by the ceasing of mining activities in Almadén as a result of the French invasion of Spain in 1808 and by the practical disappearance of the Spanish State in the Peninsula, at least as far as mercury production and commercialization—a royal monopoly—are concerned. The setback experienced by the silver production proved to be long lasting. The decrease in the 1820 exceeded that of the previous decade. The recovery in the 1830s and 1840s was not fast enough as to permit reaching the levels of the 1790s and 1800s. In sum, the long-term fall in silver production in Mexico during most of the first half of the nineteenth century was a conspicuous result of post-1810 developments. As a result, estimates of total Mexican foreign trade by Cárdenas (2003) show a significant fall between the 1800s and the 1830s: 304.3 million pesos compared to 182.3, respectively. Notwithstanding, Mexico was still producing more than 50% of the—contracted—total world silver production.

Significantly enough, similar dynamics are observed in the other silver-producing territories in Hispanic America. As a consequence, world silver production in 1841–1850 was less than 90% that of 1801–1810. The first half of the nineteenth century appears to be clearly different to the second half of the eighteenth century in terms of the supply of silver to the world economy. Our hypothesis is that these developments did affect an international monetary system which was strongly dependent on silver. In this respect, the pre-1810 global monetary context contrasts with the one that emerged after the beginning of the independence in Hispanic America. Moreover, the deterioration of the quality (weight and purity) of the new pesos further rarified global markets for silver (Irigoin 2009a, b).

At a national level, the disruption of silver production triggered different consequences that depended on the type and intensity of commercial and financial connections with silver-producing countries and on each country's monetary regime. Several countries worldwide depended more or less on silver as a local means of payment and considered this metal as legal tender (e.g., France, China, and most countries in Hispanic America). In those cases, an exogenous supply shock on silver would immediately affect the monetary base and could lead to different reactions by monetary authorities depending on the extent and nature of the shocks.

Salvucci (2013) also observes that the highest volatility of the silver price in London in terms of gold coincides with the period of inconvertibility. This volatility could have had an incidence on real activity, on the exchange rate Mexican peso—sterling pound or both, with lasting effects on the British monetary regime.

In the case of China, some authors attribute "the net outflow of silver from China to the rising value of silver in the international markets" (Demigny 1964 *apud* von Glahn 2016) instead of blaming the opium imports. According to Lin (2006 *apud* von Glahn 2016), "falling global production of silver", along with a weak demand for tea and silk in Europe, are the reasons why China experienced a net outflow of silver during the first half of the nineteenth century. Von Glahn (2016) disagrees with Lin as to the relevance of the two factors proposed by her to explain the shortage of silver in China. Part of evidence upon which Von Glahn (2016) builds his argument is empirically flawed as he clearly underestimates the real fall in Mexican silver production during the first decades of the nineteenth century.[4] However, he offers a convincing monetary argument: "the principal evidence for a shortage of silver in China during the first half of the nineteenth century is the sharp appreciation of silver (relative to bronze coin) beginning in the mid-1830s" (Von Glahn 2016, p. 368). Contrary to Von Glahn's assertion, the exchange ratio between silver and bronze started to rise before than the 1830s. Reinforcing our conclusion drawn from Von Glahn's own figures, Chen (1975) shows clearly that depreciation of copper begun early in the nineteenth century—see Fig. 2.[5]

This evidence for China is consistent with our hypothesis that the pervasive reduction of silver production in Hispanic America from 1810

[4] It is a common limitation in some works dealing with money and prices in China the lack of careful attention paid to the pre-1810 years in New Spain. Thus, it may seem that growing production in Mexico after 1821 implied a certain return to normal, which is clearly untrue, as the accumulated silver produced was clearly lower than before 1810. Between 1790 and 1809, the accumulated production of silver in Mexico nearly amounted 450 million pesos compared with the 300 million total of 1810–1839. A similar fall in other Hispanic American producers significantly changed the world supply of silver. In this new playground, the United States outperformed Europeans countries as carrier of silver to China.

[5] Both Von Glahn (2016) and Chen (1975) suggest that other factor might contribute to the explanation of the increase in rate of exchange between silver and bronze—i.e., debasement of bronze coin by the state and changes in the price of agricultural products. However, we find that their reasoning is somehow contradictory and/or unconvincing.

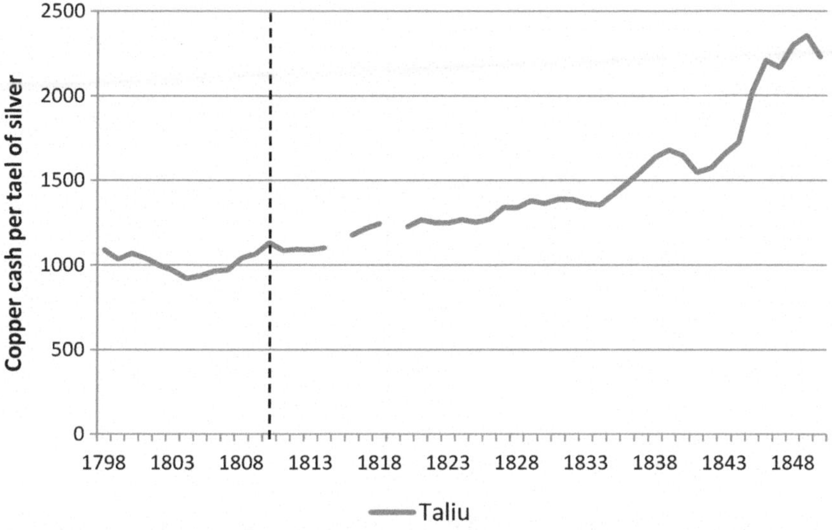

Fig. 2 Cash-silver bimetallic rates, 1798–1850 (*Source* Chang 1975)

somehow created a new monetary world in which silver became less abundant and more expensive in terms of other goods.

These global interactions can be established through an initial observation on the relationship between silver production and prices of silver in different locales. This is shown in Fig. 3, where we report the price of silver in the West, which clearly reflects, albeit less than it could be expected, the change in the supply of silver after 1810—see Fig. 3.[6]

Silver Scarcity and Decline of Prices

During the two last decades of the eighteenth, the price of gold in terms of silver increased. Interestingly enough, it experienced a significant fall in 1810 and from 1814 to 1820. Until the 1820s, the evolution of the gold/silver ratio is compatible with the hypothesis that it reflects the ups and downs of silver production. From the 1820s on, that ratio remained rather stable within bands of variation not far from the average values

[6] Details on the methodology used to construct this series are offered at https://measuringworth.com/docs/GoldInterpretation.pdf.

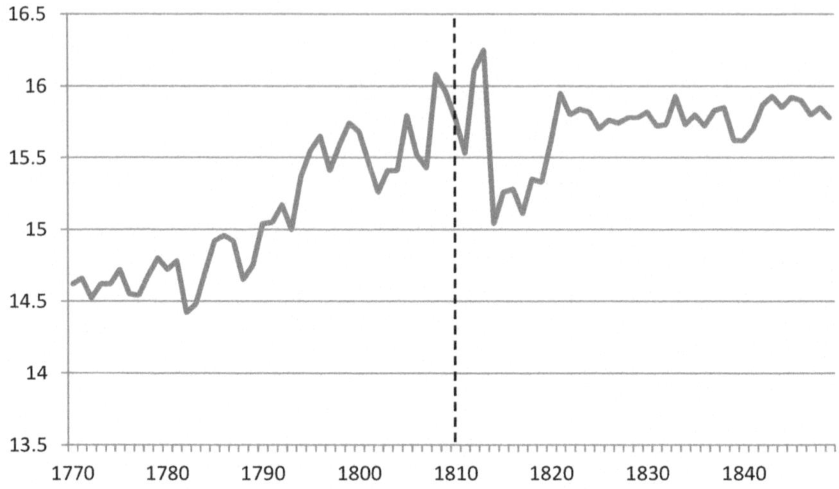

Fig. 3 Gold/silver ratio, 1770–1849 (*Source* Officer and Williamson 2017)

reached before 1810. Certainly, it is beyond the scope of this research to propose an explanatory formal model of the long run behavior of the gold/silver ratio in a period of increasing monetary and financial complexity such as this one. In any case, for the first part of the nineteenth century the respective production of gold and silver do not seem to capture the dynamics of their relative prices; see Table 2. Likely, changes in the demand for the two precious metals in response to the diverse and

Table 2 World production of silver and gold, 1801–1850 (metric tons)

	Ag	%Δ	*Au*	%Δ	*Ag/Au*
1801–1810	286.6		5.8		49.4
1811–1820	173.4	−39.5	3.8	−34.5	45.6
1821–1830	153.5	−11.5	4.7	23.7	32.7
1831–1840	197.4	28.6	6.6	40.4	29.9
1841–1850	253.4	28.4	17.1	159.1	14.8

Source White (1930a)

important economic developments in the real and monetary sectors could be considered in a future research.[7]

The link between the levels of prices and the production of gold and silver mines was reported by contemporaries (Ricardo 1811; Tooke 1838). These observations were later analyzed and named as the "price revolution", which described the economic effects in Europe from the specie flow stemming from the Spanish colonies (Clark and Hamilton 1934). Bordo (1984) provides a general picture of the classical economists, all of which emphasized the role of bullion (quantity theories of money such as the one raised by Richard Cantillon or the more elaborated international specie standard analyzed by David Hume, which emphasized the role of the balance of trade on the determination of prices and wages). These authors raised already the law of one price or the theory of purchase power parity (Rogoff 1996). Accordingly, prices in open economies should behave similarly once the effects of the exchange rates are taken into account. This reasoning justifies why authors such as McCloskey and Zecher (1984) and Flandreau (1996) have estimated that, regardless of the monetary regime blocks to which open economies belonged, the correlation in prices series during the nineteenth century—since around 1840—are high and positive and show no difference between blocks. We have reasons to believe that these forces were already in place since at least the late eighteenth century. The fall in prices that we report in the next section has also been taken as evidence in favor of the existence of common business cycles in Europe and as part of in the national historiographies of different countries. Regarding the former, Silbering (1923) reports different indexes of prices of international traded commodities and shows that they experience a general fall during the 1810s (starting close to 1810). Craig and García Iglesias (2010) reckon a downward cycle in Europe's economic activity around 1810–1811, though they insist that price expectation may vary according to an economic shock, while this relationship may be dissociated from the cycles in the real activity. Nevertheless, they recognized that the specie flows had an important effect on business cycles in Europe.

[7] A skyrocketing rise in manufactures exports from Britain to Hispanic America occurred between the 1780s and the 1820s (O'Rourke 2006). The new trade resulting from the Napoleonic Wars and, especially, from the independence of the American territories of the Hispanic Monarchy forcedly increased the inflow of silver into the UK and reduced that with Spain as destination.

Salvucci (1987, 1994) reports such a mechanism in the case of Mexico's bilateral trade. While increased production of silver allowed for more import capacity for British cottons, Salvucci (1994) identifies a real exchange rate mechanism, in which an overvaluation of the Mexican peso in the late eighteenth century and the early nineteenth century also contributed to the fall of local woolen production. This overvaluation can be directly attributed by an increase in the price levels in Mexico which were a byproduct of increased silver stock. Given the prices and exchange rates with Great Britain, bilateral trade (and smuggling) led to an increase of imports of British cottons and substitution of Mexican woolen. This effect is known as the *Dutch disease*.[8]

Following the same reasoning, the fall of silver production may have led to the reverse mechanism. The deflation reported in Mexico could have been accompanied by this same process in other countries in South America. Moreover, the interruption of silver imports to Great Britain could have other, international trade effect as Great Britain was a major player in the world's silver market. In the case of Asia, Bowen (2010) argues that in the late eighteenth century silver was exported from Britain to Asia, but that these flows reversed precisely after 1810. Most of this silver came from Hispanic America and was re-exported. Again, London emerged as a major place in which the Bank of England and the English East India Company participated in the market of "silver bullion for good". He provides figures for the period 1802–1811, in which 43.8% of silver imported by India arrived from Great Britain, 16% from Europe (other) and 40.2% from America. Bhattacharya (2008) reports that China absorbed 18% of the New World's silver output.

Silver as International Mean of Payment and Price Comovements

In this chapter we will present the evolution of different price measures in distinct locales worldwide during the eighteenth and nineteenth centuries, paying special attention to the period in which New Spain silver production collapsed.

[8]The reader can learn more about the *Dutch disease* in the chapter by Abad and Palma (2021) included in this book.

A close inspection of the price series—i.e., grain prices, rice prices, Consumer Price Indexes, Retail Price Indexes, etc.—for a relevant group of countries shows more than superficial similarities over the period under consideration (see Map 1 for a geolocation of the data used). Most of these markets may be included in a "silver world" increasingly integrated by the intra- and intercontinental trade in goods and *reales de a ocho* over the Early Modern Era. In this respect, Flynn and Giráldez (2004) "propose [critiquing O'Rourke and Williamson (2002)] that globalization began when the Old World became directly connected with the Americas in 1571 via Manila."[9] We agree with this claim. Departing from Acapulco, in the Pacific coast of New Spain, the *Galeón de Manila* was loaded with important quantities of silver that were redirected to China and other countries of the region.[10] For some time, Peru was also permitted to export silver to the Philippines in exchange for Asian goods. Trade between Veracruz and Spain had very much in common with the *Galeón de Manila* in that it consisted basically in silver. Once arrived to Seville (sixteenth and seventeenth centuries) or Cadiz, trade conducted by Portugal, the Netherlands, Britain and even Denmark, and Sweden successively joined the new commercial route through the Cape of Good Hope to the Indic and the China Sea, with an active participation of merchants from the East, where silver was very much appreciated as to permit the appearance of a market for arbitrage of precious metals. After their independence, the United States rapidly developed a fruitful trade with China. For the first time in history, trade was practically global and the main currency was the Spanish dollar.

The role played by the flexible supply of reliable, worldwide accepted, silver *reales de a ocho* minted in Hispanic America was indispensable. During some decades of the sixteenth and seventeenth centuries, Japan became an important silver producer whose exports had Korea and, mainly, China as destination, and kept alive a significant trade between the three countries (Flynn and Lee 2013).[11] The seclusion of Japan in the 1630s very much reduced its participation in international markets.

[9] Most estimates of silver exported, between 1550 and 1645, from Japan to China exceed those of the silver arriving from America through the Pacific and the Atlantic routes (Von Glahn 2013, p. 32).

[10] More information about the *Galeón de Manila* can be found in this book in the chapter by Arturo Giráldez (2021).

[11] This article presents an alternative model to conventional microeconomic theory, termed the *Hydraulic Metaphor*, to describe the functioning of the supply and demand of money in this period.

According to de Vries (2003), in 1725–1750, intercontinental silver flows were as follows: slightly more than three quarters of the Hispanic American silver production (nearly 50% higher than in 1600–1650) were sent to Europe, while direct exports across the Pacific route to Asia amounted to between 2.5% and 8%; from Europe roughly 8% and 10% were, respectively, exported to the Baltic and the Levant; and between an quarter and a third makes its way to Asia by the Cape. Therefore, we contend that the inclusion into this expanding "silver world" should have certainly affected the dynamics of prices across continents.

Albeit some country-specific or more general circumstances—i.e., bad harvests, military invasions, maritime blockades, war effort and its financial requirements—might cause the appearance of influent observations in the series, an underlying common trend becomes apparent. It adopts the shape of an inverted "U" centered sometime in the 1810s (Calderón-Fernández et al. 2019). This trend is shared by countries with different economies and varied historical trajectories across continents. This widely diffused behavior of prices—inflation in the second half of the eighteenth century and the early nineteenth century, followed by deflation and/or stagnation of prices in the rest of the first half of the nineteenth century—resembles that of the European countries in the sixteenth and seventeenth centuries (Martín Aceña 1992). Might the ascending part of the inverted "U" in the eighteenth century be considered a peculiar form of price revolution? Behind these two developments of the Early Modern era, we find a huge increase in silver flows from Hispanic America to most of the world.

In the case of Spain, the main gate of entry of silver from Hispanic America into Europe until 1821, the series of consumption baskets for Barcelona (a coastal, grain-importing, commercial and manufacturing town that pioneered Spanish industrialization) and Palencia (a distant from the sea, wheat producing, second-rate location in the peninsular urban hierarchy) follow the trajectories depicted in Fig. 4.[12] The existence of two clearly different periods is also evident in terms of prices growth rate.

[12] Details on the construction of the series may be found in Moreno (2001) and Nogués (2005). The choice of representative consumption baskets constitutes the starting point of the CPIs series. The similarity between the two series, despite the fact that the one for Barcelona is built upon prices in silver *pesetas* while that for Palencia prices are denominated in *reales de vellón*, is somewhat striking.

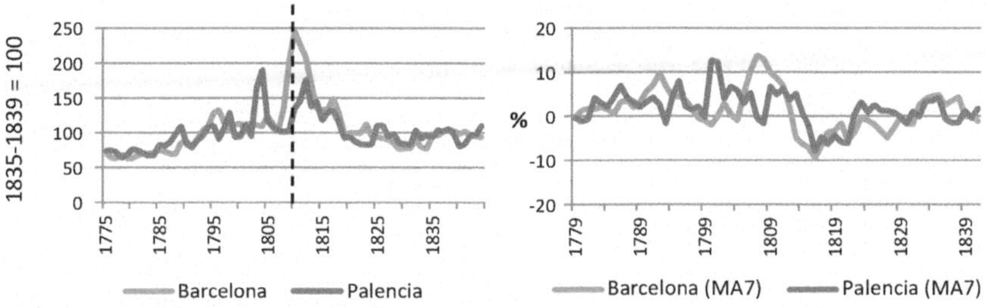

Fig. 4 Consumer price indexes in Spain, 1775–1849 (left: levels; right: growth rates) (*Source* Moreno 2001 and Nogués 2005)

The usual explanation for the Spanish inflation looks at the problems posed by the agrarian sector. Technically and institutionally, especially in inner Spain, the agrarian sector could not increase its supply at the pace required for matching the growing demand from an increasing population. Bad or very bad harvests at the end of the eighteenth and the beginning of the nineteenth century can be seen as a extreme manifestation of the structural difficulties experienced in the previous years. The Napoleonic invasion came to distort even further the instability of the market for agrarian products.[13] As to the inflationary effect resulting from the supposedly mismanagement of public finances, more particularly regarding the "excessive" issuing of *vales reales*, White (1987) finds a "lack of reaction of prices to the variations in the circulation of vales" [our translation], except after the financial collapse of the Hispanic Monarchy at the end of the eighteenth century. Tedde de Lorca (1987, p. 547) proposed a monetary explanation for the inflation, in the absence of an increase in the circulation of *vales*, of the years 1784–1788: a huge increase in the inflow of American silver. Thus, he considers that the inflationary effect of the pre-1793 issues of *vales reales* was "*moderate*". By that year, prices in Barcelona and Palencia had been already growing at historically high rates, coinciding with peaks of New Spain silver production.

[13] However, it should be noticed that the yearly average rate of growth in prices in Palencia between 1752 and 1789 was 2.6%. These rates exceed those of the two Castilles and Valencia during the price revolution of the sixteenth century (Martin Aceña 1992, Table 3, p. 367).

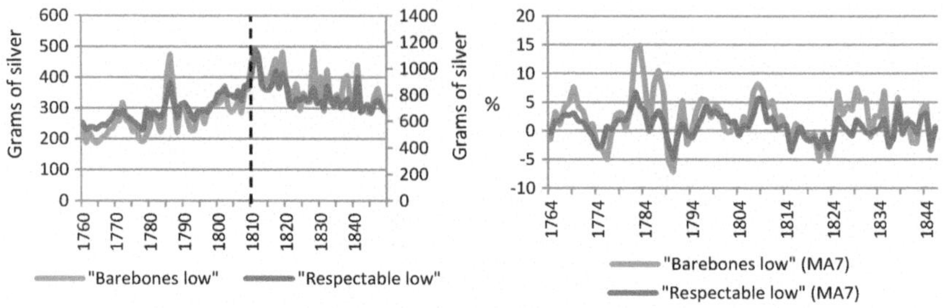

Fig. 5 Price consumption indexes for Mexico City, 1760–1849 (left: levels; right: growth rates) (*Source* Challú and Gómez-Galvarriato 2015)

The effects of Hispanic America's independence were recently summarized and reported by Tedde de Lorca (2009). This author argues that the fall in specie inflows from the Americas led to demonetization, further aggravated by the deficits in the Spanish balance of trade. According to Tortella and García, Spanish deflation was especially intense between 1815 and 1830. From around 1830 to the mid-1850s, prices "steadied [...] although with ups and downs around a horizontal trend" (Tortella and García-Ruiz 2013, p. 29). Their explanation of the Spanish deflation points out to the outflow of coins because of its high content in silver and the chronic trade deficit as well as hoarding. These might well be the main problems confronted by the Spanish monetary system but it is not necessarily true regarding other countries that were experiencing deflation as well. In this respect, Nogués (2005) finds that deflation is not a Spanish peculiarity as it was shared with other Western countries like Germany, the USA, France and Great Britain.

In this respect, Mexico City features an interesting case (see Fig. 5). Despite certain contrasting features behind the Mexican series, they do not set apart Mexico City from the basic sequence of inflation-deflation observed in Spain.[14] These differences include those stemming from consumption patterns (corn as main staple in the "barebones low" basket

[14] The "barebones" or subsistence baskets are similar to that of Allen et al. (2012) for Milan. In turn, the "respectable" basket attempts to capture the more complex diet of the urban workers and is comparable to others estimated for Beijing and London (Challú and Gómez Galvarriato 2015, p. 91). These two basic types of baskets are then divided into "low" and "high" versions. Our choice of the "low" levels of the two baskets likely represents better the real consumption of a larger share of the population. In any

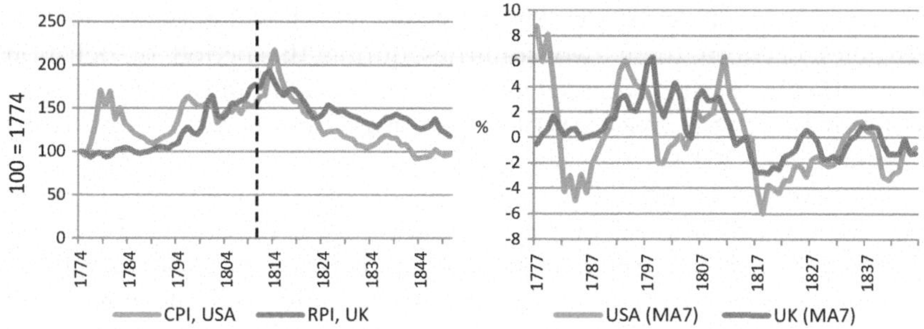

Fig. 6 Consumer price index (USA) and Retail price index (UK), 1774–1849 (left: levels; right: growth rates) (*Source* Officer and Williamson 2017 and Clark 2017)

and some wheat and much more meat in the "respectable low" one), along with especially meagre harvests in a non-negligible number of years, plus years of civil war after 1810. However, deflation is more intense in the "respectable low" basket since it was less sensible to the fall in corn harvests repeatedly suffered by the traditional Mexican agrarian sector after the independence. Nonetheless, the two-phase cycle of prices between 1760 and 1849 is perceptible, albeit somewhat less than in Spain, where intense fluctuations of the agrarian production were less frequent after the 1810s.

The inverted-U shape of prices is also perceptible in two well-integrated and relatively rich Atlantic economies, such as the United States and the United Kingdom—see Fig. 6.[15]

Once again, similarities between the two countries and their consistency with international norm are noticeable. In the United States, both inflation before 1814 and deflation afterwards were somewhat more intense. As to the inflationary phase, the effects of the War of Independence (1775–1783)—among them intense monetary instability—and the "Panic of 1796–1797"—in which Britain was involved—further increased

case, only minor dissimilarities in levels may be observed between the "low" and "high" versions of the two baskets.

[15] Details on the building of the Consumer Price Index (USA) and the Retail Price Index (UK) may be found in https://www.measuringworth.com/inflation/.

the growth in prices in the United States.[16] The similitude in prices dynamics between these two countries during the period of deflation is remarkable, what reinforced the idea of a highly integrated Atlantic economy before the canonical time span of globalization, as proposed by Dobado et al. (2012)—see, again, Fig. 6.

Our attempt to present a global picture of the influx of silver on the "Early Globalization" and the price comovements during the period 1770–1848 needs to complement developments in the West with those in East, especially in China, the largest economy until the nineteenth century. The trade of Western countries with China enormously grew during the eighteenth century and was basically based on the exchange of silk, porcelain and, increasingly, tea in exchange for silver. It is not surprising, then, that, given the parallel with the sixteenth-century Europe, a debate on the effect of the huge amount of silver inflows on Chinese prices has arisen. From a monetary point of view, China is particularly interesting since the "Chinese imperial government did not issue a silver currency before 1889" (Von Glahn 2013, p. 17).

As to the sixteenth century, Flynn and Giráldez (1995, p. 203) propose that inflation "was a global phenomenon." Moreover, they claim that, instead of main protagonists, Europeans were just "intermediaries in the trade [in silver] between the New World and China" (ibid.). Be it true or not—at least a similar quantity of silver remained in the West (Hispanic American and Europe)—China acted for centuries as the final destination of a significant part of the silver world production. But what can be safely proposed about prices and silver in the eighteenth-century China? Von Glahn (2013) reckons that imports of silver—mostly from New Spain—into China reached historical maxima in the last quarter of that century (Von Glahn 2013, p.44).[17] Cheung (2013) discusses whether the concept

[16]The crisis started when the bubble resulting from land speculation burst in 1796. It was worsened by the Bank Restriction Act passed, in 1797, by the Parliament of Great Britain. The long-lasting convertibility into gold was suspended until 1821. The controversy on the suspension of specie payments took the following factors into consideration. "The unbalancing of the budget and is possibly inflationary results; the premium on gold in Paris that accompanied the destruction of the assignats; abnormal imports of grain necessitated by inadequate British harvests; and large imports, at extremely high prices, of naval stores" (Gayer et al. 1953, vol. 1, p. 47).

[17]"Carolus pesos", after Carlos III, and "Buddha-head", issued during the reign of Carlos IV, were highly appreciated since 1790s—Irigoin (2009b) is cited by Von Glahn—and valued at an increasing premium during the first half of the nineteenth century.

of "price revolution" is appropriate for eighteenth-century China. For this author, the idea that the enormous influx of silver into China was followed by a high inflation is still widely influential among specialists. Evidence in favor of this idea is shown in Fig. 7.

A first problem with this source is recognized by Wang (1992) himself. The series for the Suzhou Prefecture, including Suzhou City, "*the largest grain market in the country*", are based on the reports submitted by the provincial authorities to Beijing. The "other series" has been assembled with shorter series for Xiaoshan, Changshu and Shanghai. Until 1785–1787, the two series basically comove. However, afterwards they clearly separate one from each other. For Wang (1992), this divergence might respond to errors in the reports from Suzhou Prefecture. Cheung (2013) proposes an alternative explanation for such a divergence. The decline in silver imports during most of the 1790s "would have led to a fall in commodity prices in terms of silver" (Cheung 2013, p. 128). In turn, the same factor might contribute to the increased value of silver in terms of copper cash in Xiaoshan, Zhejiang. In any case, rice prices in silver increased at an average yearly growth rate of 2.7% between 1711 and 1786. This was higher than that estimated by Martín Aceña (1992) for

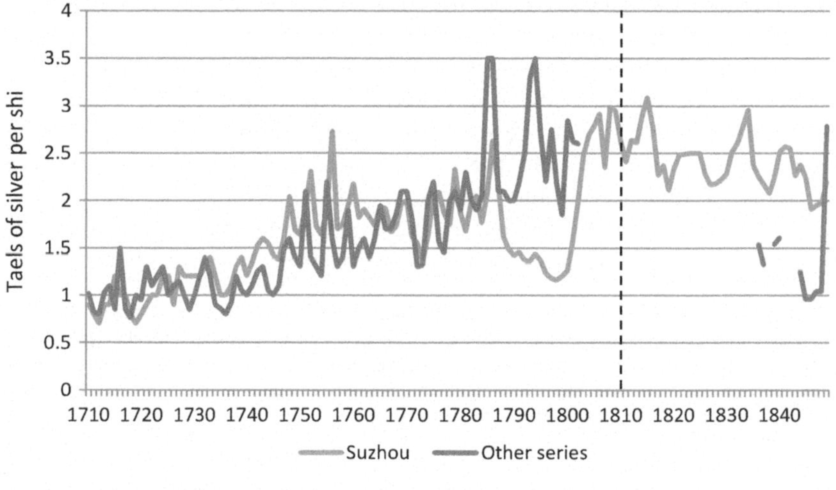

Fig. 7 Rice prices in China, 1710–1848 (*Source* Wang 1992)

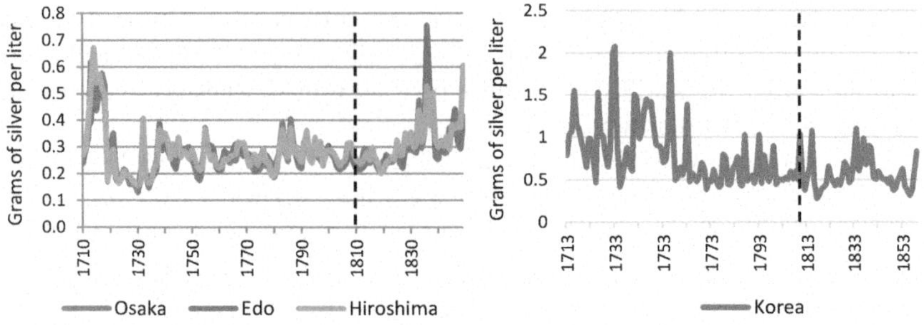

Fig. 8 Rice prices in Japan and Southern Korea, 1710–1860 (*Source* https://www.iisg.nl/hpw/data.php#japan (Japan) and https://gpih.ucdavis.edu/Datafilelist.htm (Korea)

Spain during the sixteenth century. This finding favors the notion of a "price revolution" in eighteenth-century China.

Within the East, the contrast between China and Japan or Korea is apparent—see Fig. 8. Neither in Osaka, the main and highly sophisticated Japanese rice market, nor in Edo and Hiroshima, prices show the inverted-U shape that may be observed in the previous considered cases. The same happens with the rice prices in Korea, which have a higher mean (and, especially an outstanding volatility) up to the beginning of the 1760s and a constant lower mean (and volatility) since then, for about one century. We first compare China and Japan because of two main reasons.[18] On the one hand, they were two big economies, especially the former.[19] On the other hand, they represent polar cases in terms of their economic openness. This difference between China and Japan is important to understand their price dynamics during the

[18] India has not been included in our discussion. Following Studer (2008): "Prior to the mid-nineteenth century, the grain trade in India was essentially local, while more distant markets remained fragmented" (p. 424). A visual inspection of grain prices in India reveals the existence of several well-differentiated regions. On the contrary, grain markets in China and Japan were well-integrated since the eighteenth century (Bassino 2006; Shiue and Keller 2007; Dobado et al. 2015). On the contrary, no statistical evidence of trade in grain between China and Japan is found by Dobado et al. (2015) in spite of the existing differential in prices.

[19] According to Maddison estimates, China GDP was still at the top of the world ranking by 1820, while Japan occupied the seventh position, well ahead of the USA and Spain.

period under study. Thus, while China played an active role in the flows of silver and goods of the increasing global economy from the second half of the sixteenth century—especially from mid-eighteenth century, Japan remained comparatively closed from the adoption of the *sakoku* policy in 1633–1639 by Tokugawa Iemitsu until the openness of the country forced by the arrival, in 1853, of the "black boats" of the US Navy commanded by Commodore Perry and the subsequent treaties with Western powers.[20] The rationale behind the divergent paths of foreign trade followed by China and Japan from mid-seventeenth century is exposed by Miyamoto and Shikano.[21] Rice prices movement over the long-term reveals the implications of the contrasting policies chosen in the two countries. A summary of the evidence regarding price dynamics during the period under consideration is depicted in Tables 3 and 4.

Table 3 shows the average price annual growth rate between 1775 or 1776 and the year in which the maximum of the inflationary phase is reached. Table 4 shows inter-decennial growth rates in order to avoid the effect of a possible selection bias. The two estimates reflect a similar price dynamic. The long run evolution of prices—Japan and Korea excepted—very much resembles that of Europe in the two fist centuries of the Early Modern era. In some cases, both inflation and deflation are even more intense.

The case of Korea is somehow similar to that of Japan. At least, regarding economic openness, it is clearly closer to Japan than to China. After repeated Japanese (1592 and 1597) and Manchu (1627 and 1636) invasions, Korea significantly limited exterior contacts—commercial or otherwise.[22]

[20] The isolation was incomplete since China and the Netherlands were allowed by the Shogunate to conduct trade under very restrictive conditions.

[21] "After the second half of the seventeenth century, rice prices in both countries began to diverge, and the synchronized movement was completely lost by the eighteenth century. The crucial period was the second half of the seventeenth century. Both countries suffered from shortages of silver, in Japan because of the outflow of silver and the growth of demand for money, in China because of the government's isolationist policy. However, the two countries came up with different solutions. Japan reacted by withdrawing from the international system, while China responded by re-entering it. Thus, the two economies took different paths in the eighteenth century and after" (Miyamoto and Shikano 2003, p. 185).

[22] "The main foreign contacts officially sanctioned by the Choson Dynasty were diplomatic missions to China three or four times a year and a small outpost of Japanese merchants in the southeastern part of Korea near the present-day city of Pusan. Few

Table 3 Rates of growth of prices, 1775–1849

USA (CPI)		UK (RPI)		Japan (Rice price in silver grams)			
1775–1814	2.4	1775–1813	1.9	Osaka			
1814–1849	−1.9	1813–1849	−1.1	1775–1808	3.1	1808–1849	3.5
Mexico City (CPIs)				China (Rice price in silver grams)			
	BL		RL	Yangzi delta[a]		Yangzi delta[b]	
1775–1811	3.5	1775–1811	2.1	1776–1802	1.0	1776–1802	3.28
1811–1849	0.9	1811–1849	−0.1	1776–1815	2.0	n.a	–
				1815–1849	0.4	n.a	–
Spain (CPIs)							
	Barcelona		Palencia				
1776–1810	4.3	1776–1812	4.0				
1810–1844	−1.6	1812–1844	−0.1				

[a]Suzhou prefecture, [b]Other series
Source Calderón-Fernández et al. (2019) and see text

Therefore, it was not so the distance among the markets that makes the commercial relationships possible, but the openness of the economies. And openness and trade in the eighteenth century made the markets (New Spain) silver-dependent. Obviously, this dependency was very heterogenous and, as explained in different chapters of this book, it was based on the idiosyncrasy of each country/economy. Map 1 showed the distances between some integrated economies in the West (see Dobado et al. 2012), while Map 2 presents the distances of non-integrated economies in the East (Dobado et al. 2015). As we will see in the next section, China could also be included in the *integrated economies club* that emerged during the second half of the eighteenth and the beginning of the nineteenth centuries, which illustrates that policies and silver dependence were far more important than distances in the integration game at that time. The basic findings displayed in these lines are complemented with a statistical analysis in the next section.

Koreans left the peninsula during the late Choson Dynasty, and even fewer foreigners entered." Armstrong, C. K., "Korean History and Political Geography", Center for Global Education, Asia Society (https://asiasociety.org/education/korean-history-and-political-geography. Accessed on April 28, 2020).

Table 4 Rates of growth of prices, 1775–1849

	USA (CPI)		UK (RPI)		
	Index	%Δ	Index	%Δ	
1774–1779	81.7		97.0		
1810–1819	174.0	113.1	175.7	81.2	
1840–1849	98.4	−43.5	130.7	−25.6	
	Mexico City (CPIs)				
	BL		RL		
	Index	%Δ	Index	%Δ	
1774–1779	211.6		589.2		
1810–1819	432.3	104.3	944.5	60.3	
1840–1849	325.6	−24.7	730.2	−22.7	
	Spain				
	Barcelona		Palencia		
	Index	%Δ	Index	%Δ	
1775–1779	66.3		70.5		
1810–1819	162.7	145.4	132.7	88.2	
1840–1844	96.8	−40.5	93.7	−29.4	
	Japan and Southern Korea (Rice price in silver grams)				
	Osaka		Southern Korea		
	Price	%Δ	Price	%Δ	
1774–1779	0.29		0.22		
1810–1819	0.33	15.0	0.25	13.6	
1840–1849	0.45	34.6	0.36	44.0	
	China (Rice price in silver grams)				
	Yangzi delta[a]			Yangzi delta[b]	
	Price	%Δ		Price	%Δ
1774–1779	1.95		1774–1779	1.89	
1810–1819	2.58	32.1	1800–1802[c]	2.69	42.6
1840–1849	2.26	−12.6	1840–1849[d]	1.41	−47.7

[a]Suzhou prefecture, [b]Other series, [c]1803–1819 are not available, [d]1841 and 1843 not available
Source Calderón-Fernández et al. (2019)

Statistical Analysis of Prices and Silver Production Series

This section uses some findings from Dobado et al. (2012, 2015), for the Atlantic grain prices and rice prices in Asia, obtained with data that cover the second part of the eighteenth and first half of the nineteenth century. The previous works find pairwise cointegration relationships between series from Amsterdam and Holland, Arévalo (inner Spain), London and Southern England, Gdansk, Milan, Strasbourg and Vienna, in Europe,

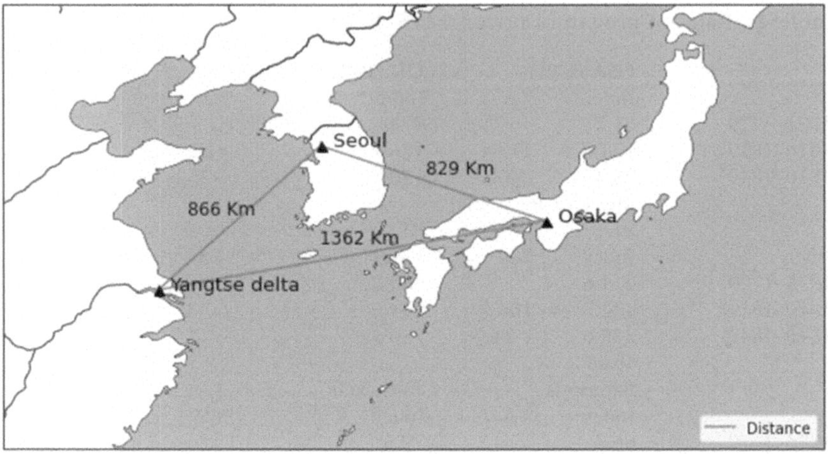

Map 2 Distance between three Asian markets

and Pennsylvania, in North America. On the other hand, by using rice prices, they also reveal that China and Japan were disconnected during the same period.

Bearing these results in mind, we use these and other eighteenth-nineteenth centuries price series (grain prices, consumer price indexes, retail price indexes, etc.) with a twofold objective: (1) understanding the behavior of the prices and their statistical similarities compatible with our hypotheses of (almost) worldwide price comovements; and (2) looking for relational patterns between prices and silver production in New Spain.

To achieve our first aim, we analyze the price series database. Statistically speaking, we find that all the price series are I(1), meaning that they need one difference (i.e., $p_t - p_{t-1}$) to be transformed into a stationary series. The results of the stationarity analysis, by means of the Augmented Dickey Fuller (ADF) test, are shown in Table 5.

As said in the previous sections, most of price series show an inverted U-shape during the period of the analysis, being Osaka and Southern Korea exceptions to this pattern. As all the price series studied are I(1), we can determine whether there is a long-run relationship between pair of prices by performing a cointegration analysis using the Engle-Granger two-step method. This consists of regressing the two cointegrated candidate prices and testing for a unit root in the residuals obtained in the

Table 5 Unit root test for the (logarithm of) price series

Series	*Sample*	*# obs*	*ADF-stat*	*# lags AIC*	*p-value*	*Decision*
America						
Pennsylvania[a]	1720–1868	149	−0.719	4	0.8418	Unit root
CPIMexResHi	1760–1868	109	−2.321	1	0.1654	Unit root
CPIMexResLow	1760–1868	109	−2.561	3	0.1014	Unit root
CPIUsa	1774–1850	77	−2.175	2	0.2153	Unit root
Europe						
Holland[a]	1720–1868	149	−2.321	3	0.1653	Unit root
London[a]	1700–1868	169	−1.941	4	0.3132	Unit root
Milan[a]	1701–1860	160	−2.365	4	0.1519	Unit root
Strasbourg[a]	1700–1868	169	−2.000	3	0.2864	Unit root
Vienna[a]	1700–1868	169	−1.953	4	0.3075	Unit root
Lisbon	1750–1855	106	−1.968	3	0.3004	Unit root
Pesaro	1720–1824	105	−2.588	2	0.1000	Unit root
Barcelona	1775–1844	70	−1.996	2	0.2882	Unit root
Palencia	1775–1844	70	−2.517	2	0.1115	Unit root
RPIUk	1680–1860	181	−1.014	3	0.7481	Unit root
France	1726–1868	143	−2.020	4	0.2779	Unit root
Asia						
Osaka[b]	1710–1864	155	−1.866	2	0.3484	Unit root
YangziRev[b]	1680–1868	189	−1.686	5	0.4382	Unit root
Seoul	1713–1859	147	−2.379	5	0.1478	Unit root

[a]Series analyzed in Dobado et al. (2012); [b]Series analyzed in Dobado et al. (2015)
The source of the rest of the series is given in previous figures or the text

auxiliary regression. Table 6 shows the results of the cointegration analysis using the ADF as the tool for testing a unit root in the residuals.

The formal test rejects the null hypothesis of a unit root in most of the cases, evidencing, in such cases, the existence of a long-run relationship of prices. This statistical result means that the cointegrated price series did not drift away from each other during this period even if they are nonstationary. So, as we perform the analysis by pairs, it also means that they were growing and falling together, likely impulse by a third force common to both of them. Interestingly enough, the only relationships that do reject the cointegration hypothesis are those involved with Osaka or Southern Korea rice prices. This result was somehow expected due to the isolationist foreign policy carried out in this period by the Tokugawa Shogunate in Japan and the so called Korean "hermit kingdom". Charts included in Fig. 9 depict the evolution of some cointegrated

Table 6 Cointegration in the (logarithm of) price series

Pair of series	*# obs*	*ADF-stat*	*# lags AIC*	*p-value*	*Decision*
Pennsylvania—CPIMexResHi	107	−4.493	1	0.000	Cointegrated
Pennsylvania—CPIMexResLow	107	−4.641	1	0.000	Cointegrated
Pennsylvania—Lisbon	106	−4.031	3	0.006	Cointegrated
Pennsylvania—Barcelona	68	−5.909	1	0.000	Cointegrated
Pennsylvania—Palencia	67	−5.512	2	0.000	Cointegrated
Pennsylvania—France	135	−4.333	3	0.000	Cointegrated
YangziRev—CPIMexResLow	106	−4.401	2	0.000	Cointegrated
YangziRev—CPIMexResHi	106	−4.019	2	0.001	Cointegrated
YangziRev—Pennsylvania	127	−5.626	1	0.000	Cointegrated
YangziRev—Holland	146	−4.662	2	0.000	Cointegrated
YangziRev—Lisbon	106	−4.200	2	0.003	Cointegrated
YangziRev—Osaka	149	−2.076	5	0.254	Not cointegrated
Pennsylvania—Osaka	139	−1.799	5	0.381	Not cointegrated
CPIMexResLow—Osaka	100	−2.461	4	0.125	Not cointegrated
France—Osaka	130	−2.211	4	0.202	Not cointegrated
YangziRev—Seoul	147	−2.570	3	0.249	Not cointegrated
Pennsylvania—Seoul	140	−2.638	3	0.222	Not cointegrated
CPIMexResLow—Seoul	130	−2.418	2	0.316	Not cointegrated
France—Seoul	134	−2.702	4	0.199	Not cointegrated

Source See Table 5

pairs of prices selected from Table 6 and the residuals of regressing one on the other (dashed lines). Figure 10 shows some examples of non-cointegrated pairs of prices. Logically, only the residuals (dashed lines) from pairs including Osaka or Southern Korea rice prices do not present a stable mean. Dobado et al. (2015) showed there was a strong degree of market integration in Japan at that time (with a sample of rice prices in eight Japanese markets) and so, Osaka has been chosen in this work as a representative market for Japan as a whole.

However, one thing is that most of the price series analyzed are cointegrated and another question is what is the cause of this long-run relation

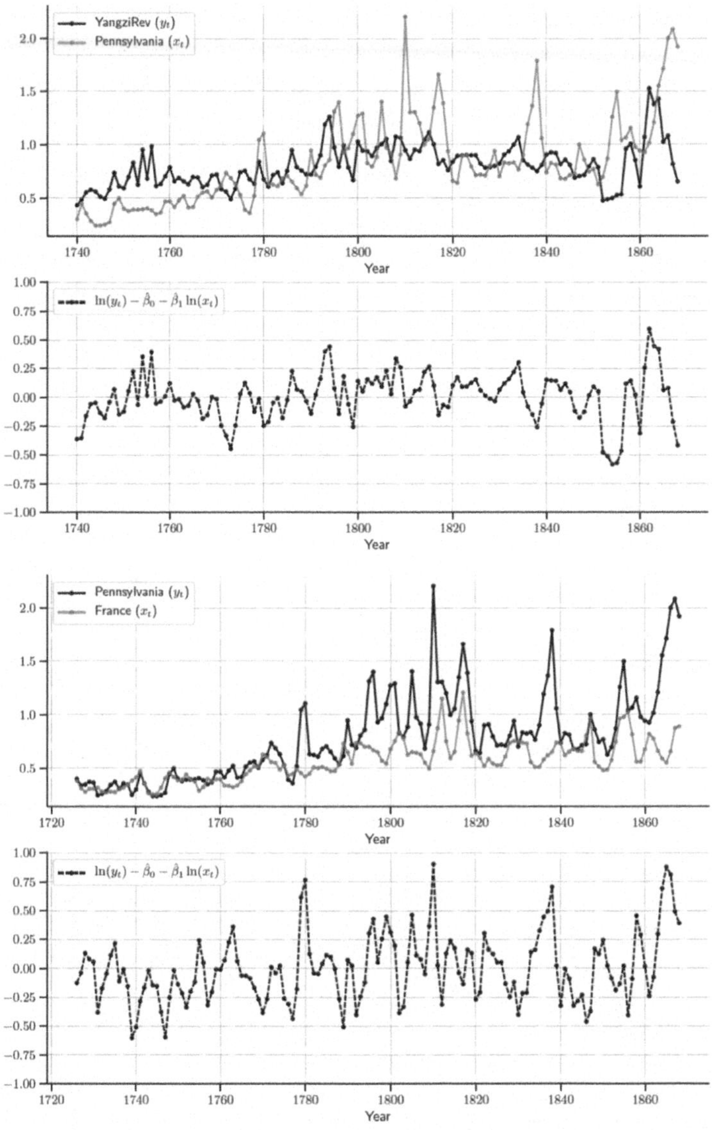

Fig. 9 Pairwise relationships of some prices worldwide (examples of cointegrated series from Table 6). Top: price levels. Bottom: residuals from the regression of one price on the other (*Source* See Table 5)

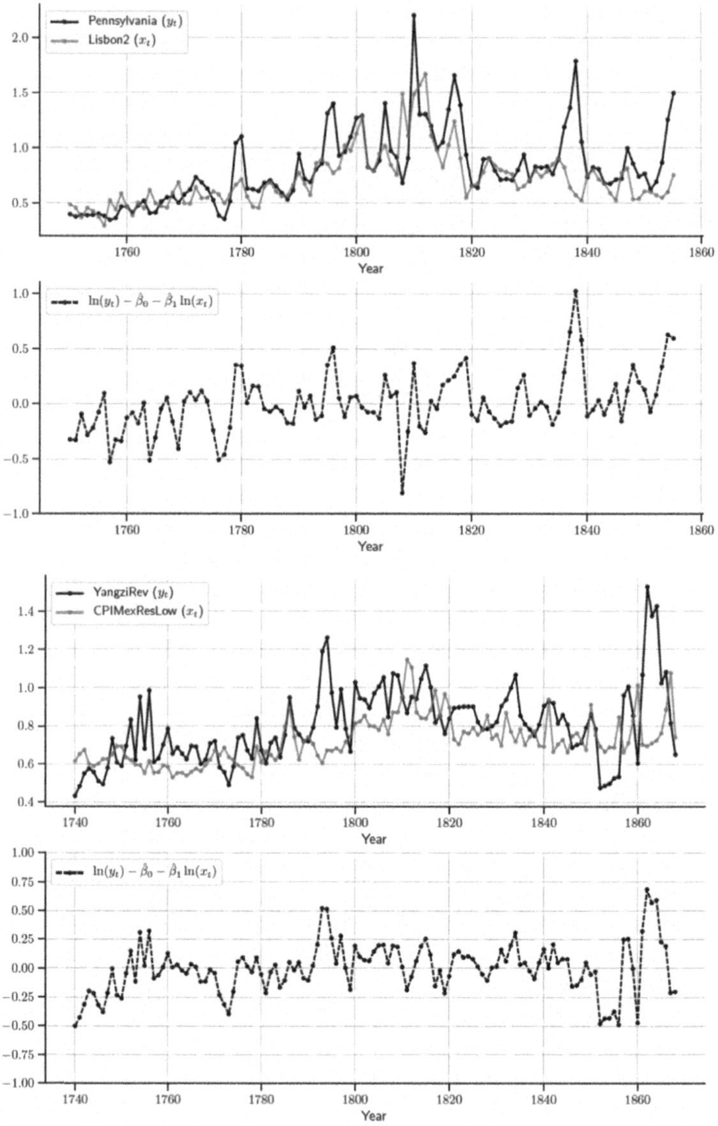

Fig. 9 (continued)

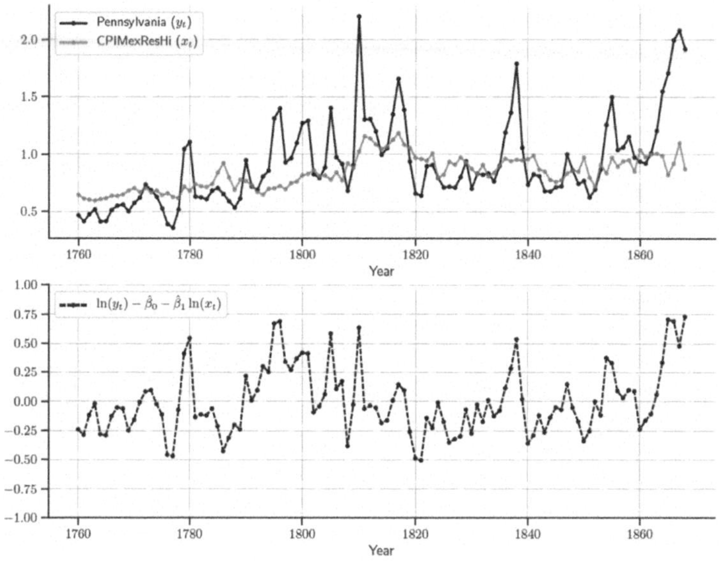

Fig. 9 (continued)

of prices in those, in many cases, quite different economies. As previously said in this chapter, our hypothesis is that Hispanic American silver production, from which New Spain was the most important part, could have been the hidden force behind the curtains driving the price comovements. A visual inspection does not reject this hypothesis, as the evolution in time of New Spain silver production also draws a similar inverted U-shape. Figure 11 presents some charts that jointly depict silver production in New Spain and price series previously analyzed. Some price series (specifically of grain) are now named with a "C" at the end because they include a dummy correction for removing the impact of the so-called *Year Without Summer*.[23] In most of the cases, the dramatic reduction of silver production suffered around years 1810–1812 seemed to have a

[23]The year 1816 is known as the Year Without a Summer (also the Poverty Year, the Summer that Never Was, Year There Was No Summer, or Eighteen Hundred and Froze to Death) because severe climate abnormalities derived from the eruption of the Tambora volcano caused average global temperatures to decrease by 0.4–0.7 °C. This resulted in major food shortages and dramatic increases in prices across the Northern Hemisphere.

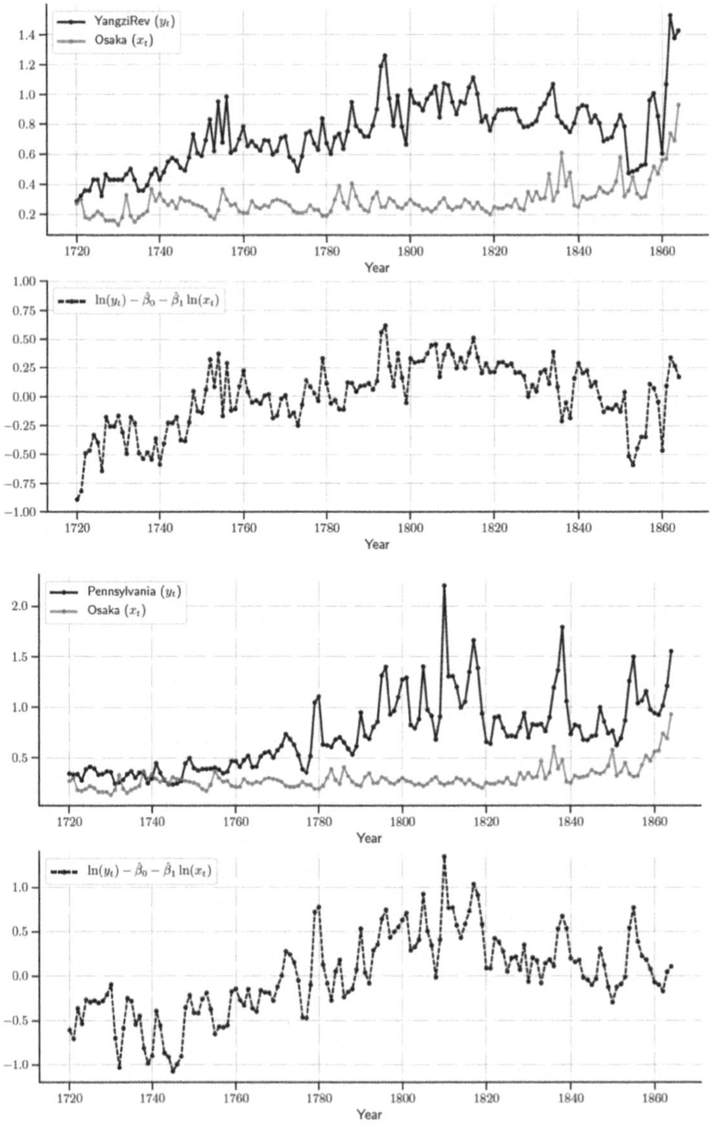

Fig. 10 Pairwise relationships of some prices worldwide (examples of non-cointegrated series from Table 6). Top: price levels. Bottom: residuals from the regression of one price on the other

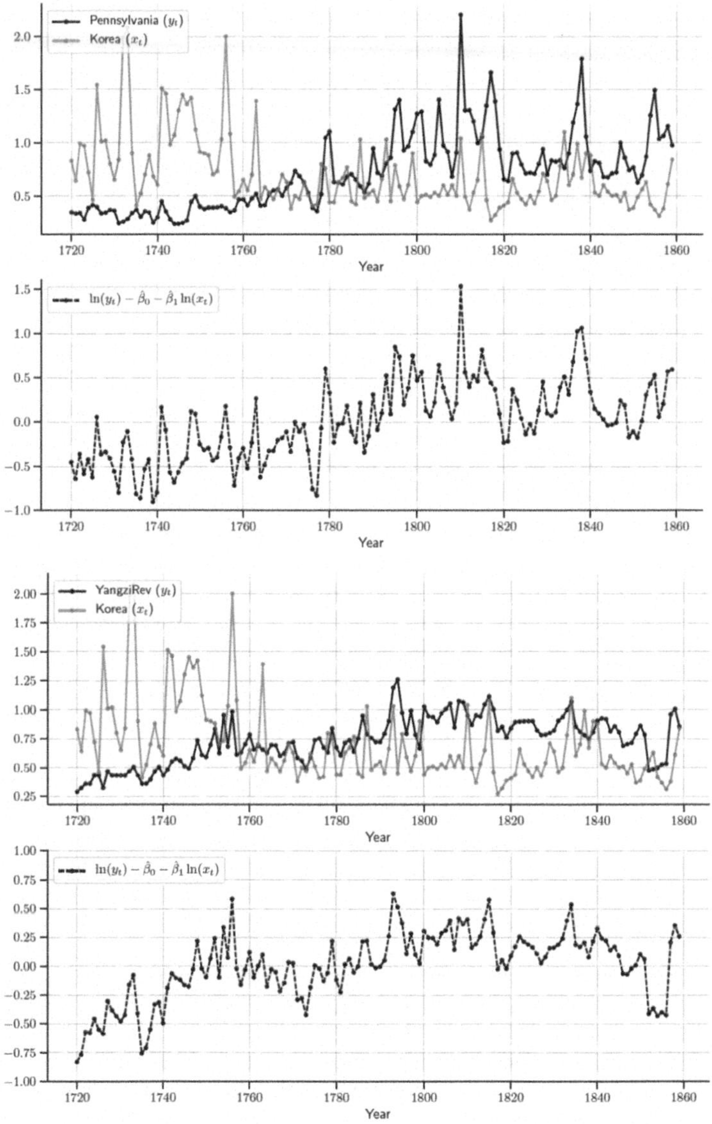

Fig. 10 (continued)

Fig. 11 Evolution of the (logs of) grain prices in different cities and the (log of) silver production in New Spain and Mexico (*Source* see Table 5)

remarkable impact in price series, generally around three years latter or so (although this delay in the response likely depends on the idiosyncrasy of each economy, like distance from New Spain, degree of openness, dependence on silver, etc.). Unfortunately, we do not find a clear statistical effect in all the cases, probably due to the instability of the relationship and the different lags in the response across markets. In such a long period, more than a century in most of the cases, we think that the relation between the production of silver and prices could certainly vary in time and intensity, which violates the assumption of constant parameters and makes the identification more difficult.

Bearing this in mind, instead of a formal statistical test, we decide to globally depict the price growth rates in different periods for the data presented in Map 1. Figure 12 illustrates the results of this calculation. All the series are separated in two periods regarding New Spain silver production: (1) the golden period, which we roughly delimit from 1751 to 1811 (period of accelerated growth; see Fig. 1), and (2) the collapse and slow recovery period, which we delimit from 1812 to 1840 (period of dramatic fall and posterior low production; see, again, Fig. 1). The choice of year 1840 at the end of the second period has more to do

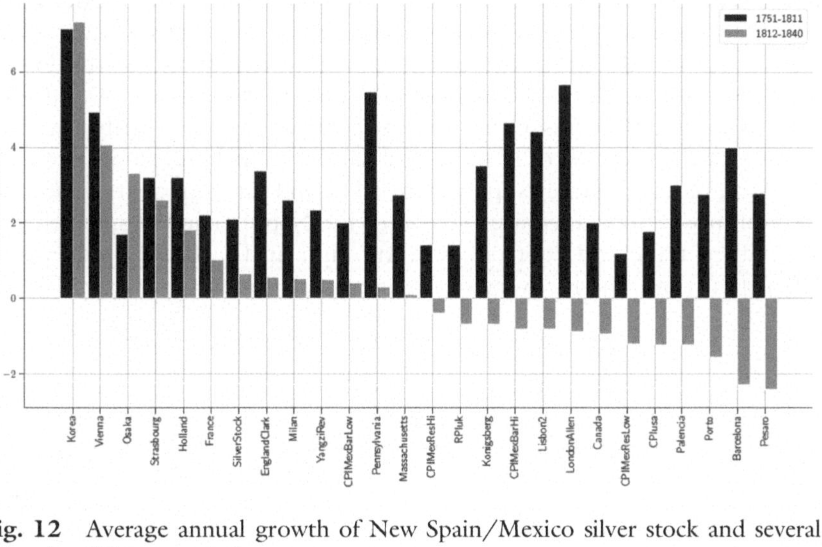

Fig. 12 Average annual growth of New Spain/Mexico silver stock and several prices in different periods

with the size of our series than with any specific event date.[24] The series in Fig. 12 are sorted by its growth rate in the second period, 1812–1840. The main conclusions drawn from this graph are the following: (i) New Spain/Mexico silver stock grew by more than 2% per year during the first period, while it did so by around 0.5% in the second one[25]; (ii) only Southern Korea and Osaka (precisely the most isolationist countries and independent of American silver) reveal a higher growth in prices in the second period than in the first one; (iii) Vienna and Strasbourg (two European inland markets) show a small difference between their annual growth in prices of the periods (less than 1 per cent point); and, (iv) the remaining markets exhibit a remarkable difference in their inter-period prices growth rates and most of them present an average inflation around 2% in the first period and around 0% or below in the second one. This markets which could be included in the above mentioned *integrated economies club* are: Holland, France, England (London, UK RPI), Italy (Milan, Pesaro), China (Yangzi delta), New Spain (New Spain CPIs), the United States (Pennsylvania, Massachusetts, USA CPI), Spain (Barcelona, Palencia, Arévalo), Portugal (Lisbon, Porto) and Königsberg.

As a consequence of these results one could wonder why a much lower, but still positive, growth rate of silver stock could imply such a negative inflation in some markets. Our hypothesis is that several important events took place around the 1820s. First, even if the New Spain silver stock growth rate was slightly above zero, the truth is that these figures do not take into account the amount of silver coins that disappeared annually. Even assuming that this value was low, this could have easily reverted the sign of the increase of silver in circulation by making it negative and, therefore, reduced money supply from 1811 and for some years. A second event of most importance was the end of the Napoleonic Wars, which had constrained trade and kept prices pretty high up to 1815 or so. Finally, also at that time, the recovery of the previously mentioned *Year Without*

[24] Robustness checks have been performed, by changing de initial date in period (1) and the final one in period (2). These shifts do not vary the result of the analyze.

[25] We define silver stock as the cumulated silver production starting from 1700. We have checked the impact of changing the starting date from which we cumulate silver production to 1600. This, logically, reduces the annual increase of silver stock (as the initial stock is bigger) but it does so in both periods and, therefore, the conclusions are pretty similar.

Summer took place, which had caused agricultural prices to peak as a consequence of the extraordinary negative supply shock.

Concluding Remarks and Further Research

This chapter is an attempt to provide historical, quantitative and statistical evidence on the role played by the production—largely exported—of silver in New Spain/Mexico in the world's commercial and monetary systems between, roughly, 1750 and 1849. In those years, New Spain/Mexico was by far the main world silver producer. In 1810, after several decades of remarkable growth, its production suffered a collapse to which an incomplete and slow recovery followed after 1821. This change, from abundance to scarcity, could not but have far-reaching consequences on an international monetary system in which silver greased the wheels of economic activity (see Abad and Palma 2021; De Zwart and Flynn 2021). Those consequences were reinforced by the similar trend registered in the other Hispanic American silver-producing countries.

Our research confirms previous claims on the extent and intensity of the economic integration across distant parts of the world long before the beginning of the—canonical—globalization of the nineteenth century. Hispanic American silver—mainly in the form of reliable, worldwide-accepted *reales de a ocho*—was indispensable for the continuity of the complex and fascinating inter- and intra-continental economic ties that were developed during almost three centuries.

Thus, a major conclusion of this chapter is that, despite differences in political and military shocks, consumption patterns, trade policy, economic development and monetary regimes, the correlation of prices within the West—or at least an important part of it—and between West and East—including China but neither Japan nor Korea—emerged before it is usually assumed. These countries, linked thanks to the Hispanic silver, made up what we name an *integrated economies club*. The price dynamics of this international area is divided by the 1810s into a pre-date phase of inflation and post-date phase of deflation. The difference between periods is clearly perceptible in both the West and the East, albeit not in the isolated Japan and Southern Korea. Inflation is already generally observable in the decades preceding the "abnormal" conditions resulting from the military conflicts of 1792–1815 and their monetary and financial consequences on prices. Admittedly, while major economic players undertook fiscal and monetary policies that led to deflation in the post-Napoleonic Wars period, the price movements that followed cannot be solely attributed to these factors. As we have shown, other, major events led to monetary disruptions in America and Asia.

Varied evidence provided in this chapter suggests that changes in the rhythm of silver production have some non-minor explanatory likelihood regarding our finding of generalized comovements of prices that adopt the shape of and inverted-U centered in the 1810s.

Recently we have been able to start building a reliable series of legal silver exports from New Spain/Mexico. While similarities with the series of production may be observed, differences also exist. At first sight, it seems that it might correlate even better, especially after 1810, with the evolution of international prices. Thus, we could conduct a deeper statistical analysis in order to test the robustness of our hypothesis and compare its results with those presented in this chapter.

Acknowledgements We thank Juan H. Flores and Andrés Calderón for their work in a previous version of this document.

References

Abad, Leticia Arroyo, and Nuno Palma. 2021. "The Fruits of *El Dorado*: The Global Impact of American Precious Metals." In *The Fruits of the Early Globalization*, edited by R. Dobado-González and A. García-Hiernaux. Cham: Palgrave Macmillan.

Allen, Robert, Tommy Murphy, and Eric Schneider. 2012. "The Colonial Origins of the Divergence in the Americas: A Labour Market Approach." *The Journal of Economic History* 72: 863–894.

Bassino, Jean-Pascal. 2006. "Market Integration and Famines in Early Modern Japan, 1717–1857." https://federation.ens.fr/ydepot/semin/texte0708/BAS2007MAR.pdf.

Bhattacharya, Bhaswati. 2008. "Making Money at the Blessed Place of Manila: Armenians in the Madras–Manila Trade in the Eighteenth Century." *Journal of Global History* 3 (1): 1–20.

Bordo, Michael D. 1984. "The Gold Standard the Traditional Approach." In *A Retrospective on the Classical Gold Standard, 1821–1931*, edited by Michael D. Bordo and A. Schwarz. Chicago: University of Chicago Press.

Bowen, Huw. 2010. "Bullion for Trade, War, and Debt-Relief: British Movements of Silver to, Around, and from Asia, 1760–1833." *Modern Asian Studies* 44 (3): 445–475.

Calderón-Fernández, Andrés, Rafael Dobado-González, and Alfredo García-Hiernaux. 2019. "Del 'real de a ocho' a los muchos pesos: plata, precios y tipos de interés en Hispanoamérica y el resto del mundo, 1750–1850." In *Estudios de Historia Económica del Banco de España*, 75. Madrid: Banco de España.

Cárdenas, Enrique. 2003. *Cuándo se originó el atraso económico de México.* Madrid: Biblioteca Nueva.

Challú, Amílcar, E., and Aurora Gómez Galvarriato. 2015. "Mexico's Real Wages in the Age of the Great Divergence, 1730–1930." *Revista de Historia Económica* 33 (1): 83–122.

Chen, Chau-Nan. 1975. "Bimetallic Exchange Rates in China, 1650–1850: A Historical Example of Optimum Currency Areas." *Journal of Money, Credit and Banking* 7 (3): 359–376.

Cheung, Sui-wai. 2013. "Copper, Silver, and Tea. The Question of Eighteenth-Century Inflation in the Lower Yangzi Delta." In *The Economy of Lower Yangzi Delta*, edited by Billy K. L. So, 118–132. New York: Routledge.

Cipolla, Carlo. 1999. *La odisea de la plata española.* Barcelona: Crítica.

Clark, Gregory. 2017. "What Were the British Earnings and Prices Then? (New Series)." Measuring Worth. https://www.measuringworth.com/ukearncpi/.

Clark, George N., and Hamilton Earl Jefferson. 1934. "The Price Revolution." *The Economic History Review* 5 (1): 128–130.

Coatsworth, John, H., and Jeffrey G. Williamson. 2004. "Always Protectionist? Latin American Tariffs from Independence to Great Depression." *Journal of Latin American Studies* 36 (2): 205–232.

Craig, Lee, and Concepción García Iglesias. 2010. "Business cycles." In *The Cambridge Economic History of Modern Europe, Volume 1, 1700–1870*, edited by Sephen Broadberry and Kevin H. O'Rourke. Cambridge: Cambridge University Press.

Crouzet, François. 1964. "Wars, Blockade, and Economic Change in Europe, 1792–1815." *The Journal of Economic History* 24 (4): 567–588.

Demigny, Louis. 1964. *La Chine et l'Occident: le commerce à Cantona au XVIIIe siècle.* Paris: SEVPEN.

De Vries, Richard. 2003. "Connecting Europe and Asia: A Quantitative Analysis of the Cape-Route Trade." In *Global Connections and Monetary History, 1470–1800*, edited by Dennis O. Flynn, Arturo Giráldez, and Richard Von Glahn. Aldershot: Ashgate.

De Zwart, Pin, and Dennis Flynn. 2021. "The Significance of Early Globalization: Arguments and Evidence." In *The Fruits of the Early Globalization*, edited by R. Dobado-González and A. García-Hiernaux. Cham: Palgrave Macmillan.

Dobado, Rafael, and Gustavo Marrero. 2014. "El mining-led growth en el México borbónico, el papel del Estado y el coste económico de la independencia." In *Oro y plata en los inicios de la economía global: de las minas a la moneda*, coordinated by Bernd Hausberger and A. Ibarra, 177–216. Mexico City: El Colegio de México.

Dobado, Rafael, Alfredo García-Hiernaux, and David E. Guerrero. 2012. "The Integration of Grain Markets in the Eighteenth Century: Early Rise of Globalization in the West." *The Journal of Economic History* 72 (3): 671–707.

Dobado, Rafael, Alfredo García-Hiernaux, and David E. Guerrero. 2015. "West Versus East: Early Globalization and the Great Divergence." *Cliometrica* 9 (2): 235–264.

Flandreau, Marc. 1996. "The French Crime of 1873: An Essay on the Emergence of the International Gold Standard, 1870–1880." *The Journal of Economic History* 56: 4862–4897.

Flynn, Dennis O., and Arturo Giráldez. 1995. "Born with a "Silver Spoon": The Origin of World Trade in 1571." *Journal of World History* 6 (2): 201–221.

Flynn, Dennis O., and Arturo Giráldez. 2004. "Path Dependence, Time Lags and the Birth of Globalization: A Critique of O'Rourke and Williamson." *European Review of Economic History* 8: 81–108.

Flynn, Dennis O., and Marie A. Lee. 2013. "East Asian Trade Before/After 1590s Occupation of Korea: Modeling Imports and Exports in Global Context." *Asian Review of World Histories* 1 (1): 117–149.

Gayer, Arthur D., Walt W. Rostow, and Anna Jacobson. 1953. *The Growth and Fluctuation of British Economy, 1790–1850*. 2 vols. Oxford: Clarendon Press.

Giráldez, Arturo. 2021. "The Last Link of an Emergent Global Economy: The Manila Galleon." In *The Fruits of the Early Globalization*, edited by R. Dobado-González and A. García-Hiernaux. Cham: Palgrave Macmillan.

Irigoin, María Alejandra. 2009a. "Gresham on Horseback: The Monetary Roots of Spanish American Political Fragmentation in the Nineteenth Century." *The Economic History Review* 62 (3): 551–575.

Irigoin, María Alejandra. 2009b. "The End of a Silver Era: The Consequences of the Breakdown of the Spanish Peso Standard in China and the United States, 1780s–1850s." *Journal of World History* 20 (2): 207–243.

Lerdo de Tejada, Miguel. 1853 (1967). *Comercio exterior de México desde la Conquista hasta hoy*. Mexico City: Banco Nacional de Comercio Exterior.

Lin, Man-houng. 2006. *China Upside Down. Currency, Society and Ideologies, 1808–1856*. Cambridge: Harvard University Asia Center.

Martín Aceña, Pablo. 1992. "Los precios en Europa durante los siglos XVI y XVII: Estudio comparativo." *Revista de Historia Económica* X (3): 359–395.

McCloskey, Donald N., and J. Richard Zecher. 1984. "The Success of Purchasing Power Parity Historical Evidence and Its Implications for Macroeconomics."

In *A Retrospective on the Classical Gold Standard, 1821–1931.* National Bureau of Economic Research.

Miyamoto, Matao, and Yoshiaki Shikano. 2003. "The Emergence of the Tokugawa Monetary System in East Asian International Perspective." In *Global connections and Monetary History, 1470*–1800, edited by Dennis O. Flynn, Arturo Giráldez, and Richard Von Glahn, 169–185. Aldershot: Ashgate.

Moreno, Javier. 2001. "Precios de las subsistencias, salarios nominales y niveles de vida en Castilla la Vieja. Palencia, 1751–1861." Documento de trabajo de la AEHE, n. 0101.

Nogués, Pilar. 2005. "Análisis de la deflación española de la primera mitad del siglo XIX: una comparación internacional." *Revista de Historia Económica* 23 (2): 371–405.

Officer, Lawrence H., and Samuel H. Williamson. 2017. "The Annual Consumer Price Index for the United States, 1774–2015." Measuring Worth. https://www.measuringworth.com/uscpi/.

O'Rourke, Kevin H. 2006. "The Worldwide Economic Impact of the French Revolutionary and Napoleonic Wars, 1793–1815." *Journal of Global History* 1: 123–149.

Ricardo, David. 1811. *The High Price of Bullion: A Proof of the Depreciation of Bank Notes. The 4th ed., To Which Is Added, an Appendix, Containing Observations on Some Passages in an Article in the Edinburgh Review, On the Depreciation of Paper Currency: Also Suggestions for Securing to the Public a Currency as Invariable as Gold, With a Very Moderate Supply of That Metal.* London: J. Murray.

Rogoff, Kenneth S. 1996. "The Purchasing Power Parity Puzzle." *Journal of Economic Literature* 34 (2): 647–668.

Romero, María Eugenia. 1997. *Minería y Guerra. La economía de Nueva España, 1810–1821.* Mexico City: El Colegio de México.

Salvucci, Richard. 1987. *Textiles and Capitalism in Mexico: An Economic History of the Obrajes, 1539–1840.* Princeton, NJ: Princeton University Press.

Salvucci, Richard. 1994. "The Real Exchange Rate of the Mexican Peso, 1762–1812 a Research Note and Estimates." *The Journal of European Economic History* 23 (1): 131–140.

Salvucci, Richard. 2013. "Some Reflections on a Pamphlet by Alvaro Flores Estrada and the Monetary Consequences of Spanish American Independence/Algunas Reflexiones Sobre Un Panfleto de Álvaro Flores Estrada y Las Consecuencias Monetarias de La Independencia de La América Española." Segundas Jornadas de Historia Económica. Organized by: *Asociación Mexicana de Historia Económica*, Ciudad de México, 14–16 August.

Shiue, Carol H., and Wolfgang Keller. 2007. "Markets in China in the Eve of the Industrial Revolution." *The American Economic Review* 97 (4): 1189–1216.

Silbering, Norman. 1923. "British Prices and Business Cycles." *Review of Economics and Statistics* 5 (Suppl. 2): 223–247.

Studer, Roman. 2008. "India and the Great Divergence: Assessing the Efficiency of Grain Markets in Eighteenth- and Nineteenth-Century India." *The Journal of Economic History* 68 (2): 393–437.

Tedde de Lorca, Pedro. 1987. "Los negocios de Cabarrús con la Red Hacienda (1780–1783)." *Revista de Historia Económica* 3: 527–552.

Tedde de Lorca, Pedro. 2009. "Oro y plata en España: un ensayo de cuantificación (1770–1850). La economía monetaria española y la independencia de América." In *Latinoamérica y España, 1800–1850. Un crecimiento económico nada excepcional*, coordinated by Enrique Llopis and Carlos Marichal. Madrid: Marcial Pons: 211–252.

Tooke, Thomas. 1838. *A History of Prices, and of the State of the Circulation, from 1793 to 1837; Preceded by a Brief Sketch of the State of Corn Trade in the Last Two Centuries*. London: Longman, Orme, Brown, Green, and Longmans.

Tortella, Gabriel, and José Luis García-Ruiz. 2013. *Spanish Monetary and Banking: A History*. London: Palgrave Macmillan.

Von Glahn, Richard. 2013. "Cycles of Silver in Chinese Monetary History." In *The Economy of Lower Yangzi Delta*, edited by Billy K. L. So. New York: Routledge.

Von Glahn, Richard. 2016. *The Economic History of China: From Antiquity to the Nineteenth Century*. Cambridge: Cambrigde University Press.

Von Humboldt, Alexander. 1814. *Political Essay on the Kingdom of New Spain*, III. London: Longman.

Wang, Yunjong. 1992. "Secular Trends of Rice Prices in the Yangzi Delta, 1638–1935." In *Chinese History in Economic Perspective*, edited by Thomas George Rawsky, 35–68. Berkeley and Los Angeles: University of California Press.

White, Charles. 1930a. *Summarized Data of Silver Production*. Washington: Department of Commerce.

White, Charles. 1930b. *Summarized Data of Gold Production*. Washington: Department of Commerce.

White, Eugene N. 1987. "¿Fueron inflacionarias las finanzas estatales en el siglo XVIII? Una nueva interpretación de los vales reales." *Revista de Historia Económica* V (3): 509–526.

The Impact of Early Iberian Globalisation on Austrian Mining Ventures

Renate Pieper

"Bella gerant alii, tu felix Austria nube" is the famous motto describing the marriage policy of the Austrian Habsburgs at the beginning of Iberian globalisation in the mid-fifteenth century. It illustrates the important political relationship between Austria and the Iberian kingdoms, bridging a distance of more than three thousand kilometres and offering the Habsburgs access to the riches from Iberia's overseas territories (Erbe 2000). Less well-known is the economic background of the marital-political relationship between the Iberian empires and the centre of the Holy Roman Empire between the fifteenth and seventeenth centuries. Although the ties between Austria and the Iberian world evolved over time, metals from the Alps and Andes—especially silver, copper, iron and quicksilver—were a constant, binding their disparate territories into a single globalised world. The study of the connection between Central Europe and the Iberian empires and their global relations during the early modern period will be at the centre of this chapter.

R. Pieper (✉)
Institute of History, University of Graz, Graz, Austria
e-mail: renate.pieper@uni-graz.at

R. Dobado-González and A. García-Hiernaux (eds.), *The Fruits of the Early Globalization*, Palgrave Studies in Comparative Global History,
https://doi.org/10.1007/978-3-030-69666-5_6

Central Europe and the Iberian Empires were connected by princely family ties from the mid-fifteenth century. The marriage of Emperor Frederick III to the niece of the Portuguese Henry the Navigator laid the foundation in 1452. In 1500, the birth of the future King of Spain and Emperor, Charles V, cemented those developments. Ties between the Austrian Habsburgs and the rulers of the Iberian Peninsula were severed by the War of the Spanish Succession in 1700. Family bonds had, therefore, been important for more than two centuries. These long lasting connections had been maintained especially through long distance trade of precious metals, iron and quicksilver. The goods were traded across large areas and circulated in faraway markets. In the early modern Austrian Hereditary Lands, silver and copper mining was concentrated in Tirol and for some periods in modern Czechia and Slovakia, iron mining in Styria and quicksilver in modern Slovenia. This analysis focuses on these mining regions as an element of royal politics with respect to the impact of Iberian globalisation in the early modern period.

Historiography has dealt with the political connections between the Iberian Peninsula and Central Europe. Friedrich Edelmayer has published extensively on the Spanish king Philipp II's patronage in Austria but did not connect this idea to mining in Austria (Edelmayer 2017). Studies on the Central European mining industry generally focus on the business of large merchant houses like the Fuggers and Welsers. Mark Häberlein analysed the activities of these important Upper German traders and bankers during the early stages of globalisation in the Iberian world, but gives little attention to the impact of overseas developments on Central European mining (Häberlein 2016). The purpose of this study is to examine the influence of the Iberian globalisation process on Central European mining regions, and the relation of those developments to royal politics.

Relations between European and overseas realms have been studied with a range of terminology. Recently, the concept of *entanglement* has been used to describe the intertwined histories of distant regions in the context of a globalising world (Conrad and Randeria 2002). This approach focuses on the two-way interactions and influences between European and non-European regions. Another term is *hybridisation*, which analyses the active adoption of foreign cultural elements in societies (Acheraiou 2011). This study uses both concepts to capture the mutual influences of European and non-European cultures and the productive integration of foreign elements in each of them during the early modern era. Nonetheless, it is important to emphasise that the impact of globalisation was neither reciprocal nor simultaneous in the regions it affected, and it led to new hybrid cultures everywhere.

This study will present a history of the entanglement and hybridisation of Austrian mining ventures in order to stress the range of Europe's transformation. Outstanding examples will illustrate general trends and mechanisms of connectivity between Austria and the Iberian Empires. In a chronological order, two noteworthy cases of the global demand for Austrian ores and its implications up to the early-sixteenth century will be discussed first. Afterwards, we will deal with three remarkable effects of the Spanish American silver mining industry on mining and politics in the Austrian Hereditary Lands from the sixteenth to the seventeenth centuries. We will cover the impact of Iberian globalisation on across all the evolutions of the Central European mining industry during the period of far-reaching Habsburg family ties.

Austrian Mining Industries as an Asset

In 1452, the Portuguese princess Eleanor married Frederick III, elected Holy Roman Emperor. Considering the benefits of this alliance, historiography assumed that the house of Habsburg had been interested in the Portuguese ventures in the Atlantic and that the house of Avis was mainly attracted by the imperial status. For the Portuguese, though, considerations beyond the status of the groom would have been important. The Hereditary Lands of the Habsburgs included profitable mining regions such as Tirol, with copper and silver deposits, and Styria, with iron ores. Frederick's realms encompassed the so called Erzberg ("ore mountain") in Styria. Its iron mines were famous—one of the largest producers of iron in Europe at the time (Pickl 1986). Trade in iron to North-Eastern Europe has been studied thoroughly (Fischer 1971). In addition, Styrian iron was traded south through the Austrian city of Leoben via Venice to the Levant and Northern Africa; another route brought iron north via the Austrian city of Steyr to Nuremberg and from there to Antwerp, although merchants from Steyr also had a chamber at the Fondaco de Tedeschi in Venice. In Antwerp a large Portuguese merchant community and a Portuguese royal warehouse offered connections to Lisbon and on to Portuguese outposts overseas. Iron from the Erzberg, or "Styrian steel" as it came to be called, especially scythes, blades and nails, were in considerable demand. Commercial connections like the trade in iron formed the background of the marriage contract between Eleanor and Frederick, which had been favoured by the Portuguese aunt of Eleanor, the duchess of Burgundy, whose realms encompassed the city of Antwerp.

The marriage with the Emperor had more tangible impact for the Portuguese crown than princely rank. It offered them the ability to compete with Venice for better access to iron from Styria for the Portuguese trade in Africa. The Emperor was fully aware of the importance the alliance with Portugal had for him and the riches offered by commerce with the Iberian Peninsula and its overseas possessions. The final decoration added to his new cathedral in the Austrian city of Graz, one of his preferred residences, is telling. Construction of the church started in 1438 when Frederick had settled his position amongst the Austrian nobility. Four years after Frederick's marriage to Eleanor, in 1456, the main entry of the cathedral in Graz was decorated with coats of arms of the Holy Roman Empire, Portugal, Austria and Styria. In 1464 the building was almost finished. In less than thirty years Frederick had erected a gothic cathedral reflecting his ambitions for Austria. Erecting an imperial residence in Graz required considerable funds, raised from the levies on iron export, triggered by the Portuguese trade with Africa. Iron tools were in demand as money needed amongst other things for the African slave trade (Béavogui 2000), where Portuguese merchants were engaged and which supplied Portuguese sugar plantations on Madeira with labour. At the same time Antwerp became the mayor hub in Northern Europe for sugar trade and refining.

It is noteworthy that in 1453, one year after his marriage, Frederick III awarded the two main iron mining sites in Austria, Vordernberg and Eisenerz, the right to hold local fairs. The next year, in 1454, Empress Eleanor founded the parish church of Vordernberg (Göth 1839), and in 1556 the shields of Portugal and Austria decorated the cathedral in Graz. By that time, the first sugar mills were put into use on the Portuguese plantations of Madeira, financed by the Genoese and with know-how from Flanders (Butel 1999, p. 38). The growing demand for Styrian iron impacted on Frederick's legislation as well. Between 1459 and 1462 alone he issued four decrees concerning the iron trade (Muchar 1867, pp. 13–27). Clearly, the trade of iron supporting the Portuguese expansion into Africa strengthened the links between the Habsburg Emperor and the Portuguese monarchy and spurred increased iron production in the Austrian Alps. Further research might illuminate whether or not African demand affected the form of the iron objects produced in Styria.

In any case, the entanglement was so close that after the death of Eleanor in 1467, contacts between Austria and Portugal via Antwerp remained. In 1477, Frederick's only son, Maximilian I, married Maria of Burgundy, heiress of the duchy with an important Portuguese merchant community established in Antwerp.

In 1490, new opportunities tightened the links between the Iberian possessions overseas and Austria's mining regions. Maximilian I, the future emperor and guardian of his son Philip, Duke of Burgundy, obtained the guardianship of his cousin Sigismund, duke of Tirol as well. Sigismund was heavily indebted, despite booming silver and copper production in his realms. At the beginning of the fifteenth century new methods for silver refining had been developed. Adding lead to copper ores allowed extraction of much lower content silver (Saigern). This new metallurgical method spread across Central Europe's mining regions. So much silver was minted at Schwaz, the most important Tirolian mining site, that in 1486 Sigismund issued new large silver coins equivalent to the value of a gold ducat. These coins, called Guldiner, set the standard for the Taler, later the peso and the dollar. The guardianship of Tirol, and inheritance of the duchy after the death of Sigismund in 1496 offered Maximilian I direct access to the wealth of the silver mines. These were valuable assets for Maximilian I in his treaties with Ferdinand of Aragon. By then, Ferdinand was co-regent in Castile, king of Sicily and claimed the kingdom of Naples against the French. Ferdinand's Italian realms needed the import of silver, copper and iron for the sugar plantations in Sicily run by African slaves. Silver was especially beneficial for African trade because silver in Africa was far more valuable in terms of gold than in Europe (Kindleberger 1989, pp. 73–74). Thus, the exchange of Austrian silver for African gold offered considerable gains. In addition, copper from Tirol and iron from Styria were in demand by the Portuguese, who exported iron and copper bracelets (manillas) to Africa where they were used as money. When Castilian expansion into the Caribbean began in 1492, it demanded iron tools as a medium of exchange and to improve native technology. For Maximilian I the alliance with Ferdinand of Aragon provided two economic benefits: it improved his realm's access to the markets of Northern and Western Africa and connected his territories to the riches expected from the other side of the Atlantic. In January 1495, in Antwerp, the marriage of both children of Maximilian with Castilian infants was agreed upon. The marriage ceremonies took place in Flanders and Castile in 1497.

In addition to the alliance with Castile, Austrian contacts with Portugal intensified as well. The connections between Austrian mining and Iberian overseas expansion became very clear at the beginning of the Portuguese Estado da India. In 1498 the Portuguese explorer Vasco da Gama reached India, where the price relation between silver and gold was even more favourable to silver than in Africa, and offered huge gains relative to Europe. Thus, trading silver for Asian spices, textiles and porcelain offered more profit than paying for the exotic wares in gold (Flynn 2019). In 1505, 22 vessels commanded by Francisco de Almeida, the first Portuguese Viceroy to India, set sail from Lisbon. Despite the general policy to exclude foreign ships from Portuguese maritime ventures, in this case, the Portuguese crown authorised a merchants' consortium from Upper Germany to equip four ships of the fleet sailing to India. The German company included the Welser and the Fugger, creditors of Emperor Maximilian I. To secure their credits the German merchant houses had been allowed to engage in the Tirolian silver trade. By that time, Tirolian silver production was nearing its peak, especially at the most important mining site in Schwaz (Breitenlechner et al. 2012; Westermann 2005; Palme 2000; Egg 1964, pp. 3–10). This mining area is located near Innsbruck, the residence of Maximilian I in Tirol. To supervise the German-owned ships on their way to India the Welser Company appointed Balthasar Sprenger as factor, who started his voyage from Antwerp to Lisbon in 1503 (Elvert 2018). Sprenger was born in Vils, near Innsbruck, and his father had administered Castle Fragenstein in the vicinity of Innsbruck for duke Sigismund of Tirol before the latter was placed under the tutelage of Maximilian I. Thus, the commissioner of the German merchant houses for the voyage to India belonged to the lower Tirolian nobility and had personal links to the Emperor Maximilian I. In 1505 the Portuguese fleet—including the German-owned ships—left Lisbon and in 1506 Balthasar Sprenger returned from Asia with a rich cargo of pepper. The successful return of Balthasar Sprenger and the considerable wealth obtained by the exchange of Tirolian silver for Indian pepper led to an extensive information campaign.

In Europe, Balthasar Sprenger not only delivered Asian spices but presented the Welser an illustrated travel account. In 1508, the painter, Hans Burgkmair the Elder used Sprenger's illustrations to publish a series of woodcuts representing a triumphal procession of the "King of Cochin" with the typical inhabitants of Africa and India (Pieper 2014). It is noteworthy that Burgkmair lived in Augsburg, were the Welser and Fugger had their headquarters. Furthermore, the painter belonged to the inner circle of artists working for Maximilian I. designing woodcuts to illustrate an allegorical triumphal procession of the Emperor (Asendorf 2017, pp. 72–73). Maximilian I might have intervened so that Burgkmair designed the woodcuts for the triumphal procession of the "King of Cochin". In 1508, the same year that the Indian procession was published, Burgkmair's woodcut was copied by the printer Jan van Doesboch in Antwerp. The text of the broadsheet printed in Antwerp associated the voyage to India with the expeditions to the Americas. Sprenger's text was printed one year later in 1509, and stressed the role of the Portuguese king, but mentioned the members of the German merchant company only once. The illustration on the title page of the broadsheet shows the Habsburg coat of arms with the Austrian shield at its centre. The second woodcut displays Sprenger's coat of arms (Sprenger 1509). Accompanying the text, the broadsheet included copies of Burgkmair's woodcuts. In 1511, the painter Georg Glockendon from Nürnberg reprinted the woodcuts from the triumphal procession of Burgkmair, adding new scenery and natives from America to the triumphal procession. In depicting the Tupinamba, Glockendon used elements of their supposed anthropophagy from the broadsheet *Mundus Novus* attributed to Amerigo Vespucci, published in Augsburg in 1505. In addition, Glockendon included a reference to the Paradise presented in Albrecht Dürer's copper engraving *Adam and Eve*, printed in Augsburg in 1504 (Pieper 2018). These additions had no obvious link to the journey of Balthasar Sprenger, but added to the glory of Maximilian I and underlined his connection with the expanding Iberian Empires.

Balthasar Sprenger's impressive voyage and its further communication by various publishers illustrate the strong links between Austrian mining and the development of Iberian globalisation. A member of Maximilian I's Tirolian entourage personally supervised the exchange of Austrian silver for Indian pepper. The importance of Austrian silver for the Portuguese in India was underlined by the Portuguese exceptional concession, allowing German merchant companies to participate directly in the expedition to India. Maximilian I's ties to Iberian globalisation also strengthened the Austrian mining industry and bolstered his position in Southern Germany. Further, the ostentatious publications surrounding the success of the silver-pepper trade suggest that Maximilian I was following the example of his father, Frederick III. The latter made his alliance with Portugal public with visible representations on representative religious buildings across Austria. Half a century later, Burgkmair, the Maximilian I's court painter, spread the news of a fruitful Austrian engagement in Portuguese India (Silver 2008). The name of the artist and the quality of the imprint guaranteed public attention in the Imperial city of Augsburg. The swift reproduction of the woodcut in the Habsburg town of Antwerp and again in the Imperial city of Nuremberg is noteworthy, showing that the message was addressed to cities associated with the house of Habsburg and engaged in the handling and commerce of silver, copper and iron from Austria. The close relations with Portugal and Portuguese expansion would have created high expectations for the future of the Austrian mining industries. Nonetheless, the juxtaposition of Portuguese voyages to India with exploration in the Americas, as portrayed by Glockendon in 1511, and the shift of the centre of Habsburg propaganda from Austria to Southern Germany suggested there were considerable changes to come.

Austrian Mining Industries Contested

One hundred years later, silver production in Schwaz had almost ceased due to both the depletion of its mines and the competition from Spanish America. From 1560 on, precious metals from Spanish America rather than Austria paid for the Asian riches imported to Europe, and would continue to do so for more than two centuries. Nonetheless, links between the Austrian mining industry and Iberian overseas territories remained. Historiography stresses the adoption of Central European technologies in the Americas (Westermann 2005; Torales Pacheco 2003). The impact of newly developed American technologies on European mining sites has received less attention. This section will outline the lengthy exchange of technology between the Austrian and American mining industries, using examples of significant changes in a chronological order.

Mining in the Americas started in the Caribbean in the early 16th century. In 1528, the Welser sent miners from Saxony's silver mines to Hispaniola (the modern Dominican Republic) to improve the gold mining operations there. These miners did not stay for long time, but left for Venezuela in the search of El Dorado. Beginning in the 1530s, gold remittances to Europe from Caribbean mining and looting on the American mainland surpassed the Portuguese gold trade with Africa. American gold mining overshadowed the first silver mining attempts in the Americas as well (Pieper 1992). At first, none of these enterprises notably affected Austrian iron, copper and silver mining; silver production at Schwaz peaked in 1523. In the 1540s, however, circumstances changed for Tirol when large silver deposits were uncovered in New Spain (modern Mexico) and Upper Peru (modern Bolivia), driving massive growth in Spanish American silver production. Improvements in metallurgical processes in New Spain in 1556 were adapted to the conditions of Upper Peru in the 1570s. This led to sustained growth of silver production in Spanish America for more than half a century. At the same time, silver production at Schwaz declined from the 1540s on. In the 1550s social and religious unrest increased in Tirol. Although the depletion of Tirolian silver mines is largely attributed to the depletion of the mines at Schwaz, competition from the American silver mines was an important factor. From the mid-sixteenth century onwards, Spanish American output surpassed Central Europe.

The influx of Spanish American silver led to the development of a new minting technology in Tirol. Afterwards, this invention was adopted in Spain, and transmitted to Spanish America. During the 1550s and 1560s so much silver poured from Spanish America into Central Europe that it was profitable to introduce a new kind of minting machine in the Habsburg mint of Hall in Tirol in 1567. Instead of hammering each coin, the new machine had water driven rollers which produced silver sheets and embossed the coins afterwards (Schmitz-Esser 2013; Marsoun-Kaindl 2011). In the 1580s, when a new method for silver refining had been successfully introduced in Upper Peru, Spanish American silver remittances to Spain multiplied further. To improve the minting process in Spain, Philipp II established a new mint at Segovia, not far from his new palace at El Escorial. Despite the opposition of his advisors, he ordered a minting machine from Hall. In 1585, the new machine arrived in Segovia, accompanied by technicians from Hall. The success of the minting press in Segovia was limited by the lack of water in Central Spain. Furthermore the Segovian mint lacked silver, which was handled by the banks at Seville first and then at the court of Madrid. Moreover, most of Spanish American silver circulated unminted in the form of silver bars. Its short period of operation notwithstanding, the fame of the Tirolian minting machine survived for centuries. When King Charles III of Spain introduced his reforms in Spanish America in the late eighteenth century, he ordered the construction of a similar minting machine driven by horses instead of water in Potosí. It went to work in 1767, two hundred years after its first installation in Hall (Lane 2019).

The development of the silver mining industry in Tirol and the construction and later diffusion of the minting machine from Hall clearly illustrates the impact of early Iberian globalisation on Austrian mining in the 16th century. Tirolian silver mining remained profitable during the first American gold rush of the early sixteenth century; the premium paid for Tirolian silver in Africa, channelled through Portuguese middlemen, compensated for the costs of production; but in the second half of the century the situation changed rapidly. From the 1540s silver rather than gold from the New World poured into Central Europe. This triggered the invention of new machinery which set the standard for two centuries and spread across Europe and the Americas. In Spain the usability of the new roller machine was reduced and its installation in Potosí in the late eighteenth century met with opposition from the local mining elite. Nevertheless, the machine worked effectively until the end of the eighteenth century. In all of these cases, it was the sovereigns who induced the development and spread of new Austrian technology in response to silver production in the Americas. The entanglement between Austrian mining and Iberian globalisation, although based on economic links, was favoured and strengthened by political ties.

Besides minting, new metallurgical techniques developed as well. In this case developments in Spanish America flowed back the other way, influencing Austrian mining industries for more than two centuries. In 1556, in Mexico, Bartolomé de Medina received a patent from the Viceroy of New Spain. Medina had found a new fuel-saving method to extract silver from ores by adding mercury instead of the lead used for the Saiger process (Guerrero 2017). Furthermore, Medina determined that additional chemical agents were necessary for silver amalgamation in Spanish America. As well as salt, copper sulphat or iron sulphate (magistral) had to be added to the silver ores because American silver veins, unlike European ores, lacked those sulphates. The moistened mixture of crushed silver ores, mercury, salt and magistral was left in the open air without any heating for several weeks (método del patio). This energy-saving innovation spread rapidly across the mining sites of New Spain. It needed the support of the crown officials to circulate, as mercury mining was a royal monopoly and the most important royal mercury mines were those of Almadén in Andalusia (Dobado 1997). Ten years later, when the first silver boom in Potosí came to an end the Spanish crown sent Viceroy Francisco de Toledo to Peru and ordered him to introduce the process of silver amalgamation in Potosí, providing enough mercury to the miners. In Potosí, the climate was harsh and cold but the miners swiftly and successfully adapted the amalgamation process to the weather conditions and the ores of the Bolivian highlands. Nevertheless, it took several months to extract silver from the ores. As a result, the clergymen Alonso Barba experimented with ways of speeding up the amalgamation process. He used heated copper cauldrons, but had to avoid producing silver-copper alloys. The Spanish administration published Barba's results in Madrid in 1640. In 1676 the treatise was translated into German. In the first half of the eighteenth century, further editions appeared in Spanish, German, English and French.

Despite considerable publicity in Europe, Barba's method was not applied regularly in Potosí. The cost of the fuel and the copper pans and especially the problems with separating the silver from the copper cauldrons persisted. It was only in the second half of the eighteenth century, in 1786, that the mineralogist Ignaz von Born published, at the court of Vienna, a treatise that described the adaptation of Barba's method to the geological and climactic conditions of the Slovakian mines in the Habsburg territories. Born was a well-known courtier and freemason, acquainted to Wolfgang Amadeus Mozart who addressed Born in his opera *The Magic Flute*. Born's treatise on amalgamation in closed containers became so famous that in the next year the newly appointed General Director of Mines in New Spain, Fausto de Elhuyar, visited Vienna to meet Born during a tour through Europe before his departure to New Spain (Torales Pacheco 2003; Reinalter 1991). In New Spain, the opposition against Elhúyar (Peset 1987, p. 416) was fierce and despite Elhúyar's efforts, the privately-run silver mining enterprises did not introduce the Barba-Born method of applying heat to copper recipients to accelerate silver amalgamation. Obviously, the enormous quantities of silver ore handled in New Spain, could be amalgamated more effectively by the fuel-saving *patio method* than by the Barba-Born procedure requiring a large number of expensive copper vessels and equally costly heating. Thus, the silver boom of the late eighteenth century in New Spain was based mainly on the old process of Bartolomé de Medina. In Europe, in the Slovakian mines, the Barba-Born method did not work neither and was improved at the mining school of Freiberg in Saxony. It was this version which spread to the Habsburg silver mines and was known to Alexander von Humboldt.

The diffusion of the silver-amalgamation technique within the Habsburg territories shows that serious obstacles had to be overcome in order for industrial methodologies to spread. As in the case of the Tirolian minting machine, which was only adopted in the Andes in the late eighteenth century, the amalgamation method from New Spain also took almost two centuries to be successfully applied in the Habsburg mining regions. It is noteworthy that this happened not immediately after the War of the Spanish Succession (1701–1713), when family ties between the Iberian monarchies and Austria had been cut, but following the 1750's, when the Habsburgs approached France and Spain once again. Now, alongside political ties enlightened professional links paved the way for modernisation, hybridisation and the diffusion of technologies from the other side of the Atlantic.

Silver-amalgamation in Spanish America had an even greater effect in the Austrian mining regions. The demand for mercury rose. In Spain, the Fugger were leaseholders of the royal mercury mine at Almadén. Second in importance was the quicksilver mine of Idrija in the Austrian Hereditary Lands (in modern Slovenia). In Idrija mining operations were at first run privately (Valentinitsch 1981). But in 1580, when demand for mercury rose considerably in Peru, Archduke Charles of Inner Austria bought out the private miners of Idrija. Italian merchants, amongst them the important Genoese merchant house of the Balbi, took over the leasehold. The continuing huge demand for mercury from Spanish American mines deprived other European users of mercury from Almadén and shifted demand to Idrija, where representative buildings emerged.

As well as these mainly indirect effects of Spanish American mining on Idrija, which led to an increased demand for mercury in general, the Austrian Habsburgs tried to gain contracts with Spain to deliver mercury directly via Spain to Spanish America. During the Thirty Years War, Idrija supplied quicksilver to New Spain between 1621 and 1645. Another major contract was signed under Emperor Joseph II in 1785, and extended under his successor in 1791 (Hicinger 1860, pp. 28–29, 34, 43, 69–70; Crailsheim and Wiedenbauer 2005).

Besides furnishing Spanish American silver mines with mercury, the connection between the mining regions went further. Technology from the Peruvian mine of Huancavélica was adopted in Idrija. In 1633, an oven to separate quicksilver from crushed ore (*horno de aludeles*) was been developed in Huancavelica. The technique was brought to Almaden in 1646 and finally adopted in Idrija in 1750, where it was later improved. The time needed for the diffusion of this metallurgical innovation was less than in the cases of the silver minting machine and the silver amalgamation, but period between the innovation in Huancavelica and its implementation in the Austrian territories was still significant.

Conclusion

Mining ventures in the Austrian Hereditary Lands of the Habsburgs experienced a range of influences from Iberian globalisation during the early modern period. Silver and copper from Tirol were produced for the African and Asian markets at least until the mid-sixteenth century. Iron ore was mined in Styria, to be sold mainly in Africa and Ibero-America from the fifteenth century. Quicksilver from the mines of modern Slovenia supplied Spanish America for some decades of the seventeenth and eighteenth centuries. The relationship between the Austrian mining regions and the Iberian world evolved over time, encompassing supply for monetary purposes, like the trade in iron, copper and silver objects as well as iron tools and quicksilver for industrial application in Spanish America. Whereas during the period before the mid-sixteenth century Iberian globalisation increased the demand for Austrian mining products, after the mid-sixteenth century Spanish American silver mining *competed* with Austrian silver mining, and enhanced the demand for quicksilver. As well as impacting production in the Austrian mines, Iberian globalisation affected metallurgical processes and minting. Innovation in the Austrian mining regions responded to the growing competition from overseas. The exchange or transfer of techniques from one mining region to the other usually took decades or centuries, but saw productive adoption and hybridisation of industrial methodologies from both sides of the Atlantic. It is noteworthy that Austrian mining sites both imported and exported technologies from the Iberian empires. The broad variety of mining sites, ores, techniques and forms of influence that linked Austrian mining to the Iberian world makes it a perfect example of the entanglement and hybridisation that characterised early modern globalisation.

Bibliography

Primary Sources

Springer, Balthasar. 1509. *Die Merfart vn[d] erfarung nüwer Schiffung vnd Wege zu viln onerkanten Jnseln vnd Künigreichen von dem großmechtigen Portugalische[n] Kunig Emanuel Erforscht funden bestritten vnnd Jngenomen, Auch wunderbarliche Streyt ordenung leben wesen handlung vnd wunderwercke des volcks vnd Thyrer dar in[n] wonende findestu* ..., [Oppenheim] [VD16 S 8379]. https://mdz-nbn-resolving.de/urn:nbn:de:bvb:12-bsb00045403-6. Accessed on March 12, 2020.

Secondary Sources

Acheraiou, Amar. 2011. *Questioning Hybridity, Postcolonialism and Globalization*. London: Palgrave/Macmillan.

Asendorf, Christoph. 2017. *Planetarische Perspektiven: Raumbilder im Zeitalter der frühen Globalisierung*. Paderborn: Wilhelm Fink.

Béavogui, Facinet. 2000. "Circulation monétaire en Afrique de l'Ouest: Le cas du guinzé (Guinėe, Liberia)." In *Outils aratoires en Afrique: innovations, normes et traces*, edited by Yasmine Marzouk, Christian Seignobos, and François Sigaut, 175–190. Paris: Karthala and IRD.

Breitenlechner, Elisabeth, Marina Hilber, Joachim Lutz, Yvonne Kathrein, Alois Unterkircher, and Klaus Oeggl. 2012. "Reconstructing the History of Copper and Silver Mining in Schwaz, Tirol." *RCC Perspectives* 10 (Mining in Central Europe: Perspectives from Environmental. History), 7–20.

Butel, Paul. 1999. *The Atlantic*. London and New York: Routledge.

Conrad, Sebastian, and Shalini Randeria, eds. 2002. *Jenseits des Eurozentrismus. Postkoloniale Perspektiven in den Geschichts- und Kulturwissenschaften*. Frankfurt: Campus.

Crailsheim, Eberhard, and Eva-Maria Wiedenbauer. 2005. "Central Europe and the Atlantic World: The Mines of Idria and the American Demand for Mercury (1556–1646)." In *Latin America and the Atlantic World/El mundo atlántico y América Latina (1500–1850). Essays in Honor of Horst Pietschmann*, edited by Renate Pieper and Peer Schmidt, 297–318. Cologne/Vienna: Böhlau.

Dobado, Rafael. 1997. "Las minas de Almadén, el monopolio del azogue y la producción de plata en Nueva España en el siglo XVIII." In *La savia del Imperio. Tres estudios de economía colonial*, edited by Julio Sánchez Gómez, Guillermo Mira Delli-Zotti, and Rafael Dobado, 403–495. Salamanca: Ediciones Universidad de Salamanca.

Edelmayer, Friedrich. 2017. *Philipp II. Biographie eines Weltherrschers*, 2nd ed. Stuttgart: Kohlhammer.

Egg, Erich. 1964. "Schwaz ist aller Bergwerke Mutter." *Der Anschnitt* 16: 3–63.

Elvert, Jürgen. 2018. *Europa, das Meer und die Welt: Eine maritime Geschichte der Neuzeit*. Munich: Deutsche Verlagsanstalt.

Erbe, Michael. 2000. *Die Habsburger 1493–1918. Eine Dynastie im Reich und in Europa*. Stuttgart: Kohlhammer.

Fischer, Franz. 1971. "Die Sensenausfuhr aus Österreich nach dem Norden und Osten 1450–1650." In *Der Aussenhandel Ostmitteleuropas 1450–1650*, edited by Ingomar Bog, 286–319. Cologne and Vienna: Böhlau.

Flynn, Dennis O. 2019. "Fifteenth-Century European Silver and Chinese End-Markets." In *Italien als Vorbild? Ökonomische und kulturelle Verflechtungen europäischer Metropolen am Vorabend der 'ersten Globalisierung' (1300–1600)*, edited by Joerg Oberste and Susanne Ehrich, 163–180. Regensburg: Schnell & Steiner.

Göth, Georg. 1839. Vordernberg in der neuesten Zeit, oder geschichtliche Darstellung der Vereinigung der Radgewerken. Vienna: J. G. Heubner.

Guerrero, Saul. 2017. Silver by Fire, Silver by Mercury: A Chemical History of Refining in New Spain and Mexico, 16th to 19th Centurie. Leiden-Boston: Brill.

Häberlein, Mark. 2016. *Aufbruch ins globale Zeitalter. Die Handelswelt der Fugger und Welser*. Stuttgart: Theiss.

Hicinger, Peter. 1860. *Das Quecksilber-Bergwerk Idria: von seinem Beginne bis zur Gegenwart*. Ljubljana Ign. v. Kleinmayr u. Fedor Bamberg.

Kindleberger, Charles P. 1989. *Spenders and Hoarders: The World Distribution of Spanish American Silver 1550–1750*. Singapore: Institute of Southeast Asian Studies.

Lane, Kris. 2019. *Potosí: The Silver City that Changed the World*. Oakland: University of California Press.

Marsoun-Kaindl, Sandra. 2011. "Der Einfluss des regionalen Silberbergbaus auf die Entwicklung der fürstlichen Darstellung auf Münzen." In *Bergbau und Kunst 9. Internationaler Montanhistorischer Kongress 2010*, edited by Wolfgang Ingenhaeff and Johann Bair, vol. 1, 259–261. Innsbruck: Berenkamp.

Palme, Rudolf. 2000. "Überblick über den Stand der Forschungen zur Bergbaugeschichte Tirols. unter besonderer. Berücksichtigung der Krisen und Konjunkturen." In *Konjunkturen im europäischen Bergbau in vorindustrieller Zeit. Festschrift für Ekkehard Westermann zum 60. Geburtstag*, edited by Christoph Bartels and Markus A. Denzel, 23–36. Stuttgart: Steiner.

Peset, José Luis. 1987. "Los orígenes de la enseñanza técnica en América: El Colegio de Minería de México." In *Universidades Españolas y Americanas: época colonial*, edited by Mariano Peset, 415–431. Valencia: Consejo Superior de Investigaciones Científicas.

Pickl, Othmar. 1986. "Die Steiermark als Gewerbe- und Industrielandschaft vom Spätmittelalter bis zur Gegenwart. Zur Entstehung moderner Industriereviere in alten Fortschrittsregionen." In *Gewerbe- und Industrielandschaften vom Spätmittelalter bis ins 20. Jahrhundert*, edited by Hans Pohl, 18–36. Stuttgart: Steiner.

Pieper, Renate. 1992. "American Silver Production and West European Money Supply in the Sixteenth and Seventeenth Century." In *Economic Effects of the European Expansion, 1492–1824*, edited by José Casas Pardo, 77–98. Stuttgart: Steiner.

Pieper, Renate. 2014. "Between India and the Indies: German Mercantile Networks, the Struggle for the Imperial Crown and the Naming of the New World." In *Culture & History Digital Journal* 3 (1, January). https://doi.org/10.3989/chdj.2014.003. Accessed on March 12, 2020.

Pieper, Renate. 2018. "Amerika in Europa Europa in America: Die Geschicke transatlantischer Verflechtungen in der Frühen Neuzeit." In *Vokalpolyphonie zwischen Alter und Neuer Welt. Musikalische Austauschprozesse zwischen Europa und Lateinamerika im 16. und 17 Jahrhundert*, edited by Klaus Pietschmann and Cristina Urchueguía (Troja, Jahrbuch für Renaissancemusik 14/2015), 13–26. https://doi.org/10.17879/68139520931. Accessed on March 12, 2020.

Reinalter, Helmut, ed. 1991. *Die Aufklärung in Österreich: Ignaz von Born und seine Zeit*. Frankfurt, Bern, New York, and Paris: Peter Lang.

Schmitz-Esser, Romedio. 2013. "Roller Press Coining in the Hall Mint and Its Progress Throughout Europe. A Model for Increasing Efficency and Its Obstacles in the Early Modern Era." In *Centre for Innovation: Hall in Tirol's Mint*, edited by Ursula Kampmann and Björn Schöpe, 26–39. Hall in Tirol: Münze Hall.

Silver, Larry. 2008. *Marketing Maximilian. The Visual Ideology of a Holy Roman Emperor*. Princeton and Oxford: Princeton University Press.

Torales Pacheco, María Cristina. 2003. "Apuntes para el estudio de la presencia de la Ilustración alemana en México." In *Jahrbuch für Geschichte Lateinamerikas* 40: 123–150.

Valentinitsch, Helfried. 1981. Das landesfürstliche Quecksilberbergwerk Idria 1575–1659, Produktion, Technik, rechtliche und soziale Verhältnisse, Betriebsbedarf, Quecksilberhandel. Graz: Historische Landeskommission für Steiermark.

von Muchar, Albert. 1867. *Geschichte der Steiermark als Herzogthum in den Jahren 1458–1558*. Graz: Leuschner-Lubensky.

Westermann, Ekkehard. 2005. "Gold, Silver, and Copper in the European Economies and Their External Trade Relations from the End of the 15th to the End of the 16th Century." In *The road to Japan: Social and Economic Aspects of Early European-Japanes Contacts*, edited by Josef Kreiner, 63–90. Bonn: Bier'sche Verlagsanstalt.

Trade and Consumption of Textiles in the Early Globalization

“The Last Link of an Emergent Global Economy: The Manila Galleon”

Arturo Giráldez

The Age of Commerce of the Philippines Before the Galleons

The Pacific Ocean’s 63.8 million square miles represent 46% of the Earth’s water cover and one third of its total surface, making it larger than all of the globe’s landmasses together. The difficulties of a sailing ship crossing such a body of water explain why continents on either side did not communicate until the foundation of Manila on the Philippine Islands in 1571.

The 7,100 islands of the Philippine archipelago form an arc that extends from Taiwan and southern China to Borneo. The largest islands are Luzon and Mindanao with a combined extension that represents 95% of the country’s total area. The rugged relief of island’s geography has shaped a settlement pattern of relatively small communities located on rivers, lakes and seacoasts. At the time of Spanish arrival, this rough-hewn geography contributed to the Philippines’s diverse polities, which encompassed Muslim sultanates, chiefdoms of varied size and complexity, upland

A. Giráldez (✉)
Department of Modern Languages and Literatures, University of the Pacific, Stockton, CA, USA
e-mail: agiraldez@pacific.edu

R. Dobado-González and A. García-Hiernaux (eds.), *The Fruits of the Early Globalization*, Palgrave Studies in Comparative Global History,
https://doi.org/10.1007/978-3-030-69666-5_7

tribal groups, and small bands of hunters and gatherers (Lee Junker 1999, pp. 16, 61). The Islands belong to the Pacific "ring of fire" that causes volcanic activity and earthquakes, as well as deposits of gold, silver, and copper.

The archipelago has a wet season that coincides with monsoons, known to the Spaniards as *vendavales*, which blow from June through part of September. Dry months correspond to the northeastern monsoon, the *brisas*, which begin in November or December. Tropical cyclones, called typhoons or, locally, *baguios*, are prevalent between July and November. Each year these tropical storms move west from the Caroline and Mariana Islands to the Philippines. The Manila galleons' track coincided with the typhoon belt, obviously a dangerous route for any vessel. In addition to dangers posed by cyclones and adverse winds, the archipelago's shoreline and submerged hazards were constant dangers to these heavy sailing galleons.

Historically, demographics in the Philippines followed Southeast Asia's prevailing trends. At the time of Spanish arrival, total population of the Philippine archipelago was between 1.25 and 1.57 million people. A large proportion of islanders were concentrated in trading centers or areas of intensive wet rice cultivation, in Ilocos, Pampanga, and Manila (Reid 1988, vol. 1, p. 45; Corpuz 2005, p. 618; Newson 2009, p. 251). Filipinos engaged in subsistence agriculture and did not produce surpluses. Until the late eighteenth century, there was little population growth.

Before Spain's era of colonization, the majority of the archipelago's inhabitants resided in small communities called barangays ruled by a chief or datu. These datu, in addition to exercising political and judicial authority were leaders of trading expeditions and maritime raids. Raiding rival settlements resulted in the seizure of a conquered community's accumulated export commodities, and people in order to eliminate unwanted competition. Captured slaves augmented the agricultural labor force, allowed local artisans to concentrate on making goods for exchange, and freed people to engage in trade. Foreign merchants redirected their voyages to better-supplied ports of call, increasing datus riches. When the Spaniards arrived in the sixteenth century, all Filipino groups were engaged in raiding for captives (Scott 1985, p. 22). There was a widespread servile dependent class some of them captured in raids, or because men pledged themselves for loans of food, for dowries, etc.

Lively commercial activities formed a tight network throughout the islands as shown by use of gold dust, and "gold-cast pellets stamped with Tagalog characters" of 0.09 to 2.00 grams used as currency since the tenth century. In the Visayas salt was small change before the colonial era (Arcilla 1998, p. 41; Alzina 1996, p. 205).

Different from the lowland Tagalogs were native groups in the highlands. Their social and economic lives were quite diverse; they ranged from small bands of hunter-gatherers to tribes of swidden cultivators and groups with intensive agriculture ruled by emerging hierarchies. The upland peoples received names like Tinguians, Zambals, Igorots, and Ifugaos in colonial sources. Igorots, who were located in gold mining regions, are particularly relevant. Before the conquest, Agoo in the Ilocos region—known to the Spaniards as *Puerto del Japón* (Japan's Port)—was a trading colony in which Chinese and Japanese merchants bartered for gold. The Igorot's mines were not the only source of bullion in the Philippines; in fact, the most productive gold mines were in the Visayas. In the last years of the seventeenth century, the governor confided to Italian traveler Gemelli Careri that metal collected by the natives was equivalent to 200,000 gold pesos. Bullion percolated through economic networks of the islands before reaching international markets of which India exercised the highest demand. Filipinos also harvested cowry shells (*Cypraea moneta*) from the coasts which they sold by weight to Siam, Cambodia, Malaysia, and Bengal.

After the "Black Death" of 1346–1348, there was a surge in demand for exotic products in the northern hemisphere coinciding with two centuries of growth in wealth and population in Ming China, along with the revitalization of the spice trade to Europe. Anthony Reid considers 1405—the year of the first trade mission under Chinese Admiral Zheng-He—to signal the beginning of Southeast Asia's "age of commerce" (1993, p. 12). Filipino societies participated in regional trend propelled by population growth and growing markets. Tropical forest hunter-gatherers and upland tribal groups exchanged products with more complex organized chiefdoms that engaged in economic circuits encompassing states in Southeast Asia, as well as China and Japan.

Throughout centuries, Islam had expanded across the Indian Ocean, and Muslim mercantile communities had appeared in East Africa, India, and Southeast Asia. This network of long distance trade that connected Southeast Asia with African, Middle Eastern, and European markets constituted in the words of Henry Scott a "Mediterranean Connection" (1992, pp. 24–39). Points of departure of this trade network were the Moluccas and Banda archipelagos. From these islands, cloves and nutmeg arrived at Malacca and Sumatra. Arab and Indian vessels delivered spices and other Asian products to Africa, the Red Sea and Persian Gulf. From Egyptian and Syrian ports (Alexandria, Beirut, Cairo, and Damascus), Venetians distributed these commodities to European markets. Predominance of Muslim merchants in the Indian Ocean and Southeast Asia—Turks, Persians, and Arabs—lasted until the first two decades of the seventeenth century at which point European powers, principally the Dutch, displaced them (Reid 1992, p. 494).

During China's Sung dynasty, (960–1279) exchanges between the Philippines and the Empire grew substantially. Sultanates and chiefdoms in the Philippines and Brunei were intermediaries between China and the Spice Islands. From the Moluccas, and the Banda Islands, cloves nutmeg, mace, and sandalwood arrived at Jolo in the Sulu Islands where hardwoods, pearls, forest and maritime products joined the cargo. These commodities followed a western route in the direction of Java and Malacca or travelled northward to the Philippines where local products—gold, wax, betel nuts, cotton goods, shells, animal skins, carabao horns, slaves, etc.—were added to the freight. These goods transported to southern China received in return porcelain, ironware, lead, tin, glass beads, copper gongs, bells, silks, and "trade gold" (Legarda 1999, p. 10).

In 1368, the Ming established a system of officially recognized trade missions as a means of controlling trade. In 1373, the first embassy from Luzon arrived with tributes (Lee Junker 1999, p. 219). The late fourteenth and early fifteenth centuries witnessed a peak in missions to the Chinese court, which, was related to increased competition among northern communities in Luzon to control the Moluccas-Borneo-Luzon-Fujian eastern trade route. As well as, rivalries in the southern Philippines for hegemony along the Moluccas-Java-Melaka route. Both processes resulted in trade supremacy of Manila in the north and Sulu in the south.

Maynila, "the Place of the Water Lilies,' was a thriving market in 1570 with a plaza and quarters for Chinese and Japanese merchants. This enclave was located on routes connecting Ming China, Japan, the Spice Islands and Southeast Asia. There, large Chinese junks brought goods and smaller boats manned by Muslim Filipinos distributed them among numerous islands. A Filipino merchant class established in Malacca, the entrepōt between the Indian Ocean and the China Sea where merchants from Luzon became rich businessmen. Each year two or three vessels sailed from Maynila to Malacca carrying gold, forest products, and foodstuffs.

Spanish Settlement in the Philippines

Shortly after Hernán Cortés' conquest of México, a number of expeditions were organized to reach the Spice Islands. Failure of the Spanish voyages resulted nonetheless in increased geographical knowledge and familiarity with Asian trade. When Philip II became king in 1556, a royal order charged Viceroy Luis de Velasco of New Spain with the organization of a new fleet for "the discovery of the Western Islands toward the Moluccas," (Blair and Robertson 1903, vol. 2, pp. 80–81). Andrés Urdaneta—an accountant in the 1542 Ruy López de Villalobos' expedition and at the time an Agustinian friar—received a letter from the king ordering him to put his knowledge and experience in the service of a planned enterprise under command of Miguel López de Legázpi.

With Legázpi in charge and with Urdaneta,who spoke Malay, acting as chief pilot, two galleons, three pinnaces (small boats), and a patache (tender), left the port of Navidad on the Mexican coast on November 21, 1564. After reaching the Philippines, Legázpi established an enclave on the island of Cebu and sent a ship back to New Spain with Urdaneta on board. On Monday October 8, 1565, after four months and eight days at sea, they entered the port of Acapulco. Urdaneta marked a map with the route details of winds and geographical features establishing the course of galleons for the next 250 years.

During his time in Cebu, Legázpi had heard about the Island of Luzon where Japanese and Chinese merchants came to trade every year. Spaniards were familiar with connections between Mindanao, Malacca, Borneo, and the Moluccas. The puzzling question for Legázpi was the presence of Chinese merchant junks in the archipelago. After a skirmish with a Bornean vessel, he received an answer. The ship had a Portuguese owner, but the cargo belonged to the king of Brunei. Legázpi returned the vessel to its owners, and commenced an exchange with the Moro pilot, which Urdaneta translated from Malay to Spanish. By combining new information with previous knowledge, a clear picture emerged of Philippine trade networks. Large Chinese junks went to Manila and smaller ships throughout the islands delivered cargo. Settlements in Mindoro guaranteed a Muslim—"Moro" to the Spaniards—monopoly on inter-island distribution: Indian products arrived from Malacca to ports in Butuan and Cebu. In addition, the pilot mentioned a route to the Moluccas that bypassed the Sulu Islands and the island of Sarangani. This state of affairs dictated Legázpi's future strategy, which aimed to eliminate Moro intermediaries in island exchanges. With varying degrees of success, Spaniards followed this course of action between 1570 and 1582 followed by the Moro Wars. In the words of Gregorio F. Zaide, "the conquistadors of Spain met their match in Islam's warriors of Mindanao and Sulu, because after 300 years of fighting, the Moros preserved their independence, religion, and culture" (1972, vol. 1, p. 306).

In 1570, Legázpi wrote to Mexico seeking guidance regarding the next step in Spain's strategy. Cebu was the ideal location to occupy if trade with the Spice Islands was the aim. This implied conflict with the Portuguese. Meanwhile, for trade with China the settlement ought to be in Luzon. Tributes from Visaya people subsidized military operations and soldiers continued in expectation of future encomiendas (grants of land). Native contributions largely financed colonization of the Philippines (Alonso Álvarez 2009, p. 92). On June 24 of 1571, Manila became capital of the Philippines and the center of colonial power.

Spanish arrived in the Philippines in 1565 during a propitious period. The climate had improved since the 1470s and heavier monsoon rains increased agricultural yield, encouraging cultivation of marginal lands (Lieberman 2009, vol. 2, p. 33). To increase agricultural production the Spaniards would introduce buffalos and the plow in order to sustain the colonial economy. The new arrivals met fierce resistance from sultanates in the south, but Islam had not yet spread widely throughout the archipelago and the Dutch were still absent, giving Spaniards four decades to consolidate their position. Yet perhaps most importantly silver production was increasing in Mexico and Peru, which enabled the newcomers to penetrate established trade networks and expand across the Pacific. The Spanish position improved further in 1567 when the Ming emperor rescinded the ban on private trade.

Manila was the Pacific linchpin of this global commercial network. Juan Pablo Carrión, an officer who served under Legazpi, saw the future clearly: "No profit can be expected from the islands until trading connections can be opened with China and the rest of the Indies" (In Schurz 1959, p. 33). During early decades in the Philippines, the situation for the Spanish was precarious, but for he empire, at large, portentous events were taking place. In 1578 Sebastião I, King of Portugal, died fighting in Morocco. His successor and granduncle, Cardinal Dom Henrique, was advanced in years and in poor health and he soon passed away. In January 1580, troops under the Duke of Alba arrived in Lisbon, and one year later, Spain's Philip II sovereign of the kingdom in 1581. Spain and Portugal were united until 1640.

Trade with China was flourishing. In 1587 Santiago de Vera president of the Philippine Audiencia, reported to the king arrival of a large number of junks with plenty of merchandise, Vera estimated that “in New Spain they gain two hundred percent and in certain goods much more” (Colín 1900, vol. 2, p. 356). It was clear that the Manila galleon could expect a quite profitable future.

Colonists were mindful of discussions in the Council of the Indies regarding administrative costs of the Philippines and of complaints from Seville about the competition that Chinese silks presented in American markets. In communications to Philip II, the Portuguese added their voices, arguing that direct economic relationships between America and Asia implied that viceroyalties in the New World would be economically independent of Spain due to abundance and variety of products from China, and that revenue from Seville's taxes would disappear.

The Manila galleon carried plants from America: maize, indigo, maguey, cacao, papaya, pineapple, peanuts, eggplant, cassava, tomatoes, sweet potatoes, tobacco, and more unknown cultivars. Conversely, colonizers sent back plants to America like, tamarinds, mangoes and the coconut palm brought by Alvaro de Mendaňa from the Salomon Islands (Schurz 1959, p. 68; Palazuelos Mazars 2016, p. 224; Machuca 2018, p. 52). Benito Legarda assesses the major importance of the exchange: “Of greater future significance, although of inconsequential invoice value, was the carrying of plants product from Mexico and Central America, some of which enriched the diet of Filipinos while others became important in trade and public finance” (1999, p. 34).

Europeans also brought deadly diseases. By 1500, smallpox was devastating populations in Indonesia and the Philippines. Widespread illnesses of unknown nature resulted in large population losses in years 1574, 1591, and 1595. From Africa, Portuguese sailors brought yaws—an infection of the skin, bones, and joints—to Asia, and syphilis arrived with both Iberian persons and African slaves (Newson 1999. p. 22). Nonetheless, Filipinos avoided the demographic disaster visited upon American peoples. Between 1565 and 1655, the numbers of Filipinos in Luzon and the Visayas diminished by around 33%. Lower population densities, widespread settlement patterns, and slow transportation diminished impact of epidemics (Newson 2009, p. 258).

The Economy of the Line & the Peruvian /Japanese Cycle During the Sixteenth and Seventeenth Centuries

Until the Opium War, writes monetary historian Frank Spooner, "The avidity of the Chinese for silver established a commercial epoch for the international economy". To illustrate this, he quotes a 1586 letter from a Florentine merchant: "The Chinese among all the peoples of Asia are wild about silver as everywhere men are about gold" (Spooner 1972, pp. 26, 45). Behind this preference, were important changes in Chinese monetary policy. Over-issue of paper money in China had reduced its value to virtually nothing by 1430s. Silver penetrated the Chinese economy from the coastal area and local governments in these places began specifying that taxes be paid in silver. Ming rulers eventually abandoned resistance to silver and implemented Single-Whip system consolidating taxes and requiring tax payments to be made in silver. China contained as much as one-fourth of the earth's population at that time (Flynn and Giraldez 1995, pp. 207–209). China's tributary system also converted to silver. Japan also fed the "silverization" of China. By 1570 differing gold-to-silver prices between both countries rendered it profitable to send silver for the purchase of Chinese's silks and gold. The output of the Japanese mines of Kai, Idzu, Iwami, and Sado Island amounted in the sixteenth and seventeenth century to about 30 and 16% respectively of the total silver mined (Barret 1990, p. 225; Giraldez 2010, p. 31).

Conversion of the world's largest economy to silver caused its value to become by far the highest in the world. In the words of John Maynard Keynes "never in the annals of the modern world has there existed so prolonged and so rich an opportunity for the business man, the speculator and the profiteer" (1950, vol. 2, p. 159).

Silver was the commodity that settled accounts on all continents and allowed the European to trade in the extremely lucrative Asian markets because. As Juan Grau y Monfalcón, procurator general of the Philippines, explained, "In Asia and the regions of the Orient, God created some things so precious in the estimation of men, and so peculiar to those provinces, that, as they are only found of manufactured therein, they are desired and sought by rest of the world" (In BR 1903, vol. 27, p. 88). Spices, silk, tea, and porcelain were exchanged for silver since the sixteenth century until the Industrial Revolution in England radically altered this basic structure of trade.

During the sixteenth century the market value of silver in the Ming empire was double that of Europe. Relative prices of silver and gold (bimetallic ratios) are striking: "From 1592 to the early seventeenth century gold was exchanged for silver in Canton at the rate of 1:5.5 to 1:7 while in Spain the exchange rate was 1:12.5 to 1:14, thus indicating that the value of silver was twice as high in China as in Spain" (Chuan 1969, p. 2). In Persia, the ratio was 1:10, and in India it was 1:8. This phenomenal state of affairs justifies the letter of the Viceroy of New Spain, Count of La Coruña (1580–1583) to the king indicating that merchants in México obtained 300% of profits with Chinese silks and only 100% with gold (Alonso Alvarez 2013, 49). The high price of silver in Asian markets would continue for decades until the amount of silver accumulated in the Chinese empire pushed its value down like in the rest of the world. This happened around 1640 (Flynn and Giraldez 2002, p. 7). From 1571 to 1640, "The opportunities for arbitrage profits were staggering" (Legarda 1999, p. 31). Merchants in New Spain and Peru accrued large profits avoiding competition with European intermediaries while directly trading with merchants from Asia in Manila and occasionally elsewhere.

The Crown established the Acapulco-Manila line for the support of such a distant colony. Every Spanish citizen in Manila participated in the galleon business; each Spaniard received an allotted space on the galleon to ship merchandise to Acapulco. The hold was divided into equal parts of uniform size called a bale, or fardo divided into four piezas, each one was represented by a boleta. The boleta's official value was 125 pesos. However, not all citizens had capital required to engage in trade, and as a result, a market for boletas came into being. In addition to citizens and government officials, the cathedral, chapter, regular orders, individual ecclesiastics, and *obras pias* received boletas. In the words of Schurz, the system was "a dignified form of dole, with a high market value in itself, the sale of which would provide the funds for the support of the original recipient until the drawing of the next year." Oskar H.K. Spate described the galleon's trade as a joint-stock company whose social seat was located in Luzon (1979, p. 161; Schurz 1959, p. 159).

By 1576 trade was firmly established, and Chinese junks made Manila a customary port of call. Mexican merchants began to settle on the island, providing knowledge and capital necessary to conduct business. Peruvian merchants sent money to Mexico and some of them ventured to China to do business there. Manila collected commodities from a multitude of places. From India came cottons, which in the eighteenth century became an important item of export. Earthen jars and a wide variety of porcelain arrived from China, rugs from Persia and goods from Japan until the Tokugawa "closure", *sakoku*, of the country in 1639. Words like: *catana*, *quimono*, or *biombo* entered in the Spanish language from Japanese during the first decades of the seventeenth century due to commercial exchanges with Japan (Kawamura 2018, p. 10). Spices were brought from the Moluccas, Java, and Ceylon. In the eighteenth century, borax, camphor, minium, and musk, as well as tea and cigars joined other commodities. The galleon also carried jewelry and precious stones. The Philippines sent fabrics like *lampotes* or cotton gauze from Cebu; cotton cloth, mantas, from Ilocos; and other textile products. But, Chinese silk was the most important item. In the words of William L. Schurz, "Silks in every stage of manufacture and of every variety of weave and pattern formed the most valuable part of their cargoes" (1959, p. 83). Chinese merchants, recognizing how popular Asian products had become in New Spain, soon learned to copy designs preferred by customers. From México, "some great gentlemen" of extravagant tastes sent their suits to China to be embroidered with gold and silver ornaments" (Machuca 2012, p. 84).

Chinese were adept at packing silks efficiently to maximize space. Bales, called *tinajas*, were tightly wrapped to protect contents from seawater and insects, with cheaper goods on the outside to deceive zealous officials as to value. On the way out to the open Pacific illegal goods joined the cargo. Each galleon's hold was full to maximum capacity and additional chests and bales obstructed passages, cabins, and decks. Bundles of merchandise occupied spaces reserved for necessary supplies and filled powder magazine. Guns were stored in the hold, which meant that weapons were not ready during encounters with the enemies. Often galleons took to sea lacking extra sails and spars required for such a difficult navigation. Also lacking were the amounts of water and food necessary for a voyage that could take up to seven months. Several times galleons had to turn back to Manila to unload excess weight; in other cases ships were lost.

In addition to Asian products, the galleon carried slaves. The Portuguese brought to Manila captives from Indonesia and the Indian

Ocean including Africans. This trade diminished at the end of the Iberian Union (1640) but smuggling continued (Souza 2004, p. 166; Seijas 2014, pp. 58–61, 63). There are no definitive numbers of Africans and Southeast Asians sold in Acapulco. Tatiana Seijas estimates: "One hundred and forty ships landed in Acapulco from 1565 to 1700, which is the approximate period of the Pacific slave trade. Given that number, we can estimate that the trade overall involved at least 8,100 individuals" (2014, p. 84). Profits were considerable. Adrian, a Filipino, was acquired in Manila for 37 pesos in 1637 and sold one year later in Acapulco for 200 pesos. African slaves fetched higher prices; Ignacio in Manila was purchased for 100 pesos and bought in New Spain for 380 (Seijas 2014, p- 95). In the last years of the seventeenth century, Gemelli Careri upon arrival in Acapulco sold his black slave for 400 pesos (Careri 1963, pp. 229–230).

The Church played a crucial role in the financial life of the Islands through *obras pias*, funded by merchants and churchmen and overseen by high-ranking laymen to support charitable work in the Philippines. Capital reserves amounted to millions of pesos. The most prominent of the *obras pias* was the Brotherhood of Mercy, or *Misericordia*. In addition to their roles as charitable organizations, these confraternities transferred inheritances to distant heirs, acted as commercial banks, provided interest-free loans to the government when the *situado* failed to arrive or in times of emergency. Since 1668, the *Misericordia* maritime insurance began. Calculating investment risks depended on the merchant's creditworthiness, the economic prospects of the fair at Acapulco, and the possibility of enemy capture (Legarda 1999, p. 40; Yuste 2015, p. 106).

Two galleons typically crossed the Pacific each year during the first half century of the line, but a single vessel became customary after initial years, with few exceptions. The cost of building and maintaining two ships was overly high, and the prevailing practice of sending only one galleon is reflected in regulations of 1726 and 1734. There was an economic rationale behind the dimensions of such large merchant ships. A vessel of seven hundred tons was much more cost-effective than one of three hundred; the larger ship with a crew of eighty or ninety, would demand stores of foodstuffs and other supplies that only occupied 10% of its capacity; providing for fifty or sixty men on the smaller vessel required 13 to 15% of storage space. Such economic realities explain why such ships dominated the East Indian and Atlantic trades (Marley 1993, p. 180).

At least two thousand trees were necessary for the construction of one galleon. Over time, forests in proximity of shipyards were depleted. Transporting logs from long distances presented considerable difficulties, which explains the practice of building galleons near a ready supplies of timber. The main shipyard during the Spanish regime was Cavite. The entire process of building a galleon could take two years, although there were exceptions like the San José, at the time one of the largest ships in the world; in 1693 it was built in a record nine months. Galleons were royal property. The Treasury financed the cost of building the liners and the expense of careening and refitting them. For instance, in 1573, the Royal Treasury spent 5,455 pesos to caulk one galleon (García-Abásolo 2013, p. 19).

The galleons travelling from Acapulco to Manila were guided by northeast trade winds. These airstreams reliably carried ships in the direction of the Philippines at good speed in two to three months. The sailing from Manila to Acapulco, about 8,500 km, took longer between four and six months. The galleon followed the westerlies north, pushed by the Kuroshio and North Pacific currents. It was essential to clear the Philippines between July and October because a late sailing meant encountering a typhoon. June was the best month for departure, as ships encountered winds blowing from Cavite to the Strait of San Bernardino—the *Embocadero* in colonial times—where the expected monsoon would propel it northward. It usually took a galleon about two months to reach open sea. Along this dangerous course, Le Gentil observed, "she picks up many things from the alcaldes and the friars to be transported to Mexico" (1964, p. 163). After the galleon sailed through the San Bernardino Strait the monsoon carried it on its way, but a zone of storms and variable winds often required the galleon to turn back to the Philippines before it could attain the necessary latitude. Worsening of climate during the seventeenth century affected each voyage's duration. Sailing was speedy between 1590 and 1630 but slowed greatly between 1640 and 1670. Sailings returned to their customary duration toward the last decades of the seventeenth and eighteenth centuries. That was the case with the San Joseph's 1662 sailing to Acapulco; only 14 of 115 people survived due to unplanned increase in crossing time that exhausted provisions (Herrera Reviriego 2011, p 107). Gemelli Careri, an Italian globetrotter, relating adventures in his 1669 *Giro del Mondo* (Travels around the World), wrote: "The voyage from the Philippine islands to America may be called the longest and most dreadful of any in the world" (1963, p. 13).

In 1734 the galleons made a stop at Jesuit missions of the Lower California: Santiago de las Coras (1721) y San José del Cabo Aňuití (1730). Higher California was colonized after 1769 but it would be some years before galleons would call at San Diego or Monterrey (Bernabéu 2013, p. 276). Related to the California expansion was export of sea otter pelts in exchange for Chinese mercury—always in demand by Mexican miners. The idea originated with Vicente Vasadre y Vega. Jars of quicksilver arrived in Acapulco from 1789 to 1793 and 9,729 otter and some seal skins were sent to Manila (Ogden 1941, p. 24). Vasadre's business was discontinued due to official opposition.

Upon arriving at Acapulco, galleons were repaired and readied to receive passengers and cargo. In addition to silver, merchandise typically consisted of cacao from Guayaquil (today the main port of Ecuador); cochineal, a dye pigment from Oaxaca; oil from Spain; wines; and other goods in smaller quantities. From Acapulco the galleons carried royal officials, family and retinue, friars and merchants from Mexico and Peru, convicts from New Spain, and banished persons. Contingents of soldiers also sailed on the galleons. From Manila, a number of Filipino sailors manned the ship.

In the last decades of the seventeenth century, Mexico City merchants organized in the *Consulado* to control marketing of the Seville fleet's merchandise coming via Veracruz and also galleon goods from Acapulco. The *Consulado* managed the textile distribution to New Spain, Guatemala, Havana, Ecuador and Peru. Occasionally they sent some of those textiles to Spain on the returning fleet. These merchants were financiers of the viceroyalty's internal commerce, advancing funds for mining operations, textile manufacture, and agricultural development as well as exercising absolute control over retail trade (Yuste 2007, pp. 11–12).

The lower price of Chinese textiles, compared with those carried by fleets, was the reason for high returns in American markets. Colonial authorities in the Philippines required the natives to cover their bodies as they had done in the New World, which meant that indigenous peoples purchased affordable garments of silk and cotton. Authorities wrote to the king complaining that "from these islands before the Chinese took away for clothing 30,000 pesos, now given the natives' disorder and excess they take 200,00 pesos from his Majesty's kingdoms" (in Chuan 1975, p. 114). The same policies in America created powerful demand reflected in transformation of New Spain silk manufacturing. After 1579 large quantities of silk reached Acapulco; consequently, Mexican silk culture began to decline. Meanwhile arrival of large supplies of Chinese yarn benefited local manufacturers in Mexico City, Puebla, and Oaxaca, which altogether employed more than fourteen thousand people (Borah 1943, p. 97).

A substantial portion of Mexico's finished silk products headed for Peru. In a 1594 letter, a Spanish official in Lima wrote to Philip II: "A man can clothe his wife in Chinese silks for two hundred reals, whereas he could not provide her clothing of Spanish silks with two hundred pesos" (Borah 1954, p. 122). A royal officer compared prices of silk goods in Manila and Lima, capital of the Viceroyalty of Peru, and calculated profit to be approximately 200% in 1620. For instance, the price of a picul of raw silk—about 60.47 kilograms, or 133 pounds—was 200 pesos in Manila; in Lima the same quantity fetched 1,950 pesos, while a picul of Canton satin was worth 5 pesos on the Islands and 50 pesos in Lima (Schurz 1959, pp. 366–370). When in 1718 the Crown forbade galleons from carrying silks, Baltasar de Zúñiga, viceroy of New Spain and future president of the Council Indies, simply refused to implement the decree, alleging that Chinese textiles were cheaper than fabrics coming from Spain and adding that the majority of people in Mexico preferred products from the Manila Galleon (in BR 1903, vol. 27, p. 88; pp. 148–150). The City of Mexico soon had a makeshift market in the Plaza Mayor, the *Zócalo*, to sell galleon's merchandise, called the Parian like the Chinese neighborhood in Manila. Permanent facilities were inaugurated in 1692, earning substantial annual income for the City Council—15,000 pesos—from rent of 144 shops (Chong 2014, p. 66).

Since 1604, the Crown reiterated decrees forbidding trade between Acapulco and Lima. The decree of 1634 was nonetheless partially successful in blocking Mexican silks products, but this measure encouraged flow of finished Chinese silk to Peru, thereby contributing to destruction of New Spain's powerful silk manufacturers (Legarda 1999, p. 42). Margarita Suarez explains that this last decree was not opposed by Lima merchants because it allowed them to avoid the glut of Asian goods in the viceroyalty (2015, p. 133). Smuggling and fraud between Mexico and Peru "became far more lucrative and took place on a scale that can be described as gigantic" (Borah 1954, p. 114). On Lima's Street of Merchants, forty shops sold luxuries from Europe and Asia; some of the owners had over one million pesos in capital. A viceroy in 1602 described Lima and its inhabitants to the king: "All wear silk, and of the finest and costly quality. The gala dresses and clothes of the women are so many and so excessive that in no other kingdom of the world are found such." Woodes Rogers of England wrote in 1712, "The ladies, who are extravagant in their apparel, impoverish the country by purchasing the richest silks." Two Spanish navy officers, in 1735, Jorge Juan y Santacilla and Antonio de Ulloa, saw Chinese porcelain for sale in shops of Lima and observed Chinese silks sent from Chile to Panama. Lima was known as "Pekin's Fair," because from this city Asian goods were redistributed widely across the Andes reaching Salta, Cajamarca, Tucumán, Córdoba and the port of Buenos Aires (Bonialian 2014, p. 22).

The official monopolistic fleet system that connected Spain with America was based on an economy of scarcity in American markets; a permanent high demand above the offer in order to secure a maximum of prices and profits (Bonialian 2019, p. 131). Asian goods demand in Colonial America was related to a culture of massive purchases depending upon lower prices and ordinary quality (Bonialian 2014, p. 25). Mariano Bonialian distinguish between goods brought by the Acapulco galleon for everyday use and fabrics for a sumptuary market provided by Spanish fleets (2019, p. 32).

Precise figures on silver sent to Manila are not available. Numbers from New Spain and Peru are estimates because official reports could not take into account fraud and smuggling, which greatly increased during periods of economic crisis. Schurz estimates "that the average for the most prosperous periods was about 2,000,000 pesos ...even more were quite possible, though not common." He indicates that during the war with the Dutch the value of silver cargo could have fallen under one million pesos. Later historians give higher numbers. According to Pierre Chaunu, between 1570 and 1780, two-thirds of Mexican silver was exported from Acapulco. Louisa S. Hoberman wrote that during the seventeenth century the Philippines received between 29 and 35% of New Spain's production. Chuan Han-Sheng calculates that exports via Acapulco maintained a consistent level of two million pesos annually—the equivalent of 55 metric tons—during the seventeenth century. Hoberman gives somewhat higher estimates at least until 1634. She calculates closer to four million pesos in 1630, 6 million in 1637, and another 4 million in 1638. Mariano A. Bonialian adds that from the end of the seventeenth century through the first four decades of the eighteenth century, large quantities of Peruvian-coined silver were shipped alongside Mexican pesos without being included in Acapulco's official accounts. Bonialian's figures are consistent with those of Jerónimo de Uztáriz—a knowledgeable Spanish administrator—who estimated in 1724 annual shipment from Acapulco of 3 million pieces of eight (Schurz 1959, p. 190; Chaunu 1960, p. 269; Hoberman 1977, p. 493; Hoberman 1991, p. 219; Chuan 1969, p. 219; Bonialian 2019, p. 215).

Over the course of two and half centuries, the Spanish Crown issued decree after decree establishing detailed legislation covering all aspects of the line in Manila and Acapulco. Enforcing such laws was a different matter. In Manila the whole citizenry from top to bottom, including the church, was united in ignoring regulations. Governors in the Philippines and viceroys in New Spain actively participated in the galleon trade. It was customary to retire as a viceroy or from the governorship with considerable holdings. Enforcing collection of taxes had ominous consequences. The riot of 1624 was provoked by Viceroy Gelves strict tax collection and confiscation of Philippine contraband; it was worse in Manila: Governor Fernando de Bustillo y Bustamante collected large sums of money from government debtors, antagonizing clergy and citizens. In 1719, a mob of citizens lead by friars assaulted the governor's palace and killed him and his son (Zaide 1972, p. 219). In the words of Guillermina del Valle Pavón, "The regulations were flagrantly and systematically violated due to the collusion between merchants and vice-regal authorities" (2005, p. 236).

Chinese merchants communities abroad including Manila connected Ming and Qing empires with global networks of trade. Chinese profits from maritime trade were quite high. However, Gang Deng wrote that returns declined over time during the Ming dynasty (1368–1644). Average profit of Sino-South Asian trade was 150%. During this same period, profits from high-quality silk exports fell from 200 to 140%; "In spite of this tendency, the high yield from maritime trade was an economic fact" (Deng 1997, pp. 147–148). The Chinese had several advantages that allowed them profit more from trade than Europeans: They operated small firms that responded efficiently to market trends and merchants had institutional and personal connections to foreign countries. These merchants with small capital borrowed money at high interest rates, leaving wives and children with the lender as security. Usually, a junk was hired by a wealthy merchant who rented space in the hold for others at a rate of 20% of gross sales. Merchandise was stored below deck in watertight compartments, in which merchants slept atop their cargo during the ten-day voyage to Manila, located 650 miles from ports of origin. When junks arrived in Manila, agents were waiting for them. These intermediaries knew how much silver the galleon had brought and prices that merchants could quote to the Spaniards and had connections with colonial inspectors to distribute required bribes. These brokers charged between 20 and 30% of the sales price. Then officers inspected incoming junks and collected taxes.

As was the case with other Southeast Asian destinations, trade to the Philippines required a junk of about 350 tons, with crew and passengers between two and four hundred. Chinese captains transported immigrants, dropping them in safe places before reaching Manila. It seems that some larger junks could carry up to five hundred people. A large number of Chinese—*sangleys* in colonial documents—were officially relegated to the Chinese neighborhood, the Parian, under the range of Spanish artillery (Schurz 1959, p. 87; Corpuz 2005, p. 305).

As early as 1589 these emigrants had acquired landed property in the vicinity of Manila. Chinese vegetable growers became an integral part of the capital for centuries. From early on the Spaniards realized that Chinese were indispensable to the colonial life. In 1583 Bishop Salazar wrote to Philip II about the Parian in enthusiastic terms: "In it is carried the whole commerce of China, involving every sort of merchandise"; he continued in this vein by enumerating the number of craftsmen, marveling at cheapness of their work in construction, and praising many services provided by such an industrious people (Schurz 1959, p. 71). In the seventeenth century, Chinese spread outside the Parian, settling in surrounding provinces or on other islands, where they engaged in trade with smaller junks and sampans. Chinese in Manila who were Christian or had married Christians resided in the Binondo and Tondo quarters of the city. Relations among Filipinos, Spanish and Sangleys were far from uniformly cordial. Chinese rebellions puntuacted the seventeenth century the last one in 1686. The underlying reason for such hostilities was fear generated by Chinese numbers to a small Spanish population. In the seventeenth century about 2,000 Spaniards lived in Manila in the middle of 10,000, 20,000 and sometimes 30,000 Chinese (García-Abásolo 2013, p. 24). The natives and other subaltern groups resented economic roles played by *sangleys* and joined colonizers against them.

The Eighteenth Century: The Mexican Cycle and the End of the Line

American plants powerfully contributed to the Qing dynasty's economic and social development. John K. Fairbank has enumerated three eighteenth century processes that determined the course of Chinese and world history: European presence in coastal China, doubling of territorial size of the Chinese Empire, and doubling of Han Chinese population (Fairbank 1978, vol. 10, Part. 1, p. 35).

In the last decades of the eighteenth century Russia and China had divided Central Eurasia signaling the end of the steppe-people's political power. Peter C. Perdue explains the interdependences among monetary issues, merchants, and Qing expansion. Taxes paid in silver, required that officials provide support to markets in which farmers sold goods and acquired bullion. "Although the bulk of its tax revenue came from the land, that revenue itself depended on an extensively monetized agrarian economy, which relied on extensive cooperation with the merchant class" (Perdue 2005, p. 516).

Demographic and market growth in China heightened demand for silver which increased its value to 50% above its price in the rest of the world. Spanish American mines produced more silver in the eighteenth century than in the sixteenth and seventeenth centuries combined. Peru's production in the eighteenth century more than tripled and surpassed even its seventeenth-century maximum, while Mexico's output was well over double Peru's for most of the 1700s (Fisher 1998; Burkholder and Johnson 1988, p. 140). In the first half of the eighteenth century, the gold-to-silver ratio in China remained at 1:10 while in Europe this ratio was 1:15 (Coatsworth 1986, pp. 26–27). Much of this silver was again destined for China, with India as a transit route. Once again, arbitrage profits entered merchant's calculations. Isaac Newton, master of the Mint in London, wrote in Minute of 1717; "In China and Japan one-pound weight of fine gold is worth but nine or ten pounds' weight of fine silver, and in the East India it may be worth twelve. And this low price of gold in proportion to silver carried away the silver from all Europe." John Conduitt, who succeeded Newton as Master of the Mint, added with further precision in 1730; "The importation of gold into Europe has been much increased, by the discovery of the new mines in Brazil, and, consequently, it is less valuable, and the real intrinsic value of silver is much enhanced by the great demand of silver for the several

East India Companies set up in Europe" (in Shaw 1896, pp. 192, 295). During the eighteenth century, silver flowed to Asia mainly in the form of Mexican pieces of eight known as *dos mundos* and *bustos* according to their symbols. Mints manufactured half a billion *dos mundos* between 1732 and 1772 and nearly 900 million *bustos* between 1772 and 1822 (Chaudhuri 1978, pp. 181–182).

Asian-European trade flourished anew during the first half of the eighteenth century. Importation of hundreds of million pesos in silver eventually saturated the Chinese marketplace, as before, to the extent that from 1750 onward the gold-to-silver in China was above 1:15, while in Europe the ratio declined to between 1:14.5 and 1:14.8. The Qing Empire continued to import silver pesos during the second half of the eighteenth century, but the profit rate per unit of silver was modest compared with the heights reached during the upward trends of the Potosi/Japan or Mexico cycles. Ordinary profit margins continued while Mexican mines kept producing large quantities of silver until the end of the century. Fluctuations in the silver market explain why Commodore Anson brought silver from his capture of the Acapulco galleon to London. In the year 1700 a similar haul would have been destined for China because the price of silver fetched a 50% premium vis-à-vis Europe (Flynn and Giraldez 2002, pp. 410–411).

Silver's purchasing power diminished as British commercial activities became increasingly influential in global marketplace. Since the 1750s British had steadily solidified its hegemonic position in the east, whereas French and Dutch influence waned. Independence of the American colonies in 1781 turned British efforts toward Asia, where India became the center of its empire. Their East India Company managed to gain control of a new, rapidly growing market involving importation of Bengal opium into China in exchange for Chinese tea. "The point is not that silver discontinued its journey into China during the second half of the eighteenth century—it did not—but rather that opium and tea became the high-profit markets, with silver playing a complementary role in terms of profitability" (Flynn and Giraldez 2002, p. 411).

In the Philippines since the middle of the eighteenth century the local economy was transformed due to Spanish attempts to produce exportable crops like sugar, indigo, cotton, abaca, and tobacco. During the reigns of Fernando VI (1746–1759) and Carlos III (1759–1788), there were significant changes in imperial policies. It was necessary to develop Spain's agriculture and manufactures and to sell its products in American markets, and better exploit colonial resources by excluding European and Asian competitors. Fundamental pieces of the plan involved dismantling the system of fleets crossing the Atlantic from Seville and Cadiz, implementing administrative reforms, and establishing a more efficient tax collection system. Politically the reforms tried to diminish the power exercised at the time by the church and merchants guilds, or *Consulados*, in the hands of the Mexican and Peruvian businessmen (Yuste 1987, p. 80).

Attempts to initiate trade from Cádiz with Asia via the Cape of Good Hope were taking shape. In 1765 the frigate *Buen Consejo* from Spain arrived to Manila following the Cape of Good Hope route with merchandise to exchange for Asian goods. There were fourteen voyages of these frigates up to 1784. After 1778, with the law of free trade between Spain and America, there was dramatic reorganization of colonial commerce. Restrictions on intercontinental trade were removed, and taxes were reduced to facilitate exchanges among American territories. The system of fleets from Spain to America was discontinued, and the House of Trade in Cadiz closed its doors in 1790. This atmosphere of liberalized regulations encouraged private traders to engage in colonial ventures. A company formed by the five major guilds of Madrid, *gremios mayores*, sent a cargo of goods to the Philippines in 1778, accompanied by commissioners who moved their residence to Canton and Manila in the following year. It seems that the real intention was to participate in the galleon trade and send goods to New Spain (Alonso Álvarez 2009, p. 318).

In the Philippines appointment of Governor Jose Basco y Vargas (1778–1787) encouraged cultivation of indigo, pepper, and hemp, as well as manufacture of silk and cotton textiles. On March 1, 1782, the tobacco monopoly, estanco, was established in the islands. In 1785 the Royal Philippine Company, *Real Compañía de Filipinas*, initiated activities after previous attempts to create a commercial company did not come to fruition. In addition to direct trade between Cadiz and Manila, company ships were permitted to trade directly with Canton, Calcutta, and Lima. Lacking strict oversight and in some cases enticed by large profits of opium commerce, agents and other officials neglected their work for the company and engaged in private business. The company petitioned the Crown to participate in the galleon trade, showing where the real profits remained. After 1789, the Royal Philippine Company's activities began to decline (Legarda 1999, p. 80; Cheong 1971, p. 147). During those years, the company was involved in ongoing efforts to commercialize the islands' products. One unintended consequence was establishment in the

Philippines of foreign commercial agents from France, United States, and Britain. Finally, a decree of 1789 that allowed European vessels to land at Manila made the city an actual free port.

From the last two decades of the eighteenth century the galleon trade suffered a series of loses due to discontinuation of voyages. Oversupply in American markets became prevalent due to smuggling of European and Indian textiles. From 1778 to 1786, three galleons and two small vessels lost cargoes valued at 3.5 million pesos. There were no ships from Manila in 1788, 1790, 1792, 1802, 1803, 1805, and 1812, and impoverished investors could only partially stock holds of several galleons. Arrival in Acapulco of three vessels from Manila in 1800 and four in 1801 ruined the Acapulco market for almost a decade. The galleon was discontinued during the war with Napoleon in Spain. In China, exportation of tea and importation of cotton and opium carried by the Europeans at Canton brought about decline of the junk trade.

The last galleon returned to Manila in 1815. From this date until 1821, smaller ships from Manila sailed not to Acapulco but to other Mexican ports, such as San Blas, Tepic, Sonsonate Guyamas, and Mazatlán. American wars of independence resulted in final collapse of the system based on extraction of silver and supply of Asian textiles.

The Beginnings of Globalization

The Acapulco-Manila galleons navigated the Pacific Ocean for about 250 years. Compared to commercial organization of today's large container ships or oil tankers, it was not a smooth operation. Wars, shipwrecks—more than thirty galleons were lost at sea—and various other misfortunes frequently disrupted the line. The British captured four ships, thousands of people died crossing the oceans, and property losses were considerable. According to Beatriz Palazuelos in the seventeenth century between sixteen and eighteenth percent of the galleons ran aground or sank, "constituting a high risk rate" (2016, p. 92). However, the large vessels kept sailing, supported by Filipino labor and resources, the work of miners in Peru and New Spain, and ongoing exchange of American silver for Asian textiles. Ecological exchanges of gigantic importance, as well as movement of American, Asians, and Spaniards on both sides of the Pacific were related to the sailing of ships. The manifold aspects of this line were linked to its lucrative operations. Considering high profits accrued by participants in the trade, from an actuarial point of view, Benito

Legarda affirms, "total losses were comparatively few and the percentages of missing and captured crew men would have caused no great concern to modern underwriters" (Legarda 1999, p. 44). These galleons originated the first planetary economy, the intercontinental market from which emerged the globalized world in which we live.

Acknowledgements I am extremely thankful to Paulina Machuca and Margarita Suarez who generously gave me their books and articles. Tatiana Seijas answered my queries diligently. Susan Giraldez edited the article. I would like to mention the interlibrary loan service of our university that has always fulfilled petitions promptly and without fail. Errors or shortcomings are only mine.

Bibliography

Alonso Álvarez, Luis. 2013. "E la nave va. Economía, fiscalidad e inflación en las regulaciones de la carrera de la Mar del Sur, 1565–1604." In *Un oceano de seda y plata: el universo económico del Galeón de Manila*, coordinated by Bernabéu Albert, Salvador and Martínez Shaw, Carlos, 25–84. Sevilla: Consejo Superior de Investigaciones Cientificas.

Alonso Álvarez, Luis. 2009. *El costo del imperio asiático: la formación colonial de las islas Filipinas bajo dominio español, 1565–1800*. La Coruña: Universidade da Coruña.

Alzina, Francisco Ignacio. 1996. *Una Etnografía de los indios bisayas del siglo XVII*, 2 vols., Victoria Yepes edition. Madrid: Consejo Superior de Investigaciones Científicas.

Arcilla, José S. 1998. *The Spanish Conquest: KASAYSAYAN. The Story of the Filipino People*, vol. 3. Hong Kong: Asia Publishing Company.

Barret, Ward. 1990. "World Bullion Flows, 1450–1800." In *The Rise of Merchant Empires: Long-Distance Trade in the Early Modern World, 1350–1750*, edited by James Tracy, 224–254. Cambridge: Cambridge University Press.

Bernabéu Albert, Salvador. 2013. "Entre la desconfianza y la indecisión las relaciones entre el Galeón y las Californias," In *Un océano de seda y plata: el universo economico del Galeón de Manila*, 271–3340. Sevilla: Consejo Superior de Investigaciones Cientificas.

Blair, Emma Helen, and James Alexander Robertson, eds. 1903. *Philippine Islands 1493–1803*, 55 vols. Cleveland, OH: A. H. Clark Company (BR).

Bonialian, Mariano Ardash. 2019. *La América española entre el Pacífico y el Atlántico. Globalización mercantil y economía política, 1580–1840*. México: El Colegio de México.

Bonialian, Mariano Ardash. 2014. "Tejidos y cerámica de China en la gobernación de Tucumán y Buenos Aires, siglo XVIII. Apuntes sobre su circulación y consume." *Anuario de Estudios Americanos* 71 (2): 631–660.

Borah, Woodrow. 1954. *Early Colonial Trade and Navigation Between Mexico and Peru*. Berkeley: University of California Press.

Borah, Woodrow. 1943. *Silk Raising in Colonial Mexico*. Berkeley: University of California Press.

Burkholder, Mark A., and Lyman L. Johnson. 1988. *Colonial Latin America*. New York: Oxford University Press.

Careri, Gemelli G. 1963. A Voyage to the Philippines: And an Appendix of the Chapters on the Philippines in the Travels of Fray Sebastián Manrique. Manila: Filipiniana Book Guild.

Chaudhuri, Kirti N. 1978. *The Trading World of Asia and the English East India Company, 1660–1760*. Cambridge: Cambridge University Press.

Chaunu, Pierre. 1960. *Les Philippines et le Pacifique des Iberiques (XVI, XVII, XVIII siècles)*. Paris: S.E.V.P.E.N.

Chong, José Luis. 2014. *Historia general de los chinos en México 1575–1975*. México: Turner.

Chuan, Han-sheng. 1969. "The Inflow of American Silver into China from the Late Ming to the Mid-Ch'ing period." *Journal of the Institute of Chinese Studies of the Chinese University of Hong Kong* 2: 61–75.

Chuan, Han-sheng. 1975. "The Silk Trade with Spanish-America from the late Ming to the Mid-Ch'ing Period." In *Studia Asiatica. Esays in Asia Studies in Studies in Felicitacion of the Seventy-Fith Anniversary of Professor Ch'en Shou-yi*, edited by Laurence G. Thompson. San Francisco: Chinese Materials Center.

Cheong, W. E. 1971. "The Decline of Manila as the Spanish Entrepot in the Far East, 1786–1826: Its Impact on the Pattern of Southeast Asian Trade." *Journal of Southeast Asia Studies* 2 (2): 142–158.

Colín, Francisco. 1900. *Labor evangélica, ministerios apostólicos de los obreros de la Compañía de Jesús*, 3 vols., Pablo Pastells Edition. Barcelona: Imprenta y Litografía de Henrich y Compañía.

Corpuz, Onofre D. 2005. *The Roots of the Filipino Nation*. Quezon City: University of the Philippine Press.

Coatsworth, John H. 1986. "The Mexican Mining Industry in the Eighteenth Century," In *The Economies of Mexico and Peru During the Late Colonial Period, 1760–1810*, edited by Jacobsen Nils and Hans-Jurgen Puhle. Berlin: Colloquium Verlag.

del Valle Pavón, Guillermina. 2005. "Los mercaderes de México y la transgresión de los límites al Comercio Pacífico en Nueva España." *Revista de historia económica. Número Extraordinario. La economía en tiempos de Don Quijote*, 213–240.

Deng, Gang. 1997. *Chinese Maritime Activities and Socioeconomic Development c. 2100 b.c.–1900 a.d.* Westport, CT: Greenwood Press.

Fairbank, John K., ed. 1978. *The Cambridge History of China, Vol. 10, Late Ch'ing, 1800–1911.* Cambridge: Cambridge University Press.

Fisher, John R. 1998. "Mining and Imperial Trade in 18th-Century Spanish in America." In *Monetary History in Global Perspective, 1500–1808: B6 Proceedings, Twelfth International Economic History Congress*, edited by Clara Eugenia Nuñez. Sevilla: Universidad de Sevilla.

Flynn, Dennis, and Arturo Giraldez. 1995. "Born with a 'Silver Spoon': The Origin of World Trade in 1571." *Journal of World History* 6 (2): 201–221.

Flynn, Dennis, and Arturo Giraldez. 2002. "Cycles of Silver: Global Economic Unity Through the Mid-Eighteenth Century." In *Journal of World History* 13 (2): 391–427.

García-Abásolo, Antonio, 2013, "Españoles y chinos en Filipinas. Los fundamentos del comercio del galeón de Manila." In *España, el Atlántico y el Pacífico y otros estudios sobre Extremadura.* XIV Jornadas de historia en Llerena. Llerena: Sociedad Extremeña de Historia, 9–29.

Giraldez, Arturo. 2010. *The Age of Trade. The Manila Galleons and the Dawn of Global Economy.* Lanham: Rowman & Littlefield.

Herrera Reviriego, José Miguel. 2011. "Acapulco, centro de comunicaciones: comercio, consumo y corrupción en los galeones de Manila de mediados del siglo XVII." *Fòrum de Recerca* 16: 103–118.

Hoberman, Louisa S. 1977. "Merchants in Seventeenth-Century Mexico City: A Preliminary Portrait." *Hispanic American Historical Review* 57 (3) 479–503.

Hoberman, Louisa S. 1991. *Mexico's Merchant Elite 1590–1660. Silver, State and Society.* Durham, NC: Duke University Press.

Kawamura, Yayoi. 2018. "Manila, ciudad española y centro de fusión. Un estudio a través del inventario del gobernador de Filipinas Alonso Fajardo de Tenza (1624)." *e-Spania* 30 (June): 1–11.

Keynes, John M. 1950. *A Treatise on Money*, vol. 2. London: Macmillan.

Legarda, Benito J. 1999. *After the Galleons: Foreign Trade, Ecomic Change and Entrepreneurship in Nineteenth-Century Philippines.* Madison: Center for Asian Studies/University of Wisconsin-Madison.

Le Gentil, Guillaume. 1964. *A Voyage to the Indian Seas.* Manila: Filipiniana Book Guild.

Lee Junker, Laura. 1999. *Raiding, Trading and Feasting: The Political Economy of Philippine Chiefdoms.* Honollulu: University of Hawaii Press.

Lieberman, Victor. 2009. *Strange Parallels: Southeast Asia in Global Context, c. 800–1830. Vol. 2 Mainland Mirrors: Europe, Japan, China, South Asia, and the Islands.* Cambridge: Cambridge University Press.

Machuca, Paulina. 2012. "De porcelanas chinas y otros menesteres. Cultura material de origen asiático en Colima, siglos XVI–XVII" *Relaciones* 131 (Summer): 77–134

Machuca, Paulina. 2018. *El vino de cocos en la Nueva españa. Historia de una transculturación en el siglo XVII*. Zamora: El Colegio de Michoacán.

Marley, David F. 1993. "The Great Galleon: The *Santisíma Trinidad* (1750–1765)." *Philippine Studies* 41 (2): 167–181.

Newson, Linda A. 2009. *Conquest and Pestilencia in the Early Spanish Philippines*. Honolulu: University of Hawaii Press.

Ogden, Adele. 1941. *The California Sea Otter Trade. 1784–1848*. Berkeley: University of California Press.

Palazuelos Mazars, Beatriz. 2016. *Acapulco et le galion de Manille. La réalité quotidienne d'un port au XVII siècle*. Paris: L'Harmattan.

Perdue, Peter C. 2005. *China Marches West: The Qing Conquest of Central Eurasia*. Cambridge, MA: Harvard University Press.

Pérez Lecha, Manuel. 2013. "Una revisión del período final del Galeón de Manila, 1785–1821." *Fòrum de recerca* 18: 197–214.

Reid, Anthony. 1988. *Southeast Asia in the Age of Commerce 1450–1680. Vol. 1. The Land below the Winds*. New Haven: Yale University Press.

Reid, Anthony. 1992. "Economic and Social Change, c. 1400–1800." *The Cambridge History of Southeast Asia, Vol. 1. From Early Times to c. 1800*, 460–507, edited by Nicholas Tarling. Singapore: Cambridge Univerity Press.

Reid, Anthony. 1993. *Southeast Asia in the Age of Commerce 1450–1680. Vol. 2. Expansionand crisis*. New Haven: Yale University Press.

Schurz, William L. 1959. *The Manila Galleon*. New York: E.P. Dutton.

Scott, William Henry. 1985. *Cracks in the Parchment Curtain and Other Essays in Philippine History*. Quezon City: New Day.

Scott, William Henry. 1992. *Looking for the Prehispanic Filipino and Other Essays in Philippine History*. Quezon City: New Day Publishers.

Scott, William Henry. 1994. *Barangay: Sixteenth-Century Philippine Culture and Society*. Quezon City: Ateneo de Manila University Press.

Seijas, Tatiana. 2014. *Asian Slaves in Colonial Mexico. From Chinos to Indios*. New York: Cambridge University Press.

Shaw, William A. 1896. *Select Tracts and Documents Illustrative of English Monetary History*. London: Clement Wilson.

Souza, George B. 2004. *The Survival of the Empire: Portuguese Trade and Society in China and the South China Sea, 1630–1754*. Cambridge: Cambridge University Press.

Spate, Oskar H. K. 1979. *The Spanish Lake*. Minneapolis: University of Minnesota.

Spooner, Frank C. 1972. *The International Economy and Monetary Movements in France, 1493–1725*. Boston: Harvard University Press.

Suárez, Margarita. 2001. *Desafíos Transatlánticos. Mercaderes, banqueros y el estado en el Perú virreinal, 1600–1700*. Lima: Pontificia Universidad Católica del Perú. Instituto Riva-Aguero/Fondo de Cultura Económica/Instituto Francés de Estudios Andinos.

Suárez, Margarita. 2015. "Sedas, rasos y damascos: Lima y el cierre del comercio triangular con México y Manila en la primera mitad del siglo XVII" *America Latina en la Historia Economica* 22 (2, May–August): 101–134.

Yuste, Carmen. 1987. *El comercio de la Nueva España con Filipinas, 1500–1785*. México: Instituo Nacional de Antropología e Historia.

Yuste, Carmen. 2007. *Emporios transpacíficos: Comerciantes mexicanos en Manila*. México: Universidad Nacional Autónoma de México.

Yuste, Carmen. 2015. "Las fundaciones piadosas en correspondencia de riesgo de a premio de mar en la Casa de la Santa Misericordia de Manila en el transcurso del siglo XVIII." *Espacio, tiempo y forma* 28: 99–115.

Zaide, Gregorio F. 1972. *Philippine Political and Cultural History. Vol. 1*. Manila: Philippine Education Company.

Weaving a Global Trade Pattern: The Portuguese Role in the Globalisation on Asian Textiles, 1500–1800

João Teles e Cunha and Maria João Ferreira

On November 7th 1615, the East Indiaman *Nossa Senhora da Luz* shipwrecked off the coast of the Azorean island of Faial, but most of her cargo was salvaged during the following weeks. The salvage, carried by local authorities, revealed the extent of the precious stones smuggled aboard, especially diamonds, and, what is relevant for us, the quantity of Asian textiles washed ashore, more than 26,000 pieces (Bettencourt 2008, p. 55; Viana 1999, pp. 105, 113, 117). This shipwreck exposed the cargo revolution that had taken place in the *Carreira da Índia* (India Run) in the second half of the sixteenth century, whose fulcrum turned around the private trade made with Asian textiles. Spices have been traditionally associated with the commerce made between Asia and Europe after the opening of the Cape Route in 1498, particularly pepper

J. Teles e Cunha · M. J. Ferreira (✉)
Universidade Nova de Lisboa, Lisbon, Portugal

M. J. Ferreira
Carnaxide, Portugal

Museu de São Roque/CHAM-FCSH, Lisbon, Portugal

Universidade Dos Açores, Ponta Delgada, Portugal

R. Dobado-González and A. García-Hiernaux (eds.), *The Fruits of the Early Globalization*, Palgrave Studies in Comparative Global History,
https://doi.org/10.1007/978-3-030-69666-5_8

(Godinho 1984; Godinho 1985; Godinho 1987; Godinho 1991). This trade, connoted with the Crown, attracted usually all the scholarly attention, but a new trend emerged in the 1990s more interested in the traffic carried by private traders, namely the leading New Christian families, that is, Jews forcibly converted after 1496 (Boyajian 1992). This new perspective disclosed not only the role played by them in building a global commercial network encompassing the two Iberian empires, chiefly from 1580 to 1640[1]; and also the part played by Asian textiles in this process, which became a staple commodity traded all over the world, predating the role usually ascribed to the Dutch and the English East India Companies.

Moreover, this cargo revolution centered around Asian textiles explained the contemporary complaints made against the bulky bundles obstructing the *naus*' decks which, according to several authors and official reports, was responsible for capsizing ships during storms, or sudden wind gusts; as well as making them vulnerable in case of attack by Dutch, English, or Barbary corsairs, because it hampered maneuverability, the firing of cannons, and to fend off attacks (Guinote et al. 1998). Asian textiles, however, had been traded between Asia and Europe long before this mid-century shift, and together with precious stones (Matos 1989, pp. 93–102), had been two commodities not monopolized by the Crown.

We must wait for the second half of the sixteenth century to witness major commercial changes, because until then most of the Asian textile traded through Portuguese networks, either belonging to the Crown, its officials, or to private traders, was made mostly in Asia or in the Indian Ocean, following an established pattern. After 1560, coinciding with the relative liberalization of the *Carreira da Índia* (Boyajian 1992, pp. 81–82),[2] innovations were introduced in the Cape Route by the New Christians. These had less to do with the trade made with Europe, despite the growing consumption of Indian "panos" and Chinese silks in the European market, and more to do with the use of cheap Indian cottons in the African slave trade.

[1] Portugal and Spain shared the same sovereign during this period, known as "Union of the Crowns", though politically and institutionally the two kingdoms remained separate polities.

[2] The Crown leased the *Carreira da Índia* to private investors in exchange for money in a three-year contract from around 1554 to 1614. At first the whole operation was leased, and then in separate parts (shipping, pepper, spices, etc.), see Cunha (2009).

This created for the first time a commercial pattern linking India and the Indian Ocean with the Atlantic which would endure until the nineteenth century, though with other European players after 1600. Another pattern emerging at this time was the supply of Asian textiles to America made by the Manila Galleon (linking the Philippines to Mexico from 1570 onwards),[3] or through the Atlantic Ocean, particularly to Brazil, after 1550 (Alencastro 2000). Indian cottons were sold to cloth slaves and their masters in America, who had enough money to buy pricier textiles, like silks. The growing craves for Asian textiles in Europe, Africa and America slowly built-up diversified markets according to geography and the consumer's purchasing power and tastes. The Portuguese were responsible for creating this new demand, particularly in Africa and in America, by taking advantage of the possibilities offered by the choice of textiles at their disposal in Asia, which appealed to everyone thanks to their quality, price and variety (Ferreira 2014; Ferreira 2015; Ferreira 2017).

These middlemen impacted in other ways, namely in the chronology of the Asian textile trade carried in Portuguese networks supplying Europe, Africa and America, which created a growing demand for this type of commodity earlier than is usually considered by modern historiography (Ferreira 2015, p. 162). New Christian family networks dominated textile commerce made roughly between 1500 and 1640, despite other private players. Portuguese Restoration in 1640 ended their ascendency, particularly in the connection with Spanish America, made either through the Atlantic or the Pacific; as an anti-Portuguese New Christian wave swept them from the Spanish Empire leading to the end of their networks (Studnicki-Gizbert 2007, pp. 151–179). Furthermore, the Inquisition targeted New Christian merchants in Portugal and in her empire after 1640, who were eventually replaced by Old Christian businessmen in key ports like Lisbon, Bahia (Smith 1975)[4] and Goa (Cunha 2006).

A second period emerged between *ca.* 1640–1710, characterized by the commercial crisis induced by Dutch and English competition in Asia, and by the steady decline of the *Carreira da Índia*, reducing the

[3] Comprising Peru until the beginning of the seventeenth century. About this subject see also the essay by Arturo Giráldez, "The Last Link of an Emergent Global Economy: The Manila Galleon" in this volume.

[4] Whose thesis defends that the New Christians businessmen were outnumbered by their Old Christians rivals in Lisbon and Bahia after 1660.

Portuguese offer of Asian textiles in Europe. Lisbon lost its leading position to Amsterdam and London, but by the end of the seventeenth century an interesting development had taken place, which would last until the early 1800s. Lisbon evolved to be a port of convenience to supply the Mediterranean with Asian commodities, namely textiles, especially to Italian ports like Livorno and Genoa, but also to Marseille whenever the French lost maritime access to Asia in the course of European conflicts (Cunha 2009, pp. 140–141). The crisis led to an overall commercial rearrangement marked by two major phenomena until the beginning of the nineteenth century. Firstly, it was the creation of a Portuguese inter-colonial market between the Indian Ocean and the South Atlantic (Africa and Brazil); and secondly the *naus*' crew acted as middlemen between Lisbon and Bahia (demand), and Goa (offer). A cross-cultural trade emerged involving Portuguese, French, and Italian merchants in Lisbon, and also Livorno-based Jews on the side of demand in Europe; the *naus*' crew acting as middlemen carrying money to India and bringing commodities back to Bahia and Lisbon; and Goan Saraswat Brahmins who bought goods in India (Trivellato 2012).

Once the crisis was harnessed, the Portuguese managed to carve a niche for themselves as distributors of Asian textiles between 1710 and 1800, first and foremost in the South Atlantic. The discovery of gold (1695) and diamonds (1728) led to the growth of Brazilian income (Sousa 2006; Costa et al. 2013), enabling a growing number of people to acquire luxury items. Brazilian economic growth depended in slave workforce, which was acquired in Africa with Indian cottons. Asian textiles, like silks and Indian cottons, became staple goods to supply Bahia, Rio de Janeiro, Luanda, and the Bight of Benin. The Atlantic steady economic growth triggered by increased income and available capital had another consequence in the *Carreira da Índia*, namely the emergence of private shipping after 1710. Private shipping came initially from joint-stock companies with limited duration (Cunha 2009, pp. 367–390, 429–649); but after 1770 most ships operating in the Cape Route belonged to Lisbon family firms which established factories in Asia (Carreira 2014, 303–455), investing mainly in Chinese silks and Indian cottons. New developments followed after 1750, when raw silk and cotton, or plain-woven cotton, was acquired in China and India to supply the embryonic Portuguese textile and printing industries (Pinto 1994, 1995).

On the supply side, however, the impact seems less noticeable. Asian manufacturing capacity was able to respond to Atlantic demand, also satisfying the newcomers' taste, like they had done in the past for other markets. The Portuguese fell under the spell of Asian textiles, giving birth to a cross-cultural consumption, even if they failed to understand the meaning of motives; or, likewise, Asian artisans missed the significance of the pieces they were creating for them, namely vestments. This cross-cultural trade had other repercussions. In Portugal, for instance, it influenced embroideries (especially those of Arraiolos and Castelo Branco), and the textile industry after 1775, whose chintzes (called "chitas" in Portuguese) competed with the Indian originals for the African and Brazilian markets.

Portuguese demand only contributed to strengthen Asian textile industry, though we lack figures to estimate the percentage of its demand in the overall Indian and Chinese production, but this was probably small. Conversely, we have little information on the impact of Asian textiles in the development of a substitution industry in Portugal. Unlike European countries like France and The Netherlands, whose laws reserved the home market to its own production to protect the national industry, with varied success, nothing analogous happened in Portugal. This was probably due to Portugal's industrialization process, whose evolution, with many ups and downs since the second half of the seventeenth century (Macedo 1982; Madureira 1997; Pedreira 1994), and insufficient output was never able to satisfy fully home and imperial demand. Portugal still had to import in the second half of the eighteenth century Indian raw cotton whenever Brazilian output was insufficient; as well as plain woven Indian cottons to supply her printing mills when Portuguese production fell short of demand. Paradoxically, it was these agricultural and industrial shortcomings that led Portugal to trade with Asia in order to buy silk and cotton textiles.

Despite the pioneering role played by Portuguese traders in globalizing Asian textiles, particularly in the Atlantic, we still lack a comprehensive study of their overall importance and impact.[5] The task to write such a comprehensive history is daunting, because we have little information on the private trade up to 1700, since the extant documentation

[5] There is, however, research carried on some Asian producing centers, or products, see for example: Cunha and Ferreira (2019, pp. 103–104), Cristóvão (2018), Karl (2016), Ferreira (2013, pp. 46–55), and Barreto (2001).

for this period deals mostly with the Crown's commerce, and most of it is dispersed in different archives and libraries in Portugal and abroad (Ferreira 2015, pp. 149–150). Therefore, what we propose in the following pages is an interpretation based on our research, the existing studies and material evidence.

Building-Up a Market (ca. 1500–1640)

The two great works written by the Portuguese on Asia soon after their arrival, Tomé Pires' *Suma Oriental* (1512–1515) and Duarte Barbosa *Livro* (1515–1518), provided references to Asian main textile producing areas, together with its names, fibers and quality. Gujarat was referred as to the greatest textile production centre in Asia, since Chinese silk was only available in Melaka by the 1510s, something already noticed by the informer of Vasco da Gama in 1498–1499, "And there is [in Melaka] many porcelains and silk (...)" (Marques 1999, p. 123), though he failed to mention China by her name. Melaka was still given as the place of origin for the satin and brocade sent as gifts to Muzaffar Shah II of Gujarat (r. 1511–1526) in 1514,[6] though its origin was unmistakably Chinese. The Portuguese craze for Chinese silk and brocades started early, even if direct and official access to China was only obtained in the middle of the sixteenth century. Afonso de Albuquerque complained to King D. Manuel (r. 1495–1521) that their fellow countrymen wasted money "(...) in very vain things of no benefit; they dress in Indian cotton cloth, silk and taffetas, which are clothes that last little, and other silk fabrics of the land", and that "(...) plain silk and satins from Melaka were not enough (...)" to meet their growing demand in India.[7] Ten years later, in 1525, a maund[8] of Chinese silk was worth 800 "fedeas"[9] in Cambay, as much as Khorasan (Iranian) silk, but more than Sumatran silk (Felner [III] 1868, p. 47), which may imply that it was raw fiber and not fabric. In Hormuz,

[6] "License of Afonso de Albuquerque" Goa 12.06.1514, Mendonça (1915, p. 97).

[7] "Afonso de Albuquerque to King" Goa 23.10.1514, Pato (1884, pp. 296–297).

[8] *Man*, an Indian weight equivalent to 12.2 kgs in Cambay and Diu.

[9] From the Arabic *fadda*, coined in Egypt, but it was a currency of account used in Gujarat.

however, raw silk was sold with a smaller weight called "faraçola",[10] and it was traded free of commissions (Felner [I] 1868, p. 15).

These random examples show how textiles circulated widely in the Asian maritime world and in the Indian Ocean when the Portuguese arrived, changing its price from one port to the next. The Portuguese started discovering this complex interdependent world after 1498, whose different markets ranged from the great emporia at the core of this commercial world, to the peripheral markets were barter still ruled. Vasco da Gama, for instance, carried surprising information to Portugal on his return from India in 1499, namely that cheap Gujarati cottons were used to obtain gold and ivory in the Swahili coast, namely in Sofala, and this type of barter was favorable to the Indians (Radulet and Thomaz 2002, p. 112). Later, the Portuguese discovered that Coromandel textiles were needed to buy clove in Maluku (Pires 1978, p. 342). The vision of a commercial world spreading from East Africa to Japan centered around great emporia as Aden, Hormuz, Cambay, Calicut and Melaka, with satellite ports and markets, was established by the founding texts of Tomé Pires (Pires 1978) and Duarte Barbosa (Barbosa 1996, 2000), though this was a relatively recent change dating from the beginning of the fifteenth century. But the way these two narratives were written also reflected the strategic vision the Portuguese had for the Indian Ocean, with their desire to capture or control these emporia, which they did in some cases, like Melaka conquered in 1511 and Hormuz taken in 1515.

The maritime and commercial nature of the Portuguese Empire in Asia, known as *Estado da Índia*, which included East Africa, meant that its networks competed with others already in place, namely the Gujarati. A close look at Pires and Barbosa works showed, correctly or not, that India occupied a central place of the Indian Ocean trading system, and that Gujarat and Cambay were at its core (Pires 1978, pp. 163–165, 192–204; Barbosa 1996, pp. 174–233). Textiles was one of the key commodities traded in this commercial world, being distributed in Asia and the Indian Ocean, but also in the Middle and Near East, and the Mediterranean. After 1500 two major changes occurred: one was the Europeans entering in the trading world of Asia, and the other was the introduction of Indian cotton textiles in the European commercial networks in the Atlantic via the Portuguese. There is evidence that Indian cotton

[10] From the Arabic *fârsala*, worthing 8,262 kgs.

fabrics were consumed in Egypt before the arrival of Vasco da Gama to India (Goitein and Friedman 2008, pp. 17, 413; Barnes 1997), and that its Egyptian copies were shipped to Europe since Mameluke times (Walker 2000, pp. 186–187). Asian silk was something different. Most of the Asian silk fabrics consumed in Europe came from the Islamic world, particularly from the Middle East (Iran), and its decorative patterns had a lasting influence in European taste and silk textiles.

A side effect of this textile interdependency in the Indian Ocean and in Asia, was the need the Portuguese had to get hold of Asian fabrics if they wanted to obtain desired spices, namely clove in Maluku; but also, gold and ivory from Mozambique. Furthermore, as the Portuguese would soon discover, the conquest and creation of factories and fortresses in Asia and in East Africa also meant that the Crown officials had to acquire textiles if they wanted to trade locally. More so in non-monetized economies of the periphery, like Mozambique, where cheap Indian cottons were used as currency to buy all kind of commodities, namely slaves (Santos 1999, pp. 252–253). Other changes contributed to increase the involvement of private Portuguese merchants in Asia and Southeast Africa textile commerce during the sixteenth century, particularly with the opening of trade to everyone made by governor Lopo Soares de Albergaria in 1516. This move, known in Portuguese sources as the "Great Opening", led to the creation of a "Shadow Empire" and the establishment of settlements in two major Indian producing areas: the coast of Coromandel and Bengal (Winius 1983, pp. 83–101; Subrahmanyam 1990). This continued with the expansion towards East Asia after 1550, with the creation of factories and communities in China (Macao) and Japan (Nagasaki), with the objective to look for Chinese and Japanese silk (Boxer 1959; Souza 1986; Kaisong 1997). After 1580, these intra-Asian maritime routes were connected with Manila, from where many Portuguese sailed to America (Acapulco), something made possible by the union of the Portuguese and Spanish crowns (1580) and the settlement of New Christians in major Spanish American urban centers (Studnicki-Gizbert 2007, pp. 17–121).

Textiles was one of the many commodities traded in these routes. No one invested solely in fabrics, but in different goods in order to diminish risk involving investment, capital recovery time and eventual transport liabilities associated with long and hazardous maritime voyages. In India, for instance, merchants tended to invest in indigo if they were in

Gujarat,[11] or bought diamonds if they traded in the Deccan. In East Asia, Chinese silk was exchanged for silver, but porcelain and lacquers were also traded there (Loureiro 2010, pp. 95–123; Canepa 2016). Commerce in indigo began to decline after 1615, as its price in India rose due to the English and Dutch East India Companies purchases of this dye-plant in Gujarat, and the New Christians preferred to buy the cheaper Guatemalan variety.[12] But diamonds continued to be a safe investment in the Deccan, as India remained its only purveyor until the discovery of the Brazilian mines *ca.* 1730, with Goa keeping its role as a major diamond redistributive hub to Europe.

Traditionally, historians tend to turn around spices and its trade made with Europe, describing it as the most important commerce made by the Portuguese in Asia. Actually, home trade carried by Portuguese and Asian traders in the Estado's networks in Asia, was twice the volume of the commerce made with Europe already around 1520, and its volume kept growing until the middle of the seventeenth century. Certain groups, like the New Christians, Banyans and other Indian merchants, got hold of a great share of the market, as they used existing loopholes in the law to their advantage, especially while transshipping commodities in the Estado ports. In 1597, for instance, viceroy Matias de Albuquerque issued a law, renewed twenty years later (1617), curtailing the value of commodities that could be transshipped in Goa without paying exit taxes: up to 30,000 *réis* if the merchandise came from China and Melaka, and 60,000 *réis* if it came from Sind and Cambay.[13] Noticeably the two last ports were situated in textile producing regions, with Gujarat being the main supplier of fabrics to the Portuguese networks. The apex of this Asian home trade was probably attained during the period of the Union of Crowns (1580–1640), when the New Christians became one of its major players.

[11] The two were closely linked, as in 1609, when not a single bale of indigo or of Gujarati textiles reached Goa to go to Lisbon, 'Letter of viceroy Rui Lourenço de Távora to King Philip II' Goa 08.12.1609 in Biblioteca Nacional de Portugal (henceforth BNP) (Lisbon), *Fundo Geral*, cod. 1975, fls. 316–318.

[12] 'Imports of Indian indigo to Portugal', Lisbon 16.01.1620 in Arquivo Nacional Torre do Tombo (henceforth ANTT) (Lisbon), *Miscelâneas Manuscritas do Convento da Graça*, caixa 3, 6.° D, fl. 321. For an overview of the indigo trade carried by the Portuguese see Cunha (1995, pp. 407–412); and for the trade of the Guatemalan production see Zamora (2017, pp. 584–607).

[13] 'Order of Philip II', Lisbon 27.03.1617 in BNP, *Fundo Geral*, cod. 2702, fls. 67v-68v.

Estimates made for this period show how they invested 180,000,000 *réis* annually in commodities only for the Manila Galleon, and a similar amount in the intra-Asian trade to supply this route, which amounted their total investment to 360,000,000 *réis*. Such large investments gave them a share of 30% in the commerce made between the Philippines and Spanish America (Boyajian 1992, pp. 81–82).

Similar sums of money were invested by the New Christians to buy textiles in India for Europe. In comparison, the money sent from Portugal to buy spices in Asia, though its amount always shifted a lot (Godinho 1987, pp. 7–214), was only a fraction of the overall private investment. This can be seen in the capital invested to buy pepper in 1615, including the spice found aboard the *Nossa Senhora da Luz*, whose value only amounted to 42,334,800 *réis* (Cunha 1995, pp. 464–465).[14] We can only estimate the share and value of the textiles belonging to this private trade to Europe because we lack records, but we have some indirect evidence of its importance, namely if we use the legislation. The ever-increasing expenses needed to keep the *Estado* working, meant that the Crown had to find new sources of revenue, namely taxing textiles, which revealed the growth of its trade. As early as 1601, attempts were made to end legislative loopholes dating from the late 1500s with new laws, which targeted the textiles traded through Goa to the Atlantic. For the first time an attempt was made to create pieces of Indian cloth with standard measures in order to facilitate its taxation. It was also the first time that a European law tried to tie Indian weavers and middlemen to a set of rules fixing textile measurement and quality, but it met with little success as it was renewed in 1607.[15]

This law of 1607 is also important for another reason. It lists the four main Asian producing centers which supplied the Portuguese for their Atlantic markets: Gujarat (with thirteen types of cloth), Deccan and Sind (with seven types of cloth each) and finally Coromandel (with only four types of cloth).[16] Noticeably all these producing centers are Indian, as India remained the most important supplier of fabrics to Portugal and her empire since 1500. Other Indian regions would occupy the forefront

[14] But the total invested in the following year amounted to twice that figure, 81,377,600 *réis*, though the general tendency of the period was to decrease the investment made in spices.

[15] Law of Philip II, Goa 13.08.1607 in BNP, *Fundo Geral*, cod. 2702, fls. 48–51.

[16] Law of Philip II, Goa 13.08.1607 in BNP, *Fundo Geral*, cod. 2702, fls. 49–51.

at later dates, namely Bengal, which disputed with Gujarat for the first place to supply textiles for the Portuguese home and imperial market in the eighteenth century. If Cambay was the greatest emporium to obtain fabrics for the Portuguese in the sixteenth century, Surat replaced it in the seventeenth century, only to be succeeded by Calcutta in the eighteenth century. However, a close look at the few surviving records of Portuguese private trade, namely the fabrics listed aboard the *Nossa Senhora da Luz* in 1615,[17] show more cloth names than those mentioned in the 1607 law, as well as more fabrics coming from those four Indian producing centers. The same diversity of names and origins continued, as can be seen 150 years later in the bill of landing of the ship *Santo António e Justiça* recorded at Bahia in 1757.[18]

Moreover, as they never held sizable manufacturing centers in Asia, excepting a small output in Diu and Daman (Bocarro 1937, pp. 114–117, 154–155), and as the factory in Goa (Cambarjuá) worked only for a short period in the middle of the eighteenth century due to lack of home-grown cotton and dyes (Antunes 2018), the Portuguese always depended on Indian supply, which could be interrupted easily.[19] Furthermore, even when Portuguese private investors travelled inland to buy textiles, they continued to depend on Indian middlemen.[20] Dependency meant that the supply line could be interrupted for various causes, particularly natural disasters. In the 1630s, for instance, the lack of rain, followed by bad

[17] 'Copy of the roll of the commodities aboard the nau *Nossa Senhora da Luz*', Faial 09.12.1615 in Arquivo Histórico Ultramarino, (henceforth AHU), *Caixas da Índia*, n.º 4 [3A], doc. 152. For this period see Afzal Ahmad, Indo-Portuguese Trade in Seventeenth Century (1600–1663), New Dlhi: Gyan Publishing House, 1991, chapter 4. Portuguese Trade in Textiles, pp. 90–109.

[18] 'Book of the receipt of the commodities coming from the Estado da Índia aboard the ship *Santo António e Justiça*' in AHU, cod. 682, fls. 3v, 4, 5, 6-6v, 7, 911v, 12, 13, 13v-14, 14v-18, 19, 21, 21v-25. It is very difficult to bind the name of a textile to its likeness, since we have little or no iconographic sources to help identify them, so most of the time we don't know how these fabrics looked like. For the names see also Luz (1968).

[19] In 1614–1615, for example, the war with the Mughals meant that no fabrics from Gujarat or Sind arrived at Goa to supply the ships of the *Carreira*, so alternative sources had to be found in the Deccan (Bijapur), though of a coarser quality 'Letter of D. fr. Cristóvão de Lisboa to Philip II', Goa 05.02.1615 in AHU, *Caixas da Índia*, cx. 3, doc. 46.

[20] On the vitality and characteristics of the Indian textile industry, namely the putting-out or domestic system behind its production, see Riello and Roy (2013).

harvest and a plague of locusts in Gujarat and in the Deccan impacted in the Indian textile industry, as many weavers working in rural areas died of starvation or disease, thus disrupting production and supply (Moreland 1988, pp. 211–213, 215–218).[21] Prices in Goa rose as the offer diminished steeply, leading viceroy Count of Linhares to seize and sell to everyone the few fabrics bought by the New Christians in the Deccan. Linhares, however, reverted his decision in 1632, since the New Christians threatened to stop risking their money and lives buying textiles in the Deccan if the law wasn't repealed.[22] Attempts to find alternative sources of supply in Sind and Coromandel had limited success, as textile prices soared all over India due to a decrease in production and an increase of demand (Cunha 1995, 510–512).

The Portuguese began sending Asian textiles to the Atlantic in greater numbers during the sixteenth century. We have no series in this trade, though there are some quantitative insights regarding its value and increase. In 1552, for example, João Brandão de Buarcos estimated that the annual cargo of Indian textiles arriving at Lisbon had a net value of 14,000,000 *réis* per vessel (Brandão 1990, p. 59), which given the average number of ships arriving in Lisbon at that date (four) amounted to 56,000,000 *réis* (Cunha 2009, p. 48). The number of vessels sailing in the *Carreira* declined after 1550, even if its average tonnage increased to reach 1,000 or more tons per ship by the late 1500s. In 1616, for instance, the textiles sent by private traders to Portugal ascended to 101,668,200 *réis* in a single hull,[23] seven times more than the value appraised half a century earlier. Textiles, however, only amounted to *ca.* 15% of the overall cargo aboard carracks like the *Nossa Senhora da Luz* (Bettencourt 2008, p. 55), but its percentage in the total cargo value was around 92%, including other commodities like diamonds and indigo (Boyajian 1992, p. 42).

Two phenomena occurred as the number of ships in the *Carreira* declined even further after 1650. On the one hand, the percentage of

[21] The viceroy count of Linhares estimated in more than three million the number of deaths in the Mughal Empire alone in 1630–1631; cf. Letter of viceroy to Philip III, Goa 11.08.1631 in ANTT, *Livros das Monções*, n.º 29, fl. 75.

[22] 'Letter of Francisco de Lucena to Philip III', Goa 30.12.1633 in AHU, *Caixas da Índia*, n.º [10], doc. 105.

[23] 'Commodities sent in the 1616 fleet', Goa 06.01.1617 in AHU, *Caixas da Índia*, n.º [4A], doc. 136.

cargo belonging to the Crown diminished to 10% by the end of the seventeenth century, the remaining belonged to private investors, thus inverting the previous trend. This tendency continued during the eighteenth century, particularly after 1710, when private shipowners and joint-stock companies started investing in the commerce with Asia. On the other hand, Lisbon lost its role as leading distributor in the Atlantic to Amsterdam and London, but it preserved Portugal's imperial market, and gained some subsidiary markets in the Mediterranean, the south of France through Marseille; and Livorno and Genoa in Italy (Cunha 2009, pp. 159–261).

The annual growth rate of 1% in world trade from 1500 to 1800 fueled globalization and established trade routes encompassing the globe by the end of the sixteenth century (O'Rourke and Williamson 2002, pp. 417–456). Asian textiles were omnipresent in this globalization process, with the Portuguese playing an innovative role in the Atlantic (including Europe, America and Africa), especially south of the Equator, and they also had a relevant share in the commerce made between Asia and America through the Pacific from 1580 to 1640.

The South Atlantic became one of the most important market for Asian textiles, especially Indian woven and printed cottons, which were used in the slave trade, and Lisbon was its main European distributor in the early 1600s. Various commodities were used to buy slaves, spices and ivory in West Africa, namely European and Moroccan textiles (Mota 1969), but the colorful and cheap Indian cottons began to be more relevant in the sixteenth century (Bato'ora 1993, pp. 311–314), thanks to the Portuguese participation in the Spanish *Asientos*. The *Asiento* was a contract celebrated by the Spanish Crown to supply slaves for its American colonies, and the Portuguese New Christians hold these lucrative deals until ca. 1640 (Ventura 1999; Scorsch 2009, pp. 51, 147–149, 278; Mouta 2017, pp. 707–728). These New Christians began using Indian cottons to buy slaves in West Africa in the second half of the sixteenth century, taking advantage of their family networks established in India. A sign of its growing weight in the Atlantic slave trade can be seen in King D. Sebastião (r. 1557–1578) decision to maintain the royal monopoly over the"panos de pretos" [Black-men cloth], or "Panos da Mina" [Elmina cloth], when he liberalized the commerce of Indian spices in 1570 (Rivara [1865] 1992, pp. 715–726). The agricultural development of Brazil after 1570, whose exporting crops of sugar and tobacco depended on slave labour force, helped this commerce to grow even further in the South Atlantic. Indian cottons were used to buy slaves in Africa, and to clothe them in America.

Economic connections between the Indian Ocean and the Atlantic can be perceived in another level, namely in the commercial and family ties linking these holders of royal contracts in Portugal and Spain. Manuel Caldeira was one of such men. He held the spice contract in 1583–1587 and married his daughter to Luís Mendes de Vasconcelos, who in turn commanded the Indian fleet of 1583 (Couto [1788] 1974, pp. 423–425), and was a close associate of slave contractors during his tenure as governor of Angola (1617–1621). António Fernandes d'Elvas was another of such men. His father-in-law, Jorge Rodrigues Solis, held the ships contract for the *Carreira* until 1614, while d'Elvas had the slave contracts of Angola, Cape Verde and the Spanish "Asiento". Solis failed to obtain the São Tomé slave contract in 1618, which would establish an Atlantic slave cartel in the hands of the same family if he had pulled the deal out (Alencastro 2000, 95–101; Cunha 2009, 72–73, 84, 91–92). Similar connections can be seen in the iconography, namely in the paintings of the Dutch artist Albert Eckhout (*ca.* 1610–*ca.* 1666). One depicts an African woman with a child by her side, and another an armed African man, the two were painted in Brazil around 1641, and both sitters are wearing a blue and white checkered Indian cotton at the waist (Fig. 1).[24] This commercial connection between Asia and the South Atlantic continued for the seventeenth and eighteenth century, as seen in the commodities traded by a Crown official in Angola during the 1680s named António Coelho Guerreiro, whose ledger book testifies to the importance of Indian cottons used to buy Angolan slaves, and his connections with Brazil (Rau 1956; Lopes and Menz 2019).[25]

Asian textiles were the commodity used to set in motion a complex and intertwined commercial world in the Atlantic. Though Indian cotton fabrics remained the most consumed Asian textile in the South Atlantic until the nineteenth century, silk was demanded by the American elite of the two Iberian empires. Indian cotton, however, was also the most sought-after Asian fabric in the North Atlantic, particularly in Europe, though the Europeans also developed a craving for Chinese silk (Ferreira

[24] Kept in the National Museum of Denmark, Etnographic Collection, Copenhagen (Inv. EN38 A7 and EN 38 A8).

[25] Coelho Guerreiro ended his official career in Asia, as governor of Timor (1702–1705), and during his sojourn in the Estado he traded mostly in Indian textiles.

Fig. 1 ***Black Woman with Child***, 1641, Albert Eckhout (ca. 1610–ca. 1666), Oil on canvas, 267 cm × 178 cm, National Museum of Denmark (Inv. N.38 A8) (© Nationalmuseet https://samlinger.natmus.dk/ES/asset/25493)

2006, pp. 119–139). But it was Indian printed and woven cotton textiles that, again, revolutionized European taste, being accepted for its bright colors and decoration, which withstood better the test of time and wash than European fabrics. It was common to recycle these valuable textiles from very early dates, as it happened with some chintzes belonging to D. Beatriz, the mother of King D. Manuel I, which were converted into stoles and maniples for church use after her death in 1506 (Freire 1914, p. 71). Recycling also shows the value Asian textiles still had after being worn, because they were bequeathed, repurposed, sold in second-hand, or pawned. In Portugal, however, Asian textiles remained the appanage of the privileged, the Church, or of those less well-off who had family in *Estado da Índia*. Queen D. Catarina, the wife of King D. João III (r. 1521–1557), had chintz curtains and other "panos da India" [India cloth] in her oratory,[26] a material option which became common in Portuguese altarpieces during the sixteenth century, whose older reference dates from 1505 and is connected with the royal chapel of King D. Manuel I (Marques 1940, p. 586). D. Catarina also had white Chinese silk thread among her possessions,[27] and was known for sending Asian exotica to her Habsburg relatives, but most of her subjects used coarser fabrics for themselves. This trend persisted in Portugal until the eighteenth century, partly because Catholic Reformation implied a sober clothing style in black or dark colors, partly due for the sumptuary laws which forbade non-privileged strata of the population to wear silk, brocades and embroideries, pushing these gaudy and rich Asian textiles into the realm of domesticity or, paradoxically, to be used by the Church (Ferreira 2011, p. 228; 2016, pp. 22–39).

Another revolution in taste can be ascribed to the acceptance of these Asian textiles decorated with a fluid all-over pattern of vegetal motives unlike anything previously seen by the Europeans (Lemire 2003, p. 500). Although their meaning was alien to their culture (like the peony, or the cranes in Chinese textiles) (Fig. 2); some symbols—like the "Tree of Life" and the peacock—were shared by Europe and Asia alike, and were usual motifs in either Indian and Chinese coverlets exported to Portugal, or in Portuguese embroidered coverlets inspired by Asian designs (Fig. 3).

[26] Livro da Recâmara dos Reis D. João III e de D. Catarina, Biblioteca da Ajuda (Lisbon), cod. 50-V-26, fl. 54v.

[27] ANTT, *Núcleo Antigo*, nº 790, "Catalina de Austria, Inventario de joyas y guardaropa, 15 de Mayo de 1528", fl. 93.

Fig. 2 ***Altar frontal***, China, 1675–1700, silk and gilt-paper-wrapped thread on silk, 72 × 212 cm, Museu Nacional de Arte Antiga (Inv, 1225/A Tec) (© DGPC/LJF, Luí Piorro)

Fig. 3 ***Tree of life in Castelo Branco's embroidery***, Portugal, eighteenth century, silk embroidery on linen ground, 221 × 149 cm, Museu Nacional de Arte Antiga (Inv. 3465)

If all civilizations developed a penchant for "Exotica" since earlier times, i.e., the desire to own and exhibit foreign goods (Sund 2019, 6–14),[28] the globalization set in motion since the sixteenth century led Europeans to engage in a consumption of material culture from Asia, namely textiles, either manufactured for the Asian market, or made specifically for European consumers. The latter gave birth to hybrid styles with themes taken from European culture (namely through prints and drawings), mixed with traditional Indian or/and Chinese motifs in the overall decoration (Fig. 4). We still don't know how much of these hybrid textiles resulted from Portuguese commissions, or were produced by the initiative of native artisans and middlemen, desiring to entice demand by offering products more akin to European taste, as both trends seem to have coexisted. It is possible that even those coverlets, or hangings with Portuguese coats of arms could have been made by Indian artisans without an order, leaving the escutcheon in blank to be embroidered with the arms of the buyer. The uniqueness of these textiles, which were frequently family heirlooms passed from one generation to the next, allowed them to survive, unlike common textiles worn out until they were in tatters, of which little or nothing remains today. But there is some iconographic trace of its consumption, as in the cycle of the live of St. Francis Xavier painted for the sacristy of the church of São Roque in Lisbon around 1619 (Serrão 1993), where they are omnipresent in several scenes, though the artist André Reinoso never left Portugal to paint them.

Besides the innovation introduced by the Portuguese in creating new markets and in fostering new tastes for Asian textiles, a final novelty had to do with the nature of the commercial agents behind this trade. The Portuguese peculiarity lay not with wholesalers, like the Crown and the great New Christian merchants, but with small commerce and family gifts that fed an intensive exchange between Asia and Portugal since the sixteenth century. The Crown officials played a major role in procuring textiles in the *Estado* to supply different needs as seen in the orders issued by Afonso de Albuquerque in the early 1510s (Pato and Mendonça 1915, pp. 9–169); but other official posts, like the captains of major fortresses and trade voyages bestowed by the Crown, had to obtain fabrics if they

[28] Damião de Góis, a Portuguese humanist and diplomat, used the expression exotic in the sixteenth century as a synonym of things coming from abroad, either European or non-European; cf. Simões (2014, pp. 517–525).

Fig. 4 ***Justice of Solomon***, Colcha, India for the Portuguese market, early seventeenth century, 320 × 271.8 cm, silk embroidery on cotton ground, The Metropolitan Museum of Art (Inv. 1975.4)

wanted to profit from the position they held. A document written explicitly for the new King of Portugal Philip I (r. 1580–1598) in 1580, so that he could be aware of the riches of his dominions in Asia, mentioned explicitly how many of the commercial voyages bestowed by the Crown from Mozambique to the Maluku Islands depended on textiles to be profitable (Luz 1960, fls. 39v-40, 83v-107). This system of voyages was in shambles by 1640, though the voyage to Mozambique, where Gujarati fabrics remained a sort of para-monetary unit, survived until the eighteenth century. The Crown also procured Asian textiles for the Royal Family since 1500, as seen in the Indian chintzes sent to King D. Manuel I, which he offered to monasteries patronized by him in Lisbon (Madre de Deus and Belém) and Sintra (Pena) between 1510 and 1512.[29]

The other wholesaler, the New Christians, harbingered globalization due to their family networks covering most of the globe, and they traded extensively in Asian textiles as seen through their businesses in the Atlantic world. Around 1615, however, they were beginning to shift their investments from the Indian Ocean to the Atlantic, even if Henrique Gomes da Costa kept the India ships contract until the 1620s, when he exchanged it for the slave contract in Angola, Congo and Luango.[30] Others stayed in Asia longer, like Manuel Tinoco de Carvalho, very active from the 1610s until the 1630s, who traded with Indian and Chinese fabrics (Boyajian 1992, pp. 134–135)[31]; though he also had relatives active at key places in the Atlantic, like Duarte Tinoco in Bahia and Diogo Fernandes Tinoco in Angola (Boyajian 2001, p. 479). These closely knit family networks were periodically targeted by the Inquisition, which led them to leave for safer places in Europe and in America. The Portuguese Restoration of 1640 severed all connections with Spanish America, and despite the allegiance shown by the New Christians to the new sovereign, D. João IV (r. 1640–1656), their situation in Portugal didn't improve.

The small commerce and family gifts exchanged between Asia and Europe survived for more than three centuries thanks to a thing called "liberdades" [liberties],[32] a system typical of the *Carreira da Índia* which

[29] ANTT, *Corpo Cronológico*, parte. 1, maço 10, docs. 10 and 116;.maço 11, doc. 127 and parte II, maço 36, doc. 10.

[30] Letter of Philip III to the Governors of Portugal, Barcelona 31.031626; Letter of Philip III for the Governors of Portugal, Madrid 18.11.1626, in Boletim (1960, pp. 470, 497).

[31] Tinoco traded in Chinese silk when he was in Macao, and was agent of Queen Isabel, the wife of Phiilp III (r. 1621–1640), to whom he sent Asian exotica and spices.

[32] "Liberdade" is an amount of cargo that the ship crew and other privileged people were allowed to ship aboard East Indiamen, as an extra. Others, mainly aristocrats, like the descendants of Vasco da Gama and the Dukes of Braganza, were entitled to bring an annual amount of commodities from Asia free of charge.

allowed officials and sailors to carry non-monopolized commodities back to Portugal, whose value and amount depended on the grantee position aboard. Since not all had money to invest it was usual for them to sell their "liberdades" to someone living in Asia, who wanted to trade or to send gifts to relatives and patrons in Portugal. Even the gifts had economic value, and could be sold once arrived at the destiny. A closer look at the list of the recipients of these "Liberdades" aboard the *Nossa Senhora da Luz* (1615) revealed the omnipresence of textiles, but also a diversity of receivers that included nuns, Jesuits in Portugal and in Rome, and the Holy House of Mercy of Golegã (Viana 1999, pp. 105, 113, 117). This way textiles could be disseminated through family members, friends, agents, investors and religious institutions (Ferreira 2015, pp. 154–155). This is not surprising, since commodities like textiles replaced money with advantage in long-distance exchanges, given the added value between the price paid to buy them in Asia, and the one obtained for its sale in Europe. Religious orders, like the Jesuits for example, used textiles for their advantage instead of sending money either in Asia, or to Europe.

All this interwoven globe came to an abrupt end around 1640, when the players and characteristics changed for good, except the "Liberdades", which lasted until the beginning of the nineteenth century. On the long run, however, every Portuguese investor, the Crown or private individuals (namely the wholesalers, either the New Christians from 1500 to 1640, or Lisbon based businessmen from 1710 to 1800), always depended on Indian intermediaries to obtain textiles.

From Demise to the Rise of a Niche Market in the South Atlantic (ca. 1640–1800)

The destruction of this interwoven commercial world around 1640 had external and internal causes. The external causes can be attributed to European rivals in Asia, the Dutch and the English, whose East India Companies managed to cripple first and destroy after the commercial networks and the maritime routes of the *Estado da Índia*. The dismantling of the Portuguese system had deep consequences not only in the home trade carried in Asia, but also in the supply to Europe. Macao, for instance, was regularly cut off from Goa since the 1620s, and that isolation increased with the fall of Melaka to the Dutch in 1640. When peace finally settled in 1663, the Dutch company (VOC) did its best to continue hampering all communication between Goa and Macao, and later between Lisbon and Macao from 1710 onwards. This had to do with the fact that Batavia needed its connection with Macao to receive Chinese goods, like silk (Souza 1986, pp. 137, 144),[33] but they continued hampering Portuguese navigation even after the VOC managed to establish a factory in Canton in the 1730s.

The English company (EIC), on the other hand, ended the war with the Portuguese sooner, in 1635, but peaceful relations changed in the course of the first half of the eighteenth century, as Britain bid for commercial supremacy in Asia. In 1738, for instance, a British called Tempest Milner, the first-clerk of the *Nossa Senhora da Conceição e São Francisco Xavier*, a Lisbon based India ship, saw how his countrymen belonging to the EIC board in Calcutta seized the textiles he had bought in the Dutch factory of Chinsura or Serampore, valued at 7,200,000 *réis*.[34] Things changed for worse during the War of Austrian Succession (1740–1748), when the EIC seized Goan ships in the Arabian Sea and the Bay of Bengal, accusing its captains of being frontmen for the French, with whom Britain was at war. That was not always the case, but the EIC was partly right, as the French agents of the *Compagnie des Indes* made private trade in Asia using Portuguese as frontmen, and used Portuguese networks to repatriate their fortunes back to Europe (Manning 1996). There was even a commercial voyage to India made in a Portuguese ship manned by Frenchmen and financed solely with French capital, which included the former governor of Mauritius and Réunion, Bertrand-François Mahé de La Bourdonnais. The *Real* made mostly home trade in the Indian Ocean between 1753 and 1756, before returning to Lisbon with a cargo of money and Bengali cotton and silk fabrics (Cunha 2009, pp. 602–614). Afterwards, however, the EIC allowed the agents of Lisbon based commercial houses active in India after 1770 to establish factories and agencies in Surat and Calcutta. All other European presences in Asia, like the Danes, the Swedes, and interlope companies (like the Ostend Company) had no real impact in the Portuguese networks and commercial routes, except for the French as we have seen.

[33] The Dutch wanted Chinese fermented teas, as the European taste in the eighteenth century had moved from the Japanese green tea to the "black tea".

[34] BNP, *Fundo Geral*, cod. 550, fl. 270v.

If spices dominated the trade between Asia and Europe until the 1680s, textiles took the upper hand afterwards, particularly Indian cotton fabrics, even if the commerce of tea grew after the second quarter of the eighteenth century (Prakash 1998, pp. 116–117, 121–123).[35] All competed for Asian production, but India and China supplied Europe's increasing demand on raw materials, plain woven Indian cotton for printing, and the usual fabrics, though prices rose steadily too.

Raw fabrics and plain woven Indian. cotton had a rising importance in feeding European industry, as the incipient Portuguese textile and printing manufactures. The Royal Silk Factory of Rato (Lisbon), founded in 1734, for example, tried to obtain raw silk from China as homegrown production was insufficient to meet demand. The Crown granted a series of voyages to Macao for the purchase of raw silk in China. Several voyages were made between 1742 and 1757, but the successive managements of the factory were more interested in trading in silk textiles and other Chinese commodities, and to sell these in the Coast of Coromandel and Rio de Janeiro, than to buy raw silk for its looms in Lisbon (Cunha 2009, pp. 455–498). Growing competition for Chinese goods, namely silk fabrics, meant that prices rose, as the *Lusitânia Grande* discovered in 1752, as there were 29 European ships vying for the same goods in Canton (Noticia 1753, pp. 7, 9, 11). The first-clerk took the decision to wait in Macao for two years to buy merchandise at lower prices before returning to the Atlantic in 1754, where the ship stayed in Rio de Janeiro for more than a year to sell part of its cargo.[36] A similar trade made with Indian plain-woven cotton started after 1775 to feed the Portuguese textile printing industry as we shall see.

Dutch and, to a lesser extent, English attacks disrupted most of the trading maritime routes in the *Estado* from 1622 to 1663. Only a few survived after 1663, mostly in the western Indian Ocean, of which the one linking Gujarat to Mozambique was perhaps the most profitable. Banyan merchants of Diu ended up by controlling its trade, as they had access to Gujarati cottons which acted as currency to buy gold, ivory and slaves

[35] Though Chinese and Bengali silk remained important commodities traded with Europe.

[36] The ship arrived at Lisbon in June 1755 and most of its cargo was still in the Customs when the earthquake in the 1st of November destroyed everything; ANTT, *Junta do Comércio*, book 74, fls. 37v-38; "Letter of the Casa da Índia to the Customs of Rio de Janeiro" Lisbon 10.02.1756, Documentação (1966, p. 283).

in Mozambique (Antunes 1992, pp. 143–164). Other routes connected with Mozambique emerged in the eighteenth century, namely one to the nearby French islands of Mauritius and Réunion, which worked as a redistributive relay to provide slaves to its own plantations and also to America (Médard 2013, pp. 69–74). Cheap Gujarati cottons continued to be one of the key commodities to buy anything in East Africa, as Brazilian shipowners discovered in the eighteenth century when they began to navigate directly to the Indian Ocean to purchase slaves. In 1737, for instance, a small ship from Rio de Janeiro was sighted in her route from Mozambique to Surat with a cargo of cowries which they wanted to sell in order to buy cottons for the slave trade.[37]

This was no longer only the case of metropolitan networks active in the Indian Ocean, but also of Brazilian networks, whose presence increased in the eighteenth century as Brazil's income and available capital grew. One of such networks belonged to António Lopes da Costa, from Rio de Janeiro, who operated in the Western Indian Ocean from his base in Mozambique Island in the 1760s, engaging in every kind of traffic, namely Indian textiles. In 1767, for example, Costa send a ship to Bengal to buy textiles not for the Mozambican market but to export to Rio (Hope 1970, p. 228). The Atlantization of the western Indian Ocean was even greater in the following decades, as the former governor of Angola, Francisco de Sousa Coutinho (1764–1772), recognized in 1779 that "the trade of Mozambique is attended by people from Bahia and Rio de Janeiro, who establish their agencies in the Island from where they send ships to the French islands with slaves, and other vessels full of ivory, gold and cowrie to the ports of India, where they buy clothes with which they return to their home ports and towns" (Ahmad 1997, p. 131).

The Atlantization, a term used to describe the capture of traffics in the western Indian Ocean by the Atlantic, frequently bypassed the metropolitan economy, and was an all-pervasive phenomenon which also included Portuguese networks, particularly after 1760. One of such belonged to a man called José Rodrigues Vareiro, a captain seasoned in the Asian commerce, whose ship *Santiago Maior* traded in the route Lisbon-Mozambique-India-Mozambique-Brazil-Lisbon in the 1760s. Vareiro, though trading only in slaves, cowries and ivory between

[37] BNP, *Fundo Geral*, cod. 550, fl. 104.

Mozambique and Rio de Janeiro and Bahia, ended by sailing his ship to Daman (Gujarat), Goa and Calcutta (Bengal), in order to buy textiles. He, and later his widow and her associates, traded for their own and also freighted the ship to English and French agents of the EIC and the *Compagnie des Indes*. François-Léon Brayer, Jean-Baptiste Chevalier, and Jacques-Alexandre Gourlade were among these Frenchmen whose investment in the 1765 homebound voyage earn them a handsome profit of 150% with the sales of Indian commodities in Rio (Cunha 2009, pp. 663–665).

The Atlantization of the Indian Ocean by the Portuguese imperial economy meant not only the unstoppable penetration of Brazilian networks in Mozambique and India, but also the end of the *Estado* as a coherent and cohesive economic space as it was created in the sixteenth century. It was the corollary of a process initiated after 1640, whose major transformation lay in the formation of an intercolonial market anchored in the South Atlantic, which blossomed fully in the eighteenth century. Goa, as a result, had to rely mostly in the supply of Indian textiles, since it had difficulties in obtaining silk and other Chinese commodities, as Macao developed its own commercial networks in the Indian Ocean. These headed to the French ports in India, as Pondicherry, which they supplied with Chinese goods; though Macao shipowners also invested in other commercial activities and routes as far away as Mozambique; as witnessed in 1738 by Paulo Teixeira, the first-surgeon of *Nossa Senhora da Conceição e São Francisco Xavier*, a Lisbon based India ship.[38] Macao was venturing out of its traditional routes in the South China Sea, and its shipping continued prospecting for new markets and itineraries in the western Indian Ocean during the second half of the eighteenth century.

Macao even tried and got direct maritime access to the Atlantic, overpassing Goa, through the short lived joint-stock Company of Macao (1710–1727), which reunited local and Lisbon based investors (Cunha 2009, pp. 367–390).[39] This was only the beginning of a phenomenon characteristic of the eighteenth century, which saw an increasing number

[38] BNP, *Fundo Geral*, cod. 550, fl. 223v.

[39] Macao's *Senado* tried to establish a company to trade directly to Brazil in 1732 and again in 1734, bypassing Goa and Lisbon, in order to obtain silver and tobacco in exchange for silk and other Chinese merchandise like porcelain. The Crown refused the plan twice, but the route was eventually established in the early nineteenth century; cf. Rego (1995, pp. 7–30).

of ships being sent from Lisbon to Macao, which stopped at Rio de Janeiro to load silver in the way to China and called Brazilian ports again in the return voyage to sell goods. The continuity of such contacts, for the sale of silk and other Chinese commodities in Rio, can be attested in the commercial correspondence exchanged between the Lisbon based merchant Francisco Pinheiro and one of his local agents, Giovanni Francesco Muzzi. The Italian even considered a plan in 1722 to collect capital among his bosses in Lisbon, Pinheiro and the commercial house of Medici & Beroardi, which could be open to other investors in London, Amsterdam and Rio, to finance a commercial venture to Macao taking advantage of the silver available in Brazil.[40] The plan came to no fruition, but Pinheiro recovered the idea, since he invested 471,503 *réis* in the *Nossa Senhora da Oliveira*, when the ship called Rio to load silver on her voyage to Macao in 1726. The money was to be invested in what "could be more profitable here [Portugal] and in Brazil".[41] These Chinese goods, among which silk, were easily sold in Rio in 1728, and the sale was such a success that the *Nossa Senhora da Oliveira* sailed directly to Lisbon without stopping at Bahia as planned.[42] The gains from this maritime route led Rio based investors to put money in other commercial ventures to Macao, as in the ship *São Pedro e São João*, which in her return voyage in 1740 gave "the capital and its earnings" to Rio's nine investors; though not everything went according to plan, since later they had to pay 2,970,909 *réis* due in tariffs to the *Casa da Índia*.[43]

All these changes impacted deeply in the trade made through the *Carreira da Índia*, which underwent a complete change after 1650. Paramount to this change was the disappearance of the New Christians, though some still kept valuable Indian trades running like diamonds until the first quarter of the eighteenth century (Fabião 1973, pp. 455–519). As the number of ships declined to a record low between 1650 and 1759, people saw the investment in the *Carreira* as a liability since round

[40] Letter of Giovanni Francesco Muzzi to Francisco Pinheiro, Rio de Janeiro 28.02.1722, Lisanti (1973a, pp. 248–249).

[41] Letter of Francisco Pinheiro to Manuel Nunes and Francisco da Cunha Freitas, Lisbon 31.03.1725, Lisanti (1973b, p. 523).

[42] Letter of Giovanni Francesco Muzzi to Francisco Pinheiro, Rio de Janeiro 28.02.1722, Lisanti (1973a, p. 268).

[43] List of the investors in the ship *São Pedro e São João*, Lisbon 30.03.1742, Documentação (1966, pp. 156–157).

voyages weren't always completed. During this period there were 5 years without a ship arriving in Goa, 11 years without a vessel leaving India to Portugal, and 20 years without a single hull completing the voyage to Lisbon (Cunha 2009, pp. 166–168). The Crown had to step in order to keep the *Carreira* running despite its deficit, though most of the cargo was in private hands since 1660–1670, amounting to as much as 90% (Ames 2000, pp. 110–111). A new characteristic emerged as the ship's crew and sailors transported capital belonging to Lisbon based investors to Goa, where it was delivered to Indian merchants, who in turn bought the commodities to be sent to Portugal through the same intermediaries. In 1703, a top official of the Exchequer in Portugal stated that the *Carreira* was still running despite its deficit only for the profit that its crews took made with the "liberdades".[44] The "liberdades" remained active until the Crown finally abolished them in the beginning of the nineteenth century, but the crews had lost their role as the sole purveyors of Asian commodities to Bahia and Lisbon with the surge of Portuguese private shipping to Asia after 1770.

A second change was connected with the route followed by the *Carreira*, which after 1660 began calling Bahia in Brazil (Lapa 2000; Antony 2013). What was initially a call in the return voyage to Lisbon to be escorted for protection sake, gave place to an informal commerce first and then to an authorized one after 1700, which was the beginning of an intercolonial trade between Brazil and Asia. This may have saved the *Carreira*, while it purveyed Bahia and Brazil with much needed Asian commodities, among which Indian textiles. The bill of landing of the nau *Santo António Justiça* in Bahia in 1757 attested to that commerce, namely in Indian textiles dispatched by two crewmen, Manuel de Oliveira and Manuel da Silva. These were luxury and common fabrics like "fine chintz at 4,000 *réis*, middle quality chintz at 3,000 *réis*, common chintz at 1,500 *réis*, fine doubled chintz at 8,000 *réis*, fine and middle quality Coromandel *gargarares* at 4,000 *réis* and 3,000 *réis* each, cotton kerchiefs at 75 *réis*, *morins* at 800 *réis*, and embroidered satin bedspreads lined with a fringe at 9,600 *réis*", the lot being valued at 544,000 *réis*.[45] Part of these

[44] Consultation of the Ultramarine Council, Lisbon 13.01.1703 in AHU, *Caixas da Índia*, n.º [44], doc. 5.

[45] AHU, cod. 682, fl. 4. We don't know what are Coromandel "gargares" or "morim", nor do we know how they looked like.

Indian fabrics was intended for the Brazilian market (Souza 2012, pp. 39–40, 52), as seen in the water-colored drawings of the Italian artist and colonial army engineer Carlos Julião (1740–1811) in the 1780s, where both slave and free women wear Indian cottons (Julião 1960, pp. 42, 49, 50, 52). Other part of the cargo, however, was destined to feed the slave trade made by Bahia's businessmen in the Bight of Benin, with bales of "folhinha" and "Kaffir cloth" also unloaded from the *Santo António Justiça*.[46]

The connection of Brazil to the west African Coast dated already from the late sixteenth century, and each Brazilian region developed a special economic relation to a part of the African littoral closer to her ports (Alencastro 2018, pp. 57–63). Cheap Indian cottons were one of the most used commodities for this trade, as seen in the commercial transactions carried by a small Crown official called António Coelho Guerreiro posted in Angola during the 1680s. Though he also traded with European fabrics, namely from France (Rouen), The Netherlands and also Portugal (Covilhã), most of the textiles trafficked by Guerreiro were Indian (Rau 1956, *passim*). As slave traffic increased to meet the ever-growing demand of labour in Brazil, particularly mining and afterwards with the development of agricultural cash crops like cotton and rice in the eighteenth century, a similar demand for textiles to buy more slaves grew too. Known data for Angola alone between 1725 and 1794 reveal a total of 614 ships making the voyage to Brazil, belonging to Rio (51.1%), Bahia (27.3%) and Pernambuco (17.7%) (Venâncio 1996, pp. 172–173).

But this trade also saw an increase in the number of ships returning from the Indian Ocean that called Luanda, especially during the 1760s and 1770s, so much so that the known Portuguese economist José Acúrcio da Neves characterized Mozambique and Angola as a warehouse of Asian commodities to be "smuggled" to Brazil (Neves 1987, p. 292). This meant that Brazilian businessmen and shipowners invested in private commercial voyages to India and Macao, and arranged for the cargo to be unloaded in Luanda in the return voyage because they knew that the local customs had older and lower tariffs than in Brazil. But such legal loopholes began to disappear in the 1770s, as a tighter customs control was established in Angola, as was witnessed in the case of the ship

[46] AHU, cod. 682, fl. 16v. "Kaffir cloth" is mentioned already in the sixteenth century, and "folhinha" [little leaf] was one of the most traded Indian printed cottons in seventeenth century Angola, as seen in the ledger book of António Coelho Guerreiro.

Nossa Senhora da Ajuda e São Pedro de Alcântara, which carried a cargo loaded in Bengal valued in 320,000,000 *réis* belonging to William Bolts. The authorities forbade Bolts agent on board, a Frenchman called Louis Cantofer, to unload the cargo and dispatch part of it to Brazil (Guedes 2006, pp. 218, 220–221; Silva 2003, pp. 338–339). The volume of Indian textiles consumed in the South Atlantic seems to have augmented during the eighteenth and early nineteenth century, as well as its sources of supply.[47]

Another change had to do with the beginning of private shipping in the *Carreira* after 1710. Its impact was small between 1710 and 1759, as only 29 ships (21.1% of the total) left Lisbon for Asia belonged to private shipowners and joint-stock companies; of which 24 returned (29.2% of the total) (Cunha 2009, p. 694). But the volume increased considerably after 1770, booming during the War of American Independence (1775–1783) and in the early stages of the French Revolutionary Wars (1792–1802), when the Crown presence in the overall traffic became irrelevant (Guinote et al. 2002, pp. 222–245). That had to do with the fact that the traditional Portuguese neutrality turned Lisbon into a port of convenience for the French to have access to Asian commodities, since the ruling maritime power, Britain, had cut off her connections with India. The role of Lisbon as a port of convenience was born out of the European conflicts of the late seventeenth century, which usually severed France's links with Asia. This and a thriving French community established in Lisbon (Labourdette 1988), meant that there were ways for them to have access to Asian goods. Many of the Lisbon-based businessmen invested in the trade made by the *Carreira*, while some officers of the *Compagnie des Indes* repatriated home their fortunes made illegally in India via Portugal, many times investing in textiles and other valuable commodities, as seen already in the case of Mahé de La Bourdonais.

[47] Known figures for the beginning of the nineteenth century reveal its magnitude. In 1810, for example, Rio de Janeiro imported 506,723,400 *réis* of Asian commodities from Goa, of which 98.7% was textiles; and three years later, in 1813, the value was 577,966,890 *réis* (with 97.3% corresponding to fabrics). Perhaps as much as two thirds of it on average was used to buy slaves, but there were other sources of supply. Luanda obtained textiles directly from Portugal, Europe and Goa, besides Brazil. In 1808, for instance, Luanda received fabrics from Goa valued at 306,447,600 *réis*, while those from Portugal amounted to 194,073,165 *réis* and those from Europe at 107,055,550 *réis*; Florentino (2014, pp. 131–132).

But Lisbon also gained a new role, that of purveyor of Asian goods to the Mediterranean, either through France (Marseille) or Italy (Genoa and Livorno). The extent of this is measurable in the money seized proportionately by the viceroy in Goa from two ships, the *Nossa Senhora da Vitória* and the *Nossa Senhora do Bom Sucesso* in 1739. More than half of that cash (52.2%) belonged to non-Portuguese, as the Italian share corresponded to 47.8% of all the capital taken forcefully as a loan, which equated to all the Portuguese money sent to India in those two ships. The single greatest investor was also Italian, the family firm of Lazzaro Maria and Giuseppe Cambiazzo, whose Goan intermediary was the Saraswat Brahmin Tondre Kamat.[48] If this commerce lived of the "kindness of strangers" (Trivellato 2012), as Tondre Kamat also catered for the investment of Livorno Jews like Manuel Ergas,[49] portraying a cross-cultural trade where people from different religions living far apart trusted each other, the same can be applied to the Portuguese Crown. Not for tolerance's sake, but out of need, since there were no alternative networks operating in Goa, but for those belonging to Hindu merchants since the late 1600s. These remained in place until 1770, when Lisbon based family firms established their agencies in Goa and elsewhere in India (Carreira 1995, pp. 83–95). Hindu financiers and merchants had been renting Crown "rendas" and bidding for pepper contracts since the late sixteenth century, and they continued doing so afterwards. Two members of the same Kamat family, Suba (1759) and Vitogy (1760), bid for two contracts to supply Indian textiles to the Crown, most of them bought in Surat.[50]

Another major change linked with private shipping and investment was the destiny of these voyages. Macao emerged as the most sought-after destiny, eighteen voyages between 1710 and 1759, doubling the number of the ships that headed to India (Cunha 2009, p. 695). Chinese commodities, especially silk, were eagerly demanded in Portugal, but also in Brazil. Private shipping stopped in Brazil on their way to Macao to load silver in Rio de Janeiro, but also stopped in the return voyage to sell fabrics, porcelain, and lacquers. Such investment in these Asian commercial voyages was onerous. The cost of sending an 800-ton ship to China in the beginning of the eighteenth century (1710–1720) amounted at

[48] AHU, cod. 491, fls. 4–43.

[49] AHU, cod. 491, fl. 43.

[50] AHU, cod. 1150, fls. 8–13.

around 100,000,00 *réis*, not counting the expenditure with fixed capital; and that amount had doubled (200,000,000 *réis*) thirty years later in the 1750s (Cunha 2009, p. 695). In 1800, the cost of sending a similar ship of 800 tons to China could amount to 300,000,000 *réis* or more. Average profits in the Macao route around 1710–1712 was about 36.5%, but we lack reliable figures for later dates. Things are different in the Indian voyages, where costs were higher, even if smaller ships were involved in the traffic, like the 400 tons *Bom Despacho* and *Santa Ana* in 1754, as investment in circulating capital alone ascended to about 270,000,000 *réis*.[51] The cost per ton invested in each voyage was higher in the Indian route than in that of Macao, hinting for the preference private shipowners and investors had for China trade. In either case, however, textiles remained the most sought-after commodity.

Epilogue—A Never Ending Story

Europe became infatuated for Asian fabrics from the sixteenth century onward, especially with Indian printed cottons, whose quality, diversity, price and "exoticism" appealed to its elite, but "mass consumption" only began in England and Holland after 1650, connected with the development of urban life and the rise of a middle class (Trentmann 2017, pp. 64, 66, 70, 93–94; Lemire 2012, pp. 205–226; Lemire 2010, pp. 185–192). Nevertheless, Portugal had to wait until the second half of the eighteenth century to follow suit. In that respect, the trickledown effect, depended as much on societal behavior, as on disposable income, and Portugal only witnessed a substantial increase of the country's living condition in the eighteenth century, which allowed the less well-to-do to acquire new "luxuries" as Indian chintzes (Cunha and Ferreira 2019, 103–104).

'Mass consumption' of Asian textiles in Portugal had to do with the offer of affordable Indian cotton commodities like kerchiefs, cheaper chintzes from the Deccan, including bedspreads, available to people with smaller incomes, as is evident in the sale of Indian commodities in Bahia in 1757.[52] This shift relates with the rise of wages in eighteenth century Portugal, particularly in its first half thanks to the Brazilian gold rush,

[51] Letter of Pierre-Philippe Rocquefeuil to George Duval de Leyrit, Mahé 04.03.1755, in British Historical Society of Portugal, (Carcavelos), *Gallwey Papers*, "Copie des lettres", p. 21.

[52] AHU, cod. 682, ff. 3v, 7v, 9, 11.

even if incomes declined afterwards (Costa et al. 2013, pp. 4–5, 12, 15–19). ‘Mass consumption’ was also helped by new marketing techniques, like publishing news with the arrival of cargoes from Asia in the ‘Lisbon Gazette’, or by printing leaflets with the description of commodities offered in sale.[53]

The analyses of inventories made between 1650 and 1800 show Lisbon houses with high incomes in tune in with European consumption patterns for home décor in the use of chintzes for example.[54] Another revolution took place in the eighteenth century. Asian textiles, Chinese silk excepted, finally left the realm of domesticity for the street, as women began wearing Indian cottons. The fashion for Indian printed cottons took to the streets, after it was a common sight in Northern Europe. The same is valid for Brazil.

To this we must add other dimensions: cost and intangible values of affective and cultural nature. The fact that some pieces, namely embroidered bedspreads, have survived show a desire to leave them from one generation to the other. They are the proof of acceptance and integration of commodities produced by different cultures with colors and motifs alien to the consumer. If civil consumption is easy, in Portugal there is also its religious use, absent in Northern Reformed Europe. What began as a simple commodity had in the end a far greater importance in the social, political, and cultural sphere.

Sources

Manuscripts

AHU—Arquivo Histórico Ultramarino:
Caixas da Índia (We use the old catalogue numbers):
cx. 3, doc. 46.

[53] See for example, the cargo list of the ships *Nossa Senhora dos Prazeres*, *S. Joseph*, *Rey de Portugal* and *Santa Anna Raynha de Portugal*, 4 Setembro de 1756, Museu do Oriente, Lisbon (Inv. ASIA 09:339 LIS).

[54] Chintz pervades all interiors, from the aristocratic interiors to more humble abodes. While richer houses have India chintzes worthing 2,200 *réis* in average, homes with lower incomes have an average of 720 *réis* invested in these textiles (Madureira 1989, p. 98) (Watt 2013, p. 87). We lack similar studies for other cities in Portugal and in her empire as well, to know how Asian textiles were distributed, transported and sold, and who consumed them as well.

n.º 3A, doc. 152
n.º 4A, doc. 136
n.º 10, doc. 105
cx. n.º 44, doc. 5

Codexis, 491, 682, 1150.

ANTT—Arquivo Nacional da Torre do Tombo:
Corpo Cronológico,
Part I, bundle 10, docs. 10 and 116
Part I, bundle 11, doc. 127
Part II, bundle 36, doc. 10

Junta do Comércio,
Book 74,

Livros das Monções,
n.º 29

Miscelâneas Manuscritas do Convento da Graça,
caixa 3, 6.º D,

Núcleo Antigo:
nº 790, "Catalina de Austria, Inventario de joyas y guardaropa, 15 de Mayo de 1528"

BA—Biblioteca da Ajuda:
Codex 50-V-26.

BNP—Biblioteca Nacional de Portugal:
Fundo Geral,
Codexes: 550, 1975, 2702

British Historical Society of Portugal, (Carcavelos):
Gallwey Papers, "Copie des lettres"

Works of Art

Museu do Oriente, Lisbon
Inv. ASIA 09:339 LIS

National Museum of Denmark, Etnographic Collection, Copenhagen:
Inv. EN 38 A7
Inv. EN 38 A8

Bibliography

Afzal Ahmad. 1991. *Indo-Portuguese Trade in Seventeenth Century (1600–1663)*. New Delhi: Gyan Publishing House.

Afzal Ahmad (Ed.). 1997. *Os Portugueses na Ásia*. Lisbon: Imprensa Nacional-Casa da Moeda.

Luiz Felipe de Alencastro. 2000. *O trato dos viventes. Formação do Brasil no Atlântico Sul - séculos XVI e XVII*. Rio de Janeiro: Companhia das Letras.

Luiz Felipe Alencastro. 2018. "África, números do tráfico atlântico." In *Dicionário da Escravidão Brasileira*, org. by Lilia M. Schwarcz and Flávio Gomes. Rio de Janeiro: Companhia das Letras, pp. 57–63.

Glenn J. Ames. 2000. *Renascent Empire? The House of Braganza and the Quest for Stability in Portuguese Monsoon Asia, ca. 1640–1683*. Amsterdam: Amsterdam University Press.

Philomena Sequeira Antony. 2013. *Relações Intracoloniais Goa-Bahia 1675–1825*. Brasília: Fundação Alexandre de Gusmão.

Luís Frederico Dias Antunes. 1992. "A actividade da companhia do comércio dos baneanes de Diu em Moçambique (1686–1777)." In *Mare Liberum*, n° 4 (December), pp. 143–164.

Luís Frederico Dias Antunes. 2018. "A Fábrica Real de Cumbarjuá (1782): o estabelecimento de uma indústria têxtil em Goa?", Paper Presented at the Conference Organized in Memory of Lotika Varadarajan, *Os têxteis indianos e o império português. Arte e Contextos*, Lisbon: Museu Nacional de Arte Antiga and FCSH/ NOVA, October 10 and 11.

Duarte Barbosa. 1996. *O Livro de Duarte Barbosa (Edição crítica e anotada)*, edited by Maria Augusta da Veiga e Sousa, vol 1, Lisbon: Ministério da Ciência e Tecnologia/Instituto de Investigação Científica e Tropical - C.N.C.D.P.

Duarte Barbosa. 2000. *O Livro de Duarte Barbosa (Edição crítica e anotada)*, edited by Maria Augusta da Veiga e Sousa, vol 2, Lisbon: Ministério da Ciência e Tecnologia/Instituto de Investigação Científica e Tropical - C.N.C.D.P.

Ruth Barnes. 1997. *Indian Block-Printed Textiles in Egypt: The NewBerry Collection in the Ashmolean Museum. Oxford*, 2 vols. Oxford: Clarendon Press.

Patrícia Salvação Barreto. 2001. *Lenços e Colchas de Chita de Alcobaça*, Lisbon: Gabinete de Relações Internacionais do Ministério da Cultura - Instituto Camões.

J. Bato'ora Ballong-Wen-Mewuda. 1993. *São Jorge da Mina (1482–1637): La vie d'un comptoir Portugais en Afrique occidentale*, vol. I. Lisbon/Paris: Fundação Calouste Gulbenkian/C.N.C.D.P.

José António Bettencourt. 2008. *A Nau Nossa Senhora da Luz (1615) no Contexto da Carreira da Índia e da Escala dos Açores: uma abordagem histórico–arqueológica*, MA Dissertation Presented at the Faculdade de Ciências Sociais e Humanas of the Universidade Nova de Lisboa.

António Bocarro. 1937. *Livro das plantas de todas as fortalezas, cidades e povoações do Estado da Índia Oriental*, A. B. Bragança Pereira (Ed.), *Arquivo Português Oriental*, tome IV, vol. II, Bastorá: Tipografia Rangel.

Boletim da Filmoteca Ultramarina Portuguesa. 1960. n.° 15, Lisbon: Centro de Estudos Históricos Ultramarinos.

Charles Ralph Boxer. 1959. *The Great Ship form Amacon. Annals of Macao and the Old Japan Trade.* Lisbon: Centro de Estudos Históricos Ultramarinos.

James C. Boyajian. 1992.*Portuguese Trade in Asia under the Habsburgs, 1580–1640*. Baltimore: The Johns Hopkins University Press.

James C. Boyajian. 2001. "New Christians and Jews in the Sugar Trade, 1550–1750. Two Centuries of Development of the Atlantic Economy." In *European Expansion and Global Interaction*, vol II, *Jews and the Expansion of Europe to the West, 1450–1800*, edited by Paolo Bernardini and Norman Fiering. New York/Oxford: Berghahn Books, pp. 471–484.

João Brandão de Buarcos. 1990. *Grandeza e abastança de Lisboa em 1552.* Lisboa: Livros Horizonte.

Teresa Canepa. 2016. Silk, Porcelan and Lacquer China and Japan and Their Trade with Western Europe and the New World: 1500–1644, London: Paul Holberton Publishing.

Ernestina Carreira. 1995. "O comércio português no Gujarat na segunda metade do século XVIII: as famílias Loureiro e Ribeiro." *Mare Liberum*, n.° 9 (July 1995), pp. 83–94.

Ernestine Carreira. 2014. *Globalising Goa (1660–1820). Change and Exchange in a Former Capital of Empire*, Saligao (Goa): Goa 1556.

Leonor Freire Costa, Maria Manuela Rocha, and Rita Martins de Sousa. 2013. *O Ouro do Brasil.* Lisbon: Imprensa Nacional-Casa da Moeda.

Diogo do Couto. [1788] 1974. *Da Ásia, dos feitos, que os portugueses fizeram na conquista, descobrimento das terras, e mares do Oriente, década décima* (Reprint of the edition of the Régia Oficina Tipográfica in 1788). Lisbon: Livraria San Carlos.

Inês de Castro Cristóvão. 2018. "*A principal riqueza que dali vem*": *os têxteis bordados indianos em Portugal nos séculos XVI e XVII*, MA Dissertation Presented at the Faculdade de Ciências Sociais e Humanas of the Universidade Nova de Lisboa.

João Teles e Cunha. 1995. *Economia de um império. Economia política do Estado da Índia em torno do mar Arábico e do golfo Pérsico. Elementos conjunturais: 1595–1635*, MA Dissertation Presented at the Faculdade de Ciências Sociais e Humanas of the Universidade Nova de Lisboa.

João Teles e Cunha. 2006. "3. Economia e Finanças: a) A rede económica do Estado da Índia (1660–1750)." In *Nova História da Expansão Portuguesa*, edited by Joel Serrão and A.H. de Oliveira Marques, vol. V, tome I, *O Império Oriental 1660–1820*, coord. by Maria de Jesus dos Mártires Lopes. Lisbon: Editorial Estampa, pp. 162–338.

João Teles e Cunha. 2009. *A Carreira da Índia e a construção do mercado inter-colonial português, 1660–1750*, PhD Dissertation Presented at the Faculdade de Letras of the Universidade de Lisboa.

João Teles e Cunha and Maria João Ferreira. 2019. "Spreading Desire, Linking the World: Pintados and the Portuguese, 1500–1800." In *Cloth That Changed the World. The Art and Fashion of Indian Chintz*, edited by Sarah Fee. New Haven: Yale University Press—Royal Ontario Museum, pp. 99–105.

Documentação Ultramarina Portuguesa, vol. IV, 1966. Lisbon: Centro de Estudos Históricos Ultramarinos.

Luís Crespo Fabião. 1973. "Subsídios para a história dos chamados "Judeus Portugueses" nas indústrias dos diamantes em Amsterdão nos séculos XVII e XVIII." In *Revista da Faculdade de Letras*, n.° 15, 3rd Series (1973), pp. 455–519.

Felner [I]. 1868. António Nunes "Lyvro dos pesos da Ymdia e asy medidas e mohedas." In *Subsidios para a História da India Portugueza*, edited by Rodrigo José da Lima Felner. Lisbon: Academia Real das Ciências, [I] pp. 1–64.

Felner [III]. 1868. "Lembranças de cousas da India em 1525." In *Subsidios para a História da India Portugueza*, edited by Rodrigo José da Lima Felner. Lisbon: Academia Real das Ciências, [III] pp. 1–56.

Maria João Ferreira. 2006. "Notícias da Seda. Referências à seda chinesa na documentação impressa dos séculos XVI a XVIII e seu impacte na sociedade europeia." In *Revista de Cultura* (International Ed.), 16, pp. 119–139.

Maria João Ferreira. 2011. *Os têxteis chineses em Portugal nas opções decorativas sacras de aparato (séculos XVI-XVIII)*, vol. I, PhD Dissertation Presented at the Faculdade de Letras of Universidade do Porto in 2011.

Maria João Pacheco Ferreira. 2013. "Chinese Textiles for Portuguese Tastes." In Amelia Peck (ed.), *Interwoven Globe*. New York: The Metropolitan Museum of Art, pp. 46–55.

Maria João Ferreira. 2014. "Os "Panos da Índia" em Portugal: integração e consumo dos artigos têxteis asiáticos na sociedade portuguesa dos séculos XVI a XVIII." In Begoña Farré Torras, coord., *Actas do IV Congresso de História da Arte Portuguesa em Homenagem a José-Augusto França. Sessões Simultâneas (2ª ed. revista e aumentada)*, Lisbon: A.P.H.A., pp. 72–81. https://www.apha.pt/wp-content/uploads/docs/Actas%20IV%20CHAP%20final.pdf.

Maria João Ferreira. 2015. "Asian Textiles in the Carreira da Índia: Portuguese Trade, Consumption and Taste, 1500–1700." *Textile History*, 46 (2), (November), pp. 147–168.

Maria João Ferreira. 2016. "Os Limites no Gosto: Os Panos da Índia nas Pragmáticas de 1609 e 1677." In *O Gosto Português na Arte*, edited by Ana Duarte Rodrigues. Lisbon: Scribe, pp. 22–39.

Maria João Ferreira. 2017. "Procedência e Consumo da Seda Asiática em Portugal (séculos XVI – XVIII)". In Ricardo Franch Benavent e Germán Navarro Espinach, coord., *Las Rutas de La Seda en La Historia de España y Portugal*. Valencia: Universitat de Valencia – PUV, pp. 379–399.

Manolo Florentino. 2014. *Em costas negras. Uma história do tráfico de escravos entre África e o Rio de Janeiro (séculos XVIII e XIX)*. São Paulo, Editora UNESP.

Anselmo Braamcamp Freire. 1914. "Inventario da Infanta D. Beatriz: 1507." In *Archivo Historico Portuguez*, n.º 9, 1914, pp. 64–110.

Vitorino Magalhães Godinho. 1984. *Os Descobrimentos e a Economia Mundial* (2nd Improved Edition), vol. 1. Lisbon: Editorial Presença.

Vitorino Magalhães Godinho. 1985. *Os Descobrimentos e a Economia Mundial* (2nd Improved Edition), vol. 2. Lisbon: Editorial Presença.

Vitorino Magalhães Godinho. 1987. *Os Descobrimentos e a Economia Mundial*, (2nd Improved Edition), vol. 3. Lisbon: Editorial Presença.

Vitorino Magalhães Godinho. 1991. *Os Descobrimentos e a Economia Mundial* (2nd Improved Edition), vol. 4. Lisbon: Editorial Presença.

S. D. Goitein and Mordechai A. Friedman. 2008. *Indian Traders of the Middle Ages: Documents from the Cairo Geniza "Indian Book" Part One*. Leiden/Boston: Brill.

Fernando Guedes. 2006. "Notícia de um fracassado negócio de escravos em tempos do Marquês de Pombal." In *Revista do Instituto Geográfico e Histórico da Bahia*, n.º 101, pp. 215–232.

, Paulo Guinote, António Lopes, and Eduardo Frutuoso. 1998. *Naufrágios e outras perdas da "Carreira da Índia": séculos XVI e XVII*. Lisbon: C.N.C.D.P.

Paulo Guinote, Eduardo Frutuoso, and António Lopes. 2002. *As Armadas da Índia 1497–1835*, Lisbon: C.N.C.D.P.

Fritz Hoppe. 1970. *A África Oriental Portuguesa no tempo do Marquês de Pombal*. Lisbon: Agência Geral do Ultramar.

Carlos Julião. 1960. *Riscos Iluminados de Figurinhos de Negros e Brancos dos Uzos do Rio de Janeiro e Serro Frio*. Rio de Janeiro: Biblioteca Nacional.

Deng Kaisong. 1997. "Estatuto e papel de Macau na rota marítima nos séculos XVI e XVII." *Revista de Cultura*, n° 32 (July/September), pp. 105–116.

Barbara Karl. 2016. *Embroidered Histories. Indian Textiles for the Portuguese Market During the Sixteenth and Seventeenth Centuries*. Weimar: Böhlau Verlag.

Jean-Baptiste Labourdette. 1988. *La nation française à Lisbonne de 1669 à 1790: Entre colbertisme et libéralisme*. Paris: Fondation Calouste Gulbenkian.

José Roberto do Amaral Lapa. 2000. *A Bahia e a Carreira da Índia* (2nd Edition). São Paulo: Editora Hucitec/Editora Unicamp.

Beverly Lemire. 2003. "Fashioning Cotton: Asian Trade, Domestic Industry and Consumer Demand, 1660–1780." In *The Cambridge History of Western Textiles*, vol. I, edited by David Jenkins. Cambridge: University Press, pp. 493–512.

Beverly Lemire. 2010. "Portugal, India and the European home: reshaping European material culture, c. 1500–1700." In *As Artes _Decorativas e a Expansão Portuguesa. Imaginário e Viagem. Actas do 2° Colóquio de Artes Decorativas. 1° Simpósio Internacional*, edited by Isabel. Mendonça and Helder Carita. Lisbon: C.C.C.M. - F.R.E.S.S., 2010, pp. 185–192.

Beverly Lemire. 2012. "Revising the Historical Narrative: India, Europe, and the Cotton Trade, c. 1300–1800." In *The Spinning World: A Global History of Cotton Textiles, 1200–1800*, edited by Giorgio Riello and P. Parthasarathi. New Delhi: Primus Books, 2012, pp. 205–226.

Luís Lisanti (Ed.). 1973a. *Negócios Coloniais (Uma correspondência comercial do século XVIII)*, vol. II. Brasília/São Paulo: Ministério da Fazenda/Visão Editorial.

Luís Lisanti (Ed.). 1973b. *Negócios Coloniais (Uma correspondência comercial do século XVIII)*, vol. V. Brasília/São Paulo: Ministério da Fazenda/Visão Editorial, 1973.

Gustavo A. Lopes and Maximiliano Menz. 2019. "Vestindo o escravismo: o comércio de têxteis e o Contrato de Angola (século XVIII), *Revista Brasileira de História*, 39: 80 (January/April 2019), pp. 109–134. https://dx.doi.org/10.1590/1806-93472019v39n80-05.

Rui Manuel Loureiro. 2010. "Chinese Commodities on the India Route in the Late Sixteenth and Early Seventeenth Centuries." In *Bulletin of Portuguese Japanese Studies*, 20 (June), pp. 95–123.

Luz. 1960. "Livro das cidades, e fortalezas, que a Coroa de Portugal tem nas partes da India, e das capitanias, e mais cargos que nelas há, e da importancia delles," edited by Francisco Paulo Mendes da Luz, in *Studia*, n.° 6 July 1960 (Offprint).

Marilina Luz. 1968. *Nomes de Tecidos em Antigas Pautas Alfandegárias Portuguesas (1699–1834)*. Offprint of the *Revista Portuguesa de Filologia*, vol. XV, tomos I e II. Coimbra.

Jorge Borges de Macedo. 1982. *Os problemas da indústria portuguesa no século XVIII*. Lisbon: Editorial Querco.

Nuno Luís Monteiro Madureira. 1989. *Inventários. Aspectos do Consumo da Vida Material em Lisboa nos finais do Antigo Regime*. Lisbon: Master Thesis presented at the Faculdade de Ciências Sociais e Humanas da Universidade de Lisboa.

Nuno Luís Madureira. 1997. *Mercado e privilégios. A indústria portuguesa entre 1750 e 1834*, Lisbon: Editorial Estampa.

Catherine Manning. 1996. *Fortunes à Faire. The French in Asian Trade, 1719–1748*. Aldershot: Variorum.

João M. da Silva Marques. 1940. "Armas e Tapeçarias Reais num inventrio de 1505." In *Congresso do Mundo Português*, vol. V, tomo 3°, pp. 555–605.

Marques. 1999. *Roteiro da primeira viagem de Vasco da Gama à Índia*, Transcription, Notes and Introduction by José Marques. Porto: Faculdade de Letras da Universidade do Porto.

Artur Teodoro de Matos. 1989. "Some aspects of the Portuguese Trade in the Malabar Coast: Cochin and the 'mercadorias meudas' (1506–1508)." In *Indica*, vol. 26, 1 & 2 (March–September), pp. 93–102.

Henri Médard. 2013. "La plus ancienne et la plus récente des traites: panorama de la traite et de l'esclavage en Afrique orientale et dans l'Océan Indien." In *Traites et esclavages en Afrique orientale et dans l'océan Indien*, edited by Henri Médard, Marie-Laure Derat, Thomas Vernet and Marie Pierre Ballarin. Paris: Karthala/Ciresc, pp. 65–118.

Mendonça. 1915. *Cartas de Afonso de Albuquerque seguidas de documentos que as elucidam*, vol. VI, edited by Henrique Lopes de Mendonça. Lisbon: Academia das Ciências.

William Moreland. 1988. *From Akbar to Aurangzeb. A Study in Indian Economic History*. Delhi: Vinod Publications.

Avelino Teixeira da Mota. 1969. "A viagem do navio «Santiago» à Serra Leoa e Rio de S. Domingos em 1526 (Livro de Armação)", *Série Separatas*, LIII. Lisbon: Junta de Investigações do Ultramar.

Fernando Jorge Cruz Mouta. 2017. "*Por Virtud del Asiento*: The Naval Logistics of the Slave Trade to the Spanish Indies (1604–1624)." In *The International Journal of Maritime History*, 3: 4 pp. 707–728.

José Acúrcio das Neves. 1987. "Observações sobre o comércio da Ásia" in *Obras Completas*, vol. III, edited by António Almodovar and Armando de Castro, Porto: Edições Afrontamento, pp. 275–306.

Noticia 1753, *Notícia da Viagem que fez do rio de Lisboa na nau Europa a 23 de Fevereiro de 1752 até à praça de Macau onde chegou a 5. de Agosto.* Lisbon: Oficina de Pedro Ferreira.

Kevin H. O'Rourke and Jeffrey G. Williamson. 2002. "After Columbus: Explaining Europe's Overseas Trade Boom, 1500–1800." In *Journal of Economic History*, n.° 62–2 (June), pp. 417–456.

Pato. 1884. *Cartas de Afonso de Albuquerque*, vol. I, edited by Raimundo António de Bulhão Pato. Lisbon: Academia Real das Ciências.

Pato and Mendonça. 1915. *As Cartas de Afonso de Albuquerque seguidas de documentos que as elucidam*, vol. V, edited by Raimundo António de Bulhão Pato and Henrique Lopes de Mendonça. Lisbon: Imprensa Nacional.

Jorge Pedreira. 1994. *Estrutura industrial e mercado colonial. Portugal e Brasil, 1780–1830*, Lisbon: Difel.

Celsa Pinto. 1994. *Trade and Finance in Portuguese India: A Study of the Portuguese Country Trade, 1770–1840.* New Delhi: Concept Publishing Company.

Celsa Pinto. 1995. "Lisbon Investment in the Indian Textile Commerce: The Surat Feeder." In *Mare Liberum*, n.° 9 (July), *Actas do VII Seminário Internacional de História Indo-Portuguesa - A Índia Portuguesa e a Província do Norte*, pp. 217–232.

Tomé Pires. 1978. *A Suma Oriental de Tomé Pires e o Livro de Francisco Rodrigues*, edited by Armando Cortesão, Coimbra: Por Ordem da Universidade.

Om Prakash. 1998. *The New Cambridge History of India*, vol. II-5, *European Commercial Enterprise in Pre-colonial India.* Cambridge: Cambridge University Press.

Radulet and Thomaz. 2002. *Viagens portuguesas à Índia, 1497–1513: fontes italianas para a sua história : o códice riccardiano 1910 de Florença*, edited by Carmen Radulet and Luís Filipe F. R. Thomaz. Lisbon: C.N.C.D.P.

Rau. 1956. *O «Livro de Rezão» de António Coelho Guerreiro*, edited by Virgínia Rau. Lisbon: Diamang.

António da Silva Rego. 1995. "Relações Directas Entre Macau e o Brasil. Um Sonho Irrealizável? (1717–1810)", *Revista de Cultura*, vol. 22 (II series) (January/March 1995), pp. 7–30.

Giorgio Riello and Tirkanthar Roy (Eds.). 2013. *How India Clothed the World: The World of South Indian Textiles, 1500–1850.* Leiden/Boston: Brill.

Joaquim Heliodoro da Cunha Rivara. [1865] 1992. *Archivo Portuguez Oriental*, fasc.5, part 2. New Delhi: Asian Educational Services.

Fr. João dos Santos. 1999. *Etiópia Oriental e Vária História de Cousas Notáveis do Oriente*, edited by Manuel Lobato and Maria do Carmo Guerreiro Vieira. Lisbon: C.N.C.D.P.

Vítor Serrão. 1993. *A Lenda de São Francisco Xavier pelo pintor André Reinoso*. Lisbon: Quetzal Editores.

Jonathan Scorsch. 2009. *Swimming the Christian Atlantic, Judeoconversos, Afroiberians and Amerindians in the Seventeenth Century*. Leiden/Boston: Brill.

Andrée Mansuy Diniz-Silva. 2003. *Portrait d'Homme d'État: D. Rodrigo de Souza Coutinho Comte de Linhares, 1755–1812*, vol. I, *Les années de formation, 1755–1796*. Paris: Centre Culturel Calouste Gulbenkian.

Catarina Santana Simões. 2014. "The Symbolic Importance of the "Exotic" in the Portuguese Court in the Late Middle Ages." *Anales de Historia del Arte*, 24, (November), pp. 517–525.

David Grant Smith. 1975. *The Mercantile class of Portugal and Brazil in the Seventeenth Century: A Socio-economic Study of the Merchants of Lisbon and Bahia, 1620–1690*, PhD Dissertation Presented at the University of Texas at Austin.

Rita Martins de Sousa. 2006. *Moeda e metais preciosos no Portugal setecentista (1688–1797)*. Lisbon: Imprensa Nacional-Casa da Moeda.

George Bryan de Souza. 1986. *The Survival of Empire. Portuguese Trade and Society in China and the South China Sea, 1639–1754*. Cambridge: Cambridge University Press.

Avanete Pereira Souza. 2012. *A Bahia no século XVIII. Poder político local e atividade econômicas*. São Paulo: Alameda.

Daviken Studnicki-Gizbert. 2007. *A Nation Upon the Ocean Sea. Portugal's Atlantic Diaspora and the Crisis of the Spanish Empire, 1492–1640*. New York: Oxford University Press.

Sanjay Subrahmanyam. 1990. *Improvising Empire: Portuguese Trade and Settlement in the Bay of Bengal, 1500–1700*. New Delhi: Oxford University Press.

Judy Sund. 2019. *Exotica. A Fetish for the Foreign*. London: Phaidon Press.

Franck Trentmann. 2017. *Empire of Things. How We Became a World of Consumers from the Fifteenth Century to the Twenty-first*. London: Penguin Books.

Francesca Trivellato. 2012. *The Familiarity of Strangers: The Sephardic Diaspora, Livorno, and Cross-Cultural Trade in the Early Modern Period*. Hew Heaven/London: Yale University Press.

José Carlos Venâncio. 1996. *A economia de Luanda e hinterland no século XVIII. Um estudo de sociologia histórica*. Lisboa: Editorial Estampa.

Maria da Graça A. Mateus Ventura. 1999. *Negreiros portugueses na rota das Índias de Castela, 1541–1556*. Lisbon: Edições Colibri - Instituto de Cultura Ibero-Atlântica.

Mário Viana. 1999. *Arquivo dos Açores*, (New Series), vol. I. Ponta Delgada: Centro Gaspar Frutuoso.

Bethany J. Walker. 2000. "Rethinking Mamluk Textiles." In *Mamluk Studies Review*, IV (2000), pp. 167–217.

Watt. 2013. Melinda "'Whims and Facncies': Europeans Respond to Textiles from the East." In *Interwoven Globe. The Worldwide Textile Trade, 1500–1800*, edited by Amelia Peck. New York: The Metropolitan Museum of Art, pp. 82–103.

George D. Winius. 1983. "The "Shadow Empire" of Goa in the Bay of Bengal." In *Itinerario*, vol. 7–2 (July), pp. 83–101.

Francisco Zamora Rodríguez. 2017. "Central American Indigo. Globalization and Socio-Economics Effects (16th–17th centuries), *Análise Social*, 224, LII (3°), pp. 584–607.

Memoirs of the Fruits of Globalization: The Markets for Chinese Textiles in New Spain by Jean de Monségur

Nadia Fernandez de Pinedo and Corinne Thépaut-Cabasset

An Economic Report, or Intelligence Gathering?

This chapter discusses textile trading and smuggling in the mid-eighteenth century by using several invaluable and newly discovered resources. Following the economic difficulties arising from the wars during the reign of Louis XIV (1643–1715) and the War of the Spanish Succession (1701–1714), a series of reports, consular reports, and memoirs related to the markets of Spanish America were produced.[1] Charles Weiss (1844), in his *L'Espagne depuis le règne de Philippe II jusqu'à l'avènement des Bourbons*—which was translated into Spanish in 1846—for example, used the *Mémoire du comte de Rébenac* (1689) from the *Manuscrits Français de la Bibliothèque du roi*. Weiss first included

[1] Some of these manuscripts are in the Foreign Affairs Archives, in Spain and France.

N. Fernandez de Pinedo (✉)
Department of Economic Analysis: Economic History, Universidad Autónoma de Madrid, Madrid, Spain
e-mail: nadia.pinedo@uam.es

C. Thépaut-Cabasset
Château de Versailles, Versailles, France
e-mail: Corinne.Thepaut-Cabasset@chateauversailles.fr

R. Dobado-González and A. García-Hiernaux (eds.), *The Fruits of the Early Globalization*, Palgrave Studies in Comparative Global History,
https://doi.org/10.1007/978-3-030-69666-5_9

some data from the memoir in his dissertation thesis in 1839 *Des causes de la décadence de l'industrie et du commerce en Espagne, depuis le règne de Philippe II jusqu'à l'avènement de la dynastie des Bourbons* (Weiss 1844, pp. 8–87). *Las memorias secretas de América*, by Jorge Juan and Antonio de Ulloa (1826), are indispensable for understanding the mid-eighteenth-century mechanisms of fraud and smuggling. Albert Girard (1932) wrote several biographies of the French consuls in Spain, and especially those on Jean-Baptiste Patoulet.[2] The cornerstone of our work, Jean Monségur's *New Memoirs of Mexico* (2002), discusses efforts to recover the market share that the French held in the Spanish colonies before the wars of Louis XIV, and his work offers information now being used in current historical works on colonial studies and in the histories of material culture and decorative arts. There are also the reports of French consuls in Cadiz and Seville (Fernández de Pinedo 1986) that are rich sources of information. The information these resources provide allows us to understand some of the changes related to the production of fabrics, their commercialisation, and their consumption worldwide between the sixteenth century and eighteenth century.

Our chapter starts with Captain Monségur,[3] who at the end of 1706 left Cadiz in Spain on a small ship lightly armed with eight canons, under the orders of His Holy Majesty the King of Spain Philipp V.[4] The mission was to carry messages to Don Fernando de la Cueva Enríquez, the Duke of Albuquerque, Viceroy of New Spain from 1702 to 1711. However, when Monségur reached Saint-Domingo, on the Caribbean Island of Hispaniola, he was attacked by the Dutch and was badly injured in the head. While not yet recovered from his injuries, Monségur sailed first for Veracruz and then to Mexico. He spent one year in the City of Mexico

[2] These are in the Marine and Affaires section of the French National Archives. See https://francearchives.fr/fr/facomponent/b5cd45f1f2c7197ab648b2f72afc555ae64ddc3e.

[3] Jean de Monségur, born in Ciboure, near Saint-Jean-de-Luz, in France, carried out military duties on land and on sea in the Royal Navy of the king of Spain. The accompanying notes in his memoir, at the National Library in Paris (BnF Mss Fr. 24.228), provides a minimal autobiography with key dates about his military career, honours, and distinctions received from the king of Spain. It also sheds light on the circumstances of his journey to Mexico, his mission, and the writing process of his *New Memoirs of Mexico*.

[4] Philipp V of Spain (1683–1746), was the grandson of Louis XIV. He inherited the throne upon the death of Charles II in 1700. At the turn of eighteenth century, Europe saw a marked rise in the House of Bourbon.

(1707–1708) on the orders he had received in Cadiz from the French minister of Marine, the Earl of Pontchartrain,[5] asking for all intelligence about the country of Mexico. Monségur collected relevant information from myriad sources, which he included in his memoir, *The New Memoirs of Mexico, or New Spain*. Upon his return to Madrid at the beginning of 1709, he presented his memoir—twenty-seven chapters at the time—to the king of Spain. He later prepared copies for the Earl of Pontchartrain and for the French ambassador in Spain, Michel-Jean Amelot.[6] In addition to these three copies, he made one copy for himself and two additional copies were shared in the hope of publishing the *New Memoirs of Mexico*. Thus, six copies were in circulation at the same time, and five remain in public collections: one manuscript is in Madrid's Archives of the Foreign Office, three are in the National Library in Paris, and one is in the Arsenal Library in Paris.[7]

From the initial twenty-seven chapters, Monségur expanded his memoir by another twenty-five chapters, for a total of fifty-two chapters, with much of this later work written when he was back to Europe in 1713 and 1714. The only regret expressed by the author was that such a detailed description of Mexico would be better if paired with a similar description of Peru. In the hope that his memoir might affect the politics at the time, he was ready to rework his manuscript in 1715, as he was seeking patrons in France. Nearly sixty-seven years earlier, Englishman Thomas Gage had published *A New Survey of the West Indies* (Gage 1648).[8] Comparing his work to Gage's, Monségur believed his own on Mexico to be more explicit and filled with essential information.

Along with offering geographical, physical, and material descriptions of the country of Mexico, as well as its on people and its natural resources, this memoir was to highlight the trade and the commerce of Spain with

[5] Jérôme Phélypeaux, Count of Pontchartrain (1674–1747), was the secretary of state at the Marine department from 1699 to 1715. This department was in charge of all commercial and international activities, including intelligence gathering.

[6] Michel Jean Amelot, Marquis of Gournay (1655–1724), Extraordinary Ambassador sent to Spain, was in Madrid from 1705 to 1709. The royal instructions he received focused on the commerce and trade agreements with Spain and the organization of the trade in the West Indies. See Ozanam and Mézin (2011, pp. 67–79).

[7] Madrid: Ms. 9; Paris: BnF Ms Fr. 24.228; Ms Fr. 24.229; Arsenal Ms. 4788.

[8] Translated into French with the title, *Nouvelle relation des Indes Occidentales, contenant les voyages de Thomas Gage dans la Nouvelle Espagne*, Paris, 1676.

its ally, the French, in the West Indies, especially as related to Mexico and the neighbouring countries of Guatemala, Bolivia, and Peru.

Monségur wrote about what he witnessed in the City of Mexico, especially about the commodities traded, their provenance, and their success. Such mercantile information on Mexico was rare at the time. At the time of Monségur's work, Gage's work on the West Indies had been translated into many languages and was the only—and very successful—source of information for Europeans on New Spain. But by the early eighteenth century, the richest and largest Spanish colony in America was mysterious and unknown, as Jean-Paul Duviols states in 2002, making Monségur's *New Memoirs* a remarkable historical testimony and a necessary reference for the knowledge of Spanish America (Monségur 2002, pp. 7–23).

European Rivalry

Monségur reflects on the socioeconomic changes that had taken place throughout the seventeenth century as related to the wars in Europe and also the economic and social situations in Spanish America in the second half of the seventeenth century.

On the first point, after peace was established between Spain and the Netherlands in 1648, conflicts in Europe turned to the Anglo-Dutch rivalry. The English Navigation Act of 1651 began a three-war cycle between England and the Netherlands in the years 1652–1654, 1665–1667, and 1672–1674. There was also France's expansion to the south (Treaty of the Pyrenees of 1659), north, and east (War Devolution in 1667–1668, Treaty Aix-la-Chapelle of 1668, war from 1672 to 1678, and the Treaty of Nijmegen of 1678). The French also went to war with of the Augsburg League (Nine Years War, 1688–1697). The Treaty of Ryswick of 1697 and the Treaty of Regensburg of 1684 recognised French annexations of Spanish lands. In the War of the Spanish Succession, France became the dominant power in continental Europe, but England and the Netherlands had managed to settle permanently in the Caribbean. For Spain, the Eighty Years War (1566–1648) saw the settling of the Dutch on the islands of Curaçao (1634) and Saint Eustatius (1636), and the Anglo-Spanish War of 1654–1659 meant the settlement of the English in Jamaica (1655). These territories would become the areas for smuggling textiles.

As related to Monségur's second point, French expansionism had a negative impact on commerce, as pointed out by most of the late

Illustration 1 Panel of chintz, India (Coromandel Coast), second quarter of eighteenth century, cotton, drawn and painted resist and mordant, dyed, with applied gold leaf. The Metropolitan Museum of Art, New York, Gift of the United Piece Dye Works, 1936 36.90.121

seventeenth-century French consular sources (Morineau 1998). French competitors included not only the Dutch and English but also the Hamburgers and the Genoese, with greater or lesser success. Trade through Spain to America was more important economically for French traders than for English or Dutch traders, whose maritime hegemony allowed them to practice smuggling in America. In addition, an unexpected competitor to the French trade in silk emerged: silk brought by the Manila galleons—Spanish trading ships—which supplied a good part of silks consumed in New Spain, and even the Viceroyalty of Peru. During the War of the Spanish Succession, the French supplied the Spanish colonies with silk, which in turn financed part of the war effort (Dahlgren 1907, p. 4). However, France paid a commercial cost, from which they tried to recover with the Treaty of Utrecht. Nevertheless, they failed to ban, or even reduce, the arrival of Chinese silks from Acapulco. However, Spain managed, through a 1720 trade regulation with Spanish America, that the *derecho de palmeo* tax, established for tissues and measured by the palm of the hand (Rodríguez 1936, p. 110)[9] would benefit heavily taxed expensive fabrics. The *derecho de palmeo* implied that the tax was paid for the volume occupied by the merchandise on the ship. This meant that these costly but small fabrics were not taxed proportional to their value when compared to the medium-quality fabrics (that is, those that were heavier and bulkier but cheaper), thus favouring French silks over English cloths (Map 1).

Societal and Consumption Patterns

Monségur's information was gathered to serve French political interests, and he discovered his knowledge about local Mexican markets by studying products and consumer purchases. It is a unique and first-hand source on the textile trade and the clothing culture in the Spanish colonies in America, and the infrastructure of its commerce. The analysis of textiles, with their description, vocabulary, and economic value allows us to have a better understanding of the colonial world in Spanish America for the early modern period (Illustration 2).

[9] "The *palmo* is one fourth of a vara... The *palmo* was the span from tip of thumb to tip of little finger with the hand outstretched—7 to 9 inches—with a tendency to be close to 8 inches in observed cases on individuals of varying height and hand proportion" (Rowe et al. 1979, p. 241).

Map 1 Carte du Mexique et de la Floride, 1703. Guillaume Delisle (1703). Bibloteque Nationale de France, Cartes et Plan. Ref. GE C 10968 80

The colonisers who arrived to the already conquered Mexica empires had fewer options to make their fortune. The *repartimiento de indios*, or discovery of rich mines, had taken place in the second half of the sixteenth century. The Indian economy was slowly changing. Increased populations of Europeans and the dramatic decline of the indigenous populations led to these changes, although mining remained the main economic engine. Livestock of European origin e.g. cows, horses, donkeys, sheep—filled empty lands; and the vineyards, olive groves, and grains from across the Atlantic, linked to the diet of the conquerors, spread. Hugette and Pierre Chaunu (1955) had already pointed out that these changes could explain the reduction of fleet and galleon tonnage because they were carrying fewer heavy products such as wine, oil, and grains that were replaced by less bulky—but higher value—fabrics. Thus, the reduction in tonnage did not necessarily mean lower consumption capacity. Nuanced readings of the volume of precious metals shipped from the mines have been made, including understanding that most of the seventeenth century was not

Illustration 2 Petticoat, Coromandel Coast, India, ca. 1725. Painted and dyed cotton chintz. Victoria and Albert Museum, London. Given by G. P. Baker, IS.14-1950

necessarily in a recession, at least in America, and there is nothing to suggest a decline in sales in America of European products. The figures on precious metals arriving in Europe probably do not capture the growing consumption in Spanish America, although, as Sánchez-Albornoz (1977, p. 108) pointed out, the movement of the population was not very dynamic and the cities grew slowly. The loss of Spanish naval hegemony in the Atlantic meant the colonies had to build their own defence by spending or investing tax money on fortifications, armed forces, weapons, and even developing modest shipbuilding. The colonies also had to send considerable sums of *situados* to colonial areas with fewer resources to also build up their defence (Marichal and Grafenstein 2012). These tax expenditures, more or less in situ, led to increased purchasing capacity of those who benefitted from this expense, such as soldiers and workers in the construction sector who were building fortresses, ports, and ships (Lynch 1969, pp. 220–23; Céspedes del Castillo 1952, pp. 263–264).

A gradual increase in the tonnage allowed on the galleons (Schurz 1918) reflects New Spain's greater purchasing capacity of Chinese products; a Royal Decree in 1702 allowed an increase from three hundred to five hundred tons in the Manila galleons. This included both legal silk fabrics and illegal silks through Guayaquil—modern Ecuador–, via the Viceroyalty of Peru. However, the main factor that increased the demand for handicraft products, especially at certain prices, was the mining of silver and gold. In the 1680s, additional mines were discovered in New Spain (Bakewell 1974, p. 269). The reports of the French consuls relate the beginning of the exploitation of these mines to the rich contents of the returning fleets. During the eighteenth century, the production of the Zacatecas mines grew regularly from an index of 100 in the five-year period of 1700 to 1704, to 187 between 1730 and 1734, and continued its growth until the end of the century (Garner 1980, pp. 163–164).

Increased mining benefitted mainly the wealthy mine owners and merchants and those who profited via fraud. Other benefactors included large groups of miners, transporters of metals, and food vendors who fed the workers. The rest of the population, from indigenous to low-income Spaniards, purchased products made locally, such as cotton fabrics, but also increasingly bought imported ones. In New Spain, a great shift occurred with the arrival of cotton fabrics from India, via the Philippines. The Spanish administration, of course, wanted to limit the consumption of these foreign products in its colonies, except for the silver leak in its payment. The *indianas* (woven in dyed cotton) created competition for linen, even though Spain exported limited amounts of this material. As with linen, Spain did not export many silk fabrics to New Spain—despite what Monségur noted—so it did not concentrate on banning outright or reducing the amount of silk fabrics arriving from China via Manila. That trade depended on the maintenance of the archipelago in Spanish hands.

Monségur (2002, pp. 70–76) established that there were relationships among New Spain farmers, shepherds, miners, indigo and cochineal collectors, pearl fishermen, and masons and the workers and servants from Europe. He highlighted that some of those who were skilled and made a lot of money spent funds on parties, suing others, and alcohol. If we leave aside his peculiar (that is, racist) vision of indigenous peoples by pointing out their limited capacity for savings, the interesting thing is that he links the indigenous population to what in Europe were manual labourers and low-skilled artisans. He also mentions blacks and mulattos who were servants, breeding mistresses, and cooks, and slaves who worked in the sugar mills and in the production of indigo (Monségur 2002, p. 71). Interestingly, some of the slaves who managed to buy their freedom or who were freed by their masters rose economically, if not necessarily socially—*accomodés et assez riches* (wealthy)—which was an exception to the indigenous people. Only the *caciques* lived better than the indigenous. The indigenous dress—calzones, capas, shirts, and skirts—were made of cotton, and usually brightly and colourfully dyed. The indigenous owned almost no furniture, not even mattresses. As true worldwide for the colonised, their essential diet was reduced to cereals, and mostly corn. This might be accompanied by chili made with a little meat. For drink, there was some milk and especially *atole*, a hot drink made from corn with cinnamon. The latter was particularly drunk by males (Monségur 2002, pp. 72, 74–75).

Monségur estimates that in Mexico City, the Spaniards and their descendants were less than a fifteenth of the population. Thus, the purchasing capacity of this demographic for imported products was low, regardless of women's tendency for fashion and holding galas, according to Monségur. The economic and social structures of Mexico City were very different from those of Spain. There were spending similarities between Spaniards and Creoles, but the latter purchased items in lower quantities and of lower quality. Dobado-González research included findings that highlight "the heterogeneity of consumption patterns between Spanish America and the rest of the world and within Spanish America" (Dobado-González 2015, p. 52).

In the *Encyclopédie* (1765, vol. 10) of Diderot and d'Alembert, Mexico City, the capital of New Spain and the largest city in the New World, is described as being extremely rich in commerce. It received supplies from the north by approximately twenty large ships filled with merchandise from Christendom that landed each year at Vera Cruz. In his *Dictionnaire universel de commerce*, Jacques Savary des Bruslons (1726) writes that the West Indies, a Spanish colony, could not survive without merchandise and products manufactured in Europe. And, according to Savary des Bruslons, despite strict regulations, trade with Spanish America—theoretically reserved exclusively for the Spanish—nonetheless occurred with other European countries, especially France, England, and the Netherlands, as well as a few other Northern European countries. This commerce was in fact one of the richest and most profitable for European businesses (Savary des Bruslons 1726, p. 237).

In a precursor of world-systems theory, Fernand Braudel states that Europe 'invented' America in the early modern age. In 'The Perspective of the World', part 3 of his book *Material Civilisation, Economy and Capitalism*, Braudel quotes a document written by Le Pottier de la Hestroy in 1703, who stated that consumption for European products in the West Indies was so high it exceeded the capacity of what European manufactures could provide. According to a comment by Ernst Ludwig Carl in 1725, the Spanish colonies in America almost became a warehouse of foreign goods (Braudel 1979, p. 516).

The arrival of artisanal goods in New Spain, especially textiles, had several origins. They arrived through legal Europe trade via fleets and galleons, and through smuggling. From China, products arrived on the Manila galleons in exchange for New World silver. Another origin was indigenous production (Melvine 2006, pp. 130–131), which was aimed at Indians, mestizos, mulattos, and slaves; that is, groups that could rarely purchase imported products. Foreign merchandise was mainly intended for the colonial elite: bureaucrats, merchants, and mine owners.

By 1686, on average, ships sailing from Spain to the West Indies were loaded especially with textile products (84.34%); excepting peddling (14.26%); paper, spices, oil, eau-de-vie, and iron and steel products (less than 1% each). Spain sent almost the same in value in wines, brandies, raisins, oil, and iron, as well as velvet, double taffeta, other silk fabrics, and some Segovia cloths. Given the theoretical high purchasing power of settlers and the considerable amount of taxes and transport prices, one might think that these were very expensive fabrics. They were, and included specifically: Rouen fabrics, brocades, gold and silver *mués*,[10] taffetas of French origin, Dutch gold and silver cloths and brocades,

[10] *Mué* was similar to a silk double taffeta such as the Gros of Tours (Dávila 2004, p. 132). Taffeta is a fine, tightly woven silk fabric.

silver and silk fabrics, silk stockings, silk taffetas, Flemish white thread lace, Bruges and Brussels camels, Brabant fabrics, and Dutch and Spanish Flanders batistes[11] But it was made clear by Monségur that the *platillas* made in Hamburg, *bocadillos* coarse canvases from Silesia and Westphalia, *creas* from Germany, *terlices* for mattresses, Morlaix common *creas* and Languedoc cloths from France, and the bays or etamines from England were materials to dress the middle class. The *sempiternals* or *perpetuanas,* and especially the less fine *sempiternals* of England or the unfashionable fabrics of Brabant, were medium-quality fabrics. Shipments to New Spain, such as to Peru, also included Indian cotton fabrics dyed in England or Holland. The finest Rouen and Louviers fabrics were actually the least sought after in New Spain and Peru; instead, *floretes* and *blancardas* were highly appreciated. The Languedoc cloths "were made to dress the poor"[12] (Monségur 2002, 202). Most likely due to the frequent wars undertaken by Louis XIV, certain French fabrics lost market shares. The *estameñas* of England replaced the Amiens serge; and the Dutch brocades in silk, gold, and silver displaced those produced in Tours and Lyon. Fabrics from Brabant competed with those from Rouen, and the *contanzas* of Holland, Hamburg, and Germany replaced those from Morlaix, Laval, and Saint Quentin. At the same time, the silks transported on the Manila galleons threatened those of European origin, and the cottons of the East were beginning to gain some relevance in the colonies. The New Spain market in the mid-seventeenth century thus had to have undergone changes. The increase in smuggling via Jamaica and Curaçao, and with the *asiento de negros* (Arrazola 1848, vol. 4, pp. 140–142) with Holland, discouraged trade from Seville-Cadiz, in which European traders (sometimes of the same national origin of those who practised smuggling) actively and increasingly participated. It could be that the irregularity of fleets and galleons with legal goods was in some way linked to the growth of smuggling (Pérez-García 2020, p. 6). With smuggled goods, the supply of European products in the viceroyalties would be satisfactory. While smuggling shifted the legal trade from Spain, it also had positive effects on prices, which increased the purchasing capacity of the Novohispanos, the inhabitants of New Spain. The worst hit by smuggling would have been the French, starting in 1667 (Weiss 1844, p. 514).

[11] Batiste is a very fine, tightly woven fabric, usually made from linen or cotton.

[12] Translations of Monségur are by the authors.

In Spanish America, from at least the second half of the seventeenth century, more money was increasingly spent on defence and on the administration through the *situados* (Marichal and Souto 1994). The smuggling and fraud would have reduced the taxes received in Spain. In addition, fraud lowered the price of certain goods. Moreover, at the end of the seventeenth century, mining in New Spain increased, with some problems arising from the supply of mercury. The slow but growing export of products linked to new colonialism (from sugar to leathers to traditional dyes) would have provided additional income to New Spain. Although the social pyramid in New Spain resembled that of Europe, those considered 'well off' were not as rich as their counterparts in Spain, and in not a few cases chose to remain there than to return to Spain. Large groups with significantly less purchasing power acquired mainly indigenous products. However, even among these lower-class groups, slaves dressed in imported cotton fabrics. Those who were socially between Spaniards (at society's top end) and Creoles (at the bottom end) increasingly had more purchasing power because of the higher fiscal spending in Spanish America and the development of non-mining activities, leading to improvement for the *sayasayas* and the *indianas*. It can be inferred that the prices of certain goods brought from China to New Spain was within everyone's budget (Dobado-González 2014).

Asian Taste and New Luxury Goods for New Consumers in New Spain

When the trading route opened between Europe and America in the sixteenth century, Mexico was placed at the crossroads of the global trade routes in the Spanish colonies, whose territories stretched from Mexico City in New Spain to the Spanish West Indies in the Caribbean and to the Spanish East Indies in the Asia Pacific. Donna Pierce explains that the "influx of luxury goods helped Mexico City gain a worldwide reputation as one of the most beautiful and prosperous cities in the New World" (Pierce 2015, pp. 53–73). Asian goods arrived in Acapulco on the Pacific Coast, and from there they were hauled overland to Mexico City and sold in the city's large Parián market in the centre of the capital (Illustration 3).

In the last chapter of his updated memoir, entitled 'Reflexions to be noticed on the commerce between Manila and Acapulco,' Monségur argued that it could no longer be ignored that the Chinese were skilled

Illustration 3
Waistcoat, textile from India, mid-eighteenth century, used for a man's waistcoat made in France, 1770–1790. The Metropolitan Museum of Art, New York, Rogers Fund, 1935 35.142

and ingenious merchants, and that their manufactures and products were sought after for their singular taste. In Mexico and Peru, as well as throughout many parts of Europe, Chinese products became preferred to those made in Europe (Illustration Detail of sack made of Chinese hand-painted silk satin (1735–1760); Illustration 5). As Pierce (2016) noted in her research, textiles comprised the majority of Asian imports to the Americas, yet not much is documented about their specific nature.

Monségur comments on Chinese silks and other textiles (coming from India) that were valued for their beauty and their affordability, even though European products offered better quality and reputation. Monségur repeatedly insists that Chinese silks were less expensive but also of lower quality as compared to Spanish or French silks. For example, he highlights that the wealthiest people in Spanish America, when not wearing the *golilla* suit[13] but "dress in inexpensive silk that comes from China" (Monségur 2002, p. 234). The same thing also happened with ribbons and stockings, with him stating "there are also a lot of these kinds of stockings from China and although they are not so good, nor so beautiful [...] they are cheaper" (Monségur 2002, p. 188). According to Monségur, price differences between European and Chinese silks had to do with design: Chinese fabrics offered simpler patterns. This was also the case for *pannes*, of which Monségur said, "they are not as beautiful nor so good as those of Europe' or brocades." The latter, however, Monségur considered quite good in terms of quality; hence, the prejudice for those of European origin, but again he points out that the difference is in "designs that are not so beautiful" (Monségur 2002, p. 189). Table 1 shows Monségur's characterization of the various fabrics.

Therefore, certain products of French and European origin that were more expensive—because they were better quality and considered more beautiful—were seriously impacted by the lower prices of Chinese products. In Monségur's description of the population of Mexico, he reports that even commoners used Chinese silks for clothing instead of locally produced material.

In addition, certain expensive European productions, such as first-quality wools, were not popular in New Spain—"they had not yet found

[13] The *gollila* was in fashion during Philip IV's reign and became the national costume (Colomer y Descalzo Lorenzo 2014; Thépaut-Cabasset 2014). Sempere y Guarinos, quoting Philip V, explains that his predecessor invented the golilla to avoid linen and laces used to make the collars (Sempere y Guarinos 1788, 145).

Table 1 Chinese fabrics as compared to European fabrics, according to Jean de Monségur

	Price	*Quality*	*Design/colour*
Silk stockings	lower	lower	not as good
Ribbons	lower	lower	n/a
Panne	lower	lower	not as good
Brocades	lower	good	not as good
Taffetas/sayasayas	lower	good	not as good
Dorures	lower	lower	old-fashioned

Source Monségur (2002, pp. 188–189)

all the esteem they deserve" (Monségur 2002, pp. 204–205)—because consumers had other alternatives. Chinese production was capable of adapting to different purchasing capacities, which made their productions so appealing. Competition was not confined to expensive items. Monségur points out that certain silk stockings rivalled those made of wool. Ordinary wool stockings were in great demand, but it would have been higher if it were not for the large amount of thick silk stockings coming out of China (Monségur 2002, p. 193). In other words, it is clear that Chinese products competed with, as Monségur called them, 'common and ordinary' products. With regard to the quality and price of silk products, the governor of the Philippines himself stated that "it is the fact that the products of China benefit in New Spain people with little wealth and servants who cannot buy the fabrics of Spain" (AGI, Filipinas, 206, N1, quoted in Picazo Muntane 2020, p. 261). The wide variety and types of silks were undoubtedly advantages for Asia, but these were not the only two. Another of China's great advantages was its ability to imitate European fabrics and trends through sampling and copying (Monségur 2002, p. 307).

Monségur noted that silk stockings for women and children had begun to arrive to New Spain between 1695 and 1697 ('so far, we hadn't seen these products coming'), imitating those made in Toledo, Naples, and Milan. He reiterated that they did not match their quality or beauty, but they were cheaper and thus more affordable. Such inexpensive garments were aimed at New Spain consumers who wanted access to 'stylish' wardrobes on a regular basis. Speaking of the *dorures*, he points out that the Chinese 'have been trying to imitate them for some time' (Monségur 2002, p. 190). He said something similar of the ribbons, which the Chinese were beginning to introduce in New Spain in the same time period (Monségur 2002, p. 306), imitating the products of Genoa, Turin, Naples, Genoa, and France.

Silk products, as well as certain cotton fabrics, created changes in the international market in the late seventeenth century that led to problems for the European textile sector. Illegal Chinese silks were well received in New Spain; hence, the *Recopilación de Indias* of 1680 tried to regulate the smuggling of Chinese textiles, but without much success. Since the beginning of direct trade between New Spain and the Philippines in 1565, this route became very lucrative as quantities of silks and other Asian goods were re-exported to Peru and Spain. Satin in New Spain in the seventeenth century was manufactured from Chinese and Mexican raw silk (Schurz 1918, p. 393), but it was the imported Asian damasks and brocades that customers preferred (Rodríguez 2015, p. 231). In New Spain, the ban in 1596 against mulberry planting and the ending of the silk industry in New Spain in 1679 (Ma 2017, p. 81; Pohl 1971, p. 7) did not appear to incentivise imports from Spain. Instead, it consolidated the consumer habit of dressing in Chinese silks.

The extraordinary consumption of Asian goods in Mexico led to additional trade with Peru—even though it was sometimes strictly forbidden by the authorities—when the desire for goods exceeded the local market demand or when prices were low. Every year a ship from Peru arrived in Mexico to purchase goods originally shipped by the Manila galleons. According to Monségur, this created a yearly opportunity for Mexicans to sell European goods when it was profitable to do so. This counter-trade was both illegal and caused financial losses for Spain.

Galleon San Francisco Javier

The global cargo on the ship *San Francisco Javier*, arriving from Manila to Acapulco in 1707, is difficult to interpret. What does Monségur mean by the '2000 boxes of all kind of silks' valued at '1.000 piastras box', or the '2.000 *ballots* named *éléfantes*' each valued at 500 piastres/*ballots* (see Table 2) (Illustration 4).

In total, over the course of his study, Monségur values the goods sold in New Spain at four million pesos. We have estimated prices according to his data for Mexico City; however, given the price range for the same product, these estimates must be interpreted with caution.

Seventy-five percent of the shipment was fabrics, and made up half the cargo (in value). It must be added raw silk, representing 9% of the

Table 2 Breakdown of the cargo by product, in piastres and percentage of the *San Francisco Javier* (1707)

Products	*Piastres*			*Percentage*
Silk textiles/fabrics	2,000,000			50.00
Cotton/silk fabrics	1,000,000	Cotton fabric	630,450	25.00
		raw silk	369,550	
Wax	150,000			3.750
Gold	25,000			0.625
Cinnamon	660,000			–
Pepper	35,000			–
Clove	5,600			–
Nutmeg	300	Total spices	700,600	17.522
Porcelains	10,000			0.25
Drogues	10,000			0.25
Other items	104,000			2.60
Total	3,999,990			99.997

Source Monségur (2002, p. 298)

total (see Table 2). Cotton fabrics represented 16%. It is likely most of the metres of fabric would be cotton textiles, since cotton was not expensive. The spices took up a certain weight (18% in value), especially cinnamon, which was linked to chocolate consumption (Fernández-de-Pinedo 2018). Gold was imported because in China silver was overvalued; thus, it was not bad business to buy gold with silver (Flynn and Giraldez 2012). Porcelain appears in the shipment, but not in excessive quantities, and the type of porcelains and at what prices is not clear. Wax was imported for use in the churches of Mexico, as in other countries in the Catholic world (Fernández-de-Pinedo 2018). The Manila galleons also brought a wide range of qualities of raw silk, which amounted to 369,550 piastres, or 2,956,400 *reales de a ocho* (see Table 3).

Unfortunately, the two most important products for our study—Chinese silk and cotton fabrics from the coast of Coromandel and Bengal—are mixed. Silks include brocades and cotton includes raw silk, some brocades, and low-quality taffeta. Luckily, Monségur provides an overview in Chapter 47, and then specifies the types of fabric in both silks (Chapter 49) and cotton (Chapter 50).

In Chapter 49, Monségur noted two thousand boxes worth two million pesos. Of those two million, the value of raw silks is estimated at almost three thousand *reales*, or 356 piastres (see Table 2) of different

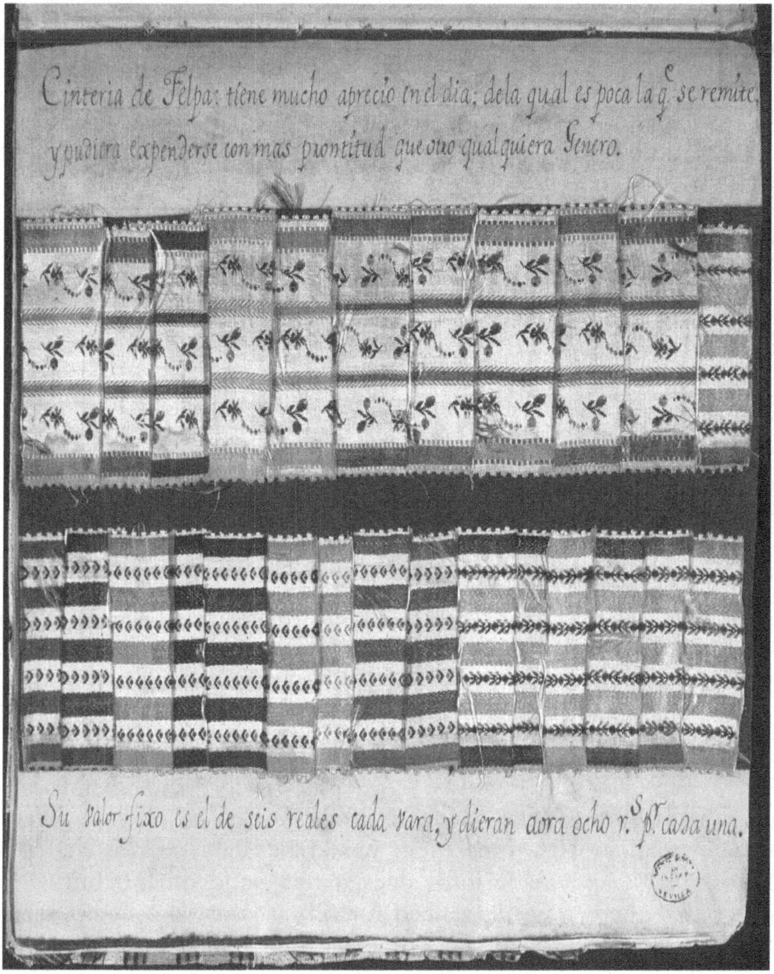

Illustration 4 Felpa Ribbons with different floral patterns. *"Quaderno de muestras de los géneros de Europa que tienen estimación en Quito y su provincia, conocidos con otros nombres de aquellos que sacan de las fábricas, con expresión del precio a que comunmente se venefician"*. Seville, Archives General de Indias, MP-Tejidos, 1780, 14, fol.

Illustration 5 Detail of sack (dress) made of Chinese hand-painted silk satin (1735–1760). The design of fanciful flowers shows the Western influence; the Chinese artists were using patterns sent to Europe to make silks expressly for the European market. The Victoria and Albert Museum, London, T.115&A-19532006AY9543_2500 and 2006AY9540_2500

types and qualities: *mazo, quina, tramas, floxa from Bengala, chagny*, and *izquierdosilla*[14] (the final item would be spun or twisted, mostly in Mexico City, and made into capes, taffeta, and other fabrics). This indicates that there was still a need for silk artisans who could use raw and spun silks from Calabria,[15] Granada, and China to produce local plain-weave silks.

[14]Ana Cabrera, curator at the Museo del Traje (Madrid) points out that raw silk is a silk from which the gum (sericin) has not been removed. Sometimes the spun threads from the broken ends and 'floss' from *B Mori* (*Bombyx mori*) cocoons are also called wild silk instead of raw silk. These 'raw silks' seems to be second-class spun silks made from short lengths obtained from damaged cocoons or broken off during processing and twisted together to make yarn.

[15]For 'soie de Calabre', see Savary des Brulons, 1742.

Table 3 Raw silks brought by the *San Francisco Javier* in 1707, in *reales de a ocho*

Product	*Average "livres" (*)*	*Prices (reales)*	*Prices* x *"livres" in reales*
a	30,000	35,33	1,059,900
b	12,000	57	684,000
c	17,500	30	525,000
d	3,500	30	105,000
e	5,500	40	220,000
f	4,500	50	225,000
g	2,500	55	137,500
Total reales	–	–	2,956,400

Note (*) as Monségur noted different quantities for the same items along the *Mémoirs* we have calculated average weight (*livres*)
a. *Sedamazo*: silk in mass quantities
b. *Quina* or *pelo*: used, for example, to make taffetas blankets
c. *Trama*: weft raw silk
d. *Bengala*: raw silk used as weft
e. *Floxa*: untwisted silk thread used to embroider shirts, cloth skirts, and church ornaments
f. *Chagny Silk*: twisted thick white silk
g. *Izquierdilla*: similar to but thinner than *chagny*

Of the silk fabrics, many were probably copies of European patterns, especially with New Spain sending samples to China. Among the most expensive were fabrics made with gold, such as silk fabrics brocaded with gold into floral patterns, which the Chinese made via a different technique from the French (Monségur 2002, pp. 301–302). There were also brocades made with gold that were of a lower quality and brocades without gold and silver in floral patterns first and second *suerte* (sort). *Primaveras* (simple inexpensive taffeta) and *fondos con trama de algodón* (cotton weft backgrounds) imitated the fabrics made in Toledo and other places in Spain, France, and Italy.

Felpas were somewhat more expensive than the *fondos*, first and second suerte, very appreciated. Shipments included double taffetas such as *pequines* and *capicholas*. *Teletones* were a mediocre imitation of *chagrins*, the latter being long and narrow satins that corresponded to the double and simple French taffetas. *Chaules*, called *dobletes* in Spain, were popular as they were used to make *caleçons* (linings and skirts for women and children), and were similar in price to *teletons*. *Chorreras* was used for garnishing beds and flags (*pavilion*), and were widely consumed by both the poor and the rich. *Guardapies*, or petticoats, were skirts worn by

Table 4 Silk with gold (piastres/pieces) (See Glossary)

		Manilla	*Acapulco*	*México*
Telas	brocades with gold flowers glued on paper and applied on the fabric	16–24	40–50	50–55
Brocados	brocades of lower quality, with glued golden flowers made of gilded paper applied on the fabric	8, 10, 12, 14	20, 24, 35	25, 30, 35, 40

Source Monségur (2002, pp. 301–302)

women at home and as undergarments when they went out. *Gorgorán* was heavily used among women. The *sayasayas* (see Glossary), a kind of simple taffeta, was shipped in three qualities and used for skirts and linings for multiple types of clothing (Monségur 2002, 305). Monségur describes them with high praise: 'The fabric of all of them is good, good quality, and long lasting; they are preferred to everything that comes from Europe and of great consumption'. Each galleon brought no less than twenty thousand pieces, and sometimes more.

The measurements of silk fabrics—except for the *sayasayas*—were fairly uniform (16 × 1 and 1 × 0.75 varas),[16] which facilitates comparison by using prices in Mexico. Among the expensive fabrics were brocades (see Tables 4, 5 and Glossary), followed by *primaveras*, *fondos*, *felpas*, *damascos de primera suerte*, *pequines*, and *capicholas*. The *sayasayas* were much shorter in length—10 to 12 rods long—and therefore their prices have to be multiplied by 1.6. Those that were doubles cost between 4 and 5 piastres, second quality between 3.5 and 4 piastres, and those of the third quality between 2.5 and 3 piastres.

Even when those prices are multiplied by 1.6 however, they are not comparable to the rest of the silk fabrics. This creates a problem in interpreting certain texts related to the quality of Chinese silk fabrics. Some were expensive, but the majority were much lower cost than European silks manufactures, which certainly used different qualities for different types of customers. Silk consumption by lower-class groups with little purchasing power was possible through this wide variety of

[16] Vara was a Spanish unit of measurement of length between 768 and 912 millimetres (mm). The standard was the Burgos vara of 836 mm (= 33 inches).

Table 5 Silk Fabrics with or without silver (piastres/pieces) (See Glossary)

	Price and type of fabrics, according to the place they were sold	*Manilla*	*Acapulco*	*México*
Tissus (original name in the document)	brocaded silk	25–30	60–70	+70
Petite flores, first-class	brocaded silk with damask ground	15–20	35–45	35–50
Petite flores, second-class	brocaded silk with damask ground	8–16	20–25	30–35
Primaveras	Brocaded silk taffeta	5–6	12–20	+20
Fondos(a)	silk fabric with cotton weft (similar to *panne*)	12–16	30–35	+35
Felpas (b)	silk fabric with cotton weft (similar to *panne*)	+12–16	+30–35	+35
Damascos, first-class	Silk damask	15–16	32–35	+35
Damascos, second-class	Silk damask (2/3 varas long)	6–8	12–20	+20
Pequines	Pekins (almost 1 vara long)	8–10	18–22	22–28
Capicholas (c)	Silk taffeta, silk thread, low quality (the majority in *musc* colour)	+8–10	+18–22	+22–28
Teletones	Silk double taffeta (similar to *chagrin* but a poor imitation; only *musc* colour)	4–5	8–9	9–10
Rasos (d)	Silk satin (the majority are *musc* taffetas)	8–10	18–22	22–28
Rasos (e)	Silk satin (simple taffeta, 0.75 varas long)	+4–5	+8–9	+9–10
Chaules (f)	Silk double taffeta	+4–5	+8–9	+9–10
Chorreadas (g)	Taffetas (mouchetés) as *chaules*	4–5	8–9	9–10
Guardapies	Petticoat, puffed fairthingale (plain taffeta like a brocade with various flowers designs and colours)	6–8	12–14	15–18

(continued)

Table 5 (continued)

	Price and type of fabrics, according to the place they were sold	*Manilla*	*Acapulco*	*México*
Sayasaya	Silk taffeta, third-class (most was white and the rest coloured), weight 5–6 ounces	5–7	14–16	20–24
Sayasaya	Silk taffeta, second-class (most was white and the rest coloured), weight 9–10 ounces	9–12	20–24	28–32
Sayasaya	Silk taffeta, double (only white), weight 12 ounces	2	4	4–5
Medias	Stockings, Milan's imitation (for men) piastras/pair	1.5–2	3.5–4	4–5
Medias	Unspecified (for women) reales/pair	12	24	28–30
Medias	Matching Manila style (for children) reales/pair	1.5–2	2–3	3–4
Rubans	Ribbons, Naple's imitation (n° 40) real/pieza	8–10 reales/pieza	18–20	24–28
Rubans	Ribbons	5–6 piastre/livre	18–20	14–16
Rubans	Ribbons, Turin's imitation (*colonias*)	10, 12, 14 reales/pieza	22, 32	35, 40
Rubans	Ribbons, Turin's imitation (raised with gold, applied on paper, and sealed on the fabric)	2 piastres/pieza	4	5–6
Rubans	Ribbons, France's imitation	2 piastres/pieza	4	5–6

Source Monségur (2002, pp. 301–306)

Note ***Pequins, gorgorans, capricholas, taffetas***, and ***damas*** measure 1 vara × 16 varas. The remaining textiles measured 1 vara × 0.75 varas

a. 'Black colours are neither good nor valued. Because the Chinese do not do well on the black colour.' The Chinese did not have access to the Palo de Campeche, thus they were not capable of dying in black as in Europe

b. A little more expensive than *fondos*

c. A little more expensive than *pequines*

d. Similar to *capicholas*

e. Not quite *teletones*

f. A little more expensive than *teletones* for underpants and underskirts, and mostly consumed in Guatemala, Guaxaca, La Veracrux, Cartagena, Havana, Campeche, and all seaport and tropical countries

g. Similar to *chaules*, and especially consumed in hot countries

quality and thus prices. The increase in what was paid for *indulto* (pardon)—attributed to the amount of silk brought in from the Philippines—indicates an increase in consumption starting in 1682 (Monségur 2002, pp. 313, 315).

This information on the large range of textile products coming from Asia, including those destined for Europe, reveals the extraordinary dynamic of the commerce in Mexico. It reveals also the fantastic appetite for textiles and fashionable goods no matter gender, race, or social rank in the colonial system.

Denis Carr, in the introduction to the exhibit catalogue for *Made in the Americas*, states that "the search for faster sea routes to Asia had led to the original discovery of America by Spain in 1492, and the enduring desire for Asian luxury goods would have a powerful influence on the culture and consciousness of the Americas for the next three centuries" (Carr 2015, p. 21). As a matter of fact, Asian goods left in wills and listed in home inventories continued until Mexico's Independence from Spain in 1821.

Fashion as Fruit of Globalisation

In Spanish America, apparel was not only a key element in "the establishment of European culture in general" (Martínez Bonanad 2013, p. 399) but also in the spread of an Asian-inspired taste in fashion that would develop into a Chinese aesthetic (Martins Torres 2019). If Asian trade had an impact in stimulating 'new European consumer wants' (De Vries 2010, p. 728), it appears that the impact was even greater in Spanish America (Bonialian 2016; Gasch-Tomás 2012; Ibarra 2017; Pérez-García 2020). In America, Asian goods changed daily consumer habits to the point of creating a hybrid fashion. Elite benefitted from these changed habits, but so did all strata of the society from this mingling of cloth, design, and colours. Careri, Humbolt or Gage, among other voyageurs, were surprised how much of the population in New Spain dressed in Chinese silks. Schurz (1918, p. 390), quoting the *Reglamento* of 1720, noted that natives of New Spain were accustomed to dressing in goods coming from China. Dahlgren (1907, p. 64), citing a text by Antonio de Ulloa, highlights that in Peru men dressed *à la francesa* (in the

French way),[17] but especially in silk in a rare mixture of bright colours, brocades, embroidered silk, and silver fabrics. De Ulloa mentioned that women wore clothing to show off their wealth, despite sumptuary laws and ordinances (Illustration 5).

The laws and royal or municipal ordinances against luxury, originating in thirteenth-century Europe, regulated dress and adornment to certain classes and aimed at controlling sartorial display.[18] Sumptuary rules, along with clothing laws (Wunder 2019, p. 243), defined social strata[19] and tended to reserve silks and brocades for the elites (Baghdiantz 2015, p. 21). Such legislation in a mercantilist framework had a twofold purpose.[20] One, it favoured national production of textiles over foreign competition; and two, it also favoured the elites as they regulated the external appearance of all social classes (Sanz 2002, p. 1629). Duplessis (2016, p. 155) pointed out that from the 1500s, Spanish America sumptuary laws constrained consumption by slaves and forbade them from wearing certain fabrics. The Ordinance of 1628 for example "was one of a number of regulations aimed at restricting the adoption of certain Spanish practices by Amerindians" (Earle 2019, p. 325). These bans were enacted to regulate legal status and to protect social and religious hierarchies in the colonies by taking into account the complexity of this hybrid society and the different types of identities within it. For Earle (2019, p. 326), "the history of sumptuary laws in Spanish America is inevitably entangled with colonial regulation of caste or race". Gonzalbo (1996, p. 64) points out, however, that there was greater laxity towards the less wealthy

[17] In Spain in 1707 it was common to wear *à la francesa*. See Sempere y Guarinos 1788, p. 146.

[18] "The English government, for example, enacted 34 royal statutes between 1327 and 1604, while Spanish kings enacted an average of one sumptuary law per decade for 600 years. France surpassed both with 135 royal statutes passed between 1229 and 1736, or an average of roughly 2.5 per decade" (Moyer 1997, p. 10).

[19] 'Edit contre le luxe des habits considérant les grandes et excessives dépenses ou le luxe et les superfluités engagent nos sujets et particulièrement notre noblesse' (24 Novembre 1639) (Decrusy et al. 1829, pp. 515–519).

[20] 'Mercantilists made several attempts to supplant Asian suppliers with a domestic calico industry. Before the 1686 statute was enacted, any type of painted cloth could be freely imported or manufactured in France' (Moyer 1997, 219). The toiles peintes, indiennes, and painted cloth or calicoes were banned in France in 1708 as well as in England in 1720 (Moyer 1997, 217).

classes, as was witnessed by numerous travellers who made their observations from a European point of view: "In the society of New Spain, the importance of clothing as a cultural symbol acquires special relevance since the Spanish Crown recognized the equality of all its subjects, but imposed differentiation on clothing".

Sumptuary laws in Spanish America were "premised on the interconnections between caste, morality, gender, and status" (Earle 2019, p. 337), whereas in Europe they focused on "gender, class, wealth and profession" (DuPlessis 2019, p. 346). A growing body of research demonstrates that prohibitions were constantly violated in both the colonies and in the metropolis (Martínez 2008; Riello and Rublack 2019).

While taste deals with habit, use, custom, and even comfort, fashion deals with novelty, creativity, and innovation (Welch 2017, p. 18). As a result, value systems, lifestyles, and identities produced a hybrid clothing culture in the colonial territories, reflected in the Mexican and Peruvian schools of painting in the eighteenth century (Katzew 2004). *Casta* paintings are good examples of the transformations that shaped Spanish America by means of clothing (Carrera 2003; Katzew 2004; Katzew et al. 2011): Mexican apparel display the impact of the Manila galleon trade while Chinese designs seem to have inspired daily life.

Starting in the early seventeenth century, it was observed that the upper-class in New Spain lived luxuriously and wore expensive silks of the finest quality. This taste for luxury, including silks, adorned cloth, and significant quantities of lace, continued into the eighteenth century, as noted by Monségur. Elena Phipps quotes Amédée-François Frézier, who travelled to Peru between 1712 and 1714, who noted: "Both men and women are equally inclined to be costly in their dress. The women not satisfied with the expense of the richest silks, adorn them after their manner, with a prodigious quantity of lace" (Phipps 2013, p. 45). Such taste for all that glitters and shimmers was the trend in the New World, too. Fabrics mentioned by Monségur include 'imitation' luxurious brocaded silk, which was gilded paper glued onto fabric (similar to Indian *sarasa* or Japanese *kirande* [gold brocade]). Lace from Spain and Belgium, and ribbons and trimmings made of gold and silver metallic threads, were extremely popular European-made goods. Despite the trade routes that were opened to the East, which provided silks from China and other Asian cloths from India and the importation of Spanish silk and woollen cloth to the Americas continued throughout the eighteenth century. The annual arrival of Manila galleons from the Philippines to Acapulco on the Pacific Coast of Mexico brought goods from Asia, which became part of the vocabulary of textiles and dress in the Americas (Phipps 2013, pp. 29–45). Monségur includes quite a number of these terms (see Table 5).

From the sixteenth to the eighteenth century, as Phipps concludes in her essay 'The Iberian Globe':

> The desire for silks, velvets, and other luxury or exotic goods was shared by much of society within the viceroyalties, a society composed of indigenous inhabitants, Europeans, Africans, and even Asians. (...) The Americas participated in the international exchange that fuelled the global trade networks, not only as a primary supplier and source of some of the most precious and sought-after materials but also as a major consumer of the international products that traversed the oceans. (Phipps 2013, 45)

Dress historians and textile historians agree that the circulation of fashion was international, and was made possible in the early modern world by using the print culture, the press, and even miniature dresses such as for dolls, among other avenues (Thépaut-Cabasset 2011). European fashion—and the shape of clothing especially—was spread throughout the eighteenth century via the second-hand market of clothing goods. Ulinka Rublack quotes Ernst Ludwig Carl, who reported in 1723 that second-hand French clothing was sent to Mexico and Peru (Rublack 2012, pp. 281–82) (Illustration 6).

Our discussion about fashion underlines Monségur's reflexion on commerce in New Spain between 1709 and 1714. In the last chapter of his *New Memoirs of Mexico*, he states that China was hyper-focused on the latest fashion in Europe, which explains why it sent to Mexico all goods made from European silk, even those they did not produce themselves, such as silk stockings and ribbons: "This nation is so attached to our fashions, that today in Mexico we see coming from their country, everything that is done in Europe in silk, to stockings and ribbons that they do not work". Fashion was the new engine for global trade, as Monségur

Illustration 6 Wedding dress made in America, 1776, Chinese silk damask. Brooklyn Museum Collection at The Metropolitan Museum of Art, New York, Gift of the Brooklyn Museum, 2009; Gift of Edith Viele, 1949 (2009.300.731)

reveals in his observation that fashion created a mercantile system before the Industrial Revolution in Europe.[21]

Giorgio Riello argues that 'in the early modern period fashion was much more about the "new in space" than the "new in time". This translates that fashion derived not so much from a process of invention (as couturiers and fashion designers claim today) but as a process of adoption of goods coming from somewhere else, and thus fashion is 'globalizing' (Riello 2017, p. 67).

Remarks on Monségur's New Memoirs

What seems clear is that *New Memoirs* was written to convince his readers that the American market had to be divided between Spain and France, as indicated by title of Chapter 37: '*Que l'Espagne alliée de la France et unie avec elle, peut-elle seule fournir les Indes Occidentales toutes les marchandises qui s'y consomment et faire seule tout le commerce de l'Amérique*'. France was not the only country trying to prohibit Chinese silk fabrics in America. However, as Monségur points out, Spain made two mistakes in relation to this industry. The first was Spain's lack of interest in incentivising its own domestic industry, and the second was its trade tolerance with China, describing it as "the pernicious license they have given to the introduction of all of China silk in America" (Monségur 2002, p. 200). Likewise, Dahlgren (1907, p. 17) also insists on pointing out "the absurd colonial legislation of Spain". In *New Memoirs*, Monségur reiterated that Spain had to export certain silk products to prohibit the importation of silk from China. A French consular report of 1709 included the same complaint[22] (Illustration 5).

Indeed, Spain brought large quantities of Asian raw silk and woven silk cloths into New Spain in the late sixteenth and early seventeenth centuries (Canepa 2015, p. 17). They were destined for the local market within New Spain and for reexport to the Viceroyalty of Peru. Meanwhile,

[21] In this line there is an ongoing research on New Spain based on a set of qualitative and quantitative data, highlighting the fact that an early Consumer Revolution can take place without any relationship with an Industrial Revolution is been carried out by Calderón, Dobado, and Fernández de Pinedo. "Asian goods in New Spain: An Early Consumer Revolution?".

[22] Archives Affaires Étrangères, Espagne. Correspondance politique, t. 197, fol. 317, 'Observations sur le commerce des Indes Occidentales Espagnoles'.

only limited quantities of silk were shipped to Spain through Acapulco. Although there were pressures to ban the importation of Chinese silk into Spain early on, it was not until the *Real Cédula* in October 1720, in which Philip V prohibited trade in silk, gold, and silver via the Philippines (Picazo 2020, p. 255). Despite the War of the Spanish Succession, the American market was well supplied, both legally and illegally. France had discovered the lucrative Peruvian market for French products, despite the prohibition of trading with these territories, and especially in silk. "The smuggling of fabrics and clothing from China also affected the actual incomes, by avoiding the tax, and therefore the prohibitions on free trade were repeated on several occasions" (Gonzalbo 1996, p. 63). Juan de Solórzano Pereira, in his two-volume book, identifies the prohibitions that started in 1596 and continued throughout the seventeenth century: "It is also forbidden even more firmly that those of Peru cannot be brought, neither in them to sell, to have, to bring, nor to spend silk, nor any clothing of the calling of China" (Solórzano 1739, pp. 474–475). Solórzano stresses that "in these ordinances there is not only a command to proceed against those who bring from China, but also against those who buy it, have or spend it, no matter how little" (Solórzano 1739, pp. 474–475), and argues that it should not stop the trade in silk coming from Spain. He added that Spain must avoid shipping silver to China.

Coastal trading between New Spain and Peru was first forbidden in 1604, and this decree was reissued until 1706, even though commerce continued illegally between both viceroyalties, especially in Chinese goods. Similar trade prohibitions were set in 1582 between Peru and Manila, as well as between Peru and China in 1591 (Schurz 1918, p. 396). These prohibitions consequently led to illicit trade spreading in diverse informal and personal ways, and bringing a variety of silk products into these countries. As Farrell explained, "pieces of cloth and garments could be folded up and hidden inside boxes and packages. Individual travellers, therefore, could make ideal 'smugglers'" (Farrell 2016, p. 274).

During the War of the Spanish Succession, Spain traded silver to France in exchange for French ships escorting the Manila galleons in the Indies as well as other vessels to Peru. French merchants understood the advantages of this trade (Dalhgren 1952, p. 4). The route followed by some French traders was France to Peru to China—either Canton or Amoy, with a stopover in Manila at times—to America (Dahlgren 1907, pp. 5, 16). The French, allies of Spain in this war, hoped to divide the American market with Spain to the detriment of third nations—particularly England and the Netherlands. However, this was not to be as trade remained Spain's monopoly. This led to the insistence of Monségur, and to France's prohibition, against this type of trafficking (Manila to Acapulco) because it directly harmed the French production of certain goods.

Savary des Bruslons (1726, p. 1165) made a similar point: "China is producing all kind of fabrics made of silk; among them flowered brocaded with or without gold, velvets, panes, satins, damasks, creps, taffetas, and many others that Europeans don't know".

The reason this French prohibition was so important was because the export of French fabrics to Spain amounted to 8 million pounds (Dahlgren 1907, pp. 78–79), and a good part was shipped to America, including silks from Rouen and Bretagne as well as other expensive cloths. In addition, Savary des Bruslons acknowledges that the French trade in silk fabrics—*galons and étoffes d'or et d'argent*—had been weakened since the Peace of Utrecht due to competition from the Dutch, which sold silks at a lower price, and from the English, which manufactured more affordable drapes and cloths (Savary des Bruslons 1726, p. 923). With the arrival of imported textiles from India and China in Europe, England and France took early steps to ban them.[23] Such bans were part of mercantilist policies to protect domestic textile manufacturers from foreign competition. Spain passed a Royal Order on 20 June 1718 prohibiting the entry of clothing, silks, and other fabrics from China and parts of Asia. The measure appears to have not been very successful, as another Royal Order on 28 June 1728 prohibited cotton fabrics and painted canvases from Asia, imitation or counter made. On the other side, French fabrics played an important role in the Mediterranean households. Pérez-García noted that "it is possible to find French fabrics emulating Chinese silks such as *cambrai*, *chalu*, *chamelotte*, *monfort* or *ruan*, as well as Asian textiles such as silk, muslins or calicoes from India and China. Such goods are

[23] Restrictions on importing Indian textiles, starting in the mid-1670s, proliferated in England as a way to increase duties before the Calico Acts (Parthasarathi 2011, p. 126). Numerous petitions addressed also to Colbert prohibited the commerce from the Levant brought into the port of Marseille (e.g. silk and cotton cloths) (Baghdiantz 2015, p. 127). The total ban on imported foreign textiles occurred in 1714 (Belevitch-Stankevitch 1970, p. 115). Increases in duties were followed by bans in the eighteenth century: 'These measures were applied in several European countries, first in France in 1689, and later in England (1701 and a total ban in 1721)'. See Lemire and Riello 2008, p. 898. Farrell (2016) draws an interesting picture on silk textiles contraband in Britain, including which were the most popular silks, where they came from, and who consumed them.

found in the inventory of the Béarnaise merchant Juan Bicaix showing that they were intended for trade. This reaffirms the theory that these foreign traders played an important role as mediators in introducing new products and materials in the Mediterranean area" (Pérez-García 2019, 28).

The Spanish American colonies were well supplied with textiles and cotton products, either legally through the Manila galleons and Seville-Cadiz or illegally by smuggling.[24] If the ban on imports from India and China to America had worked, as Monségur had suggested be done, it would have benefitted the English, French, and Dutch, among others, because they legally shipped textiles to America through Seville-Cadiz that competed with those made by in China and India. Savary des Bruslons noted that French ships arrived with Indian or Chinese products (e.g. porcelains, silks, silk stockings) in *derechura* (direct trade) through Cadiz as these goods were banned in France (Belevitch-Stankevitch 1970, p. 114).

Conversely, if the prohibition had been successful, it would have meant increases in the prices of fabrics, which would have harmed consumers in Spanish America and created problems with the Philippines. As noted earlier, Monségur and several French consular reports pointed out that indeed the French were deeply affected by the arrival of silk Chinese fabrics.[25] In one consular report was the warning that "there is a trade that affects the whole of Europe (it is understood that it is negatively), to which limits should be placed, and that is the Philippines to Acapulco".[26]

In this chapter we have explored the finding made by Jean de Monségur as related to the flow of textiles, especially Chinese silks that competed with European textiles manufacturers. While his data is vital, it

[24] The "Spanish Crown since the heavy imports of Chinese silks from Fukien, Kwang-tung, and Macao and Manila (whence some of them were re-exported to Mexico and Peru) not only deprived the Seville silk merchants of an otherwise closed market, but diverted a considerable quantity of bullion from the Peruvian silver-mines of Potosi to Portuguese and Chinese hands, as the silks were invariably paid for in specie". (Boxer 1946, p. 162).

[25] Archives Affaires Étrangères, Correspondance politique, t. 398 (1732–1733), fol, 329–332. 'Mémoire ou l´on établit que la balance du moins de débit et de la baisse du prix arrivées depuis quelques années dans les marchandises qu´on porte aux indes espagnoles...'.

[26] Archives Affaires Étrangères, Espagne. Correspondance politique, t. 197, fol. 316 'Observations sur le commerce des Indes Occidentales Espagnoles'.

must be noted that he was not a neutral observer. As Dobado-González (2020) highlights, the central role played by the Viceroyalty of New Spain has perhaps not been properly understood as an important driver of globalisation. Even if the trade in Asian goods could be considered small in proportion to overall trade (De Vries 2010), its impact on blending styles and materials is undeniable, as was its influence on economic performance. As Lemire (2018, p. 71) noted, "the Manila-Acapulco connection produced a distinctive material ecosystem in the Americas". Each demand had its own dynamics and audience, and in Mexico all strata of population wore silks of varying quality. Attempts to ban fabrics, especially from China, were indeed in vain (Rodríguez 2015, p. 231).

The Pacific Ocean was the centre of several intersecting circuits of exchange that connected textiles. This chapter considers the incorporation of Chinese silks in all its qualities, types, and price ranges as critical in cultural exchanges before the eighteenth century. Mexico City consumers had an influence beyond the Manila galleons when they stimulated new fashion patterns through a complex process of domestication. This new phenomenon of hybridised cloth consumption emerged as a result of the city's particular socioeconomic and political factors.

This chapter suggests that one way to redress the partial understanding of the consumer revolution that was centred in Europe, and to bring New Spain into the narrative, is to explore new insights on the role played by the global flow of textiles in the Pacific. That an early Consumer Revolution took place in New Spain soon after the opening in the of the commercial route across the Pacific known as the Manilla Galleon—see the chapter by Arturo Giráldez—is one of the results of the research carried by Dobado, Fernández de Pinedo and Calderón in a preliminary paper under the title "Asian goods in New Spain: An Omitted Early Consumer Revolution". In contrast to Britain, this early Consumer Revolution did not led to any Industrial Revolution in New Spain. New perspectives, in the words of Otero and Trentmann, are needed to 'de-centre' the current Latin American narrative (Otero and Trentmann 2017, p. 19).

Illustration 7 Pale blue Chinese silk damask weaved in 1710–1720 for export to America, used for a woman gown sawn in 1770–1780, Victoria and Albert Museum, London, T.35-1972

Illustration 8 The design of this *sarasa* relates to Mughal embroideries of the late seventeenth century, which drew their inspiration from earlier European embroideries. The Metropolitan Museum of Art, New York, Funds from various donors, by exchange, 2010 2010.55

Acknowledgements The Open Access of this research has been sponsored and financially supported by GECEM (Global Encounters between China and Europe: Trade Networks, Consumption and Cultural Exchanges in Macau and Marseille, 1680-1840), a project hosted by the Pablo de Olavide University (UPO) of Seville (Spain). The GECEM Project is funded by the ERC (European Research Council) Starting-Grant, ref. 679371, under the European Union's Horizon 2020 Research and Innovation Programme, www.gecem.eu. The P.I. (Principal Investigator) is Professor Manuel Perez-Garcia (Distinguished Researcher at UPO). This work was supported by the H2020 European Research Council. This research has also been part of the academic activities of the Global History Network (GHN) in China www.globalhistorynetwork.com. This research has been also supported by research funding from Ministerio de Economía, Industria y Competitividad (Agencia Estatal de Investigación/Fondo Europeo de Desarrollo Regional (FEDER), HAR 2016-78026-P).

This chapter's roots are in the research project 'Dressing the New World', awarded in 2015 by the EU Commission Marie Curie Sklodowska Individual Fellowship Horizon 2020 (EU project 661517–DRESSING THE NEW WORLD). The discovery of the unique document, *The New Memoirs of Mexico, or New Spain, ... in 1708–09 ... amended and augmented in 1713–14...*, written by Jean de Monségur, is the highlight of a two-year fellowship that framed the study on the trade of textiles and the clothing culture in the Spanish Americas in the early modern period. https://dressworld.hypotheses.org.

The authors are very grateful to Ana Cabrera and Emiliano Fernández de Pinedo Fernández who kindly provided technical support.

Illustrations/Glossary

Damask: Monségur frequently complained about lower consumption of rich European fabrics, such as dress silk damasks, because of the silk damasks produced in China. Chinese-made damask was in patterns that revealed their Chinese origin, but some of these damasks were also copies of European silks. The most detailed lists found in the galleon shipments relate to patterned silks of all kinds. These can be compared to the list of cargo conveyed by Miguel de Elorriaga on the galleon *Nuestra Señora del Rosario* in 1712, which is preserved in the General Archives of Indias in Seville.[27]

[27] Archivo General de Indias. ES.41091.AGI/16//CONTADURIA,908,N.1.

Saya: *Saya* is a single-colour damask-like textile (i.e. lightweight, monochrome, woven silk) characterised by a pattern in twill on a plain-weave background. These Chinese silks were available plain or with small or large design of flowers.

Illustr. Wedding dress made in America, 1776, Chinese silk damask. Brooklyn Museum Collection at The Metropolitan Museum of Art, New York, Gift of the Brooklyn Museum, 2009; Gift of Edith Viele, 1949 (2009.300.731).

Illustr. Pale blue Chinese silk damask weaved in 1710–1720 for export to America, used for a woman gown sawn in 1770–1780, Victoria and Albert Museum, London, T.35-1972.

Taffetas: Chinese-made *taffetas* were lightweight lustrous plain-weave silk fabric, available in a multitude of colours, often used for lining. These taffetas could be in two colours, giving a vibrant effect called 'shot' silk (Miller 2014). Taffetas like *sayasayas* in Monségur's *New Memoirs*, were used for petticoats in the New Spanish colonies, or as *guardapies*, which were worn as underskirts for formal dress but could also be worn as an informal and simple skirt.

Gold brocaded silks and other figured silks: These were most precious textiles coming from Asia. Monségur lists a number of gold brocaded fabrics produced in China with a specific technique unknown in Europe; these included the luxurious *telas* and the more modest *brocatos*, in which gold brocaded silk was replaced with gilded paper. A woman's gown made of orange and gold Chinese exported damask silk, and sewn in New York between 1740 and 1760, is preserved at the Colonial Williamsburg Foundation (Museum Purchase 1985–143).

Gold leaf or gilded paper: Following the description of Monségur in his *New Memoirs*, the glittering effect of gold leaf or gilded paper applied on fabric was very popular among the locals in Mexico. The garments' shimmer was close to that produced by more luxurious fabrics like brocaded silks with metallic threads of gold or silver. Gold leaf or gilded paper was usually fixed to Indian cottons by an aqueous gum that was painted on to chintz. The gilding and application of painted and printed flowers on cotton produced a shiny fabric, as, for example, seen in the textile of the man's waistcoat.

Illustr. Waistcoat, textile from India, mid-eighteenth century, used for a man's waistcoat made in France, 1770–1790. The Metropolitan Museum of Art, New York, Rogers Fund, 1935 35.142.

Imitation gold and silver brocaded silks: Another example of textile matches Monségur description of techniques aiming to "imitate" the gold and silver brocaded silks produced in Europe, such as this illustration of a cotton panel made in India, where the floral pattern is drawn and painted resist and mordant, dyed, with applied gold leaf. This process produced a vibrant coloured 'imitation' of popular Western patterns of floral silk used in both women's and men's fashions in Europe.

Illustr. Panel of chintz, India (Coromandel Coast), second quarter of eighteenth century, cotton, drawn and painted resist and mordant, dyed, with applied gold leaf. The Metropolitan Museum of Art, New York, Gift of the United Piece Dye Works, 1936 36.90.121.

***Sarasa*:** *Sarasa* is a colourful dye-patterned cotton fabric originally from Gujarat (India), and is also a term for textiles imported into Japan. In the first half of the eighteenth century, these textiles made of cotton and painted, mordant, dyed, and decorated with applied gold leaf were produced in Gujarat for the Japanese market. Not surprisingly, products intended for Japan could also end up in other markets through China and the Philippines, because the Manila galleon shipped Asiatic merchandises to Vera Cruz in Mexico. Could *sarasas* have been traded in the Spanish colonies and imported to Mexico? That might explain why Monségur encountered this term and used it in his *New Memoirs*.

Illustr. The design of this *sarasa* relates to Mughal embroideries of the late seventeenth century, which drew their inspiration from earlier European embroideries. The Metropolitan Museum of Art, New York, Funds from various donors, by exchange, 2010 2010.55.

Cambayas: This is another term closely related to *sarasas*, which were probably also panels of ready-made petticoats, made of cotton, mordant, painted, dyed, and with applied gilded paper. Cambaya is certainly connected to the port of Cambay in Gujarat, on the Coromandel Coast in India. The petticoat was a visible underskirt of a woman's open robe costume or covered with a jacket. Some ready-to-sew petticoat panels were Asiatic imports from India, and made of cotton painted and dyed chintz.

Illustr. Petticoat, Coromandel Coast, India, ca. 1725. Painted and dyed cotton chintz. Victoria and Albert Museum, London. Given by G. P. Baker, IS.14-1950.

Illustr. Detail of sack (dress) made of Chinese hand-painted silk satin (1735–1760). The design of fanciful flowers shows the Western influence; the Chinese artists were using patterns sent to Europe to make silks expressly for the European market. The Victoria and Albert Museum, London, T.115&A-19532006AY9543_2500 and 2006AY9540_2500.

Illustr. 1 Felpa Ribbons with different floral patterns.

"Quaderno de muestras de los géneros de Europa que tienen estimación en Quito y su provincia, conocidos con otros nombres de aquellos que sacan de las fábricas, con expresión del precio a que comunmente se venefician". Seville, Archives General de Indias, MP-Tejidos, 1780, 14, fol. 6v.

Bibliography

Abel, Fernando, Martín Martínez, and Bautista Mora. 2014. "Interdiscursividad en la serie de cuadros de castas atribuida al pintor novohispano José Joaquín Magón." *Historia y Memoria* 8: 245–295.

Alcalá; Luisa; Katzew, Ilona. 2011. *Contested Visions in the Spanish Colonial world*. Los Angeles: County Museum of Arts-Museo Nacional de Antropología.

Arrazola, Lorenzo [dir.]. 1848. *Enciclopedia española de derecho y administración o Nuevo teatro universal de la legislación de España e Indias*. Vol. Ar-Au. Tip. de Antonio Rius y Rossell.

Baghdiantz, Ina. 2015. *A History of Global Consumption : 1500–1800*. Abingdon and New York: Routledge.

Bakewell, Peter. 1974. *Silver Mining and Society in Colonial Mexico, Zacatecas 1546–1700*. Cambridge: Cambridge University Press.

Belevitch-Stankevitch, Hélène. 1970. *Le goût chinois en France au temps de Louis XIV*. Geneva: Slatkine.

Benson, Elizabeth, Ann Rowe, and Anne-Louise Schaffer. 1979. *Junius B. Bird Pre-Columbian Textile Conference, May 19 and 20, 1973*. Washington, DC: The Textile Museum-Dumbarton Oaks Trustees for Harvard University.

Bonialian, Mariano. 2016. "La "ropa de la China" desde Filipinas hasta Buenos Aires. Circulación, consumo y lucha corporativa, 1580–1620." *Revista de Indias* 76 (268): 641–672.

Boxer, Charles. 1946. "Portuguese and Spanish Rivalry in the Far East during the 17th Century." *Journal of the Royal Asiatic Society* 78 (3–4): 150–164.

Braudel, Fernand. 1979. *Civilisation matérielle, économie et capitalisme: XVe-XVIIIe siècle*, vol. 3. Paris: Librairie Générale Française.

Brook, Timothy, Mitchell Codding, and Karina Corrigan. 2015. *Made in the Americas: The New World Discovers Asia*. Boston: Museum of Fine Arts.

Canepa, María. 2015. *Silk, Porcelain and Lacquer : China and Japan and Their Trade with Western Europe and the New World, 1500–1644. A Survey of Documentary and Material Evidence.* PhD thesis, Leiden University. https://openaccess.leidenuniv.nl/handle/1887/36487.

Carr, Denis. 2015. "By the Boatload. Receiving and Recreating the Arts of Asia." In *Made in the Americas: The New World Discovers Asia*, edited by Denis Carr, Gauvin Alexander Bailey, Timothy Brook, Mitchell Codding, Karina Corrigan, and Donna Pierce. Boston: Museum of Fine Arts.

Carrera, Magali. 2003. *Imagining Identity in New Spain Race, Lineage, and the Colonial Body in Portraiture and Casta Paintings.* Austin: Univeristy of Texas Press. https://utpress.utexas.edu/books/carima.

Céspedes del Castillo, Guillermo. 1952. La defensa militar del istmo de Panamá a finales del siglo XVII y comienzos del XVIII. *Anuario de Estudios Americanos*, vol. 9, 235–275.

Chaunu, Huguette, and Pierre Chaunu. 1955. *Seville et l'Atlantique (1504–1650)*, 8 vols. Paris: Colin.

Colomer, José, and Lorenzo Descalzo, eds. 2014. *Spanish Fashion at the Courts of Early Modern Europe | CEEH*, 2 vols. Madrid: Centro de Estudios Europa Hispánica.

Dahlgren, Erik Wilhelm. 1907. "Voyages français à destination de la mer du sud avant Bougainville (1695–1749)." *Nouvelles Archives des Missions Scientifiques et Littéraries. Choix de raports et instructions* 14 (4). Paris: Imprerie Nationale.

Dávila Corona, Rosa María, Montserrat Durán i Pujol and Máximo García Fernández. 2004. *Diccionario histórico de telas y tejidos.* Burgos: Junta de Castilla y León.

de Monségur, Jean. 2002. *Mémoires du Mexique. Le manuscrit de Jean de Monségur (1709).* Edited by Jean-Paul Duviols. Paris: Chandeigne.

de Solórzano, Juan. 1680. *Recopilación de Indias.* Madrid: Julián de Paredes.

de Solórzano, Juan. 1739. *Politica indiana*, vol. 2. Madrid: Matheo Sacristan.

de Ulloa, Juan; de Ulloa, Jorge; de Ulloa, Antonio. 1826. Noticias secretas de América sobre el estado naval, militar, y político de los reynos del Perú, y provincias de Quito, costas de Nueva Granada y Chile. London: R. Taylor.

De Vries, Jan. 2010. "The Limits of Globalization in the Early Modern World." *Economic History Review* 63 (3): 710–733.

Decrusy, A., Alphonse-Honoré Taillandier Isambert, and A. Jourdan. 1829. *Recueil général des anciennes lois françaises: depuis l'an 420 jusqu'à la révolution de 1789.* Belin-Le-Prieur: Verdiere. https://archive.org/details/recueilgnraldes03jourgoog.

Diderot, Dennis, and Jean D'Alambert. 1751. *L'Enciclopedie*, 32 vols. Paris: Briasson/David/Le Breton/Durand.

Dobado-González, Rafael. 2014. "La globalización hispana del comercio y el arte en la Edad Moderna." *Estudios de Economía Aplicada* 32 (1): 13–42.

Dobado-González, Rafael. 2015. "Pre-independence Spanish Americans: poor, short and unequal... or the opposite?"*Revista de Historia Económica (New Series)* 33, 1: 15–59.

Dobado-González, Rafael. 2020. "The Hispanic Globalization of Commerce and Art in the Early Modern Era." *Studies of Applied Economics* 32 (1): 13–42.

DuPlessis, Robert. 2016. *The Material Atlantic Clothing: Commerce and Colonization in the Atlantic World, 1650–1800*. Cambridge: Cambridge University Press.

DuPlessis, Robert. 2019. "Sartorial Sorting in the Colonial Caribbean and North America." In *The Right to Dress: Sumptuary Laws in a Global Perspective, c.1200–1800*, edited by Giorgio Riello and Ulinka Rublack. Cambridge: Cambridge University Press.

Earle, Rebecca. 2019. "Clothing, Race and Identity : Sumptuary Laws in Colonial Spanish America." In *The Right to Dress: Sumptuary Laws in a Global Perspective, c.1200–1800*, edited by Giorgio Riello and Ulinka Rublack. Cambridge: Cambridge University Press.

Farrell, William. 2016. "Smuggling Silks into Eighteenth-Century Britain: Geography, Perpetrators, and Consumers." *Journal of British Studies* 55 (2): 268–294.

Fernández de Pinedo, Emiliano. 1986. "Comercio colonial y semiperiferización de la monarquía hispana en la segunda mitad del siglo XVII." *Áreas. Revista Internacional de Ciencias Sociales* (Special issue): 121–135.

Fernández-de-Pinedo, Nadia. 2018. "Global Commodities in Early Modern Spain." In *Global History and New Polycentric Approaches: Europe, Asia and the Americas in a World Network System*, edited by Manuel Perez Garcia and Lucio De Sousa. Palgrave Studies in Comparative Global History. Singapore: Springer Singapore.

Flynn, Dennis, and Arturo Giraldez. 2012. "Silk for Silver: Manila-Macao Trade in the 17th Century." *Philippine Studies: Historical and Ethnographic Viewpoints* 44 (1): 52–68.

Gage, Thomas. 1648. *The English-American, His Travail by Sea and Land, or, A New Survey of the West-India's Containing a Journal of Three Thousand and Three Hundred Miles Within the Main Land of America ... : Also, a New and Exact Discovery of the Spanish Navigation to Those Parts ... : with a Grammar, or Some few Rediments of the Indian Tongue Called Poconchi, or Pocoman / by the True and Painfull Endeavours of Thomas Gage ... 1648*. London: R. Cotes.

Garner, Richard. 1980. "Silver Production and Entrepreneurial Structure in 18th-Century Mexico." *Jahrabuch für Geschidte von Staat, Wirtschaft und Gresellschaft Late in amerikas* 17: 163–164.

Gasch-Tomás, José. 2012. *Global Trade, Circulation and Consumption of Asian Goods in the Atlantic World: The Manila Galleons and the Social Elites of Mexico and Seville (1580–1640)*. PhD thesis, European University Institute.

Girard, Albert. 1932. *Le commerce français à Séville et Cadix au temps des Habsbourg*. Paris: E. de Boccard.

Gonzalbo, Pilar. 1996. De la penuria y el lujo en la Nueva España. Siglos XVI-XVIII. *Revista de Indias*, vol. 56, nº 206, pp. 49–75.

Ibarra, Antonio. 2017. "Mercancías Globales y Mercados Locales en Nueva España: La Circulación Interior de "Efectos de China" en Guadalajara, a Fines de la Época Colonial." In *Redes, corporaciones comerciales y mercados hispanoamericanos en la economía global, siglos XVII–XIX*, edited by Guillermina del Valle Pavón and Antonio Ibarra. Mexico City: Instituto Mora, Consejo Nacional de Ciencia y Tecnología.

Katzew, Ilona. 2004. *La pintura de castas: representaciones raciales en el México del siglo XVIII*. Madrid: Turner Yale University Press.

Lemire, Beverly, and Giorgio Riello. 2008. "East & West: Textiles and Fashion in Early Modern Europe." *Journal of Social History* 41 (4): 887–916.

Lemire, Beverly. 2018. *Global Trade and the Transformation of Consumer Cultures: The Material World Remade c. 1500–1820. New Approaches to Economic and Social History.* Cambridge: Cambridge University Press.

Lynch, John. 1969. *Spain Under the Habsburgs: Spain and America, 1598–1700*, vol. 2. Oxford: Basil Blackwell.

Ma, Debin. 2017. *Textiles in the Pacific, 1500–1900.* New York: Routledge.

Marichal, Carlos, and Matilde Souto. 1994. "Silver and Situados: New Spain and the Financing of the Spanish Empire in the Caribbean in the Eighteenth Century." *Hispanic American Historical Review* 74 (4): 587–613.

Martins, Andreia. 2019. "O quimono na Nova Espanha: uma manifestação local de uma moda global nos séculos XVII–XVIII." *Conservar Património* 31: 79–95.

Martínez Bermejo, Saúl. 2008. Beyond Luxury: Sumptuary Legislation in 17th-Century Castile. In G. Lottes, E. Medijainen, and J. Vidar Sigurdsson (eds.), *Making, Using and Resisting the Law in European History*, pp. 93–108. Pisa: Plus – Pisa University Press.

Martínez Bonanad, David. 2013. Recepción y asimilación en América del traje y los textiles europeos. Mestizaje y moda en la nueva imagen de la sociedad novohispana. In Carme López Calderón, María de los Ángeles Fernández Valle, Inmaculada Rodríguez Moya (coord). *Barroco iberoamericano: identidades culturales de un imperio*, vol. 2, pp. 397–412. Santiago de Compostela: Andavira.

Melvine, Elinor. 2006. "Land Use and the Transformation of the Environment." In *The Cambridge Economic History of Latin America: Volume 1, The Colonial Era and the Short Nineteenth Century*, edited by Victor Bulmer-Thomas, John Coatsworth, and Roberto Cortes-Conde. Cambridge: Cambridge University Press.

Mézin, Anne, and Didier Ozanam, eds. 2011. Economie et négoce des Français dans l'Espagne de l'époque moderne: instructions et mémoires officiels relatifs au commerce en Espagne de la gestion de Colbert (1669) au Pacte de famille (1761). Paris: Archives Nationales.

Miller, Lesley Ellis. 2014. *Selling Silks: A Merchant's Sample Book*. London: V&A Publishing.

Morineau, Michel. 1998. "L' Etat, la fiscalité, les finances publiques et la croissance economique en France au XIXe siécle." In *Hacienda y crecimiento económico : la reforma de Mon, 150 años después*, edited by Mario García Zuñiga and Joseba De la Torre. Madrid: Gobierno de Navarra-Departamento de Economía y Hacienda.

Moyer, Johanna. 1997. *Sumtuary Law in Ancien Regime France, 1229–1806*. Syracuse, NY: Syracuse University Press. https://surface.syr.edu/hst_etd/60.

Otero, Ana, and Frank Trentmann. 2017. "Presentation: Paths, Detours, and Connections': Consumption and Its Contribution to Latin American History." *Historia Crítica* 65: 13–28.

Parthasarathi, Prasannan. 2011. *Why Europe Grew Rich and Asia Did Not: Global Economic Divergence, 1600–1850*. Cambridge: Cambridge University Press.

Pérez-García, Manuel. 2019. "Consumption of Chinese Goods in Southwestern Europe: A Multi-Relational Database and the Vicarious Consumption Theory as Alternative Model to the Industrious Revolution (Eighteenth Century)." *Historical Methods: A Journal of Quantitative and Interdisciplinary History* 52: 15–36.

Pérez-García, Manuel. 2020. "Creating Global Demand: Polycentric Approaches, Crossroads of Silk and Silver in China and Iberian Empires During the Early Modern Era." *Revista de Historia Económica—Journal of Iberian and Latin American Economic History*, 1–15.

Phipps, Elena. 2013. "The Iberian Globe. Textile Traditions and Trade in Latin America." In *Interwoven Globe: The Worldwide Textile Trade, 1500–1800*, edited by Amelia Peck and Amy Elizabeth Bogansky. New York: Metropolitan Museum of Art.

Picazo, Antoni. 2020. "El comercio de Filipinas en el tránsito al siglo XVIII: la política comercial china." *Vegueta: Anuario de la Facultad de Geografía e Historia*, 253–572.

Pierce, Donna. 2015. By the boatload: Receiving and recreating the arts of Asia. In Dennis Carr (ed.), *Made in the Americas: The new world discovers Asia*. Boston, Mass: MFA Publications, Museum of Fine Arts, Boston, New York, N.Y.

Pierce, Donna. 2016. "Popular and Prevalent: Asian Trade Goods in Northern New Spain, 1590–1850." *Colonial Latin American Review* 25 (1): 77–97.

Pohl, Hans. 1971. "Algunas consideraciones sobre el desarrollo de la industria hispanoamericana - especialmente la textil - durante el siglo XVII." *Anuario de Estudios Americanos* 28: 459–477.

Riello, Giorgio, and Ulinka Trentmann, eds. 2019. *The Right to Dress: Sumptuary Laws in a Global Perspective, c.1200–1800*. Cambridge: Cambridge University Press.

Riello, Giorgio. 2017. "Governing Innovation : The Political Economy of Textiles in the Eighteenth Century." In *Fashioning the Early Modern: Dress, Textiles, and Innovation in Europe, 1500–1800*, edited by Evelyn Welch. Oxford: Oxford University Press.

Rodríguez, Vicente. 1936. "Comentarios al Decreto y Real Instrucción de 1765, regulando las relaciones comerciales de España e Indias." *Anuario de historia del derecho español* 13: 100–135.

Rodríguez Moya, Inmaculada. 2015. Lujo textil en la corte novohispana. *Quintana: Revista Do Departamento De Historia Da Arte* 14: 229–245. Lujo textil en la corte novohispana.

Rublack, Ulinka. 2012. *Dressing Up: Cultural Identity in Renaissance Europe*. Oxford: Oxford University Press.

Sánchez-Albornoz, Nicolás. 1977. *La población de América Latina: desde los tiempos precolombinos al año 2000*. Madrid: Alianza.

Sanz, Carmen. 2004. "El patrimonio empresarial de autoras y actrices a fines del siglo XVII: vestidos de comedia." In *Memoria de la palabra: actas del VI Congreso de la Asociación Internacional Siglo de Oro. Burgos-La Rioja 15–19 de julio 2002*, vol. 2. Burgos-La Rioja: Iberoamericana.

Sanz Ayán, Carmen. 2002. El patrimonio empresarial de autoras y actrices a fines del siglo XVII: vestidos de comedia. In Francisco Domínguez Matito and María Luisa Lobato López (ed.. lit). Memoria de la palabra: actas del VI Congreso de la Asociación Internacional Siglo de Oro. vol. 2, pp. 1629–1639. Iberoamericana: Vervuert, Fundación San Millán de la Cogolla.

Savary des Bruslons, Jacques. 1726. *Dictionnaire universel de commerce, contenant tout ce qui concerne le commerce qui se fait dans les quatre parties du monde. (A-E)*, 3 vols. Amsterdam: chez les Jansons.

Savary des Bruslons, Jacques. 1742. *Dictionnaire universel de commerce, contenant tout ce qui concerne le commerce qui se fait dans les quatres parties du monde*. vol. 3. Insert City: Estienne.

Schurz, William. 1918. "Mexico, Peru and the Manila galleon." *The Hispanic American Historical Review* 1 (4): 389–402.

Sempere y Guarinos, Juan. 1788. *Historia del Luxo y de las leyes suntuarias de España*. Madrid: Imprenta Real.

Thépaut-Cabasset, Corinne. 2011. "Princely Wardrobe and International Network: The Case Study of Bavaria in the 1680s." In *Royal Wardrobes:*

Visual Culture, Material Culture, edited by Isabelle Paresys and Natacha Coquery. Lille: University of Lille.
Thépaut-Cabasset, Corinne. 2014. "Marie-Louise d'Orléans Queen of Spain." In *Spanish Fashion at the Courts of Early Modern Europe*, edited by J. L. Colomer and Amalia Descalzo Lorenzo. Madrid: CHEE.
von Grafenstein, Johanna, and Carlos Marichal. 2012. *El secreto del Imperio Español: Los situados coloniales en el siglo XVIII*, 1st ed. Mexico: Colegio de México Instituto Mora.
Weiss, Charles. 1844. *L'Espagne depuis le règne de Philippe II jusqu'à l'avènement des Bourbons*. Paris: Hachette.
Welch, Evelyn, ed. 2017. *Fashioning the Early Modern. Dress, Textiles and Innovation in Europe 1500–1800*. Oxford: Oxford University Press.
Wunder, Amanda. 2019. "Spanish Fashion and Sumptuary Legislation from the Thirteenth to Eighteenth Century." In *The Right to Dress: Sumptuary Laws in a Global Perspective, c.1200–1800*, edited by Giorgio Riello and Ulinka Rublack. Cambridge: Cambridge University Press.

Index

R. Dobado-González and A. García-Hiernaux (eds.), *The Fruits of the Early Globalization*, Palgrave Studies in Comparative Global History, https://doi.org/10.1007/978-3-030-69666-5

T

U

V

The manufacturer's authorised representative in the EU is Springer Nature Customer Service Centre GmbH, Europaplatz 3, 69115 Heidelberg, Germany. If you have any concerns regarding our products, please contact ProductSafety@springernature.com

Printed and bound by CPI Group (UK) Ltd, Croydon, CR0 4YY
30/09/2026
02225701-0011